THE LAST INVASION

The Last Invasion

War, Women and Memory, 1797–1997

Hywel M. Davies

UNIVERSITY OF WALES PRESS
2025

© Hywel M. Davies, 2025

Reprinted 2025

All rights reserved. No part of this book may be reproduced in any material form (including photocopying or storing it in any medium by electronic means and whether or not transiently or incidentally to some other use of this publication) without the written permission of the copyright owner except in accordance with the provisions of the Copyright, Designs and Patents Act 1988. Applications for the copyright owner's written permission to reproduce any part of this publication should be addressed to The University of Wales Press, University Registry, King Edward VII Avenue, Cardiff CF10 3NS

www.uwp.co.uk

British Library Cataloguing-in-Publication Data

A catalogue record for this book is available from the British Library.

ISBN 978-1-83772-237-2
e-ISBN 978-1-83772-238-9

The rights of authorship of this work have been asserted in accordance with sections 77 and 79 of the Copyright, Designs and Patents Act 1988.

For GPSR enquiries please contact:
Easy Access System Europe Oü, 16879218. Mustamäe tee 50, 10621, Tallinn, Estonia. gpsr.requests@easproject.com

The publisher acknowledges the financial support of the Books Council of Wales.

Typeset by Richard Huw Pritchard
Printed and bound by CPI Group (UK) Ltd, Croydon, CR0 4YY

Contents

Acknowledgements		vi
List of Illustrations		viii
Introduction		1
1	Popular and Official Reports, February to March 1797	15
2	Despair, Deliverance and Discord, 1797 to 1798	47
3	Invasion Propaganda, Historical Tourism and the First Jemima, 1798–1813	79
4	Remembrance and Legacy, 1813–56	109
5	The French Invasion in Popular History and Culture, 1847–85	139
6	A Laddo a Leddir: Who Slays Shall Be Slain, 1885 to the 1897 Centenary	169
7	New Prosperity, New History, an Old Story, 1897–1913	201
8	The First World War and the Legend of the Women, 1914–36	233
9	The Second World War and the Last Invasion, 1936–50	261
10	'Little Fishguard for Ever!': Two Hundred Years and Counting, 1950–97	291
Bibliography		307
Index		339

Acknowledgements

My friend and research supervisor Gwyn A. Williams was not interested in the French Invasion. To him it was a 'reactionary moment'. From very early on I became aware of the contested nature of the events in Pembrokeshire in February 1797.

As part of my administrative work with the University College of Wales Aberystwyth in the early 1990s I first made the acquaintance of Bill Fowler, head of history and head of sixth at Fishguard High School. We soon realised that we both shared an interest in the history of the revolutionary decade. His knowledge of the French invasion and his involvement in its memorialisation was infectious, and my interest was reawakened. He invited me to contribute an article to the 1997 Bicentennial Souvenir Brochure and we had several fascinating discussions on the Invasion, the role of the women and the mistreated Baptists. His early death was a great loss. At around the same time I enjoyed the friendship of a colleague, man of Pembrokeshire, and another ex-Aber student, Colin Evans O.B.E., who shared with me his childhood memories of Pencaer and Goodwick. These two men of Pembrokeshire, I hope, compensate for my comparative lack of Pembrokeshire credentials.

More recently I have benefited from the encouragement of Professor Paul O'Leary and directly from the AHRC/University of Wales funded *Wales and the French Revolution* project. Professors Dafydd Johnston and Mary Ann Constantine invited me to write an article on the Invasion for their festschrift *Footsteps of Liberty and*

Revolt (2013) and present at a conference on *Wales and the French Revolution*. This work would not have been possible without the publications of this project, which make new approaches to old stories possible. I am grateful especially to Ffion M. Jones who shared with me her article on 'The silly expressions of French revolution'.[1]

The comments of the anonymous readers at the University of Wales Press have been helpful. I am also grateful to the archivists and county librarians at Haverfordwest, Bath and those at Swansea University who have aided my research especially at a time of 'lockdown'.

My most heartfelt thanks are to my former colleague and friend Dr D. Russell Davies who gave me invaluable help in the early stages. Professor Jane Aaron has read and commented expertly on the book in its latest draft form and to her I am particularly indebted. I am also grateful to Rachel Hartell for her editing skills and advice.

This work is dedicated to two women, my mother who died just before this book was finished, and my wife Susan, the Jemima in my life.

---

1   Ffion M. Jones, '"The silly expressions of French revolution ...", the experience of the Dissenting community in south-west Wales 1797', in David Andress, *Experiencing the French Revolution* (Oxford, 2013), pp. 245–62.

Illustrations

1	Map of French Invasion, 1797, by Propert
2	The letters from Tate and Cawdor as they appeared in *The Universal Magazine*, March 1797
3	'A Fishguard Fencible'
4	James Baker engraving of Fishguard Bay
5	'Cwyn y Cystuddiedig'
6	'Specimens of French Ferocity and Brutality in Wales'
7	Dedication of *Welsh Patriotism* by John Harries to the women of Pembrokeshire
8	Commemorative medal. Text reads: '1897 Centenary of the last foreign invasion of Britain 1797. In commemoration of the surrender of the French on Carreg Wastad Point Pencaer Feby 24th 1797'
9	Reverse side of the commemorative medal, with an image of the Welsh women on Carreg Wastad Point. Text reads: '*A laddo a leddir*', and '1797 *Fishguard* 1897'
10	Photograph showing women of the area in traditional dress posing for a photograph before the parade
11	Postcard from the early 1900s showing the large memorial stone placed at Carreg Wastad to commemorate the centenary of the French Invasion

12	Postcard of Harbour Village
13	Postcard of Goodwick Harbour
14	Postcard of Fishguard Harbour
15	James Baker engraving of Goodwick Sands
16	James Baker engraving of Carngwastad
17	Title page of 'History of the Pembroke Imperial Yeomanry'
18	Order Form for 'History of the Pembroke Imperial Yeomanry'
19	Opening page of the Fishguard chapter in the GWR publication *Historic Sites and Scenes of England*
20a and 20b	Cawdor jug, and detail showing a woman in the midst of militia
21	'We Laughed at Boney': a humorous anti-Napoleonic work published in 1943
22a and 22b	Example of a promotional leaflet produced for the bicentenary of the Fishguard Invasion in 1997

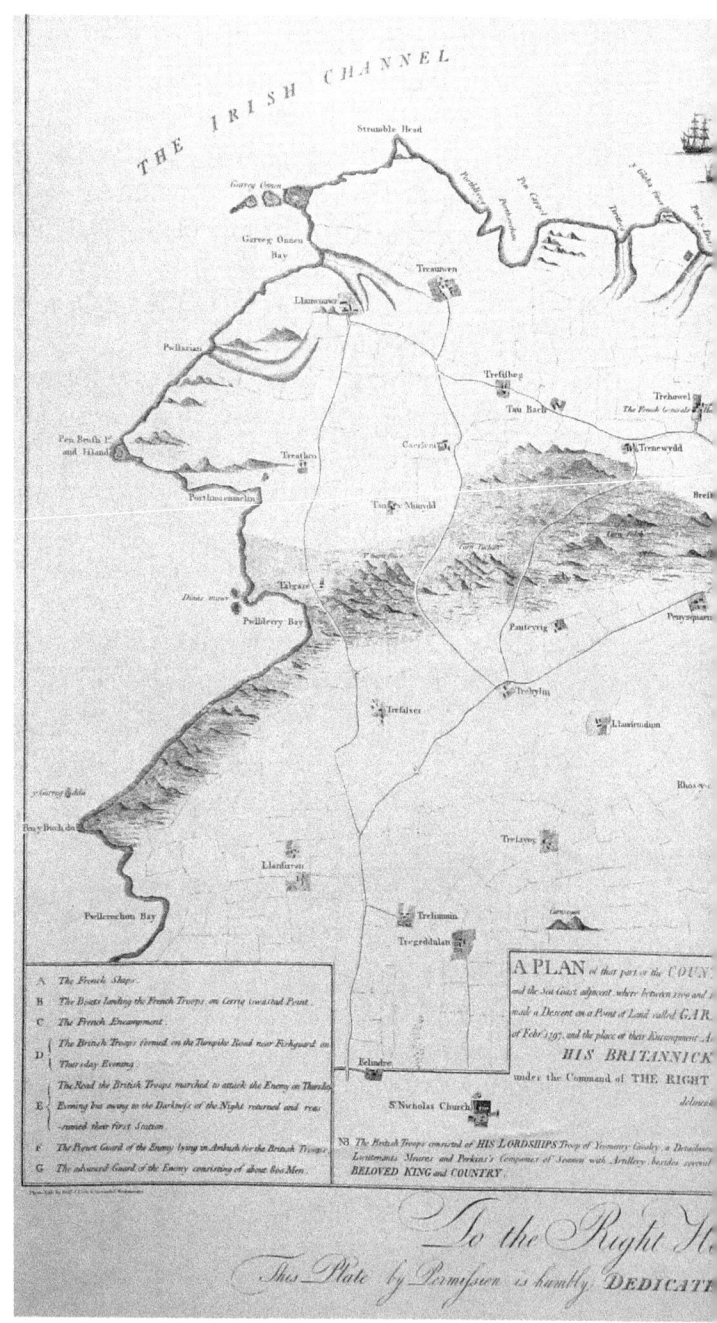

Figure 1: Map of French Invasion, 1797, by Propert[1]

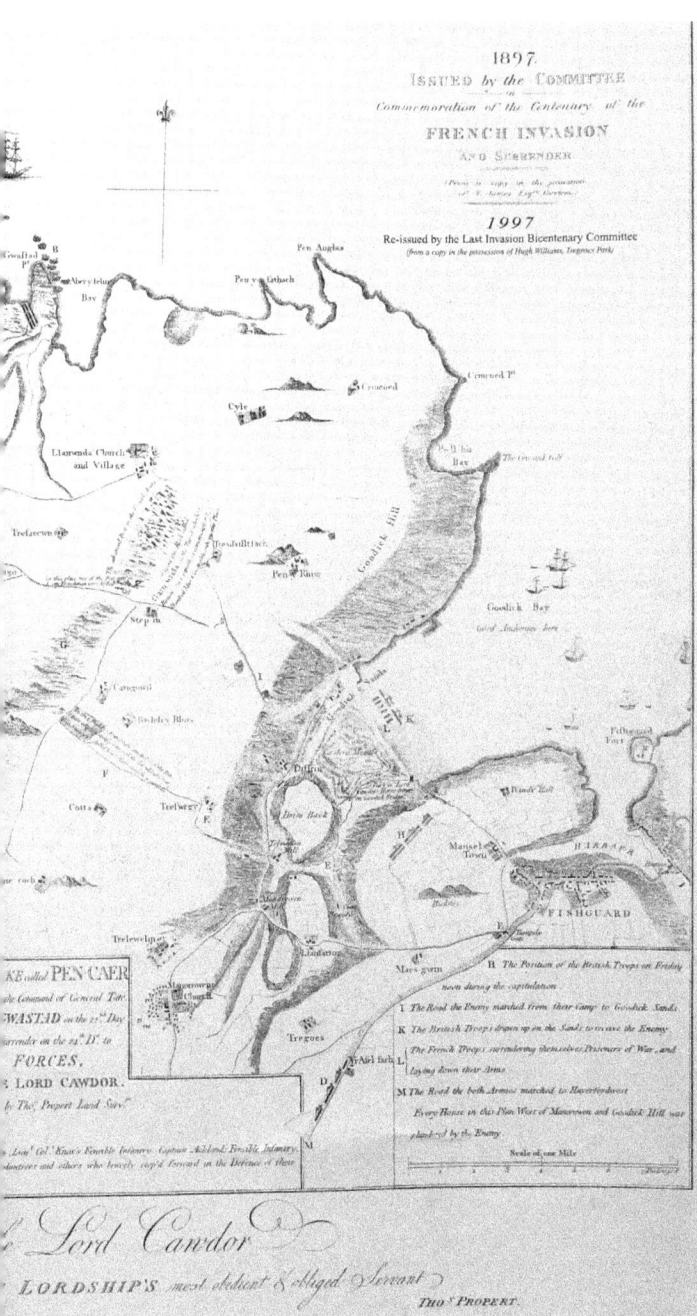

Introduction

The Last Invasion

Much has been written about the French in Pembrokeshire in 1797. The women in their red petticoats and the heroine Jemima with her pitchfork predominate in the popular mind. Jemima Nicholas is one of the most memorable and well-known figures in Welsh history, but this has not always been the case. Jemima was not identified in public, by name at least, as the heroine she was, until 1842.[2] From 1860, the figure of Jemima begins to take over the story of the women in red, to become even more prominent in the narrative. While Jemima is remembered, other women associated with the invasion, equally famous in their time, such as the God-fearing, hymn-singing Nansi Jones, have been largely forgotten. This work seeks to explain the contingency of figures such as Jemima and the anti-Jemima, Nansi Jones, by locating the story of the French Invasion in historical culture over time, in the interconnected field of study that historicises memory, public history, popular history and historiography.[3]

The significance of the French Invasion, so often dismissed as a farce or a fiasco by leading Welsh historians normally sympathetic to popular movements, has been described by Mark Rawlinson, from the first dissemination of intelligence from the Welsh coast, as a cultural and psychological mobilisation that far outweighed its physical and strategic consequences as a contest of arms.[4] The story had a life and significance of its own, separate from the history of the events that it was describing. It may be, as Rawlinson hints, that the story, the 'myth' of the invasion is greater than its historical impact.

The past is one of the most powerful tools for legitimising the present. The history of the invasion has been a partial history dominated by certain traditions, narrators and historians of all types shaped the narrative by selecting sources they judged appropriate or 'authentic' and neglecting others. Military history, written by men, ignored or at best marginalised the role of women. It is in oral tradition and in social memory that the women were remembered or misremembered.

Roland Quinault describes the popular remembrance of the French Invasion as a 'mixture of French farce and Welsh flannel'.[5] Tate's expedition, it has been said, was not serious, it was a comic opera affair set up to fail. It was dismissed by the British government, very soon after the event, as a French attempt to rid itself of unwanted criminals, to downplay the incident and to restore faith and credibility in the British war effort and system of defence. To interpret it this way, however, is to deny the experience of the invaded, who were killed and raped and terrorised.

The events in Pembrokeshire in February 1797, when 1,400 or so French men (and a few women) descended on the Pencaer peninsula near Fishguard, were largely determined by what happened, or rather did not happen, in Ireland in 1796 and in Brittany in 1795. In the autumn of 1796, the French military leader General Louis Lazare Hoche and the Irish revolutionary Theobald Wolfe Tone planned a French expedition to Ireland, to assist the Society of United Irishmen, seeking Irish independence. Ireland was seen as a potential partner in Revolution. But plans to land French troops in Bantry Bay were abandoned due to stormy weather. In anger and frustration over the Bantry Bay failure, Hoche proposed to the French Directory an expedition 'more important than that against Ireland one which will strike a more fatal blow against the interests of England'.[6] The force meant for that invasion was largely that which was supposed to provide support in the Bantry Bay attempt.[7]

One of the French soldiers, an American, thought he was in the 'North part of Ireland'[8] when he was standing on Pembrokeshire soil. Several of the officers including the commander William Tate were either Irish or of Irish origin. Tate himself was an American from South Carolina, with Irish roots. He was committed to republican ideals that stemmed from his initial commitment to America, his adopted homeland. Tate had fought with George Washington and had corresponded with him but was a mercenary and adventurer who hated the English with a passion.[9]

The precedent for the Tate expedition was a failed invasion attempt, not a French attempt, but a British one. In 1795 the British had supported and equipped *emigré* regiments to fight in the civil war that was the Vendée.[10] The failed Quiberon raid was a major incitement to the French to respond in kind.[11] The uniforms of the killed and captured were used again, dyed black (although some looked more like brown) to clothe Tate's force, which is why they were called *La Legion Noire*. *La Legion Noire* were to wreak terror on the British mainland, and the port of Bristol (originally Liverpool) in particular. This was in accordance with Tate's *Instructions* that Tone had translated from the French as preparations for Bantry Bay were unravelling.[12] Tate was to proceed with four ships, including two of their most modern frigates, to Bristol. While there, his soldiers were supposed to goad Bristolian sailors into mutiny before spreading insurrection and chaos to London.

For several days in February 1797, blustery winds prevented Tate's fleet from sailing up the Bristol Channel. Heading west, they reached Pembrokeshire on Wednesday 22 February and landed in the only place they knew from their planning: Cardigan Bay. It was from here that Tate later wrote his letter of negotiation and surrender.

Tate's force included grenadiers, criminals and prisoners of war.[13] The presence of convicts was a deliberate terrorist feature of the general strategy of *chouannerie*, guerrilla warfare, attributed to Nicolas Léonard Sadi Carnot, the organiser of Republican victory.[14] It later became British government strategy to downplay the French expedition to Pembrokeshire by exaggerating the criminal elements within the French force and discrediting any military credentials that they may have had. Tate, when questioned after his arrest, declared that he 'had with him 600 of the best troops in France, veteran, and experienced soldiers'.[15]

One of these crack troops, his second in command, Barry St Leger, an Irishman by birth but brought up in Charleston, was prominent in the landing at Carreg Wastad Point near Fishguard.[16] Overnight, Tate set up headquarters in Trehowel, a nearby vacated farm on the Pencaer peninsula, and, as planned, his ships departed. Prisoners were taken: the captain of a small sloop that they sunk before landing and forced to be their pilot, a man from Mathry who witnessed attempts to enforce discipline in the French camp and Thomas Williams, the farmer from Caerlem on the peninsula who later led two of the French officers to Fishguard to parley. The French expected to attract local dissidents to their cause, waving their flag on Carn Gelli on the Pencaer peninsula to attract local support but no one took up the offer.[17] Throughout the night, as word of the French invasion spread, locals whose houses had been raided sought shelter with neighbours and out in the open; others just fled. Thomas Knox, a local commander, was slow to gather his men due to a lack of military experience. By Thursday, he had assembled the Fishguard Fencibles, but lacking resources and not fully understanding the extent of the French threat, he moved south towards Haverfordwest to wait for reinforcements.

John Campbell, Lord Cawdor, who was at his country estate 60 miles away in the south of the county was more decisive. He marched two local militias to Fishguard and on the way picked

Introduction

up Knox and the Fishguard Fencibles and assumed overall command. The combined forces reached Fishguard late on Thursday afternoon, a force of not more than 700 men, greatly outnumbered by the French.

Meanwhile, the ill-disciplined *Legion Noire* made the most of their opportunity and went on the rampage, antagonising the peasantry that they had expected to recruit, and became almost out of control. They vandalised the ancient church of St Gwyndaf in the village of Llanwnda, ripped Bibles apart and stole the communion cup. It was during this time that violence against the local people occurred, three rapes, one victim being later identified as Mary Williams, the wife of Thomas Williams the farmer from Caerlem on the Pencaer peninsula, and several deaths. This was the time when atrocities were committed and the space where legends were created. The Welsh were not passive and, after their initial terror and flight, fought back with vengeance against a hated enemy. A very early report accounted for 'two or three [Welsh] killed and the enemy ten or more in skirmishes'.[18] Stories circulated both at the time and later stressed the bravery and bloodlust of the Welsh peasants – French bodies were pierced and skulls bludgeoned, a woman cobbler captured and imprisoned several French soldiers. This cobbler, Jemima Nicholas, was said to have singlehandedly rounded up twelve drunk soldiers and locked them up in St Mary's church in Fishguard. Her name is not mentioned in contemporary sources, but there were several occasions when civilian bravery of this type did occur, forcing the surrender of dispersed groups of demoralised soldiers who were not sure whether they were surrendering or continuing to fight.

As well as violence against civilians, the French posed a real and deadly military threat. Cawdor's force approached the French redoubt along the Trefwrgi Lane, but at dusk on that Thursday afternoon, decided to fall back to Fishguard. If they had proceeded there would have been a bloody massacre, since behind the high hedges of the lane lay St Leger and his grenadiers. The French grenadiers fell back in an orderly manner to the safety of the rocky heights of Carn Gelli, firing rolling platoon volleys into the darkness to discourage pursuit.

Morale collapsed among the French soldiers as they found themselves marooned on hostile territory. Separated from reinforcements or rescue, Tate saw no other choice but to send two officers to Fishguard seeking conditions of surrender. Tate himself never set foot in Fishguard, despite it being said that the treaty was signed in the building that is now the Royal Oak pub. Lord Cawdor, so his reports said, bluffed his way through negotiations, not letting on that the Welsh troops were outnumbered. Tate acting alone but under pressure from his officers, surrendered without engaging the various militias assembled by Cawdor or the local people who had confronted the French before Cawdor arrived. Later in the twentieth century it was called the 'Battle of Fishguard', but nothing could be more wrong – Tate deliberately avoided confrontation between the militaries to avoid unnecessary bloodshed, it was a 'surrender' not a 'battle'.

The 'surrender' was later presented as an orderly transition from the exchange of letters between Tate and Cawdor and the agreement of military gentlemen, to the signing of some form of treaty document (popularly occurring in the Royal Oak), to the regulated laying down of arms by the French troops to their British counterparts on Goodwick Sands. This is as much a later tradition as the women in red forcing a French surrender. The people, including the women, are absent from the official surrender accounts. What happened after the exchange of letters, the role of the people, as well as the nature of the surrender (or surrenders) is still not properly understood. The space between the French and the local opposition was more contested, the period more prolonged, the outcome more uncertain than the official surrender accounts supposed.

The effects of the French 'Other' in forging British identity during the long eighteenth century are well-known and well-made.[19] The more sustained and significant transnational connection for the people of Wales was not the French or later the German 'Other' but the British state and their related identities as Britons. For three days in February 1797 the men and women of the Pencaer peninsula confronted French terrorists as ancient and as modern Britons. British, Welsh, as well as local Pembrokeshire patriotisms, provide multiple permutations over time and affect the telling and retelling of the stories, as told by travel writers, historians, novelists, journalists, poets, librettists, Nonconformist ministers, and others, in both English and Welsh. When Cymru Fydd peaked in the 1890s, the French Invasion and its centenary celebrations were associated with Welsh Home Rule. The English press responded with 'Gallant Little Wales'. It was as Britons that the Welsh volunteered for the Rifle Corps, and later the Territorials to defend and fight for the Empire. It was during times of fear of invasion, at various points during the nineteenth century, and again during the two World Wars, that the actual invasion of 1797 was recalled most sharply. The story was used as a tool to allay the fears of people in all parts of Britain that current enemies – the Germans – would share the same humiliating fate as Tate and his men in 1797.

Associated with national identity, religious affiliation played a major role both in the history and in the historiography. Thomas John and Samuel Griffith were tried for treason but were identified as such largely because they were Dissenters. 'Fishguard' was a moment that allowed denominations to prove their civic loyalty, the Baptists tried to gloss over their wrongly tried preacher who was proved innocent, but the injustice and the stigma rankled for generations. Denominations had their own traditions and remembrance of the French Invasion. The telling of the story even by the remembrancers themselves reveals changing and contested attitudes among Nonconformists to volunteering, bravery, state violence and war. Anglicans had their Jemima, the Independents responded with their Nansi;

both strong women superior to the men around them but representing different values and systems.

Fishguard prospered by the new sea route to Rosslare in 1892, a new town was built in Goodwick, built largely by Irish labour, and a new Atlantic crossing. Fishguard and Goodwick celebrated this new prosperity. Local women wearing the red shawls of their grandmothers and great grandmothers brought down from their attics re-enacted their history and family memories, demonstrating the civic pride and heritage of a growing and prosperous port with its new destinations to Ireland, New York and railway connections to south Wales and London. The Women of Fishguard were iconic figures in the travel and promotional literature of the main architect of this travel boom, the Great Western Railway in the years before the Great War.

The French Invasion had become a tourism and heritage asset. A trip to Fishguard was to tread on significant historical ground, ground that had witnessed the 'Last Foreign Invasion of Britain' as it was called by the locals at the Centenary in 1897. At about the same time, the story itself, especially the role of the women, came under greater scholarly scrutiny from archival research, and the availability of new primary sources. In the 1920s professional teachers (and others) were interested in the story of Fishguard as part of a growing awareness of the importance of the French Revolution on Welsh life and literature. Academic discourse and scholarly texts conflicted with popular and local memory. What became known as 'the legend of the women' showed remarkable resilience in defiance of professional scepticism and growing public scorn.

No other event in its modern history, at least before the World Wars, has put Pembrokeshire more in the news than the landing of the French in 1797. Even the King had Pembrokeshire on his mind in February 1797. But the French Invasion was greater than Pembrokeshire; its effect lived on in those cities that were historically connected to the invasion, Bristol and Liverpool and that which had no direct connection with Fishguard either in the

Introduction

present or past. The invasion's location as the site of the 'Last Invasion of Britain' gave it a British, more often 'English', and emblematic significance in the Second World War. It was not Fishguard, nor was it Pembrokeshire or even Wales, but Britain that was invaded and polluted by the tread of the enemy. When the 'Last Invasion' imagery was at its height just after the Second World War, and the fear of invasion a recent memory, Tate was at last given his dues: 'this complete nonentity stood on British soil in command of invading troops, which is more than Napoleon or Hitler ever did'.[20]

The story of the invasion was told and written in multiple forms. Texts influenced other texts, some more than others, crossing or not crossing temporal, linguistic and cultural boundaries, to effect intertextual connections between history and popular history, fiction and non-fiction, propaganda and the press. Accounts of the French Invasion in different forms appeared both in English and in Welsh, the story offering different meanings and readings to their audiences. 'The women of Fishguard' prompted merriment and mockery from English and misogynistic directions, including Pembrokeshire men, while the Pembrokeshire military kept silent about the 'women' in celebrating their own past. However, the defiance of the women of 1797, including their success in securing compensation, inspired young working-class feminists in Wales during the years of the Second World War. Aspects of the French Invasion canon, well-known in Welsh, particularly those involving Nonconformist memories and creations such as Nansi Jones, were completely unknown in English. To understand the interaction between texts, between text and popular memory, and their genealogies, the testimonies of both the languages of Pembrokeshire are employed. Welsh-language sources (ballads and local remembrance of the landing), newspaper reportage, both contemporary and later, as well as the writings of English tourists to Wales, had a pivotal role to play in interpreting and promoting the events of February 1797 to wider English-speaking audiences. Newly available and accessible primary sources, together with a close reading of the texts, tell the history not only of the invasion but of the invasion story or stories, how it was chronicled, commemorated and re-enacted, by women especially, over time. It was a story centred on remembered and misremembered events, both local and global, on official and informal accounts, often framed in imagination and fantasy, sometimes independent of its history but always inspired by it. The formation of these memories accords with Guy Beiner's definition of social memory as collective memory shared by a community, a discursive reconstruction of the past performed and promulgated by multiple agents and relating to numerous participants, contributing towards a communal body of cultural knowledge relating to the past.[21]

The women and men central to the story are predominantly Welsh and from Pembrokeshire, but Pembrokeshire in the 1790s was micro-cosmopolitan and several national and local identities and allegiances are in evidence. One of the themes in the narrative was the tension between the military, men of the Pembroke Yeomanry from the English-speaking south of the county and the women of Fishguard from the Welsh-speaking north. The people of Tenby and Fishguard wanted to celebrate the centenary differently. The women of Fishguard and the cavalry men of Castlemartin appear in separate narratives and memory traditions but their roles are intertwined and combined, notwithstanding the absence of the women from the male-dominated military account. The French Invasion became a source of Pembrokeshire unity and pride overcoming the tensions of class, gender and language. 'Fishguard' after all was the name given on the battle honours of the Pembrokeshire Yeomanry, the only volunteer force to have defeated an enemy on British soil, which the Pembrokeshires and the community below the Landsker celebrated proudly.[22]

The Descent in Wales, the French Landing in Pembrokeshire, the French Landing at Fishguard, the French Invasion of

Introduction

Fishguard, the Battle of Fishguard, the Fishguard Invasion and the Last Invasion of Britain are some of the different English-language names used to describe the same historical events and indicate how even the titles have changed as the narrative has been told differently. In Welsh, the terms *Glaniad* or *Tiriad* – both meaning 'landing' rather than *Goresgyniad* meaning 'invasion' – were the terms usually used. The term French Invasion will be used in this work, while acknowledging what many thought at the time and since the event was not an invasion but rather a raid or a landing. The term 'invasion' had political connotations of a foreign, state-organised offensive, whereas 'landing' was more neutral in meaning. The term 'Fishguard Invasion' is avoided even though it has been widely used. The landing not only did not occur in Fishguard, but in fact deliberately avoided Fishguard. If the landing had taken place there, the consequences would have been radically different, as would the far greater potential for bloodshed. The laying down of arms took place in Goodwick, a separate place altogether. However, it is the port of Fishguard that is paramount in the public mind as the location of the 'Last Invasion of Britain'.

The key themes running through the work are the emerging narratives of the women in red whittles or shawls, then cloaks, then in red petticoats; and Jemima Nicholas, the defining figure in popular memory of the events of 1797. The other is a larger theme: the uneasy relationship between 'official' history and oral and popular culture. 'Official' history, written and endorsed by scholars, and influencing public opinion, is often partial and flawed, while popular culture tends repeatedly to return to certain events and images, making parts of history familiar and vivid, while rendering others distant or unknown.[23] Jemima has benefited from this process, but others have not. It is the aim of this work to restore the forgotten and half remembered, both chroniclers and chronicled, to the current narrative. The survey of two hundred years ends with the bicentenary in 1997, but the story continues to be told and retold.

Endnotes

1. For Propert's map, see Hywel Davies, 'The Failed French Invasion of Pembrokeshire in 1797', in D. Howell (ed.), *An Historical Atlas of Pembrokeshire* (Haverfordwest, 2019), pp. 130–1.
2. 'An Heroic Single Woman', in H. L. Ap Gwilym, *An Authentic Account of the Invasion by French Troops on Carrig Gwasted Point, near Fishguard, 1797* (Haverfordwest, 1842), p. 33.
3. For this definition of 'historical culture', see Martha Vandrei, *Queen Boudica and Historical Culture in Britain: An Image of Truth* (Oxford, 2018), p. 15.
4. Mark Rawlinson, 'Invasion! Coleridge, the defence of Britain and the cultivation of the public's fear', in Philip Shaw (ed.), *Romantic Wars: Studies in Culture and Conflict, 1793–1822* (Aldershot, 2000), pp. 110–11.
5. Roland Quinault, 'The French Invasion of Pembrokeshire in 1797: A Bicentennial assessment', *Welsh History Review*, 19/1–4 (1998–9), 618.
6. *Ipswich Journal* (28 January 1797), 2. Quoting from the Parisian paper *L'Ami des Lois* (20 January 1797).
7. *Ipswich Journal* (14 January 1797), 1.
8. David Salmon, 'A Sequel to the French Invasion of Pembrokeshire', *Y Cymmrodor*, 43 (1932), 74.
9. Tate was on the fringes of power and intrigue in the early national period in the United States. He wrote to George Washington on the 3 August 1789, see *https://founders.archives.gov/documents/Washington/05-03-02-0218* (last accessed 29 July 2024).
10. Martin Lyons, *France under the Directory* (Cambridge, 1975), p. 15.
11. Quinault, 'The French Invasion of Pembrokeshire in 1797', 618–21; Sylvie Kleinman, 'Initiating Insurgents abroad: French plans to "chouannise" Britain and Ireland 1793–1798', in B. Heuser, *Small Wars and Insurgents Theory and Practices 1500–1850* (Abingdon, 2016), pp. 48–50.
12. T. W. Moody, R. B. McDowell and C. J. Woods (eds), *The Writings of Theobald Wolf Tone 1763–1798*, vol. 2 (Oxford, 2001), 25 November 1796, p. 397; 26 November 1796, p. 399.
13. The most reliable composition but without precise numbers is Marianne Elliott, *Partners in Revolution: The United Irishmen and France* (Yale CT, 1982), p. 116.
14. Nicolas Léonard Sadi Carnot, 'Instructions pour l' Etablissement d'une Chouannerie en Angleterre', in 'Carnot's Plan for Invading England', *Fraser's Magazine*, new ser., 15/86 (1877), 201–2.
15. *The New Annual Register, or General Repository of History, Politics and Literature for the year 1797* (London, 1798), p. 245.
16. For St Leger, see *Writings of Theobald Wolf Tone*, vol. 2, 9 November 1796, p. 369
17. J. Baker, *A Brief Narrative of the French Invasion, Near Fishguard Bay* (Worcester, 1797), p. 6.

Introduction

18 *The Times*, from a letter dated 24 February (28 February 1797).
19 Linda Colley, *Britons: Forging the Nation 1707–1837* (Yale CT, 1992); see also Elizabeth Edwards, *English-Language Poetry from Wales 1789–1806* (Cardiff, 2013), p. 47, no. 42.
20 Derek Hudson, 'A Very Small Invasion', *The Spectator* (22 September 1950), 26.
21 Guy Beiner, *Remembering the Year of the French: Irish Folk History and Social Memory* (Madison WI, 2007), p. 28.
22 E. H. Stuart Jones, *The Last Invasion of Britain* (Cardiff, 1950), p. 287.
23 Tessa Morris-Suzuki, *The Past Within Us: Media, Memory, History* (London and New York, 2005), p. 17.

Chapter 1

Popular and Official Reports, February to March 1797

Pembrokeshire Men and the Official Invasion

The established account of the French Invasion is largely a story of Pembrokeshire men, substantial landowners, and men of high social and political status. The main British protagonists of the French Invasion story, Lord Milford and Baron Cawdor, headed the list of the great landlords of the county.[1] They were the political elite, members of Parliament with houses in London as well as Pembrokeshire, who at a time of war acquired military responsibility, to which not all were suited. These were the men responsible for the defence of Pembrokeshire and in military history tradition the French Invasion is their story.

The Lord Lieutenant of Pembrokeshire, the representative of the king in the county during this period was Richard Philipps (1744–1823), Baron Milford, the Whig member of Parliament for the county. In 1793, Britain had declared war on Revolutionary France and in March 1794, the prime minister wrote to all lord lieutenants, inviting them to raise additional volunteer forces. Milford received the prime minister's letter on 14 March 1794 and called a meeting of all Pembrokeshire gentlemen then in London, where they determined to raise the 'Pembrokeshire

Company of Gentlemen and Yeomanry Cavalry' under Milford's personal command. Milford, characteristically, apart from convening the meeting, took no initiative.

The Pembrokeshire landowner who led the way in raising the cavalry was John Pryse Campbell of Stackpole, later to become Baron Cawdor. Despite family connections, there were no sentimental bonds between Cawdor and Milford and their relationship was purely one of power and patronage.[2] They came to dislike one another intensely and their only common interest, like most privileged men of their class, was their passion for hunting.

Campbell in June 1794 was able to report to the Duke of Portland, the home secretary, that he had agreed a plan for the troop of Cavalry with Lord Milford. The plan envisaged two troops of fifty each, with the 'Dungleddy' to the north commanded by Milford and the 'Castlemartin' to the south commanded by himself. Both Milford and Campbell were commissioned captains of their respective troops. The Lord Lieutenant, although commissioned, never undertook any active military role and his troop, the Dungleddy, never materialised. In 1796, Campbell was elevated to the peerage as Baron Cawdor of Castlemartin in the County of Pembrokeshire as a reward for his, albeit short-lived, support for Pitt's war policy.[3] Once he had secured his peerage, his political ambitions had been fulfilled and Campbell had no further political ambition.[4] He was still known locally as Squire Campbell.

The other men in Pembrokeshire actively involved in the defence of the county included William Knox, an Irishman, who purchased the Llanstinan and Slebech estates for £90,000 after being under-secretary of state for the Americas.[5] A man of considerable public spirit, he was the organiser of many firsts in Pembrokeshire: the Agricultural Society, the Post Office, the packet service from Milford to Waterford, the market in Fishguard, and he even became the high sheriff of Pembrokeshire in 1786. When war with France broke out in 1793, he came forward at once and raised, at his own expense, a regiment of Fencible infantry, the second of its kind in the kingdom.[6] The raising of the Fishguard Fencibles was a very rapid response to the declaration of war and proof of the patriotism of the Knox family as well as their commitment to the defence of their home community. His son Thomas was appointed to the command.

The official accounts in government sources such as the *London Gazette* and *The Times* during the winter of 1796 and into early 1797 were largely concerned with managing the fear of invasion, not only against Britain but also against the sister kingdom of Ireland, which continued 'to preponderate over the public mind'.[7] When the French threat, long expected, actually occurred, it took place not on the east coast of England but in west Wales. As Edmund Burke noted in reference to the failed French attempt in Ireland, the French attack was not on any particular place but on the British Empire.[8]

The French landed at Carreg Wastad, a rocky cove out of sight of Fishguard and its fort, during the night of Wednesday 22 February. They established their headquarters at the nearest farmhouse, Trehowel (owned by John Mortimer who quickly fled), ran rampage on Thursday, and had surrendered by Friday. By the time the news of the Fishguard Invasion had reached the streets of London on Saturday, the mopping-up operation was finished.[9] News of the surrender did not come until two days later, leaving a long period for the information to marinate in agitated minds; many were terrified. When the dust had settled, newspapers reflected on the state of the 'public mind' during those anxious days between the announcements when 'the public mind was tortured with its own imaginations'.[10] The alarm in government circles triggered action. Messengers were sent off to Foreign Secretary Grenville and Dundas, the secretary of state for war, requesting their immediate attendance in London.[11] It was not the 'descent in Wales', as Windham called it, but the financial crisis and the state of the Bank of England that was their chief concern.[12] The king was informed of the surrender by a letter from the home secretary sent just after noon on Sunday, 26 February.[13]

Particulars of the landing and details of the surrender were published in *The Times* on Tuesday 28 February, when it printed three letters that had appeared initially in the *London Gazette Extraordinary*, the official newspaper of the government with a limited circulation and sent by post to subscribers.[14] These three letters are the defining official documents of the invasion, shaping the narrative from the outset. The letters came from the chief military officer on the ground in Fishguard; namely, Lord Cawdor (not Milford, it should be noted). The covering letter from Cawdor was dated Friday, 24 February 1797, and sent from Fishguard. Accompanying it were two further letters that were dramatic, for the circumstances they described and for their impact.

The letter from Tate, chef-de-brigade of the French forces, is dated in true republican style, '5th of Ventose, 5th year of the Republic'. The letter was addressed 'Cardigan Bay'. The other letter was Cawdor's reply to Tate's, dated 23 February 1797, its address 'Fishguard'. Figure 2 shows how the letters appeared in one of the news outlets of the time.

These are remarkable letters. Tate's is perhaps the most important letter ever written from Cardigan Bay. His use of the republican calendar shows his assimilation of revolutionary ideology and his allegiance to the Republic. Cawdor's letters are noteworthy for the precision of their timings, the negotiated nature of the surrender, his praise for his officers and men, and for the loyalty 'which has pervaded all ranks throughout the country'. This exchange of letters is central to the interpretation of the surrender, as it was later developed in the established narrative. They were sent as copies to the home secretary, the Duke of Portland, and were published widely in the metropolitan and provincial press. The original famous Tate letter dated '5th of Ventose' is in the Cawdor collection in the Carmarthenshire

Fishguard, Friday, Feb. 24, 1797.

My Lord,

In consequence of having received information on Wednesday night, at eleven o'clock, that three large ships of war, and a lugger had anchored in a small Roadsted, upon the coast in the neighbourhood of this town, I proceeded immediately, with a detachment of the Cardigan militia and all the provincial force I could collect, to the place. I soon gained positive intelligence they had disembarked about 1200 men, but no cannon. Upon the night's setting in, a French officer, whom I found to be the second in command, came in with a letter, a copy of which I have the honour to inclose to your grace, together with my answer: in consequehce of which they determined to surrender themselves prisoners of war, and accordingly laid down their arms this day at two o'clock.

I cannot at this moment inform your grace of the exact number of prisoners, but I believe it to be their whole force; it is my intention to march them this night to Haverfordwest, where I shall make the best distribution in my power. The frigates, corvette and lugger, got under weigh yesterday evening, and were this morning entirely out of sight.

The fatigue we experienced will, I trust, excuse me to your grace for not giving a more particular detail; but my anxiety to do justice to the officers and men I had the honour to command, will induce me to attend your grace, with as little delay as possible, to state their merits, and at the same time to give you every information in my power upon this subject.

The spirit and loyalty which has per-

Cardigan Bay, 5th of Ventose,
Sir,   5th year of the Republic.

The circumstances under which the body of the French troops under my command were landed at this place, renders it unnecessary to attempt any military operations, as they would tend only to bloodshed and pillage. The officers of the whole corps have therefore intimated their desire of entering into a negociation, upon principles of humanity, for a surrender. If you are influenced by similar considerations, you may signify the same by the bearer, and in the mean time hostilities shall cease. Salute and respect,

TATE, Chief de Brigade.

To the officer commanding his Britannic majesty's troops.

Sir,   Fishguard, Feb. 23.

The superiority of the force under my command, which is hourly increasing, must prevent my treating upon any terms short of your surrendering your whole force prisoners of war. I enter fully into your wish of preventing an unnecessary effusion of blood, which your speedy surrender can alone prevent; and which will entitle you to that consideration it is ever the wish of British troops to shew an enemy, whose numbers are inferior.

My major will deliver you this letter, and I shall expect your determination by ten o'clock, by your officer, whom I have furnished with an escort, that will conduct him to me without molestation.

I am, &c.
CAWDOR.

To the officer commanding the French troops.

Figure 2: The letters from Tate and Cawdor as they appeared in *The Universal Magazine*, March 1797[15]

Archives.[16] No surrender document, signed or otherwise, has so far materialised.

The surrender was, however, not how it appeared in the official communiqués. Two letters from Lord Milford in Haverfordwest to Portland written on the Friday of the surrender were published in the *London Gazette* and the provincial press as early as 28 February and were important because they announced the 'surrender' of the French enemy, one written, so it was noted, at six o'clock in the morning, the second at nine o'clock at night, both from Haverfordwest. [17]

In the first letter, Milford is writing as lord lieutenant to his administrative superior to impart the most recent news:

> Since I had the honour of writing last to your Grace by express I received information of the French ships having sailed and left 300 men behind who have surrendered themselves prisoners. The great spirit and loyalty that the gentlemen and peasantry has shown on this occasion exceeds description. Many thousands of the latter assembled, armed with pikes and scythes, and attacked the enemy *previous to the arrival of troops that were sent against them*.[18] [emphasis added]

Early twentieth-century historians and the press at the time end their transcript at this point.[19] However, the original letter does not end there, but continues: 'and many thousands more were ready to march could arms have been procured for them. I therefore hope an ample supply will be sent sufficient to frustrate any future attempt that might be made.'[20]

This letter carries clear evidence of a popular fury, that the ordinary people were enraged by the invasion. On that Friday morning the peasantry, armed with improvised weapons, attacked the French before the arrival of the troops. Milford at this time is appealing to the Home Secretary for firearms to arm the peasantry, including the colliers from Hook near Haverfordwest who had followed the Pembrokeshire militia to arrive on the scene. The request for arms was a dangerous step with implications for civil order, but such an extreme step was required to frustrate any further attempt that the French might make.

This request shows how desperate he was. Nobody was more afraid of the rioting colliers than Lord Milford.[21] A reason for Milford's anxiety may lie in the number of troops given in his first sentence as having surrendered at that point: 300 men were left behind by the departing ships and 'have surrendered themselves prisoners'.

Milford added a postscript: 'I do not recollect whether or not I mentioned in my last letter that the number of the French that disembarked was Twelve Hundred.'[22] Three hundred prisoners were far fewer than the 1,200 men who had disembarked.[23] Most of the enemy at the time of writing the letter on that Friday had not yet surrendered and were still potential threats of a very grave nature.

This letter, written in haste by a rattled man, from the safety of Haverfordwest about events in Fishguard 15 miles or so away, showed that the surrender was partial at best, the position confused, the outcome uncertain and in the hands of the peasantry. So confused and uncertain was the situation that Milford wrote to the mayor of Carmarthen at 12.30 p.m. to inform him, from information received from Cawdor, that the French had actually re-embarked and were not surrendering. Cawdor had seen the ships depart, and Milford assumed that most of the French were on board. They were not.[24]

Mr Mansell, the commissary of French prisoners at Pembroke (not the men from Fishguard but rather earlier French prisoners from the war), a surgeon by profession, was tasked by Milford to take the news by express letter to the home secretary in London.[25] He passed through Gloucester on Saturday 25 February on his way to London. The *Gloucester Journal* carried the earliest news of the surrender on Monday 27 February. It was not Milford's news that appeared in the *Gloucester Journal* but Mansell's own account. Mansell was criticised later for an account that seemed to contradict the official version of events.[26] The *Gloucester Journal* reported from Mr Mansell that the French 'were summoned to surrender themselves prisoners to which they did not altogether accede but in a short interval they began complying by 50 and a 100 at a time'.[27] The French had not laid down their arms before he left. This early information already challenged the official Cawdor account that had the French surrender as a whole at precisely 2 p.m. on 24 February. The timings given are deceptively precise, and it is safe to conclude from other reports that the process took longer than Cawdor described and that many of the French were reluctant to concede. These extra hours are crucial in that they allow aspects of the narrative, later disputed, that involve interplay between the people, including the women and the French, to take place while the outcome was unresolved, and both sides remained in a state of conflict. Some of the French did not give up their arms willingly, the French decision to surrender was something 'to which they did not altogether accede'.[28] These statements contradict Cawdor's official claim to Portland of 24 February that the French were 'determined to surrender themselves'. Some were more reluctant than others. John Reynolds, a local Baptist minister, wrote to his brother to say that the depredations of the French continued 'till Friday evening, when they surrendred [sic]'.[29]

It was only on Sunday that Milford could write with assurance that the French had actually and finally surrendered. His letter on Friday night had informed Portland 'that the French were inclined to surrender. I have now the Pleasure of Informing your Grace that they have Capitulated'.[30] Milford gave Cawdor's negotiation the credit for the surrender. In the space of two days, Milford's focus had changed. Before the surrender he stressed the fury of the people that led him to ask the home secretary for arms to equip the people more effectively. After the surrender, his focus changed to praise for Cawdor's negotiating skills. Later accounts praised Cawdor's master stroke but at the time in private correspondence this went largely unnoticed and was not highlighted by Cawdor himself as anything to brag about. Milford and Cawdor were working, through their carefully worded letters to the home secretary, on behalf of the government and in so doing they controlled the narrative, particularly at the point of surrender and capitulation, stressing the orderly and ordered surrender of the entire French force, the efficacy of the local militia and volunteer forces and the loyalty of all ranks of people involved. The official accounts had a lasting effect and influence in terms of the history of the narrative. The Cawdor/Tate/Portland correspondence is regularly published in the histories and accounts that follow, often alongside versions that contest the official position. Features not mentioned in the official correspondence become more evident as the story unfolded.

Popular Fury

As well as the correspondence from Cawdor and Milford to the home secretary, the newspapers published eyewitness accounts written soon after the events they describe.[31] These letters provide a new context in which to understand the invasion from the perspective of contemporaries. Each correspondent was a narrator with a story to tell. In late February and March 1797, people all over Britain were eager to listen to these stories.

The French landing was national news, not just a matter for the metropolitan newspapers or those that served Wales and the borders. The *Kentish Chronicle* gave the landing considerable exposure, using the official correspondence from the Home Office for the patriotic and propaganda purposes it was intended.[32] The readers of the *Chronicle* were no doubt relieved that the action had taken place in faraway Pembrokeshire, not on their own doorsteps. The east coast was thought by the government to be the prime target for a French invasion. The *Kentish Chronicle* reported that the Welsh peasantry armed themselves with whatever weapons they could and, in their zeal, in a proper expression of their loyalty, 'without waiting for the regular troops', returned to face the enemy. Before the militia arrived, the *Chronicle* claimed, '300 of the French were taken prisoners of the Peasantry'.[33]

The other paper serving the people of Kent was the *Kentish Gazette*. The *Gazette*, like the *Chronicle*, also published the official correspondence from the Home Office, but its editorial was more stridently loyal to Church and King than its rival. After presenting the official correspondence, the *Gazette* entered fully into a theme that would become familiar in the provincial English press, one that associated the Welsh 'country people' with the 'Ancient Britons', an identification that was widely shared.[34] The country people augmented the few soldiers and sailors and formed a force of 'near 3000 persons whose number were hourly increasing. When the Frenchmen saw this, about two o'clock on Thursday, they surrendered'.[35]

The sheer force of the popular response caused the French to surrender. The role of the military was therefore secondary to that of the people. Several newspapers repeated the descriptions of the popular and independent nature of the uprising. The country people had risen *en masse* and armed themselves with whatever weapons they could collect and 'without waiting for the regular troops returned to face the enemy'.[36] The popular enthusiasm was overwhelming and included everyone irrespective of age or gender. The children followed the examples of their parents (parents, not fathers).

Such popular enthusiasm and ferocity, although gratifying and welcome against the hated French invaders, posed a challenge to the military chain of command. Lord Cawdor was commended for his 'great spirit in leading his troop of Yeoman Cavalry', but his difficulties in 'restraining the impetuosity of the Welshmen *who were not willing to allow the invaders to capitulate*' [emphasis added][37] were also described. Several newspapers added details to what they called 'the official accounts of the landing of the French in Wales', which could not be found in the official documents.[38] Cawdor's immediate difficulties were with the Welsh not the French: 'who fell upon the French without order, instead but with irresistible fury'.[39] The reference to disorder demonstrated the serious challenge that the impetuous 'mountaineers' posed to military discipline. A few of the French men were 'killed by this irregular attack, but on the arrival of the militia and volunteers, the invaders surrendered, prisoners of war'.⁴⁰ The challenge of popular 'irresistible fury' was how to control it.

Ten days later, the *Chester Courant* received more accounts from various parts of south Wales that all concurred in praising the zeal and spirit of the exertions by the 'brave descendants of Ancient Britons'. These accounts referred explicitly to both 'men and women' who 'attached themselves to the few military then in that quarter and boldly advanced with them against the enemy'.⁴¹ These accounts specifically concerned the point when the danger of popular attack was at its highest; namely, 'during the parley that preceded their surrender'.⁴² This suggested that the negotiations concerning surrender took place or were continued in the field itself.

Hugh Meyler owned the house in the centre of Fishguard where the leaders of the British forces assembled and that they used as a guard house. This house later became the Royal Oak public house, which celebrates its role in the French Invasion to this day. Hugh Meyler's brother, William Meyler, was the founder and proprietor of the *Bath Herald*. In the issue of that paper for 11 March 1797, a long letter from his brother, dated 5 March and headed 'Fishguard, Guard House', was published, describing the landing.⁴³ The *Hereford Journal* of 15 March published another, shorter letter, slightly different, but substantially the same, dated 10 March from the same correspondent.⁴⁴ Hugh Meyler was a member of the Fishguard Fencibles and involved in the defence of Fishguard; he refered to the Fencibles in the first person plural. The letter is important for this reason and because it offers a reliable version of events by a participant. Meyler's narrative is different to the official version. His account begins as accounts so often did, with the numbers involved. Cawdor's reinforcements gave the Fishguard Fencibles a total force of 'about 500 under the name of soldiers'. But the numbers of 'country people who accompanied us, armed with fowling pieces, swords etc were immense'.⁴⁵ The country people were also 'armed with the musquets of the Supplementary Militia that were deposited at Haverfordwest'.⁴⁶ That evening they marched towards the ground near Llanwnda that was occupied by the French, but returned to Fishguard at nightfall, which was fortunate because had the French 'not been deterred from attacking us, under the idea that we were provided with field pieces, they might easily have surrounded us, and taken our little force prisoners'.⁴⁷

This early near-encounter could have been a disastrous massacre. Behind the high hedge of the Trefwrgi lane lay the grenadiers of the Irish officer Barry St Leger, and in the narrow confines of the lane the Fencibles and Militia would have been easy targets. This near-disaster was not a feature of the official accounts, which stressed the completeness of the British victory through the French surrender. The fact that it was mentioned by Hugh Meyler, an informed participant at the time, showed the small margin between victory and defeat and the uncertainty of armed conflict. A dominant official line was to discredit the French forces and to stress that they were composed largely of galley-slaves and gaol birds, but as Hugh Meyler noted, the French soldiers were well equipped and that upwards of 600 were 'chosen troops, selected from different regiments'.⁴⁸ They could have been more than a match for the local force of 'about 500 under the name of soldiers' led by inexperienced officers such as Cawdor and Knox. However, the French chose not to engage, and that night prepared to surrender. Hugh Meyler's account of the surrender differed from the official accounts: 'That night two of the enemy's officers came to town escorted by a Country Farmer, with an offer to surrender themselves and the whole body. The next morning early, one of our officers attended them to their camp, and a surrender was then *in a manner refused*' [emphasis added].⁴⁹ Hugh Meyler did not mention the exchange of letters even though the negotiations took place in his house. But the main difference was the reference to the offer of surrender being 'in a manner refused' and its timing; namely, early the next morning on Friday 24 February. The official accounts stress the success of Cawdor's tactics of negotiated bluff. The response to Cawdor's letter was, according to the official account, Tate's unconditional surrender. A letter in the Carmarthenshire Record Office suggests another step. Tate wrote again to Cawdor the day after his famous letter of the 5th Ventose; his second missive reads as follows:

> The idea of the officers of the French Corps is the same which you have expressed in your letter. I therefore authorize Lt Colonel Le Brun and Lieutenant Faucon my aid de camp, to meet such officers as you will appoint to treat on the subject of the surrender of the troops in the usual forms.[50]

This letter clearly implies that the issue of surrender was still a matter of negotiation, and that Tate wanted a further meeting to take place.

Meyler's account allows for the French decision to surrender to have been affected by the show of military and popular force early that Friday morning, saying 'Our superior force and a reinforcement expected to the amount of 10,000 were pointed out to them and they were given till ten o'clock to consider of it'.[51]

While the French were considering the offer, the local forces waited and assembled. The deciding factor was what followed:

> We were formed in a line just facing their ground, in the most advantageous manner, every Countryman that had any kind of a weapon was put in the line. The honest Farmers formed in the rear with their horses, and cut so formidable a figure altogether as terrified the French so much, that they all came down to Goodwick-Sand (half-a-mile from Fishguard) and delivered up their Arms.[52]

These early contemporary accounts from an 'active witness' both made clear that the countrymen were equipped with an array of homemade weapons, were deployed in an advantageous manner and included civilians in the line as well as the military.

It was the farmers who 'cut so formidable a figure' that they terrified the French. By early afternoon, Tate, if not all his soldiers, had had enough. Tate told two Welshmen who had been escorted under French arms to Trehowel, 'to inform their countrymen that the French were all prisoners and to leave them alone'.[53]

The letters published in the newspapers differ from the narrative of the official correspondence and portray the distinctive and crucial role of the country people in defeating the French and in so doing highlight the lesser role of the military. The French laid down their arms to the militia to save themselves from the fury of the Welsh people, not because of any surrender negotiated by their superiors. These narratives could have been troubling to government authority.

One way of managing the challenge of popular fury was to downplay the threat of the entire operation. The defeat of the French had been too easy, the French were not a serious threat after all. The government view, and the view of the commander in chief of the British army, the Duke of York, was that the French landing was a predatory expedition not an invasion, because the expedition was so easily countered and by 'honest Welshmen' at that.[54] 'Honest Welshmen' was used here as an insult suggesting that the Welsh people were not very sophisticated or clever. Another example of the downplaying was particularly insulting because a part of it was in Welsh. 'Our undisciplined Cumru [sic]' defeated the French with such ease, therefore 'we may conclude how little we have to fear from any attempt the enemy may make'.[55]

Another means of controlling the narrative of a ferociously enthusiastic people that were different from the English, was to remind readers what the English and Welsh held in common. They were not separate peoples, they were Britons, the only difference being that the Welsh were not only Britons but Ancient Britons, descendants of the original inhabitants of the island of Britain. As Kaminski-Jones has argued, the particular Britishness of the Welsh could simultaneously be a badge of unity or a mark of alterity, even in a piece of explicitly wartime propaganda.[56] English readers were reassured that they had nothing to fear from the French provided that they retained, 'as we are convinced we do, the invincible spirit of Ancient Britons'.[57] At a time of war, the historic characteristics of the Welsh, a separate cultural and picturesque entity as a new generation of tourists were discovering and writing about, could be shared by other Britons. This identification of a masculine, militaristic spirit with the Ancient Britons was particularly relevant at a time of war. It was widely believed that the Ancient Britons had never been defeated, nor submitted to an invader. The bravery of the Ancient Britons was transferable to the English. The Manchester Church and King Club toasted 'the brave and loyal Welsh; and may Englishmen repel invaders with the courage of Ancient Britons'.[58] This Welsh-inflected national defence patriotism easily travelled beyond Wales.[59] The Welsh as 'Ancient Britons' enjoyed higher status than 'honest Welshmen' or 'undisciplined Cumru' in the defence of Britain.

The key feature of the local response to the French invaders was the uneasy alignment between the military (men) and the civilians (women and men). After the popular fury had been checked or accommodated, the small military force of 660 men interacted with the country people of both sexes, of all ranks, of all ages, of different occupations, farmers and colliers from south Pembrokeshire who had equipped themselves with a range of different, but lethal rustic and homemade weapons. Detailed lists of the rustic arms used by the peasantry against the French appeared frequently in the press and in the ballads and hinted at the devastating effect that peasants could inflict even with hand-made weapons. The prospect of the peasantry armed with muskets was another matter altogether, as we have seen from Lord Milford's first letter. He was desperate enough to arm the country people because of his initial fear of being overwhelmed by the French. Some of the civilians already had access to firearms. The list of rustic weapons described by the *Hull Advertiser* and other newspapers included muskets as well as pitchforks.[60] Hugh Meyler in his careful account mentioned that the country people were armed with the muskets of the Supplementary Militia.[61] James Baker, the author of the first published narrative in May 1797, also mentioned that the inhabitants who accompanied the Fishguard Fencibles to take on the French, were 'armed'.[62] An armed peasantry was a matter of concern for the authorities in Pembrokeshire, both during and after the French invasion. First, an armed peasantry might turn their arms against them at a time of civil disorder and riot. Second, and more pressingly at this time of invasion, the armed peasantry might join forces with the French invaders. After the surrender, the military authorities made concerted efforts to retrieve the firearms, left deliberately by the French 'to put into the hands of their friends, whom they expected to join them'.[63]

In the aftermath, two local men, Thomas John and Samuel Griffith, were arrested in March on the charge of treason in that they had communicated with and collaborated with the French. An incidental by-product of the charge was the production of witness statements from the accused and the accusers, describing their comings and goings on the Pencaer peninsula in their own words.[64] The interaction between the military and civilians in these anxious hours, when the French were in uneasy and uncertain transition from hostility to capitulation, is evident in these statements. This direct evidence goes under the cover of the newspaper reports. John and Griffith interacted with the military of both France and Britain out of inquisitiveness and curiosity. The authorities later said that they had acted treasonably, but from their perspective it was more like vigilance and an instinct for self-preservation. The Welsh gathered to spectate in numbers, not only out of curiosity but to keep themselves safe (the women especially) and to keep track of the movements of the French as they threatened their property and livestock. The country people were actively involved in interacting with the French, in taking prisoners and a few even visited Tate's headquarters itself. The position was uncertain, and the French surrendered in piecemeal fashion. Mansell, in Gloucester, mentioned that before he left, the French were beginning to comply to surrender 'by 50 and a 100 at a time'.[65] The French were surrendering not to Cawdor and his troops but in fact to the country people. Thomas John saw 'twenty of the French surrender'.[66] Thomas Davies of Caswilia a near neighbour of Griffith saw the same incident as Samuel Griffith, who witnessed about twenty of the French 'breaking off with some of the Country People'.[67] The French later surrendered in larger numbers but still in an uncoordinated manner, in smaller groups.[68] These accounts under oath show the bravery of the people who took on the French in a spirit that would later be associated with Jemima Nicholas.

It was while engaging with the enemy, doing what they had been told to do, or thought they had to do, that misinterpretations of their actions and 'high words' took place. John, a young Baptist farmer from Summertown, claimed that he was asked by Lord Cawdor (under examination it turned out to be Colby, the only experienced officer among the militia) to call the rest of the French together, since they were so scattered. It was while he was performing this quasi-military role that John engaged with the French. As the French marched past, John asked if one of them could speak English. One answered that he could, and a conversation ensued between Charles Prudhomme – who was in fact an American – and Thomas John. Prudhomme stated he had no idea where he was, believing himself to be in the north of Ireland. It was John who told him he was in Wales. Prudhomme asked about the gaols and where they were situated, evidently concerned as a potential, if not actual, prisoner of war about his welfare.[69] This exchange was witnessed by others who believed that he had 'some office' with the Frenchman. John replied that he had none, he was only doing what Cawdor had told him.[70]

Griffith's story was that on Friday 24 February he went with his son and Thomas Davies to the high ground by Carn Coch, where they joined a group of Welsh people and encountered the French. As the country people were receiving the muskets of the French, one French soldier made to push at Griffith with the bayonet. Griffith was understandably afraid, but in Griffith's own words, he 'did nothing further to the said French Soldier who immediately came up to this Examinant and *patted him on the Knee shewing as this Examinant believes a Disposition to surrender but an unwillingness to deliver up his Arms*'[71] [emphasis added]. The confusion worsened with the sudden appearance of about 100 French soldiers who were meant to be surrendering, but instead, captured those who were facilitating the surrender.

In retrospect, Cawdor claimed a level of control that he may not have possessed at the time. The young, impressionable John Manners, Duke of Rutland, visited Cawdor on his tour in Wales shortly after the landing and had dinner with his host. Rutland later recorded the information that he received over dinner from Cawdor in his journal, which was published privately in small numbers for the reading pleasure of his friends in 1805. According to Rutland, Cawdor 'made the best disposition he could in dispersing his men on the different heights, to deceive the French as to numbers' late on 23 February.[72] This achieved two effects. First, it allowed Cawdor and his officers to accommodate, if not control, the popular fury of the country people, which seemed to be becoming unrestrained. Second, it allowed Cawdor to use the force of numbers to deceive the French of his superiority. The evidence of the moment does not suggest that the 'best disposition' was intended to convey the visual effect of the appearance of British troops, just the impression of superior numbers. Women were not only spectators, they were active participants, and they were there in the numbers.

The *Annual Register* reported that 'more than three thousand men were collected, of whom 700 were well-trained militia' in Fishguard and its environs on the 23 and 24 February 1797.[73] This figure of more than 3,000 people in total suggests more than 2,000 civilians, men and women. The population of the parish at the time was estimated at some 2,600, based on the number of households.⁷⁴ There were more people in and around Fishguard than the entire population of the parish of Fishguard itself (which included Goodwick). Ordinary people assembled in Fishguard from all parts of southwest Wales and beyond. The French were faced with the popular fury of the people of Dyfed, or as Iolo Morganwg (the bard of Glamorganshire, Edward Williams 1747–1826) put it, the 'ferocious Demetians'.⁷⁵

Women in Red

The ruse of deliberate or 'judicious' positioning did not take long to arrive.⁷⁶ Strongly associated with the visual deception, its vital component, was the iconic French Invasion 'myth' of the women in red. In the accounts of the surrender, the capitulation and the role of the country people, including the women, were intricately linked. One of the reasons for the invisibility of the women as active participants in the confrontation was the use of the identity of Ancient Britons in this context, as it signified masculinity and martial identity, thus excluding the women. The concept of Ancient Britons was a traditional literary and historical archetype, and it was used in several contexts.⁷⁷

There was a Society of Ancient Britons, long established, dominated largely by aristocrats and the affluent London Welsh.⁷⁸ There were no women in the Society, and women were not included in the idea of Ancient Britons.⁷⁹ Ancient Britons were masculine, Cambria was feminine.⁸⁰ The prevalence of this particular expression of identity suppressed female agency.⁸¹ Hugh Meyler in the *Bath Herald* and the *Herford Journal* described the Welsh achievement as a male affair: 'We have by tradition heard that THE WELSH WERE NEVER CONQUERED and I verily believe not a man would have disgraced his Ancestors.'⁸² This same issue of the *Hereford Journal*, 15 March 1797, included an epigram on the Welsh Haymakers:

The brave ANCIENT BRITONS were frequently told
By their Preachers, that 'all flesh was grain'
That men were cut down, both the young and the old
And thence to dry herbage did pass

So when the Invaders no longer conceal'd
Their designs on old England to pray
The Welshmen with *scythe*s went to mow the French fields
And with *pitchforks* their wives to make hay.[83]

The references to the homemade weapons of the country people carefully listed each rustic item transformed into a weapon: scythes, pitchforks, bludgeons, fowling guns, reaping hooks. However, the weapons had important gender implications, as some were weapons designated for men, others for women. Scythes were weapons for men, pitchforks for women. To the authorities, the disposition of the people who bore arms was as important, if not more important than the arms they wielded. Accounts stressed the all-embracing response of the people, men and women of all ages. An account in the *Cumberland Paquet* included both genders as: 'becoming of the character of ANCIENT BRITONS. An immense muster had assembled, who were pushing on a mass on the enemy (many of the women accompanying their husbands to the attack determined to conquer or perish with them).'[84]

The distinctive contribution of the women and girls to the civilian response is captured in a number of sources, all of which describe their actions as occurring as early as the landing itself. The first type of account is that of ridicule used to discredit the domestic and French military alike. A Mr Jenkins rode all the way from Hay to Carmarthen, with the troops ordered to Pembrokeshire, to see for himself what was taking place. Jenkins described the frantic movement of troops mobilising across south Wales and the west country and news of landings and false alarms. Some did not believe the news. On the Monday morning after the landing, he went to his neighbour Joseph Brown of Castleton who did not take the news seriously at first: 'he began joking with me with raising a false alarm about the French landing in Wales and fearing the Old Women in the Country.'[85] But news had evidently travelled fast and part of this was a story about the 'Old Women'. It was the same story that Iolo Morganwg heard at home in Flemingston in the Vale of Glamorgan: 'Our Dragooners sent us some companies of Dragoons after the old women of Pembrokeshire had secured the damned Republicans as it seems we are requested to call them.'[86]

The 'Old Women' jibe became part of anti-military banter and satire. Hugh Barlow, member of Parliament for Pembroke Boroughs, attended a subsequent county meeting in Pembroke arranged by Lord Milford to consider the contributions of the various parties in achieving the surrender of the French in order to form a Resolution of thanks. Barlow gave Cawdor a report of the meeting. After mentioning the various weightings given to the male combatants, with Cawdor's name given precedence, one man ventured, as Barlow put it, 'I think in ridicule' to thank 'the women who attended at Fishguard'.[87]

Other sources of information about the role of the women at Fishguard come from female letter correspondents who have long been known to those who have studied and written about the French Invasion, including historian Stuart Jones who refers to them in his classic work published in 1950.[88] The first known account written by a woman was a letter from Mary and John Mathias of Narberth to their sister in service in Swansea, dated 27 February 1797. It is the authentic voice of young people, contrasting sharply with the tone and content of the gentlemen and military men that appeared in the press, or the clever but sneering mockery of Iolo.[89] This remarkable letter written in distinctive south Pembrokeshire dialect references the presence of women, their number and their commitment to fight. The letter also mentions what they wore, although this is incidental to the narrative. Later the apparel of the women become almost more important than the women themselves. An extract of this letter with some alterations was published in newspapers in April 1797.[90] One difference is the assumption of a first-person female voice, that of a 'Pembrokeshire lass to her friend in Swansea'. But there are other significant differences too:

> Four hundred of us went to Squire Campbell's in *our red mantles to look like Soldiers*. He asked us, what we came for? We said, to *fight the French*. And when the French saw us, they laid down their arms. God struck their hearts with fear and took from them the spirit of War. To him be the praise. God save the King.[91] [emphasis added]

The newspaper versions of April 1797 have the writer as a participant rather than a commentator, and the purpose of the 'red mantles' has become evident: to make them look like British soldiers.

The second piece of evidence presented by Stuart Jones was a letter from John Mends of Haverfordwest to his son, a surveyor of customs at Grays in Essex, dated 27 February.[92] According to Mends, the French surrendered for several reasons. First, their ships had abandoned them. Second, the 'vigilance, alackrity and spirit of the Welch', and third 'above all, about 400 poor women with Red flannel over their shoulders which the French at a distance took for soldiers, as they appeared all Red'.[93]

This letter provides a dispassionate and non-military explanation from civilian to civilian. John Mends gives prominence to the role of the country people: 'one of the most glorious Conquest(s) ever performed by a parcel of Country people and no Soldiers amongst them.'[94] This statement would be uncharacteristic for a military participant in the Invasion since it relegates the role of the military, while promoting the role of civilians. The role of the women was soon made known to the French combatants at the time. Charles Prudhomme, the American who gave evidence against the 'traitor' Thomas John at his apprehension initially deposed on oath that he had been informed by John, who had come to the camp on that Thursday evening, that there were only 300 soldiers below and that the rest were women in red flannels.[95] Stuart Jones marshalled this evidence in 1950, but these were not new pieces of evidence and had long been known to historians of the Invasion. The contemporary evidence of the role of the women reappeared at various points to challenge the dominant male military account and later revisions, and would appear to support oral tradition with hard evidence.[96]

Since the publication of Stuart Jones's classic work, other evidence has come to light that strengthens the female, civilian narrative. Around the time of the Invasion, Ann Knight, a London Quaker, was on a visit to her cousin in Haverfordwest. It was a very female household; her cousin John was the only man among seven women in the house. Knight's letter describes the streets of Haverfordwest as the French prisoners were coming in. Her letter from 28 February to her father in London also shows the interchangeability of descriptors for the national communities of eighteenth-century Britain:

> the english or rather the welsh got together with the women and children with the red flannels over their shoulders and placed them in such a position that the french could only see their heads and they thought it was a large army of men and one of our officers spoke to the general and told him we they [sic] had ten thousand men under arms and gave him his choice either to come to engagement directly or surrender.[97]

The connection between the positioning and the women was made even more explicit. Just over a year later 28 August 1798, the *Kentish Gazette* noted:

> We scarcely recollect a better military stratagem, than that by which Lord Cawdor intimidated the French troops that landed at Fishguard-it is *not generally known* that a number of Welsh women, whose common dress is a beaver hat and a short red cloak were ranged on the surrounding hills. The French commander, when summoned to surrender, was desired to observe, that the ascents were covered with soldiers. The *uniform of the ladies* were at that distance a formidable appearance, and the heroes of the GREAT NATION surrendered at discretion to the fair.[98] [author's italics]

It had taken just over a year for the role of the women at Fishguard to be singled out as a deliberate stratagem to fool the French and insult their masculinity and military prowess. While letter writers John Mends and Ann Knight mention the 'red flannels' as civilian apparel a year later this garment has become militarised as 'the uniform of the ladies'. In view of the eyewitness accounts it becomes extremely likely that the women played an active role in the civilian response that intimidated the French.[99]

Louise Carter discusses how women in Georgian Britain were attracted to the scarlet of the men in uniform, a sexual and social attraction that was also the gendered way in which Georgian men and women were encouraged to express their patriotism during war.[100] In 1797 in Pembrokeshire, women had the opportunity to perform a martial role in masculine military red. The women appear in the accounts of the French as a contributing factor to their surrender. The precise nature of the women's martial role, whether they marched around the Bigney or were organised in any way separately as 'women', or whether they rushed down to the sands to face the French face to face, remained a matter of conjecture that later developed into the legend that resonated in popular culture and memory.

Figure 3: 'A Fishguard Fencible'

'A Fishguard Fencible', as seen in Figure 3, is a familiar image of the Fishguard Invasion. This engraving, dated early March 1797, was produced in London in Berners Street by G. M. Woodward. A satirical piece, the text signifies the direct speech of the Fishguard Fencible in a mock Welsh accent. The text in the engraving is as important as the image itself, reading: 'Py St DAVID-they took the Womens red Cloaks for Soldiers & look'd as pale as the Tiffel himself-Let em come-whose afraid-WELCH POYS-reaping hooks-toasted cheese-creen Leaks and Little FISHGUARD for ever!'

It shows categorically that the red cloaks of the women had been taken by the French to be soldiers, though whether as a *ruse de guerre* or because of French stupidity is not clear, but it was a device that succeeded. The engraving exudes confidence and bravado, 'Let em come'. The striped jacket was the uniform of the Fishguard Fencibles as supplied by Thomas Knox. The young Fencible is holding a massive reaping hook, the fighting instrument of the country people, not the musket of the Fencible. In this image we have all the components of the home defence against the French Invasion, a composite which mentions boys and women, and a young Fencible wielding the weapon of the country people. Above all, the image celebrates the victory of the people of Fishguard, the Fencible exclaiming 'LITTLE FISHGUARD for ever!'

Endnotes

1. Charles Hassall, *General View of the Agriculture of the County of Pembroke* (London, 1794) p. 10.
2. R. G. Thorne, 'The Pembrokeshire Elections of 1807 and 1812', *The Pembrokeshire Historian*, 6 (1979), 9.
3. J. E. Davies, *The Changing Fortunes of a British Aristocratic Family 1789–1976: The Campbells of Cawdor and their Welsh Estates* (Woodbridge, 2019), p. 14.
4. R. G. Thorne, 'The Pembrokeshire Elections', 9.
5. E. H. Stuart Jones, *The Last Invasion of Britain* (Cardiff, 1950), p. 85 and notes 4 and 5, p. 253.
6. Stuart Jones, *The Last Invasion*, p. 86.
7. *The Times* (24 February 1797).
8. Edmund Burke, *A Third Letter to a Member of the Present Parliament on the proposals for Peace with the Regicide Directory* (London, 1796), pp. 36–7.

Popular and Official Reports

9 'This Day's Mail London 25 February', as reported in the *Dublin Evening Post* (28 February 1797), 3.
10 *Hampshire Chronicle* (4 March 1797), 2; see also *Chester Chronicle* (3 March 1797), 2.
11 *The Times* (27 February 1797), 2.
12 Willliam Windham noted in his diary for Saturday 25 February 1797 'News of descent in Wales', the next day, Sunday 26 February, he learnt of the surrender. Mrs Henry Baring, *The Diary of the Right Hon. William Windham 1784 to 1810* (London, 1866), p. 353.
13 A. Aspinall (ed.), *The Later Correspondence of George III, vol. 2: February 1793 to December 1797* (Cambridge, 1963), pp. 544–5.
14 *The Times* (28 February 1797), 4.
15 These three letters were printed in several publications. This version is from 'French Invasion', *The Universal Magazine* (March 1797), 211.
16 Carmarthenshire Record Office, Cawdor Collection, box 223. The Duke of Portland wrote to the King, Sunday 26 February 8.25 p.m.: 'The Duke of Portland humbly begs leave to lay before your Majesty a letter which he has just received from Lord Cawdor and two enclosures, by which it appears that the French surrender'd themselves prisoners of war and laid down their arms accordingly'; Aspinall, *The Later Correspondence of George III*, letter 8335, p. 545.
17 For example, *Kentish Chronicle* (28 February 1797), 3–4.
18 H. F. B. Wheeler and A. M. Broadley, *Napoleon and the Invasion of England: The Story of the Great Terror*, vol. 1 (London, 1908), p. 58; *Kentish Chronicle* (28 February 1797), 4.
19 Wheeler and Broadley, *Napoleon and the Invasion of England*, p. 59.
20 Milford to Portland, no date but 24 February 1797 National Archives 42-40-3 no. 240.
21 A year later Milford would escape from Picton Castle to his town house in Piccadilly in fear of the colliers who had threatened to set his castle on fire. David Howell, 'Society 1660–1793' in Davies and Howell, *Pembrokeshire County History, vol. 3: Early Modern Pembrokeshire 1536–1815* (Haverfordwest, 1987), p. 297.
22 National Archives 42-40-3 no. 240.
23 National Archives 42-40-3 no. 240.
24 Milford to David Edwardes, 24 February 1797, Carmarthenshire Record Office. Facsimile of original in Syd Walters, *Fishguard and French Invasion: Cheating and Obtaining Funds by False Pretences* (Glastonbury, 1995) pp. 5–7.
25 *Gloucester Journal* (27 February 1797), 3.
26 PEMBROKIENSIS. 'To the CONDUCTOR of the TIMES', *The Times* (15 March 1797), 3.
27 *Gloucester Journal* (27 February 1797), 3.
28 *Gloucester Journal* (27 February 1797), 3.

29 British Library Add MS 25388, fol. 410; John Reynolds to William Reynolds, 3 April 1797.
30 Milford to Portland, 26 February 1797, Wheeler and Broadley, *Napoleon and the Invasion of England*, p. 60. The earlier letter, which said the French 'have surrendered' not 'inclined to surrender', was sent at 9 p.m. on Friday 24 February 1797, see David Salmon, *French Invasion of Pembrokeshire* (Carmarthen, 1930), p. 24.
31 The main letters are 'News from Haverfordwest from a friend of a Bristol Gentleman', *Chester Courant* (28 February 1797) 3; 'A person who was an active witness of all the circumstances' who attended 'the late invasion of Wales' letter dated 10 March 1797 *Hereford Journal* (15 March 1797), 3; letter from Pembroke dated 5 March, *Kentish Chronicle* (17 March), 4; letter from Fishguard Guard-House dated 5 March, *Bath Herald* (11 March 1797); letter from a 'military gentleman who was in Lord Cawdor's Army' dated 22 February, published in *Hereford Journal* (29 March 1797), 3. For a treatment based on newspapers from the border counties, see M Löffler, *Welsh Responses to the French Revolution: Press and Public Discourse 1789–1802* (Cardiff, 2012), pp. 16–18.
32 *The Kentish Chronicle* (28 February 1797), 2–4.
33 *The Kentish Chronicle* (28 February 1797), 4.
34 *Hereford Journal* (1 March 1797), 3; *Northampton Mercury* (4 March 1797), 1; *Cambridge Intelligencer* (4 March 1797), 1.
35 *The Kentish Chronicle* (28 February 1797), 4; *Hereford Journal* (1 March 1797), 3; *Northampton Mercury* (4 March 1797), 1; *Cambridge Intelligencer* (4 March 1797), 1.
36 *Caledonian Mercury* (2 March 1797), 3; *Hull Advertiser* (4 March 1797), 2; *Newcastle Courant* (4 March 1797), 2; *Leeds Intelligencer* (6 March 1797), 1.
37 *Hereford Journal* (1 March 1797), 3.
38 *Bath Chronicle* (2 March 1797), 2; *Norfolk Chronicle* (4 March 1797), 2.
39 *Bath Chronicle* (2 March 1797), 2; *Norfolk Chronicle* (4 March 1797), 2; *Caledonian Mercury* (2 March 1797), 3; *Hampshire Chronicle* (4 March 1797), 2.
40 *Bath Chronicle* (2 March 1797), 2; *Norfolk Chronicle* (4 March 1797), 2; *Caledonian Mercury* (2 March 1797), 3; *Hampshire Chronicle*, (4 March 1797), 2.
41 *Chester Courant* (14 March 1797), 3.
42 *Chester Courant* (14 March 1797), 3.
43 The letter is mentioned by Stuart Jones in *The Last Invasion*, p. 257 footnote 1, but the evidence that it contains is not used.
44 The letter in the *Hereford Journal* (15 March 1797), 3, is dated 10 March and has fewer radical anti-official statements than the earlier letter in the *Bath Herald* (11 March 1797), 2, which is dated 5 March.
45 *Hereford Journal* (15 March 1797), 3; *Bath Herald* (11 March 1797), 2.

46 *Bath Herald* (11 March 1797), 2. This alarming prospect for the authorities was omitted by the *Hereford Journal*, which used 'etc' to avoid listing all the types of weapon available to the 'country people'.
47 *Hereford Journal* (15 March 1797), 3; similar text was published in the *Bath Herald* (11 March 1797), 2.
48 *Hereford Journal* (15 March 1797), 3. This text does not appear in the *Bath Herald*.
49 *Bath Herald* (11 March 1797), 2.
50 Carmarthenshire Record Office, Cawdor Collection Box 223, Tate to Cawdor 6th Ventose, 5th year of the Republic.
51 *Bath Herald* (11 March 1797), 2.
52 *Bath Herald* (11 March 1797), 2.
53 Griffith's Own Examination, in David Salmon, 'A Sequel to the French Invasion of Pembrokeshire', *Y Cymmrodor*, 43 (1932), 89.
54 *Leeds Intelligencer* (6 March 1797), 1; *Northampton Mercury* (4 March 1797), 1; *Chester Courant* (7 March 1797), 1.
55 *Chester Chronicle* (10 March 1797), 3.
56 Rhys Kaminski-Jones, 'True Britons: Ancient British Identity in Wales and Britain' (unpublished PhD thesis, University of Wales, 2016), 199.
57 *Chester Courant* (7 March 1797), 1; *Derby Mercury* (16 March 1797), 4.
58 *Manchester Mercury*, (14 March 1797), 4. See also *The Times* (3 March 1797), 3.
59 Elizabeth Edwards, *English-Language Poetry from Wales 1789–1806* (Cardiff, 2013) p. 31.
60 *Hull Advertiser* (4 March 1797), 2.
61 *Bath Herald* (11 March 1797), 2. This statement does not appear in his *Hereford Journal* letter.
62 J. Baker, *A Brief Narrative of the French Invasion, Near Fishguard Bay* (Worcester, 1797), p. 5.
63 *Kentish Chronicle* (17 March 1797), 4.
64 For versions of this narrative see John S. Kinross, *Fishguard Fiasco: An Account of the Last Invasion of Britain*, rev. edn (Little Logaston, 2007), pp. 56–60; Stuart Jones, *The Last Invasion*, pp. 223–7 and 231–2.
65 *Gloucester Journal* (27 February 1797), 3.
66 Salmon, 'A Sequel to the French Invasion of Pembrokeshire', 73.
67 Salmon, 'A Sequel to the French Invasion of Pembrokeshire', 80 and 88.
68 Salmon, 'A Sequel to the French Invasion of Pembrokeshire', 73.
69 Salmon, 'A Sequel to the French Invasion of Pembrokeshire', 74–5.
70 Salmon, 'A Sequel to the French Invasion of Pembrokeshire', 74–5.
71 Salmon, 'A Sequel to the French Invasion of Pembrokeshire', 87–8.
72 John, Duke of Rutland, *Journal of a Tour through North and South Wales, the Isle of Man* (London, 1805) entry for 19 August 1797, p. 132.
73 *Annual Register, or a View of the History, Politics and Literature for the Year 1797*, 39, second edn (1807), p. 89.
74 'Statistical Account of the Parish of Fishguard in Pembrokeshire', *The Cambrian Register for the year 1795* (1796) p. 260,

75 Aberystwyth, National Library of Wales, NLW 1760A, 6/13. See also G. H. Jenkins, 'An Uneasy Relationship: Gwallter Mechain and Iolo Morganwg', *The Montgomeryshire Collections*, 97 (2009), 80.
76 *The Monthly Magazine or British Magazine*, 1797, p. 172.
77 Sarah Prescott, *Eighteenth-Century Writing from Wales: Bards and Britons* (Cardiff, 2008); Bethan M. Jenkins, *Between Wales and England: Anglophone Welsh Writing of the Eighteenth Century* (Cardiff, 2017); Kaminski-Jones, 'True Britons'.
78 See Kaminski-Jones for the cultural contribution and public patriotism of this group of anglophone Welshmen, '"Where Cymry United, Delighted Appear": The Society of Ancient Britons and the celebration of St David's Day in London 1715–1815', *Transactions of the Honourable Society of Cymmrodorion*, new ser., 23 (2017), 56–68.
79 Women were not members of the London Welsh societies until the Second Cymmrodorion Society in 1820, which had a few 'lady subscribers', R. T. Jenkins and H. Ramage, *A History of the Honourable Society of Cymmrodorion* (London, 1951), p. 7.
80 See Richard Fenton, *The Tears of Cambria* (1773) and portrayed by Englishmen as 'fallen', also Joseph Cottle, *The Fall of Cambria* (1808).
81 For the exclusion of 'polite women', see Kaminski-Jones, 'True Britons', p. 32.
82 *Bath Herald* (11 March 1797), 2; *Hereford Journal* (15 March 1797), 3.
83 *Hereford Journal* (15 March 1797), 3.
84 *Cumberland Paquet* (7 March 1797), 2.
85 'Landing of the French: AD 1797', *Carmarthenshire Antiquarian Society Transactions*, vol. 8, 23–4 (1912–13), 79.
86 National Library of Wales, NLW MSS 13222, fol. 131–4, Iolo Morganwg to William Owen-Pughe, 7 March 1797.
87 Carmarthenshire Record Office, Cawdor collection box 223, Barlow to Cawdor, 18 March 1797.
88 Stuart Jones, *The Last Invasion*, pp. 115–21. The Mathias letter had been in the public domain since 1869.
89 Stuart Jones, *The Last Invasion*, p. 119.
90 *Bath Chronicle* (13 April 1797), 3; *Hereford Journal* (19 April 1797), 3.
91 *Bath Chronicle* (13 April 1797), 3; *Hereford Journal* (19 April 1797), 3.
92 Stuart Jones, *The Last Invasion*, pp. 120–1. This letter was first published by David Salmon in the *West Wales Historical Society Transactions*, 14 (1929), and was presented to him by Sir James H. Seabrooke. For the Mends family, see L. Phillips, 'The Naval Family Mends of Haverfordwest', *Dyfed Family History Journal*, 10/7 (December 2010), 26–7.
93 David Salmon, 'The French Invasion of Pembrokeshire in 1797', *West Wales Historical Transactions*, 14 (1929), 155–7.
94 Salmon, 'The French invasion of Pembrokeshire in 1797', 156.
95 Stuart Jones, *The Last Invasion*, p. 121.

96 The Mathias letter was rediscovered in 1869 and again 1935, the Mends letter in 1912.
97 R. B. Rose, 'The French at Fishguard: Fact, Fiction and Folklore', *Transactions of the Honourable Society of Cymmrodorion*, new ser., 9 (2003), 98. Richard Rose says he was converted to the orthodox doctrine of the women at Fishguard on the strength of that letter.
98 *Kentish Gazette* (Tuesday 28 August 1798), 3; also in *Staffordshire Advertiser* (1 September 1798), 2.
99 Anne Brigstocke from St Clears mentions the French surrendering to the 'glitter bright' cloaks of 'our women', *God and Gideon or, the valour of ancient Britons displayed* (no date but NLW has *c*.1797, no imprint) lines 53–5, pp. 2–3.
100 Louise Carter, 'Scarlet fever: Female Enthusiasm for Men in Uniform 1780–1815', in Kevin Linch and Matthew McCormack, *Britain's Soldiers: Rethinking War and Society, 1715–1815* (Liverpool, 2014), p. 179.

Chapter 2

Despair, Deliverance and Discord, 1797 to 1798

Chouannerie, a form of guerrilla warfare or banditry used originally by the royalists in La Vendée, was a feature of republican invasion plans, to 'carry death and despair into the ranks of the enemies' and cause chaos and civil war.[1] Although the French Invasion failed, it succeeded in inciting terror.

The overwhelming emotion experienced by the people in Pembrokeshire and south-west Wales, particularly those directly involved as victims of the invaders, was fear. This is, perhaps, an obvious observation to make but it is comparatively absent from the historiography of the invasion.[2] Ordinary people did not normally write about their experiences in any autobiographical sense, their actions spoke for them. Fear was not a sentiment to be articulated publicly unless it was overcome. The civilian fury and bravery, described in Chapter 1 rose triumphantly out of fear.

The enterprising travel writer and engraver James Baker rushed the first narrative and visual representations of the invasion into print a few months after the invasion in May 1797.[3] As author of the *Picturesque Guide through Wales and the Marches* (1795), Baker was a travel writer and topographer of established reputation.[4] Not much is known of his personal history but he had spent 'a long residence' in south Wales, and this may

Figure 4: James Baker engraving of Fishguard Bay

have been in Fishguard itself.[5] Baker was at pains to stress the preparation that had gone into his *Brief Narrative of the French Invasion Near Fishguard Bay*, it contained 'every local information which the Author has been able to collect on a studious enquiry and from his own attentive Survey'.[6] The tranquil, rural locality was disrupted that memorable February day 'by so much horror and dismay' that 'every other passion became swallowed up in fear'.[7]

Welsh-language accounts were even more sensitive to the emotions of ordinary people. The Baptist minister and historian Titus Lewis, a native of Cilgerran but long associated with the church at Blaen y Waun, a few miles from Fishguard, defined the Fishguard Invasion primarily by the 'terror' that it had caused to the local inhabitants. The landing 'caused great terror throughout all the neighbourhoods' ('parodd hyn ddychryn mawr trwy'r holl cymmydogaethau').[8]

Deliverance from Despair

The emotional experience of ordinary people can be found not so much in the prose evidence of accounts and histories, but more in social memory and oral tradition, in poetry, in the Welsh-language ballads of the period.[9] In the quest for authenticity in the historical narrative of the French Invasion, the ballads provide the most reliable means, making allowance for literary form, of accessing the experiences and perceptions of contemporaries. The ballads express the fear and the common loathing of the local people towards the French.

The ballad writers were contemporaries, several were local to the area of southwest Wales, and some may have been eyewitnesses of the events or knew people who had seen the events in Fishguard themselves.[10] The ballads express loyalty to Britain and to the King, but were not loyalist propaganda pieces translated from the English or examples of a genre taken over by reactionary voices.[11] The ballads were sung in fairs and public places but also printed and traded in market squares as a source of news. They were the cultural expression of a people who were shaken to their core by these terrible events. As the ordinary people faced threat to life and limb, their instinctive reactions were to wish for their own or their communities' safety, allay their own fears, express their hostility towards the enemy and praise God for their miraculous deliverance.[12] The emphasis on a miraculous escape from the enemy is commonplace, the word 'deliverance' ('*gwaredigaeth*') and its cognates are present in several of the titles of the ballads concerned.[13] The understanding of their world was based on the received authority of the Scripture. The overwhelming priorities of the balladeers were to frame events familiar to their local audiences within the parameters of miraculous escape or deliverance. Through the ballads, the people expressed their thanks for the relief of their fears and their deliverance from the subjects of their loathing. For example, 'Fishguard, you escaped from the hands of merciless men, take care to give all the praise properly to the King of Zion for saving you'.[14] Deliverance was an occasion for praise.[15]

The people who were invaded expressed their fear in their own voices. Ebenezer Richard is more famous as the father of Henry Richard (1812–88), the member of Parliament for Wales and Apostle of Peace,[16] than for his own achievements, which included drawing up the Calvinistic Methodist Confession of Faith in 1823.[17] At the time of the invasion, he was a young man of fifteen or sixteen who lived in nearby Trefin, and the events made a profound impression on him. It was said that the invasion preyed on his mind throughout his life ('wedi effeithio ar ei feddwl ar hyd ei oes').[18] At the time of the invasion, or very soon after, Richard wrote a ballad that conveyed the emotions of a young man consumed with fear and worry. The biblical references to wailing and lament are clear, but within the literary form they had personal meaning and reference: 'Am yr amser tywyll du' ('Of the time of pitch black despair').[19] Richard referred to the thousands of people who were in a state of fear and trepidation as if they were hovering over their own graves ('Yno hongian uwch ein beddau'). On the Wednesday of the invasion, when they arose from their warm beds, little did they know that there were cruel enemies in their midst; they were too afraid to return to their beds that night. The cause of their incessant weeping and moaning was the news that a host had invaded their small island, intent on polluting God's Gospel and introducing the worst kind of Papistry into their midst. With the fear came loathing. These were the 'black enemies' ('gelynion duon'): 'Bymtheg cant o ddynion o bob rhyw, rhai o'r blacks a rhai o'r tonis, Ni hadwaenem wrth eu lliw' ('fifteen hundred men of all races, some were black and some were tawny, unrecognisable by their colour').[20] The colours here referred to their uniforms, not the colour of their skin. Throughout the period when the French ran rampage, the people moaned and groaned incessantly ('Yr oedd llefau ac och'neidiau, Yr holl amser yn parhau').[21] Then, after the all-consuming fear, came wonderful deliverance, akin to that of the children of Israel from the cruelty of Egypt.

Ballads did convey reliable information; some gave specifics confirming the accuracy of popular knowledge within the literary form and its religious framing. The balladeer Philip Dafydd supplies a litany of suffering and loss, stolen wealth, wanton destruction of food and clothing, and rape, and refers to a specific incident: 'the cursed pagans burnt our Bibles, where life is'.[22] This is a specific reference to the spoliation of the church at Llanwnda. As well as the bible, the church records and registers were destroyed, and the Communion plate stolen.[23]

The most descriptive ballad, as a source for the history of popular participation in the conflict, is the anonymously written ballad, *Clôd i'r Cymry* ('Praise to the Welsh').[24] It provides a vivid account of the invasion almost from an insider's perspective, indicating the proximity of the author to the location of the invasion.[25] The unknown author presents the mindless destruction of the French against the response of the local population who were responsible almost exclusively for their defeat. This is the most worldly of the ballads to deal with the invasion. The element of praise to God is certainly present, but as the title of the ballad suggests, praise was due not only to God, but to the Welsh and to the men of Pembrokeshire. It is likely that the author was one of these men. We have here a voice of the 'country people'. It is a very masculine voice. This claim of victory for the people is done with an astounding confidence that has an appealing freshness[26] No other ballad represents the role of the people and 'their popular fury' as well as this one does.

The ballad tells how the French gorged themselves at the local people's expense. They stole the corn from the barn and the cattle and the calves. They delved into the cellars to get fresh, strong beer, and then wastefully poured the rest away. Furniture from the houses was used to build fires to boil their food. These French soldiers were 'Llu gwrthnysig, cad mileinig / Rhai ffyrnig, milwyr Ffrainc' ('a vile host, a savage throng, fierce men, French soldiers').[27]

Other ballads also depict the French in the most loathsome terms.[28] The ballads are united in their depiction of the French as a serious threat. There is no downplaying of the peril, these French men were physical, existentialist threats to the lives, property and livelihoods of the community, from whose clutches they were graciously delivered by God. The focus of hatred is on the French as despoilers, vagabonds and thieves not as republicans, not even as atheists or Papists.[29] Ebenezer Richard's reference to Papistry is an exception.

The loss of property and possessions features prominently.[30] Injuries against the person seem to have a lower priority than loss of property. In the litany of loss, rape comes second to the ruination of food and tearing of clothes.[31] It was not until 1803, a time of even greater country-wide invasion fear and panic in the face of a renewed threat from Napoleon and a mobilisation of the population on a scale not previously attempted in Britain, that rape came to be more strongly recognised as one of the atrocities of the French.

One of the ballads reflects the linguistic divide between north and south of the county, referring to 'the valiant English and the noble, loyal Welsh', suggesting that the armed men were viewed as Englishmen from the south, while the Welsh (that is, Welsh-speaking) from the north, were the non-military.[32] Another ballad refers to 'the Welsh together with the English of Pembroke'.[33] These are differences, not tensions. The ballads reflect overwhelmingly the inclusive Pembrokeshire nature of the resistance to the French. The English language ballads preserved in oral memory from Jeffreston and Corston in the south stressed 'how we were saved in Pembrokeshire' and how 'the country folks they gathered to Fishguard from all parts'.[34] Men and women from all parts of Pembrokeshire were involved in resisting the French: the yeomanry cavalry led by Cawdor from Castlemartin; volunteers from Pembroke; sailors from Solva near St David's; Knox's Fencibles with two separate contingents, one from Fishguard the other from Newport (Trefdraeth); and the pitmen from Hook near Haverfordwest, who may have been accompanied by their women folk. The Cardiganshire militia were involved too. As another ballad writer put it, the credit lay with the gallant men of Pembrokeshire whose fame now resounded throughout Britain, 'noble Welsh, because they were faithful to the Crown'.[35]

Fear and Flight

The English-language accounts may not be as immediate as the Welsh but they do express one consequence of fear: flight. Flight was available to those with the wealth and the means to leave quickly.[36] Philip Dafydd, the Newcastle Emlyn ballad singer, wrote that when the French landed in Pencaer, 'all were weeping' and 'the inhabitants generously had to leave their wealth behind'.[37] In her English-language ballad, the genteel Anne Brigstocke talks of the 'Dread to many' that had 'Houses, Land and Money / Fear they should all them lose'.[38]

The *Leeds Intelligencer* published an extract of a letter from Haverfordwest to a 'gentleman of rank and fortune in this neighbourhood' in late March.[39] The writer of the extract, relates how the minister of Llanwnda and his family escaped with their lives, while the French soldiers destroyed all his furniture, flung his books into the sea, wantonly 'murdered his livestock' and, almost as an afterthought, 'ravished' (in other words, sexually assaulted or raped) his maid servants who were left in the house.[40] Baker tells how the French set fire to the furze and heath to give them light and security. The fire and smoke were causes of 'the most extreme distress' for the 'alarmed and scattered inhabitants' who had deserted their farms and feared it was 'their houses and haggards' that were being burnt down.[41] Richard Fenton, a resident of Fishguard and 'on the spot' when the French invaded, tells in 1811 of 'the inhabitants more immediately within the reach of the ferocious invaders', deserting their houses and hiding in the 'rocks and thick furze' – expecting their homes to go up any minute in flames.[42] The town of Fishguard itself, though a little further away, 'caught the general panic' and was soon emptied by 'the removal of their wives, children, and most valuable articles for greater security into the interior'.[43]

Not all the wealthy left. When the news was broken to the local gentry at a dance at Tregwynt, a sea-side country house situated 4 miles south-west of where the French had landed, Colonel Daniel Vaughan of the family long settled at Jordanstown, remained behind when everyone had left, loaded all the fire arms, barricaded himself in, and awaited the arrival of the enemy, who, fortunately for him, never came.[44] Mrs Harries, the lady of Tregwynt, on the other hand, got into a coach with her two sons, with what valuables they could collect and drove to Narberth. When they then heard that the French had surrendered, they returned to Tregwynt.[45]

Memories of fear and flight stayed in the local communities. The travel writer Richard Ayton and artist William Daniell visited Fishguard during their home tour of Great Britain in 1813. Ayton mentions the way fear had preyed on the imagination when the French invaded and the subsequent flight.[46] Ayton recounts how after the initial uncertainty as to whether the ships sighted off St David's Head were friendly or not, the overwhelming response was flight. The people took to the hills, 'concealed themselves among the rocks and furze brakes and before the enemy had reached the shore every house in Fishguard was deserted'.[47]

For most of the population, the farm workers, fishermen and sailors, there was no alternative but to sit it out and see what would happen. It was not because they were heroic or particularly brave, but because they had no choice. William Davies, later an Independent minister at Fishguard, was twelve years of age when the French invaded. He lived 1 mile from Rhosycaerau and about 2 miles from Carreg Gwastad Point. He hid with his mother and father in a cave for three days and nights. Terrified, they heard the footsteps and voices of the French as they passed by.[48]

The ballads also mention another fear, the gentry's fear of an armed peasantry. Philip Dafydd's ballad, when describing the removal of the French as prisoners, provides a noteworthy detail: 'they were taken to gaol and we had the rifles of the terrible ones.'[49] If discovered, this would have had serious implications for the people involved. The authorities were concerned after the surrender that the French had left three thousand stands of arms concealed in the cliffs and that Tate had supplied the country people with muskets. It was one of Lieutenant Colonel Knox's duties, after the surrender, as instructed by General Rooke, the general in charge of the entire Severn region, to investigate this claim. Knox did so and wrote later in his 1800 *Account* that he had proved 'the falsity of the story'.[50] However, General Rooke had written to Knox from Haverfordwest on 3 March 1797 requesting him to 'order the arms, and so forth, discovered, to be brought here, without giving you any further trouble'.[51] *The Times* reported that the French had concealed an even greater number – 5,000 – stand of arms in the rocks: 'deposited there for their own use and for any other vagabonds whom they could get to join them'.[52] The man in charge of actual delivery of the arms, as far as Cawdor was concerned, was not Knox but Major Bowen of Llwyngwair. Bowen wrote to Cawdor on the 2 March to inform him of progress, stating that they were:

> doing all in our power for the recovery of such of your prisoners arms and ammunition as were ignorantly carried away by some of the Peasants last Friday, who, not thinking it a crime to rob the enemy, were not a little proud of trophies, which, however, as soon as required; of them were cheerfully given up to us.[53]

Thomas John, the local man arrested on a charge of treason, purchased two cutlasses from the French on his journey to Goodwick Sands, one on behalf of an 'Old Woman', as souvenirs.[54] Cawdor went to the trouble to produce a handbill in Welsh to warn the peasantry that if they retained any of the arms left by the French and did not return them they would be putting themselves in danger.[55]

Imaginary Landings and the Contagion of Fear

One of the most memorable observations concerning the fear of the people across south Wales on hearing the news of the Invasion, and certainly the most vivid, was that made by Iolo Morganwg on 7 March 1797: 'Breeches, petticoats, shirts, blankets, sheets (for some received the news in bed) have been most woefully defiled in South Wales lately in learning that a thimbleful of Frenchmen landed on our coast.'[56]

The French could return at any moment. False alarms and news of terror continued and were deeply distressing. It is only in retrospect that we know the French Invasion had ended on 24 February 1797, but to contemporaries it was still an imminent threat. John Vaughan of Golden Grove, one of Lord Cawdor's closest friends, had initially dismissed the actual fleet that had carried the French troops to Carreg Wastad as 'imaginary'.[57] If this imaginary fleet turned out to be real, what was the probability of other landings taking place at any point along the long and unprotected Welsh coastline? The fear of another French invasion was felt in Welsh coastal communities both near and far away from Fishguard.

One such 'landing' took place in the vicinity of Fishguard Bay almost immediately after the real one. John Roach of Llethr was doing some coast-watching on his own on the night of 28 February (some have suggested that he was smuggling). He arrived at the beach of Gesail Fawr near St David's Head and heard boats coming to anchor close to shore in the dark. Thinking it was a fresh lot of troops making a landing, he raised the alarm immediately and sent word to St David's.[58] At Haverfordwest, Major Francis Edwardes, the mayor, convened a committee who discussed the consequence of the landing, including whether these new marauders should be put to death if taken prisoner.[59] Expresses were sent off to Milford and Swansea and a general alarm was raised. The popular response to this imaginary landing was as ferocious as the response to the actual invasion. Five thousand people, men and women, were in a few hours collected in the neighbourhood of Carmarthen, the roads clogged, the men with scythes straitened on poles, the women with pitchforks, 'eager to encounter and punish the presumptuous foe'.[60] This alarm also caused a rapid deployment of troops across the wider region.[61] The alarm finally subsided when it was discovered that the noise was of a few coasters bound for Milford who had anchored at this spot to wait for the tide and had employed their time in robbing fishing nets set for the night.[62]

There was an understandable fear that the French ships that had left Fishguard were still at large and ready to disembark another cargo of *banditti*. Samuel Horsley, the Bishop of St David's, wrote anxiously to his son at Oxford that if he heard reports (as had been spread in London) of another landing and the burning of Carmarthen, he 'may rest assured there is not the least foundation for any of them'.[63]

Fifty miles or so to the north of Fishguard, the port of Aberystwyth on Cardigan Bay was also in a state of alarm. Jane Johnes, the lady of the Hafod estate, Pontrhydygroes, received a message from Aberystwyth the week after the landing in Pembrokeshire announcing that the enemy was about to land on their part of the shore. She wrote to her brother in Dolaucothi: 'the sail of the French are off Aberystwyth and Aberaeron … come over and bring what Arms you can provide and shot; they will not sell any at Aberystwyth.'[64]

Twenty miles or so north of Aberystwyth, in Ynysymaengwyn near Machynlleth, the squire Edward Corbet was in contact with the home secretary 'during the last invasion in this Bay'.⁶⁵ Corbet saw himself as a linchpin in communicating the news of the landing to Liverpool, the most important commercial port for north Wales at the time. Based on Corbet's information, the Liverpool mayor George Dunbar believed that the French who had landed 'at Fiscard in Cardigan Bay' had been obliged by the armed force that they had met there to reembark and head towards Liverpool.⁶⁶ Liverpool erected batteries and called on its 'inhabitants to enrol and arm themselves'. Both Liverpool and Bristol, the latter being the commercial centre for south Wales, had substantial numbers of French prisoners, which were perceived as great security threats.⁶⁷

The French were hated for many reasons and had been even before the invasion of Pembrokeshire. The Invasion could be used to give a new pitch of intensity to existing fears. A self-styled 'FRIEND TO HIS COUNTRY' (writer's capitals) wrote to the Duke of Portland in his role as his Majesty's Principal Secretary of State for the Home department, and sent a copy to the *Chester Courant*, who published it on 14 March. The letter was addressed from Caernarfon and dated 1 March 1797.⁶⁸ It is a master expression of anti-Gallican loathing, which also contained practical proposals to improve the defences of Caernarvonshire and Anglesey. Anxiety had already spread throughout the north Wales littoral, for example the Rector of Llanrwst expressed fears that after their landing in Pembrokeshire, the French would attempt 'a Descent in Llandudno, or Llandrillo Bay, or both'.⁶⁹ 'A FRIEND' urged the government to take proper precautions to repel any invaders to 'this part of the principality'.⁷⁰

The events of Fishguard stimulated voluntaryism and boosted recruitment to militias locally in both north and south Wales.⁷¹ The sight of French prisoners in Cowbridge in Glamorganshire was an occasion for a public display of loyalty. The French Invasion accelerated local developments of national defence and national defence patriotism that were already in progress, injecting urgency and pace into pre-existing arrangements.

Discord

Not everyone involved in repelling the invaders, it was later alleged, had overcome their fear, and conducted themselves with merit or bravery. Thomas Knox was the first military man to hear of the landing. The problem was that he was slow to believe the reports and, once he knew it was true, he took a long time to assess the nature of the threat and formulate his response to it. He, too, was at Tregwynt when the news of the enemy's landing was received. He went to Fishguard via Trehowel, the nearest house to the landing spot, from where he could view the French ships, albeit indistinctly in the February evening light. He kept meeting people who were fleeing into the interior and who informed him that the French were landing and that twelve boats had come ashore. One of the communication problems was that Thomas Knox 'not sufficiently understanding Welsh' relied on his servant to interpret.[72] To some, Knox was reticent and overcautious; others thought he was a coward. He had turned his back, it was said, on Fishguard, to march with his Fencibles towards Haverfordwest, leaving the port of Fishguard undefended and at the mercy of the invaders.[73] Knox demanded a court martial to clear his name. This request was rejected by the Duke of York because 'a volunteer corps are not subject to martial laws, except during the existence of an actual invasion',[74] effectively denying that this was an invasion.

Knox was forced to resign his royal commission. His position was untenable since he had lost the confidence of his fellow officers, who wrote to resign their commissions rather than act under his command.[75] The signatories did not impugn Knox's courage, and none of the Fishguard officers joined in it. The signatories were all 'below mountains', south of the Preseli hills, and the first signature was Cawdor's.[76] Cawdor and Knox threatened to duel, whether it happened or not is unclear, but it does show that there was conflict within the home forces as well as without. This episode destroyed Thomas Knox and he was a broken man; his history demonstrates clearly how subjective and contingent interpretations of bravery and cowardice can be.[77]

While Thomas Knox suffered an attack on his reputation and standing both socially and militarily, others in inferior social positions were accused of criminality and the most serious offence: treason. The events in Pembrokeshire had been covered closely by the provincial as well as the metropolitan papers. Even as soon as mid-March, the provincial papers were making jokes about the French in Wales.[78] However, the invasion retained its shock value. An item of news, not new but becoming a disturbing theme, was the possibility of traitors among the Welsh. Three farmers had gone to greet the French on their landing and it was said that papers were found on the French 'between their shirts and their skin, that will materially affect these farmers as well as several other persons'.[79] No mention was made of the religious affiliation of the farmers but the newspapers who reported on the conjecture moved from the allegation to a general comment that the people of Fishguard had over years frequently emigrated to Pennsylvania and were 'chiefly dissenters and Methodists'.[80]

By the end of March, newspapers reported their sorrow to learn that amidst the loyalty and zeal 'some individuals were suspected of treasonable practices'.[81] A letter from a shop keeper named Thomas had been intercepted; magistrates deemed it treasonable and warranted the writer to prison. Another man was given his full name, Thomas John, a 'preacher among the Anabaptists', who was apprehended on a charge of being present in the French camp on the first night of their landing and communicating to them 'such intelligence as he thought likely to promote the success of their enterprise'.[82] Traitors were everywhere, it seemed; the *Hereford Journal* also reported that the government had obtained the names of some individuals on the coasts of Devon and Somerset who had been in correspondence with the French with the intention of encouraging them to invade.

The reactionary *Chester Courant* was the most critical of the dissenters' supposed role in the French landing.[83] It published an extract of a letter from Haverfordwest that contained specific allegations of collusion. Eight dissenters ('both Presbyterians and Anabaptists') had visited the French camp and declared that the British forces were so few that they could ride through them with ease. Religious sects, which before would not associate with each other, had been brought together through 'Republican dogmas' something that the Bible had failed to do.[84] The dissenters had local targets in mind, such as pulling down the cathedral of St David's and 'destroying every clergyman in their way', but the letter writer had to acknowledge 'what truth there may be in that, I know not, but admittedly, many falsehoods are carried about'.[85]

Falsehoods were acted on, and allegations of treason made against a number of men, all of whom were dissenters. The allegations of treason revealed deep divisions and acrimony between and within the religious communities of south-west Wales.[86] In April 1797, at the Great Sessions at the Guildhall in Haverfordwest, Thomas John and Samuel Griffith were charged with high treason for helping the enemy. The case against Thomas John, who engaged the American Charles Prudhomme in conversation, as we have seen, was based on evidence from Prudhomme. Thomas John, Prudhomme claimed, had disclosed to him: 'that half the local force were women with red flannels ... and that many local people would join the French'.[87]

John and Griffith were locked up in the dark dungeons of Haverfordwest Castle to await trial. They were treated harshly, John especially, throughout their captivity. Cawdor and his friend John Manners, the Duke of Rutland, on different occasions, visited the 'state prisoners', as Rutland called them. They considered Thomas John to be a 'desperate villain', while 'the French were all uncommonly fine men and were dressed in their uniforms'.[88] Rutland's *Journal* provides conclusive evidence of witness tampering and bribery on the part of the state. The French prisoners were treated very well while awaiting trial. Lord Cawdor personally punished a guard who had kept them locked up and he also 'gave some money to the prisoners which set everything to right'. The reason for this indulgence of the French prisoners, as Cawdor related to Rutland: 'was on account of the evidence which they had in their power to give against the state prisoners and which, if ill treated, they might possibly withhold. It was certainly therefore in our interest to treat them as kindly as possible.'[89] The government took an active interest in the preparations for the trial and Cawdor and John Colby kept Windham, the secretary at the War Office, and Portland in the Home Office informed.

The trial of Thomas John and Samuel Griffith began on 7 September amidst huge public interest. More than 120 men were chosen for jury service, but several were either rejected as infirm, or not summoned at all.[90] The foreman was a Mr Barlow, Member of Parliament for Pembroke.[91] The fact that an MP was the foreman of the jury underlines the high public profile and significance that this event had in the county. It was an event that succeeded as a *coup de theatre* but failed to deliver the outcome that many of the gentry and people of Haverfordwest wanted.

The Attorney General made a very impressive and dispassionate speech in which he described the evidence he would bring against the prisoners. After calling on two or three witnesses to relate the apprehension of the prisoners, he called Charles Prudhomme to prove the facts which the witnesses had stated at the time of apprehension. Prudhomme failed to cooperate and refused to answer any of the questions.[92] Prudhomme's non-cooperation undermined the case for the prosecution completely. The indulgence towards, and bribery of, the French prisoners by the witnessed behaviour of Cawdor had evidently not worked.

The two prisoners were not without their defenders.[93] The Welsh-language pamphlet *Cwyn y Cystuddiedig* was published in early 1798.[94] The pamphlet's preface was dated 24 December 1797, the day the case against the two accused had fallen through and when proceedings could be reported freely. Its author was anonymous but was known to be William Richards.

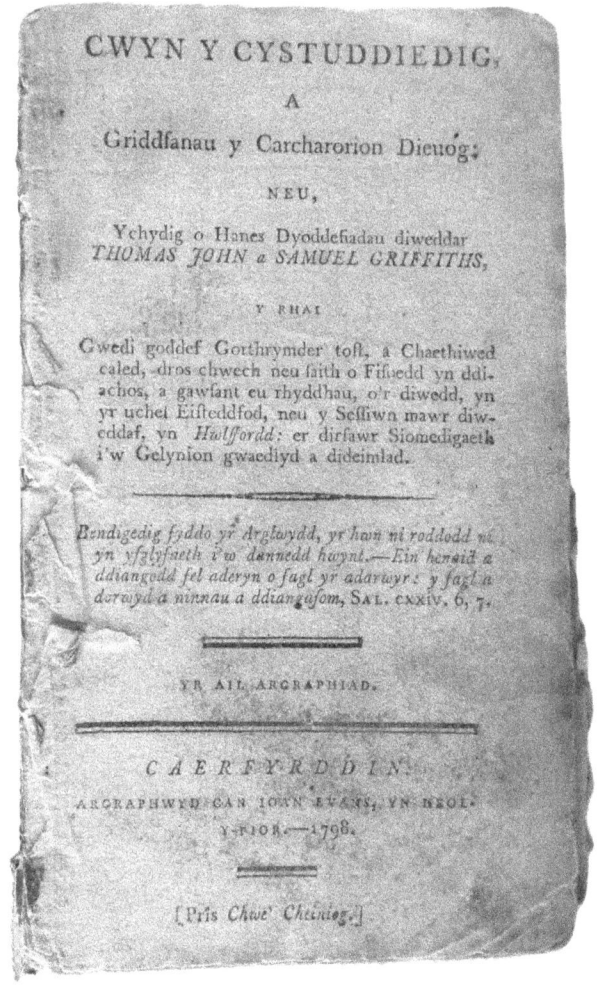

Figure 5: 'Cwyn y Cystuddiedig'

William Richards was born in the parish of Penrhydd near Haverfordwest in 1749. Born and raised a Baptist, in 1763 he went to train as a minister at the Baptist Academy in Bristol. Richards was educated in English and through the Bristol Academy was introduced to a Baptist network of ministers that spanned the Atlantic.[95] In 1776 he became the minister at King's Lynn in Norfolk, and he stayed with this church throughout most of his life. He became known by this association as William Richards, Lynn. However, he maintained a close connection with Pembrokeshire and south-west Wales, where he visited and stayed frequently. What people tended to remember of Richards was his irascibility.[96]

Richards was a closed communion Baptist. Ascetic in his personal life, a man of principle and conviction, he was also a man with radical tendencies. He translated Gilbert Wakefield's anti-war, anti-government, pro-French Fast Day sermons into Welsh and wrote a powerful critique and defence of French Atheism, which he argued was less atheistic than the Gallican Church that preceded it and preferable in many respects to established religion in England.[97] The French invasion had a personal effect on his political views, totally altering his opinion of the French revolutionaries.

In the *Cwyn* (which can be translated either as 'complaint' or 'lament'; the publication certainly has elements of both), Richards could hardly conceal or contain his anger. There may have been a personal dimension in his support for the Baptist preacher, as Thomas John, Richards told his Welsh-American correspondent Samuel Jones, was a 'friend and relation'.[98]

Richards had to tread carefully. He used scriptural terms to allege that the witnesses had been bribed by five members of the gentry and that there had been jury tampering ('Story of the five beasts and the sixty guineas and the letter of direction').[99] There may have been a legal victory, but the wrong doing and moral outrage continued since the innocent were still being accused: 'they persist still to give it out.'[100]

The accused had suffered simply because they were dissenters: John, a Baptist and preacher; Griffiths, a friend to the Presbyterians. Their neighbours were also arrested, but freed as soon as it was understood they were not dissenters.[101] This targeting of dissenters was not just a consequence of the French Invasion, but a Welsh manifestation of anti-dissenter prejudice and victimisation that had been taking place throughout Britain. Dissenters were frequently targeted on account of their alleged support for the French Revolution, their meeting houses disturbed, some places of worship burnt and their ministers 'grossly abused'.[102]

The core of Richards's diatribe arose from his reading of what had happened and what had not happened in Pembrokeshire in February 1797. The story was central to his argument. Richards was the first to give a full narrative account in print in Welsh. He started his piece with his assessment of the historic importance of what he was narrating, of all the events that had occurred in Wales at the time: 'there is not one, perhaps more worthy of remembrance than the attack which a troop of Frenchmen made on Pembrokeshire at the beginning of last spring.'[103] In Richards's narrative the military detail is sparse, the people are absent, there is no mention of rustic weapons, but there is a reference to the small number of the local force, (560, contrasting with the 1,400 of the French) to highlight the deliverance they experienced. God is the overwhelming presence in Richards's narrative. 'God saw fit, by his wondrous mercy' to hinder armed conflict 'and to prevent the frightful consequences which would have been bound afterwards to take place'.[104] The offer to end the dispute through parley came from the French and the commanders through a 'quiet and easy agreement' avoiding the spilling of blood: 'Thanks be to God for this'. Richards supports the narrative of the surrender that appears in the official accounts, adding new detail to explain the French capitulation such as the 'unruliness of the men' and the effects of wine from wrecked wine-laden ships. The French were then moved as prisoners to Haverfordwest and then to Milford Haven and then to the 'west of England [sic]'.[105] Some of the men were kept behind for the purpose of proving the 'treasonable guilt of the ill-fated prisoners'.[106]

Nobody was more overjoyed at the surrender of such a numerous troop to a small weak army than 'the scorned and falsely accused dissenters', Richards claimed. They thanked the Lord for the 'wondrous deliverance'.[107] The French who had borne false witness against the innocent were 'the dregs of the French prisons'.[108] He calculated whether there were as many as 100 out of that 1,400 who were not of that type.

Richards wrote that there were three things that made these men totally unfit to act as witnesses. First, they were enemies. Second, they were criminals. Third, they did not believe in a life to come or that there was any punishment to be expected in another world.[109] This was not the picture of French civic religion portrayed in his *Reflections on French Atheism and English Christianity* where he argued that the principles of the Jacobins were less atheistic than those of the clergy before the revolution.[110] His narrative comes alive in the aftermath of the surrender when he discusses the victims, persecuted not only by English-speaking gentry, but also by their Welsh-speaking neighbours, in fratricide akin to that of Cain in the Old Testament. Richards names the wronged: John Thomas, a responsible trader from Haverfordwest, who was imprisoned without an arrest warrant and then released; and John Reynolds, a respectable Baptist minister whose house was ransacked for some supposedly treasonable material from John Thomas, but nothing was found.[111]

Richards described the orchestrated campaign of calumny against those who were eventually tried. The Baptists were hated by the gentry and by many of their neighbours. Richards's defence may have been extreme, but the anti-Baptist prejudice of certain establishment members who either participated in the invasion or commented on it was also extreme. Richards was very vocal about the lies spread by the 'ungodly' and the Methodists but he realised that the architects of the 'treason trials' were the

'Tory Gentry', and this is what he told his friend Samuel Jones in Pennepek, near Philadelphia a year later.¹¹² The foremost of those who were spreading lies, he claimed in the *Cwyn*, 'were the five monsters and their relations'.¹¹³ These five monsters were the aforementioned Tory gentry, and one of these was John Colby of Ffynone.

Colonel John Colby of Ffynone loathed 'Anabaptists'. As a regular soldier and landowner, he was active in securing the arrests of the Baptist and other suspects. On 20 March he wrote to Cawdor from Haverfordwest to inform him of what he had achieved.¹¹⁴ He then proceeded to discuss another suspect that Cawdor had ordered to be apprehended and confined in the prison under a military guard: 'Thomas the shopkeeper in this town.' He was a Baptist and according to Colby the 'whole sect of Anabaptists … are determined lads'. Colby suggested that Cawdor take out 'a detainer against this man on suspicion of Treasonable practices'. Colby was prepared, even keen to take the fight to the Baptists:

> I am credibly informed that the Anabaptists in my neighbourhood above the hills continue to hold nightly meetings since the Fishguard affair I long to get amongst them, but have not been able to quit this Town since you left the Country. They have sent me a threatening anonymous letter, which I have treated with the contempt it deserved.¹¹⁵

Colby was not alone in his hatred of Baptists. The fullest and best articulated anti-Baptist position was that of Cawdor's young aristocratic friend John Manners, the fifth Duke of Rutland, who was in west Wales during the summer of 1797 on a tour. In Fishguard he wrote:

> When I talk of the disaffection of the peasantry, I must be understood to mean those all around the place where the enemy landed. They are chiefly anabaptists and some men

were afterwards taken up for having communicated with the enemy. In Carmarthenshire and other parts of Wales, they would have risen en masse.[116]

The strength of feeling of these Anglican gentry against the Baptists was not because they were poor or disaffected but because they were Baptists.

What antagonised Richards more about this this coordinated campaign was that it involved not only the usual suspects, the Anglican gentry, but also ordinary, orthodox Methodists. It was almost unthinkable that 'orthodox Methodists would be seen travelling together with the others, along the same Cain-like path'.[117] Richards was able to pinpoint the geographical extent of the Methodist calumny against the Baptists. The falsehoods and slander had spread some 60 miles through Cardigan and Aberystwyth, 'and on through every corner of the north as well as the east and the south; to the great distress, and defamation and shame of that Denomination in many places'.[118] In almost every community where the Methodists were numerous they were the 'cause of more trouble, scorn, and persecution to those of that Denomination than frivolous and worldly men who profess no religion'. The 'slanderous sourness' of the Methodists affected Richards personally; the hotspots of Methodist vitriol were in his own locale, specifically Narberth and Newcastle Emlyn, a few miles from where he was born. The Methodist Newcastle Emlyn ballad writer Philip Dafydd, was scorned by Richards for two lines in the ballad 'Encouragement to praise God' on account of its insinuations of Baptist collusion with the French.[119]

The Baptists in their associational meetings addressed the effects of the French Invasion. In the south-western association ('*Y Gymanfa Orllewinol*') held in Penybont, Llandysul, shortly after the invasion in 1797, the main theme of their meeting was thanksgiving for the deliverance they had.[120] The next year in Ebeneser, Eglwyswrw, Pembrokeshire, the meeting agreed to support Thomas John 'dan y gorthrymder diweddar ag oedd wedi ei gael' ('under the recent oppression he had experienced').[121] It was the first and last time that Thomas John's name would appear in their minutes, or any other Baptist publication, for at least two generations as the Baptists adopted a passive role of suffering in silence and wrestled with fallings out and dissension in their midst over theology, forms of worship and church order. William Richards's *Cwyn* was forgotten and neglected, and became increasingly rare. It did not affect the telling of the story, the treason trial was remembered only by the Baptists and only occasionally became part of the mainstream narrative when it was told by the Welsh themselves.

As the historian Prys Morgan has noted, the French Invasion of Pembrokeshire led to the punishment of dissenters; the debate that then ensued was more about the loyalty of dissenters than about reform or revolution.[122] This was not a new debate by any means, but what M. C. Jones has called the 'Fishguard Moment' gave it added impetus.[123] The debate was not only between dissenters, Anglicans, and the state, but among dissenters themselves concerning their own denominational loyalty. In the sectarian disputes concerning the French invasion, the Methodists did much better than the Baptists to prove their civic loyalty. They decided to hold their regional meetings on Goodwick Sands, and by so doing made the place of surrender almost a sacred place where God had performed great deeds and where they could give thanks. It was decided in early January 1798 that they would hold a thanksgiving service on the Sands each year on the anniversary of the landing.[124] The service held on the first anniversary was such a well-attended demonstration of loyalty and outpouring of praise that it was still remembered more than thirty years later.[125]

The role of the Methodists in the French Invasion and their commemoration of it was used by Methodist leaders as one element of evidence of their loyalty to the British state.[126] In 1798, Thomas Jones published *Gair yn ei Amser*, a statement, soon translated into English, on Methodism, Wales and the public order. There was a critical edge to Thomas Jones's writing. The people of Fishguard were under a great disadvantage, he claimed, because of a lack of suitable weaponry and ability to handle them. How much stronger and more secure a country would be, if its inhabitants, or most of them, were armed, embodied and trained and led by proper officers. Thomas Jones called on the inhabitants of Wales (note: not 'the Welsh') to 'withstand the attack of the cruel spoiler' and 'as it likewise loudly calleth on us to repent and forsake our sins'.[127]

New information concerning Tate's *Instructions* emboldened loyalist propaganda. The *Anti-Jacobin* on 12 February 1798 presented its readers 'with a very singular curiosity:- an Extract from the *Official Orders of Colonel Tate*, delivered to him preparatory to his landing in Wales'.[128] The *Instructions*, said to have been found on Tate's person, were to destroy Bristol, incite local insurrections and destroy Liverpool, among other things. This was a gift to the propaganda of the anti-Gallican, anti-Jacobins. The *Anti-Jacobin* anticipated those who doubted its authenticity by immediately pledging that the *Instructions* were authentic and printing them in full.[129] This 'historical chronicle' not only appeared in the ultra-loyalist *Anti-Jacobin* but also in the *Gentleman's Magazine* of 1798 and several provincial newspapers.[130]

Endnotes

1   Attributed to Nicolas Léonard Sadi Carnot, 'Instructions pour l' Etablissement d'une Chouannerie en Angleterre, Carnot's Plan for Invading England', *Fraser's Magazine*, 15 (1877), 201–2.
2   It is not absent from the study of poetry of the period. Ildiko Csengei connects Coleridge's 1798 poem 'Fears in Solitude' to the invasion fear and alarm of the time. Ildiko Csengei, 'The Literature of Fear in Britain Coleridge's Fears in Solitude and the French Invasion of Fishguard in 1797', *English Literature*, 5 (December 2018), 183–206.
3   James Baker, *A BRIEF NARRATIVE OF THE FRENCH INVASION NEAR FISHGUARD BAY. Including a Perfect Description of that Part of the Coast*

of Pembrokeshire, on which was effected the LANDING OF THE FRENCH FORCES, on the 22nd of February, 1797, and of their surrender to the Welch Provincial Troops, HEADED BY LORD CAWDOR (Worcester, 1797).

4   J. Baker, *Picturesque Guide through Wales and the Marches; Interspersed with the Most Interesting Subjects of Antiquity in that Principality. The Second Edition; with Considerable Alterations and Additions* (Worcester, 1795).

5   J. Baker, *The Imperial Guide with Picturesque Plans of the Great Post Roads, containing Miniature Likenesses* (London, 1802). Address to the Public

6   J. Baker, *A Brief Narrative of the French Invasion*, p. 1.

7   J. Baker, *A Brief Narrative of the French Invasion*, p. 1.

8   Titus Lewis, *Hanes, Wladol a Chrefyddol Prydain Fawr* (Carmarthen, 1810), p. 610.

9   J. J. Evans, *Dylanwad y Chwyldro Ffrengig* (Liverpool, 1928); Geraint Jenkins, 'Glaniad y Ffrancod yn Abergwaun ym 1797, Darlith Eisteddfod Genedlaethol Abergwaun 1986', in *Cadw Ty mewn Cwmwl Tystion; Ysgrifau hanesyddol ar grefydd a Diwylliant* (Llandysul, 1990), pp. 256–72; Ffion Mair Jones, *Welsh Ballads of the French Revolution 1793–1815* (Cardiff, 2012), ballad numbers 12, 14, 15, 18, 19, 20, 21, 22, 23, 24.

10 Ffion Mair Jones, '"The silly expressions of French revolution …": the experience of the Dissenting community in south-west Wales, 1797', in D. Andress, *Experiencing the French Revolution* (Oxford, 2013), p. 248.

11 Jones, 'The silly expressions …', p. 261.

12 Jones, 'The silly expressions …', pp. 259–60.

13 Jones, 'The silly expressions …', p. 256.

14 Philip Dafydd, 'Encouragement to praise God for the great deliverance which the country had when 1,400 fearsome Frenchmen landed at Pencaer', number 19 in Jones, *Welsh Ballads of the French Revolution*, lines 71–4, p. 209.

15 For example, Anon., 'A song of gratitude to the Lord for His remarkable deliverance, keeping us from the scourge of our enemies when they landed on our land', number 14, in Jones, *Welsh Ballads of the French Revolution*, pp. 170–6.

16 T. I. Ellis (1959), 'RICHARD, HENRY (1812–1888), politician', in *Dictionary of Welsh Biography*, https://biography.wales/article/s-RICH-HEN-1812 (last accessed 12 March 2024).

17 G. M. Roberts (1959), 'RICHARD, EBENEZER (1781–1837), Calvinistic Methodist minister', *Dictionary of Welsh Biography*, https://biography.wales/article/s-RICH-EBE-1781 (last accessed 31 July 2024). Henry Richard, his politician son, merits an entry in the *Oxford Dictionary of National Bibliography*: M. Cragoe (2014), 'Richard, Henry (1812–1888), politician', in *Oxford Dictionary of National Biography*, www.oxforddnb.com/view/10.1093/ref:odnb/9780198614128.001.0001/odnb-9780198614128-e-23527 (last accessed 31 July 2024).

18 Dr D. Rees, Bronant, 'Cymru Fu. Ebenezer Richard', *Y Negesydd* (1 May 1896), 1.
19 The ballad was entitled 'Am y Waredigaeth ryfeddol a gafwyd gan yr Arglwydd oddiwrth y Ffrancod yn y flwyddyn 1797, gan Ebenezer Richard (bachgenyn pymtheg mlwydd oed) wedi ei chyfansoddi yn yr un flwyddyn, sef 1797', and appears in full in 'Hen Faledau', *The London Kelt* (20 March 1897), page 3; and 3 April 1897, page 4. Select verses from it appeared in the sons' eulogy for their father in 1839, Edward W. Richard and Henry Richard, *Bywyd y Parch. Ebenezer Richard* (London, 1839), pp. 4–7.
20 'Hen Faledau', *London Kelt* (3 April 1897), 4, lines 37–40. See also Geraint H. Jenkins, 'Glaniad y Ffrancod yn Abergwaun yn 1797', in *Cadw Tŷ mewn Cwmwl Tystion: Ysgrifau Hanesyddol ar Grefydd a Diwylliant* (Llandysul, 1990), p. 266.
21 'Hen Faledau', *London Kelt* (20 March 1897), 3, lines 56–7.
22 'Hen Faledau', *London Kelt* (20 March 1897), 3, lines 25–6.
23 E. H. Stuart Jones, *The Last Invasion* (Cardiff, 1950), pp. 105–6; for the Llanwnda Bible see, *The Historic Bible in St Gwyndaf's Church, Llanwnda* (no date), for pictures of the vandalised bible, the text block torn from the binding and the missing pages. The French tore the bible to make fire or possibly to wipe their backsides.
24 'Clod i'r Cymry, gwŷr Sir Benfro, am gymeryd y rheibus elynion cythreulig, ysglyfyddwyr mileinig, sef Ffrancod pan diriasant yn Abergwaun', ballad 15, in Jones, *Welsh Ballads of the French Revolution*, pp.178–84.
25 Jones, *Welsh Ballads of the French Revolution*, p.31.
26 Jones, *Welsh Ballads of the French Revolution*, p. 32.
27 'Clod i'r Cymry', in Jones, *Welsh Ballads of the French Revolution*, pp. 180–1, lines 39–40.
28 Ballad 19, p. 204, line 6; Ballad 14, p. 170, line 9; Ballad 22, p. 234, line 5; Ballad 21, p. 233, line 10, in Jones, *Welsh Ballads of the French Revolution*.
29 One ballad attacking the French for atheism predates the French invasion: Jonathan Hughes 'A song of encouragement to the patriotic soldiers that are being raised in this kingdom to protect harbours, who are generally called the militia' (1795), in Jones, *Welsh Ballads of the French Revolution*, p. 153, line 44.
30 For example, Nathaniel Jenkin, 'An address to the Welsh, to urge them to repent of their sins and return to God, and to praise Him for delivering us from the claws of the merciless French', ballad 18, in Jones, *Welsh Ballads of the French Revolution*, p. 199, lines 41–50.
31 Phillip Dafydd, 'Encouragement to praise God for the great deliverance which the country had when 1,400 fearsome Frenchmen landed at Pencaer in Pembrokeshire, to conquer our land by murdering and burning our fellow countrymen', ballad 19, in Jones, *Welsh Ballads of the French Revolution*, p. 205, lines 23–4.

32 'A new Song on the great deliverance which the old Britons received through the hand of God and Lord Cawdor, from a host of French thieves in the year 1797', ballad 12 in Jones, *Welsh Ballads of the French Revolution*, p. 161, line 35, and introduction p. 29.

33 'A song of gratitude to the Lord', ballad 14 in Jones, Welsh Ballads of the French Revolution, p. 171, line 29.

34 'Ballads', in E. H. Stuart Jones, *The Last Invasion of Britain* (Cardiff, 1950), Appendix 1, pp. 269–74. Lines quoted are from the Jeffreston ballad, p. 269, line 5, and p. 270, lines 41–2.

35 Anon., 'Praise to the Welsh, the men of Pembrokeshire, for seizing the voracious, fiendish enemies, savage plunderers, namely the French when they landed in Fishguard', ballad 15 in Jones, *Welsh Ballads of the French Revolution*, p. 181, line 66–7.

36 Phil Carradice, *The Last Invasion: The Story of the French landing in Wales* (Pontypool, 1992), pp. 10–11.

37 Phillip Dafydd, 'Encouragement to praise God', ballad 19, in Jones, *Welsh Ballads of the French Revolution*, p. 205, lines 15–16, 19–20.

38 Anne Brigstocke, *God and Gideon or, the valour of ancient Britons displayed* (no date but NLW has c.1797, no imprint), lines 27–28.

39 *Leeds Intelligencer* (20 March 1797), 3.

40 *Leeds Intelligencer* (20 March 1797), 3.

41 Haggards are enclosures beside a farmhouse in which crops are stored. It is an Irish and Manx term used in Pembrokeshire dialect. J. Baker, *A Brief Narrative of the French Invasion*, p. 3.

42 Richard Fenton, *A Historical Tour Through Pembrokeshire* (London, 1811), p. 11.

43 Fenton, *A Historical Tour Through Pembrokeshire*, pp. 11–12.

44 Francis Jones, 'Harries of Tregwynt', *Transactions of the Honourable Society of Cymmrodorion* (1944–5), 117.

45 Jones, 'Harries of Tregwynt', 117.

46 *A voyage round Great Britain undertaken in the summer of 1813 and commencing from Land's End, Cornwall. By Richard Ayton; with a series of views. drawn and engraved by William Daniell* (London, 1814) p. 126.

47 Ayton and Daniell, *A voyage round Great Britain 1813*, pp. 125–6.

48 'Yr Hybarch William Davies, Abergwaun. Gan y Parch D. Bateman, Rhosycaerau', *Y Cronicl (Cronicl y cymdeithasau crefyddol)*, 48/565 (May 1890), 130.

49 Jones, *Welsh Ballads*, p. 215, line 210.

50 Thomas Knox, *Some account of the proceedings that took place on the landing of the French near Fishguard, in Pembrokeshire, on the 22nd February 1797* (London, 1800), p. 28.

51 Knox, *Some account of the proceedings*, pp. 47–8.

52 *The Times* (3 March 1797), quoted in *Old Wales*, 1/1 (1 January 1905).

53 Carmarthenshire Record Office, Cawdor MSS; Bowen to Cawdor, Llwyngwair, 2 March 1797, in Syd Walters, *Truthful History of the Last Invasion of Britain* (privately printed, 1992), p. 149.
54 David Salmon, 'A Sequel to the French Invasion of Pembrokeshire', *Y Cymmrodor*, 43 (1932), 75.
55 Bowen to Cawdor, in Walters, *Truthful History*, p. 145.
56 National Library of Wales MS13222 fo. 131–4; Iolo Morganwg to William Owen Pughe, 7 March 1797, in Trevor Herbert and Gareth Elwyn Jones (eds), *The Remaking of Wales in the Eighteenth Century* (Cardiff, 1988), p. 138.
57 Francis Jones, 'The Vaughans of Golden Grove', *Transactions of the Honourable Society of Cymmrodorion*, 1 (1966), 179.
58 Stuart Jones, *The Last Invasion*, p. 149.
59 Stuart Jones, *The Last Invasion*, p. 149.
60 *Hereford Journal* (8 March 1797), 3.
61 *Hereford Journal* (8 March 1797), 3.
62 H. L. Ap Gwilym, *An Authentic Account of the Invasion by French Troops on Carrig Gwasted Point near Fishguard, 1797* (Haverfordwest, 1842), p. 35.
63 Samuel Horsley to his son, 3 March 1797, in F. C. Mather, *High Church Prophet: Bishop Samuel Horsley (1733–1806) and the Caroline Tradition in the Later Georgian Church* (Oxford, 1992), p. 253.
64 Elisabeth Inglis-Jones, *Peacocks in Paradise* (Llandysul, 2006 reprint), p. 146.
65 National Archives, HO-42-40-1; Corbet to Pelham 15 March 1797.
66 National Archives, HO-42-40-3; Dunbar to Portland 27 February 1797.
67 Stuart Jones, *The Last Invasion*, p. 159.
68 *Chester Courant* (14 March 1797), 4.
69 National Archives, HO-42-40-4; Rector of Llanrwst to Portland, 27 February 1797. For a poetic description of the effect and the extent of this contagion of fear on north Wales, see Anon, 'A False Alarm', in Elizabeth Edwards, *English Language Poetry from Wales 1789–1806* (Cardiff, 2013), pp. 162–3.
70 *Chester Courant* (14 March 1797), 4.
71 For example, in Flintshire, see Paul Evans, 'The Flintshire Loyalist Association and the Loyal Holywell Volunteers', *The Journal of the Flintshire Historical Society*, 33 (1992), 62. For example, in Glamorgan, see William Linnard, 'John Perkins of Llantrithyd. The Diary of a Gentleman Farmer in the Vale of Glamorgan 1788–1801', *Morgannwg*, 31 (1987), 26–7.
72 Knox, *Some Account of the Proceedings*, p. 3.
73 Stuart Jones, *The Last Invasion*, pp. 87–99, pp. 176–204.
74 James Rooke to Thomas Knox, 2 April 1797, Knox, *Some Account of the Proceedings* Appendix 24, p. 61.
75 Stuart Jones, *The Last Invasion*, p. 189.
76 Stuart Jones, *The Last Invasion*, p. 189 and p. 199.

77 Stuart Jones discovered that Knox's later life became clouded with insanity; Knox compared himself to Napoleon, got deeply into debt, spent his last years in poverty and died in London in seclusion in 1824 or 1825. Stuart Jones, *The Last Invasion*, p. 203.
78 'The trade of punning seldom decays. The Welsh who repulsed the French with pitch-forks, spades etc are said to have been well-provided with *field* pieces', *Hull Advertiser* (18 March 1797), 3; *Norfolk Chronicle* (18 March 1797), 2.
79 Extract of a letter from Haverfordwest, to a gentleman of rank and fortune in this neighbourhood, *Leeds Intelligencer* (20 March 1797), 3.
80 *Leeds Intelligencer* (20 March 1797), 3; *Bath Chronicle* (9 March 1797), 2.
81 *Hereford Journal* (22 March 1797), 3; *Northampton Mercury* (25 March 1797), 1.
82 *Hereford Journal* (22 March 1797), 3; *Northampton Mercury* (25 March 1797), 1.
83 *Chester Courant* (28 March 1797), 1.
84 *Chester Courant* (28 March 1797), 1.
85 *Chester Courant* (28 March 1797), 1.
86 See also Jones, 'The silly expressions of French revolution …', pp. 243–62.
87 This is a summary of the deposition against John from the examination of Charles Prudhomme, in David Salmon, 'A Sequel to the French Invasion of Pembrokeshire', *Y Cymmrodor*, 43 (1932), 63–4.
88 John Henry Manners, Duke of Rutland, *Journal of a Tour through North and South Wales* (London, 1805), pp.159–60.
89 Manners, Duke of Rutland, *Journal of a Tour*, p.160.
90 Transcripts by E. A. Lewis of documents in the Public Record Office relating to the trial – PRO W.R. Miscellanea 208D, in NLW MS Henry Owen Papers 1419C.
91 R. G. Thorne, *The History of Parliament: The House of Commons 1790–1820*, vol. 3 (London, 1986), pp. 143–4.
92 Marion Löffler, *Welsh Responses to the French Revolution: Press and Public Discourse 1789–1802* (Cardiff, 2012), p. 136.
93 Marion Löffler and Bethan Jenkins, *Political Pamphlets and Sermons from Wales 1790–1806* (Cardiff, 2014), p. 63.
94 *Cwyn y cystuddiedig, a griddfanau y carcharorion dieuog: neu, Ychydig o hanes dyoddefiadau diweddar Thomas John a Samuel Griffiths, Y Rhai Gwedi goddef Gorthrymder tost, a Chaethiwed called, dros chwech neu saith o isoedd yn ddiachos, a gawsant eu rhyddhau, o'r diwedd, yn yr uchel Eisteddfod, neu y Sessiwn mawr diweddaf, yn Hwlffordd: er dirfawr Siomedigaeth I'w Gelynion gwaedlyd a dideimlad* (Carmarthen, 1798). For the full text in Welsh with an English translation and an excellent overview, see Marion Löffler and Bethan Jenkins, *Political Pamphlets and Sermons from Wales 1790–1806* (Cardiff, 2014) pp. 235–92. For the avoidance of any doubt on authorship, Richards mentioned that he was the author in a letter to Samuel Jones on 19 March 1798: 'the narrative was drawn up

by me'; Philadelphia, Historical Society of Pennsylvania, Mrs Irving H. McKesson collection (Jones section); see also John Oddy, *The Writings of the Radical Welsh Baptist Minister William Richards (1749–1818)* (Lampeter, 2008), p. 52.
95 See Hywel M. Davies, *Transatlantic Brethren: Revd Samuel Jones and his Friends, Baptists in Wales, Pennsylvania and Beyond* (Bethlehem PA, 1995), pp. 131, 181–2, 185, 194, 211–12, 214/
96 R. T. Jenkins, 'William Richards o Lynn', *Trafodion Cymdeithas Hanes Bedyddwyr Cymru* (1930), 19.
97 William Richards, *Reflections on French Atheism and on English Christianity* (Lynn, 1795).
98 Historical Society of Pennsylvania, Mrs Irving H. McKesson Collection (Jones section); Richards to Samuel Jones, 19 March 1798. Also in Oddy, *The Writings of the Radical Welsh Baptist Minister William Richards*, p. 52.
99 Löffler and Jenkins, *Political Pamphlets*, p. 265.
100 Löffler and Jenkins, *Political Pamphlets*, p. 266.
101 Löffler and Jenkins, *Political Pamphlets*, p. 266.
102 Joseph Cornish, *A Brief History of Nonconformity from the Reformation to the Revolution: with Remarks on Church-Establishments* (London, 1797), p. 140.
103 Löffler and Jenkins, *Political Pamphlets and Sermons*, p. 268.
104 Löffler and Jenkins, *Political Pamphlets and Sermons* p. 269.
105 He meant the 'east of England', Löffler and Jenkins, *Political Pamphlets and Sermons*, p. 270, footnote 5.
106 Löffler and Jenkins, *Political Pamphlets and Sermons*, p. 270.
107 Löffler and Jenkins, *Political Pamphlets and Sermons*, p. 270.
108 Löffler and Jenkins, *Political Pamphlets and Sermons*, p. 270.
109 Löffler and Jenkins, *Political Pamphlets and Sermons*, p. 271.
110 Richards, *Reflections on French Atheism and on English Christianity*, p. 8.
111 Löffler and Jenkins, *Political Pamphlets and Sermons*, p.272.
112 Historical Society of Pennsylvania, Mrs Irving H. McKesson Collection (Jones section); Richards to Samuel Jones, 19 March 1798. Also in Oddy, *The Writings of the Radical Welsh Baptist Minister William Richards*, p. 52.
113 Löffler and Jenkins, 'Cwyn y Cystuddiedig', *Political Pamphlets and Sermons*, pp. 273–4.
114 Carmarthenshire Record Office, Cawdor Collection box 223; Colby to Cawdor Haverfordwest, 20 March 1797, also quoted in Walters, *Truthful History of the Last Invasion of Britain*, p. 150
115 Walters, *Truthful history of the Last Invasion of Britain*, p. 151.
116 Manners, Duke of Rutland, *Journal of a Tour*, p. 129.
117 Löffler and Jenkins, *Political Pamphlets and Sermons*, p. 274.
118 Löffler and Jenkins, *Political Pamphlets and Sermons*, p. 275.
119 Jones, *Welsh Ballads of the French Revolution*, no. 19, p. 209, lines 81–4.
120 William Jones, *Hanes Cymmanfa y Bedyddwyr Neillduol yn Nghymru, o'i dechreuad hyd y flwyddyn 1790* (Cardiff, 1831), p. 70.
121 Jones, *Hanes Cymmanfa y Bedyddwyr*, p. 71.

122 Prys Morgan, *The Eighteenth-Century Renaissance* (Llandybie, 1981), p. 144.
123 Matthew C. Jones, '"Weak Heads and Worse principles?" Church and State, Conservatism and identity in Welsh Calvinistic Methodist Literature 1797–1802', *The Journal of Religious History, Literature and Culture*, 4/1 (June 2018), 96.
124 Löffler, *Welsh Responses to the French Revolution*, p. 121
125 Thomas Dugdale assisted by W. Burnett, *Curiosities of Great Britain: England and Wales Delineated: Historical, Entertaining and Commercial*, vol. 2 (London, 1830), p. 784.
126 For the wider context, see Matthew C. Jones, 'Weak Heads and Worse principles?', 79–99.
127 *A Word in Season* was at pains to avoid politics, but this did not deter others from using it as loyalist propaganda at a later time of invasion fear. See 'A Welsh Minister's Address', *The Loyalist*, no. 12 (October 1803), pp. 204–5, which was a precis of Thomas Jones's statement, adapted for an English audience and stripped of its sectarian affiliations.
128 'Instructions for Col Tate', *The Anti-Jacobin*, no. 14 (12 February 1798), in William Gifford (ed.), *The Anti-Jacobin or Weekly Examiner*, vol. 1 (New York, 1970), p. 480.
129 'Instructions for Col Tate', p. 480.
130 *Kentish Gazette* (16 February 1798), 2; *Northampton Mercury* (17 February 1798), 4; *Caledonian Mercury* (17 February 1798), 2; *Reading Mercury* (19 February 1798), 4; *Chester Courant* (20 February 1798), 4; *Hereford Journal* (21 February 1798), 4; *Derby Mercury* (22 February 1798), 3.

Chapter 3

Invasion Propaganda, Historical Tourism and the First Jemima, 1798–1813

The French Invasion was not the only occasion on which the Welsh had defeated the Jacobin enemy. The Welsh played a conspicuous part in defeating enemies of the British state in Ireland at the same time as they were overthrowing the French in Pembrokeshire. In 1797–8, men from north Wales and the Cheshire border country, aptly named the Ancient (or 'Antient') Britons, a regiment of fencible cavalry, raised and financed by their commander Sir Watkin Williams Wynn, 5th Baronet, fought in in Ireland the name of Church, King and Country. Their atrocities in the Irish rebellion in 1797 and 1798 are still remembered with bitterness in Ireland but are now almost totally forgotten in Wales.[1]

The French Revolution in Wales has for too long been seen as a conflict of ideas carried out in press and public discourse. It was more complex and much uglier, a real war that killed many in Ireland and Wales. While 30,000 Irish men, women and children were being killed with inhuman savagery, the reading public of Britain was being entertained by stories of noble savages, Edward Williams was taking pebbles out of his pocket to lay out a stone circle inside which druidical rituals could unfold and Walter Scott was dreaming at Abbotsford of mist-shrouded glens and Jacobite heroes.² The key transnational relationship for the people of Wales was their relationship, not to the French "Other", but to their own British state and their related identities as Britons.³ The role of Welsh men in the revolutionary war demonstrated the Welsh martial contribution to the British state. These connections held lethal consequences in the late 1790s. Whether as victims or victors of the French in Pembrokeshire in 1797, or as instruments of state terror themselves in Ireland in 1797–8, the Welsh were fighting as modern Britons as well as Ancient Britons. The 'Antient Britons' were known and hated for their violence in Ireland against innocent civilians including misogynistic practices and torture.

The contribution of Welsh military success to the cause of Britain was celebrated as early as October 1797 in Anglesey in the form of the *Anglesea Volunteer Song* and coupled the defeat of the French in Pembrokeshire with the achievements, even before the events at Naas, Arklow and Vinegar Hill, of the 'Antient Britons' in Ireland:

> Hibernia's blood stain'd rebel dread,
> A Welshman's resolution,
> Prepar'd Life's last, best blood to shed,
> For King and Constitution.
> When France on Pembroke's Plains did flee,
> She met her just reward, Sir,
> And Cambrian courage still shall be
> A freeborn's Briton's Guard, Sir⁴

'A Welshman's resolution' consisted of torture, burnings, floggings and general harassment, which the Antient Britons carried out too effectively during the rest of their stay in Ireland to August 1798. Its author was Thomas Ellis Owen, one of several Welsh clerics in north Wales to defend the Anglican Establishment by attacking the Methodists.⁵ It is a simple, loyalist song celebrating a catalogue of Welsh, rather than English or British, military successes from Roman to modern times, the defeat of the French at Fishguard (lines 33–6) and Welsh involvement in the Irish rebellion (lines 29–30). The Welsh victory is also a British victory. Owen connects in a seamless whole, the defeat of the French on the 'Pembrokeshire Plains' with the defeat of the Irish rebels by Sir Watkin Williams Wynn.[6]

The connection between Welsh success in Pembrokeshire and Ireland was noted at the highest level. After the turbulence in Ireland had been partially suspended in the hot summer of 1798, newspapers noted: 'The Prince of Wales has it in contemplation to solicit his Majesty for an order of St David, in honour of his brave Welshmen, who so nobly distinguished themselves when the French landed in South Wales and on every occasion in Ireland.'[7]

The cause of Church, King and Constitutio, held sway in Wales, Britain and Ireland, culminating in the union between Ireland and Britain of 1801. Support for the union was a demonstration of the unionism that was central to the identities of Ancient and Modern Britons, and the Antient Britons of Watkin Williams Wynn were celebrated as facilitators of the Irish Union of 1801.[8] A Welsh version of British martial history lauded Welsh and British achievement and hostility to the French revolution and Napoleon: the connection between Welsh/British victory in Pembrokeshire in 1797 and in Ireland in 1798 is celebrated in the Rector of Aberporth, Thomas Thomas's *Memoirs of Owen Glendower (Owain Glyndwr) With a sketch of the History of the Ancient Britons*. Published in Haverfordwest in 1822 but written earlier in stages, it was inspired by the union of 1801 as much as by Glendower, and featured Sir Watkin Williams Wynn as a hero. Thomas's account of Glendower finished with his history of the French Invasion. A fitting climax, it portrayed the struggle for Welsh independence culminating in a show of Welsh loyalty to the British Crown. The Welsh repelled the French revolutionaries who had invaded Wales 'to fraternize a nation inflexibly affected to the existing government'. Their reception in Wales was the 'reverse of a fraternal hug'.[9] The principality of Wales, once a turbulent district, was now 'incorporated with England under one august monarch'. They could now rapturously say, in Latin, 'We Are All One People and May We Be So Forever'.[10] Owen's War Song and Thomas's account of Owen Glendower bristle with masculine and martial glory.

In March 1802, the Treaty of Amiens was signed, which gave a temporary peace in Europe until May of the following year. The subsequent breakdown of the peace renewed the threat of invasion and raised a series of troubling questions. How would the renewal of war be greeted by the British people? How far could the government count on the loyalty of its own subjects in resisting the French? If Napoleon should invade, would he be welcomed or repulsed?[11] However, the renewal of hostilities was greeted with what seems to have been an outpouring of loyalty to the Crown and Constitution.

The *Association for the Preservation of Liberty and Property* (APLP), an organisation supported by government, led by John Reeves, which had been active during 1792–4, was revived and met again at the Crown and Anchor tavern in the Strand on 12 July 1803.[12] John Reeves was again in the chair. The threat was not now how to counter 'French principles' but how to counter the physical threat of 'our malignant enemy'. It did so through an intense but short-lived blast of anti-Gallican and anti-Invasion literature that, as with the works of the earlier incarnation of the APLP, was targeted carefully and distributed widely.[13] As in 1792–3, the literature produced was also translated into Welsh, but this time with more centralised control than the earlier translations that were organised at a far more local level.[14] Their first sponsored publication, titled *Important Considerations for the People of this Kingdom*, was rushed into print on 25 July 1803.[15] That same month, a Welsh translation was published, *Ystyriaethau Pwysfawr*.[16] The government spent thousands of pounds sterling in distributing them to the minister of each parish in England and Wales, enough for one copy in every pew and several more in the aisles, where the poor worshipped.[17] The purpose of the propaganda effort was to make all the inhabitants of Britain aware of the destruction, pillage and cruelty that Bonaparte had wreaked in every place he had been. France was preparing to 'make England, Ireland and Scotland the scenes of their atrocities'.[18] In the English-language version, Wales was subsumed into England and rendered invisible, but in the Welsh-language version, Wales was included in the list. The addition of Wales to the list of nations made the statement directly relevant to its Welsh readers and demonstrated the desire to ensure that Wales partook of the defence arrangements for Britain on the same footing as the other nations in this new United Kingdom. In so doing, it was a Welsh expression of Britishness.[19] The author was not identified until 1809, when it became known that William Cobbett was responsible.[20]

Invasion Propaganda and Brutal Reality

Although the patriotic publications of 1803–5 were directed at the people, they were not for the most part produced by the people.[21] Shortly after the publication of Cobbett's *Important Considerations*, the APLP rushed another anti-French diatribe onto the market: *An Address to the People of the United Kingdom of Great Britain and Ireland on the Threatened Invasion* (1803), also intended for mass distribution and even more focused than *Important Considerations* on the horrors of a French invasion. This barbarous people, having preyed enough on each other, were now turning their thoughts 'to the invasion, conquest and *destruction* of Great Britain'.[22] *An Address* concluded with half a dozen lines of atrocity pornography, centred on the rape of women and the associated undermining of the masculinity of their fathers, brothers and husbands. The rape of women was secondary to the undermining of masculinity: 'to shock the feelings of fathers and brothers and husbands!'[23] The call to action was clear and immediate; the question was posed: 'Will you, my Countrymen, while you can draw a trigger, or handle a pike, suffer your daughters, your sisters and wives to fall into the power of such monsters?' In some editions the pamphlet ended there, but in the editions that bore the 'Printed by Order' of the APLP there was an addendum. The addendum was titled (in italicised print) *Specimens of French Ferocity and Brutality in Wales*, the text is brief, but explosive:

> It is well known, that in the last war, some French troops succeeded in effecting a landing in Wales. They were greatly superior to the regular force which happened to be in the part of the country where they landed; but, upon seeing at a distance, a number of Welsh women with red cloaks, whom they mistook for soldiers, they surrendered! – The following proofs of their ferocity and brutality are well attested:-
>
> A peasant whom they had compelled to assist them in landing their stores, presumed to ask for some compensation, upon which the commanding officer drew a pistol and SHOT THE POOR PERSON THROUGH THE HEART.
>
> Two officers went to a house, in which was a woman in child-bed, attended by her mother, who was upwards of 70 years old. The French brutes tied the husband with cords, and, in his presence, defiled both the wife and the mother!![24]

The reference to the 'women with red cloaks' as the cause of the French surrender is one of the earliest references in print to a narrative theme that in later years would become the defining trope of the French Invasion in popular perception and memory. Women usurping the role of men and the ridicule that this caused is in stark contrast to the atrocity committed on women by men in the same paragraph. The humiliation of menfolk is present in both aspects, the humiliation of the French men by the women in red cloaks, and the abject humiliation of the man who was forced to watch the rape of his wife and his mother-in-law.

This day was published,
AN
ADDRESS to the PEOPLE
OF THE UNITED KINGDOM OF
Great Britain and Ireland,
ON THE THREATENED
INVASION.

EXTRACTS FROM THE ABOVE WORK.

AMONG the inexpressibly dreadful consequences which are sure to attend the conquest of your Island by the French, there is one of so horrible a nature, as to deserve distinct notice. This barbarous, but most artful people, when first they invade a country in the conquest of which they apprehend any difficulty, in order to obtain the confidence of the people, compel their troops to observe the strictest discipline, and often put a soldier to death for stealing the most trifling article. Like spiders they artfully weave a web round their victim, before they begin to prey upon it. But when their success is complete they then let loose their troops, with resistless fury, to commit the most horrible excesses, and to pillage, burn, and desolate, without mercy, and without distinction. But the practice to which I particularly allude will make your blood freeze in your veins. These wretches are accustomed, whenever they prevail, to subject the women to the most brutal violence, which they perpetrate with an insulting ferocity, of which the wildest savages would be incapable. To gratify their furious passions is not however their chief object in these atrocities. Their principal delight is to shock the feelings of fathers and brothers, and husbands! Will you, my Countrymen, while you can draw a trigger, or handle a pike, suffer your daughters, your sisters, and wives, to fall into the power of such monsters?

Specimens of French Ferocity and Brutality in Wales.

It is well known that in the last War some French troops succeeded in effecting a landing in Wales. They were greatly superior to the regular force which happened to be in the part of the country where they landed: but, upon seeing, at a distance, a number of Welsh women with red cloaks, whom they mistook for soldiers, they surrendered! The following proofs of their ferocity and brutality are well attested.

A peasant whom they had compelled to assist them in landing their stores, presumed to ask for some compensation, upon which the commanding Officer drew a pistol, and SHOT THE POOR FELLOW THROUGH THE HEART.

Two Officers went to a house, in which was a woman in child-bed, attended by her mother, who was upwards of Seventy Years old. The French brutes tied the husband with cords, and, in his presence, defiled both the wife and the mother!!!

LONDON
Printed by H. Bryer, Bridewell Hospital, Bridge Street.
The Address is sold by J. Downes, Temple Bar; J. Spragg, King Street Covent Garden; J. Asperne, Cornhill; and J. Hatchard, Piccadilly.
Price Two-pence each, or Twelve Shillings the Hundred, and Eighteen-pence per Dozen.

Figure 6: 'Specimens of French Ferocity and Brutality in Wales'[25]

This addendum's purpose is to provide 'specimens' of French ferocity and brutality. It is a propaganda piece and includes exaggerated distortions of what may have happened. The case of the 'peasant' shot through the heart is a good example. It was claimed that the French used the tactic of putting one of their own soldiers to death over a trifling incident to win over the confidence of the people.[26] In this addendum, the specimen is pitched at a higher level of atrocity. It is not a French soldier who is put to death but a poor Welsh peasant who dared to complain. There is no evidence of this taking place; however, James Baker, the earliest narrator of the Fishguard Invasion, tells of William Thomas (of the parish of Mathry) who was captured by the French and badly treated. He had the audacity to complain of his ill treatment, Tate threatened to court martial the soldiers who stole from William Thomas not Thomas himself.[27]

The *Specimens of French Ferocity and Brutality in Wales* received much greater exposure and visibility than might have been expected of an addendum to an anti-invasion, anti-Gallican pamphlet. It was also used as part of a broadside to advertise the full *Address* (see Figure 6).

The Welsh translation, by Edward Davies, the Rector of Llanarmon, did not appear until 1804.[28] The language used in the translation is as vivid as the English, particularly in its depiction of the hated Bonaparte. The English version refers to him as 'the monster', Davies's translation describes him as a *'diawl ddyn'* ('devil man').[29] The ending of the pamphlet focuses faithfully on the atrocities inflicted on mothers, sisters and wives.[30] In the Welsh, as in the English, women are not seen to be suffering as women, but by proxy in relation to the shock felt by their fathers, brothers and husbands. The rape of women was a weapon of war against men.

Cobbett's *Important Considerations*, written in July 1803, and the Welsh translation the same month, provided the shocking scenario of the rape of women of all ages, irrespective of the condition that they were in. Women could be raped in childbirth or they could be raped on their deathbeds. The pleading actions of the women themselves – 'shrieking, tears, supplications, were of no avail'. There is a clear reference to the onlooking gaze and involvement of fathers, brothers and husbands in Cobbett's *Important Considerations*, 'where fathers, husbands or brothers interfered, murder seldom failed to close the horrible scene', a reference entirely absent from earlier anti-Gallican accounts.[31] The closing paragraphs of *An Address to the People* coupled with the *Specimens of French Ferocity and Brutality* show a further intensification in the anti-Gallican, fear of invasion literature that verges on the pornographic. The primary object of rape was not 'to justify their furious passion' but 'their principal delight is to shock the feelings of fathers, brothers and husbands'.[32] Or as the Welsh language account had it, 'y peth hyfrytaf ganddynt ydw peri braw a dolur i galonau, tadau a brodyr a gwyr'.[33] The *Specimens of French Ferocity and Brutality in Wales* heightens the horror of the narrative to undermine masculinity further. The husband is tied with cords, the abject spectator not only of the rape of his wife in child bed (a theme that Cobbett includes in his *Impartial Considerations*) but also the rape of his mother-in-law who was upwards of seventy years old. The sentence ends with three exclamation marks. The writers of the *Specimens* want their readers to believe that these incidents were common in Pembrokeshire. The Invasion Fear of 1803 used the 1797 French Invasion as part of an orchestrated campaign to highlight and exaggerate French atrocities and the terrible consequences for Britain should France invade successfully. The *Specimens* attempted to present women, not the same women, as red-cloaked heroines and as rape victims. The defeat of French men by Welsh women was a direct assault on their masculine martial identity.

There is no mention of damage or loss or injury of person or property in the earliest newspaper accounts that concentrate on the loyalty and bravery of the militia and country people and the surrender of the French. But, by mid-March 1797, several had commented on the consequences for those who lived there; the response of the government to these reports was that 'the only mischief which they did in Wales was the plundering of two or three farmhouses', the occupants of which received compensation from the government.[34]

The 'mischief' perpetrated by the French was in fact far greater than just damage to property, theft of livestock and general squandering of food and drink. The French were also guilty of what would have, in later times, been classified as war crimes. As early as 25 February, General White, the military commander for the region, wrote to the Mayor of Liverpool, who then wrote to his counterpart in Dublin, that the French had 'landed men at Fisgard and plundered and did much mischief in the neighbourhood'.[35] 'Much mischief' covered a multitude of sins. On 20 March the *Leeds Intelligencer* published an extract of a letter from Haverfordwest sent to a local gentleman 'of rank and fortune' in the Leeds area. The letter refers to the landing and its immediate aftermath:

> Their instructions were to murder, pillage and devastate the country. The minister of Llanunda and his wife and children luckily escaped with their lives, but they destroyed all his furniture, flung his books into the sea, wantonly murdered his livestock and ravished his maid servants, who were left in the house. Wherever they went, their outrages were horrid and almost incredible! To mention only one species of their brutality, they ravished the women, and *tyed the husbands with cords, to oblige them to look on.*[36]

The reference to the treatment of the husbands as 'one species of their brutality' provides the imagination with a catalogue of horrors to convey the fear and loathing of the inhabitants of Fishguard to a wider audience. This is not some adherence to an unwritten narrative or script. The Revd John Reynolds wrote to a Baptist brother in London shortly after the invasion and described what took place. They stole clothes and provisions and money 'and ravished many women and thus they went on till Friday evening, when they surrenderd [sic]'.[37] The ravishing of women was listed after the theft of meat, clothes and money.

James Baker's first published narrative of the invasion mentions atrocity but does so obliquely. His *Brief Narrative* was intended to convey the general horror of the invasion but does have enough specifics to place the atrocities in a certain place and time. He relates that the prisoners taken by the French from the sloop that they captured and sunk accompanied them to the heights of Carreg Wastad, probably acting as guides. They 'were the sorrowful witnesses of acts the most cruel, atrocious and brutal, the more poignantly afflicting as the family of one of them was within a small distance of the horrid scene'.[38] John Owen, master of the captured and sunk sloop lived in Pontiago on the Pencaer peninsula, 'a small distance' indeed from the place where the atrocity occurred.[39] Baker provided no further detail; it was not his intent to identify victims, to shock or offend people who had suffered so recently. There is another eyewitness account; Richard Fenton, a nearby resident, mentioned in his *Historical Tour* published in 1811 the 'brutal excesses' and 'execrable orgies, disgraceful to nature' perpetrated, as was to be expected, by 'wretches commissioned to confound and desolate'.[40] The 'veil of night' was drawn over these acts so he spared his readers the detail, which 'humanity shudders to mention'.

Portland, the home secretary, had promised that the king would compensate the sufferers for their loss. This was done with bureaucratic thoroughness. The investigator, Mr H. Mathias, drew up an account of the losses, which was laid before the Haverfordwest Grand Jury for approval to 'prevent fraud and imposition'. In the covering letter he sent to Milford with a book containing the account of the losses, Mathias said simply that he had 'sent affidavits of two women who suffered by acts of violence, one of whom after the act, had the small bone of her leg broke by a musket ball'.[41]

Mathias indicates that the woman, who was not named, was shot in the leg 'after the act'; that is, after an act of violence had taken place. There is no mention of the husband in the compensation account. The sparse but reliable information supplied by Mathias for accounting purposes can be supplemented by information from Cawdor himself who confided in August 1797 to the young Duke of Rutland who wrote in his journal that on the Thursday the French marauding parties 'met three women on the road, one of whom, and who was two months gone with child, they shot in the leg, and afterwards ravished her in the presence of her husband'. Rutland continued: 'One of their officers also, a man of the name of St Leger (an Irishman) went to a farm house and ravished a virgin 60 years old. This man afterwards informed Lord Cawdor that he had only come over for that amusement and intended no harm to any one.'[42] This account confirms in part the *Specimens* propaganda narrative. Rutland mentions two 'ravishments', one on the road, of a pregnant woman in the presence of her husband. Separately, there is mention of an older woman, not related to the first, who was also a virgin. The *Specimens* could easily have conflated the two accounts for propaganda effect into a mother and daughter episode and converted the presence of the husband into a forced presence tied with cords.

The Duke of Rutland has St Leger ravishing a 'virgin 60 years old'. St Leger was not the rapist of Mary Williams, despite the insinuations.[43] Mary Williams was pregnant and not sixty years old. Rutland held strong anti-Gallican views that were used for purposes of propaganda; his 1803 speech at Belvoir castle on forming a corps of Leicestershire volunteers was published by William Blair in *The Loyalist*, a government sponsored and, as the title suggested, a strongly loyalist magazine.[44] It was a little later, in 1805, that Rutland published his *Journal of a Tour in Wales in 1797* for private circulation. There is no reason to doubt the authenticity of Rutland and it is an excellent source for Cawdor's views. However, it is strongly anti-Gallican, anti-Baptist, anti-Methodist and anti-Irish. St Leger, whom Rutland specifically identifies as 'an Irishman' was certainly no saint, but he was also not a rapist.

The name of one of the alleged rapists was known well before any of the victims were identified. It was not until 1842 that one of the victims was named. Ap Gwilym in his *Authentic Account* identifies Mary Williams for the first time in public from local knowledge: 'Mary Williams, Carlem, seeing the enemy approach her house attempted to escape from them through a field; the Frenchmen fired at her, wounded and otherwise ill treated her.'[45] This 1842 account did not mention that Mary Williams was pregnant when the rape occurred. Ap Gwilym writes that she was from the farm Caerlem, confirming the Baker narrative that the atrocity occurred a 'short distance' from where John Owen lived in Pontiago. She was the wife of Thomas Williams who escorted the French officers to Fishguard to parley. Mary Williams received a pension in 'compensation' and it is the pension of £40 a year that commentators tended to stress, not the violence that had occurred.[46]

Male commentators tended to use euphemisms such as 'acts of violence' or 'wounded and otherwise ill treated her'.[47] Mary Williams was raped. In the 1850s, David Meyler, the Methodist minister in Fishguard, claimed, without naming her, that she had not suffered any ill treatment (*'sarhâd'*), 'er y buwyd yn dweyd hyny' ('even though people have said so').[48] Meyler was a boy in 1797 and published his reminiscences as an old man in 1856. In his recollections, he did however confirm that she had been shot by the French in trying to escape and that she was pregnant when this violence occurred. Just two months after the incident she gave birth to a son, whom she named Jabez, but the infant lived only a few months. The pension is again a prominent feature of the narrative relating to Mary Williams. Meyler knew about the pension first hand because he had to testify to London each year that she was still alive so that the Paymaster General could send her the pension. The issue of the pension and the envy that it clearly engendered clouded remembrance and pointed bias. Outside of the local communities of Pencaer and Fishguard, Mary Williams was unknown. This changed when Mary Williams died on 12 September 1853 at the age of eighty-eight. Her death was reported by several newspapers who mentioned she had been 'maltreated' by one of the French soldiers while in an advanced state of pregnancy.[49] This confirms at least part of Rutland's account of the unnamed woman, shot in the leg, 'who was two months gone with child ... and afterwards ravished'.[50] However it was her pension and the amount she had earned over a long lifetime that was most newsworthy.

The Times reported on 27 July 1799 on the items that appeared in the Distribution Money granted to His Majesty towards defraying the Extraordinaries of the army for 1798: 'For expenses, etc incurred, and compensations for losses sustained by sundry persons, when the French landed in Wales £1311 16s 10d had been distributed.'[51] The generous compensations that 'sundry persons' such as Mary Williams and others received may have soothed local feelings of anger and loss, but the pensions they received became recurrent themes of envy in popular memory, particularly since several of the affected – Mary Williams, for example – lived long lives.

Historical Tourists

Most people got to know about the events in Pembrokeshire in 1797 through the writings of tourists who had visited the area and had written about them. When tourists mentioned Fishguard, they also mentioned the invasion: 'the place is chiefly known on account of its neighbourhood to the spot where the French landed in 1797'.[52] The Fishguard Invasion was packaged for tourist consumption from the start.[53] Several accounts mention the

Invasion without making any mention of the women, knowingly or unknowingly following the official position. Neither Rutland nor others such as Thomas Evans in his *Cambrian Itinerary or Welsh Tourist* (1801) and Clement Cruttwell in his account of a tour from London to Cardigan and St David's in 1801 make any specific mention of a role for women in the invasion, although both had enough to say about the Invasion in other respects.[54] The story was as old as the Invasion itself, but so too was denial or rejection of the story or simply just not telling. Things were changing though, and the story of the women was being told more often and growing in importance.

Theophilus Jones reflected wearily in his critique of Welsh Tours written in 1798 'how much the colour and the garment contributed, on the occasion just alluded to, to strike the enemy with consternation is too well known to be mentioned'.[55] But as befitting the lawyer and historian that he was, gave equal weight to the role of Pembrokeshire men, and the role of Pembrokeshire labouring men at that, in the defeat of the French. The working men of Pembrokeshire, he contended, were 'mostly thick set, short men from five foot two to five foot six, muscular, bony, brave, determined and resolute (as the French desperados who lately landed on their coast can attest)'.[56]

Jones adopted an even-handed approach in dealing with the sexes, but in so doing, he was swimming against the tide. The 'Welsh Tour' presented an attitude to Welsh women that was decidedly chauvinistic. Tourists were predominantly male, young, undergraduates from Oxford and Cambridge and generally moneyed and leisured. As far as these English tourists were concerned, Welsh women were markedly different from their counterparts in England, and not only because Welsh people and their manners were different from the English. There was a different quality to Welsh women, often inferior but occasionally superior to their more polished sisters in England. Welsh women inhabited the two extremes of the English male imagination, Cambrian beauties on the one hand and the Welsh landlady caricatured by Thomas Rowlandson on the other, the epitome of the woman as man.[57] The attribution of masculine features and characteristics to Welsh women by male observers was well established long before the description of Jemima as a 'masculine female' in 1842.[58]

George Lipscomb was among several who paid attention to how Welsh women dressed and how their apparel changed from place to place. Lipscomb's account was criticised for being superficial: although his tour was of south Wales he only got as far as Cardigan, he did not venture into Pembrokeshire nor did he enter Glamorganshire or Monmouthshire.[59] Lipscomb, a doctor and an officer in the Warwickshire militia, was an observant traveller and he noticed that the colour of women's jackets and petticoats changed from blue in the north part of Cardiganshire, to white and red in the middle of the county, with the red jacket over the white as they moved south.

He was not the first to make this observation, Theophilus Jones had also done so in 1798 in his *Cursory Remarks*.[60] Lipscomb makes explicit what Jones held as implicit; namely, the connection between the apparel and the French decision to surrender. The Mathias correspondence that did appear in a few newspapers in April 1797 stressed the girls' readiness to fight, and their appearance as soldiers, but did not make the connection between the 'red flanes' and the French decision to surrender.[61] Lipscomb seems to have been the first to have made the explicit connection in print:

> These Cambrian Amazons, having on their red mantles, struck a terror into the French whose general immediately waited on Lord Cawdor, commanding officer of the militia force stationed nearest to the spot and surrendered himself a prisoner at discretion.[62]

In Lipscomb's account we have the first reference to 'Cambrian Amazons' and a national and gender reversal, instead of the

French men striking terror into the hearts of Welsh women, Welsh women were striking terror into the French men. Lipscomb may be the source for the red cloaked ladies in the *Specimens of French Brutality*. The focus on the women's apparel took on a role to such an extent that it became as, or more important than the wearers.

What the women wore at the time of the invasion also occupied Benjamin Heath Malkin who wrote an encyclopaedic history of south Wales in 1804.[63] He writes with insight about Pembrokeshire, a county that he declared was historically 'partly Dutch, partly English, partly Welsh'.[64] However, he had low opinions of the ports of northern Pembrokeshire and Cardiganshire.[65] His disdain for Fishguard was the worst: the streets were filthy, the church was a mean building with no registers, the people were inbred, and considered 'themselves as marked out for depredation … the landing of the French in the late War in some measure justifies their habitual jealousy'. The enemy would have given 'some trouble to the country, had it not been for a collection of women on a distant hill, clad in red mantles peculiar to these parts, who were taken for a large reinforcement coming on to the attack'.[66] The red mantle (a cloak or shawl) was known locally, Malkin explained, as the 'whittle': 'a short red mantle, with a very deep fringe, hanging over the shoulders, and communicates a most awfully military appearance, as General Tate can testify.'[67]

By the end of the first decade of the new century, dress, manners and cultures developed from being subjects of the male gaze to an accepted subject for historical enquiry, reflecting a new type of tourist, the historical tourist, tourists of the type of Malkin and the Samuel Rush Meyrick. Meyrick realised that the only people who wore distinctive Welsh dress were the peasantry as the 'superior persons followed the English fashion'. Meyrick also saw an intimate connection between this clothing and the French Invasion. The red flannels, 'since the taking of the French who landed at Fishguard last war, have been termed "the Frenchman's terror".'[68] During the Peace of Amiens a 'French lady of rank' visited the camp at Pencaer and 'purchased one of the scarlet flannels, to take home to France, in order to ridicule the French military'.[69]

Of all the historical tourists, the Fishguard resident, antiquarian, linguist, lawyer and wit Richard Fenton had the most to say about the Fishguard Invasion.[70] Born at St David's into a Pembrokeshire family in 1747, he became a lawyer, mixed in political and literary circles in London but also maintained his connections with Wales. He seems to have appointed himself unofficial poet to the Society of Ancient Britons. He dedicated his *Poems* in 1790 to none other than John Campbell of later French Invasion fame, whom Fenton described as 'the Discerning Judge and Munificent Patron of the Fine Arts'.[71] Fenton assisted William Owen-Pughe in editing *The Myvyrian Archaiology of Wales* (1801); his son, John married Owen-Pughe's daughter, Elen in 1814.

Fenton, a man of means, retired in 1792 at the age of forty-five to devote all his time to his antiquarian and historical work and to tour Wales, often with his friend Richard Colt Hoare. In 1796 following the death of Samuel Fenton, his uncle and adoptive father, Fenton moved to Fishguard, where he had inherited his uncle's considerable commercial and property interests. He now owned Fishguard's entire mackerel fleet and the greater part of lower Fishguard.[72]

Fenton was particularly qualified to write of the Fishguard invasion, not only was he a historical tourist, but he had also been involved in the invasion himself. The five pages of prose on the invasion that appeared in his *Historical Tour* was not the first time he had written about the event.[73] When James Baker wrote the first published narrative in April 1797, the advert in the *Hereford Journal* noted that to this number would be 'added a POEM, written for the occasion, and presented to the work, by the ingenious MR FENTON'.[74]

Fenton published two Tours in 1811, the anonymous *Tour in Quest of Genealogy through Several Parts of Wales, Somersetshire and Wiltshire by a Barrister* and the more substantial *A Historical Tour through Pembrokeshire*. The *Tour in Quest* has been described as 'lightly written'.[75] It was a *jeu d'esprit*, a light-hearted display of wit and cleverness. The text was probably written a year or so before the text of the *Historical Tour*.[76]

Fenton's *A Historical Tour through Pembrokeshire* appeared in 1811, the only county history that he succeeded in completing and publishing. Written after the period of intense anti-Gallican fear of invasion propaganda, Fenton's *A Historical Tour* reshaped the French Invasion narrative. As a resident of Fishguard, Fenton would have heard the stories, memories and recollections as told by his neighbours, servants, the fishermen on his boats and the people of Fishguard and Goodwick. His account of the recent events was intended to be different, more elevated, reflecting his status, his scholarship, his talents and above all his detachment, even though he was 'one on the spot'.[77] He wished to avoid a narrative 'which, if narrowly observed, would often leave to the greatest heroes but little of the merit of those victories they presume to challenge', a reference to the redirection of the credit from the men of the military to the women in their red cloaks.[78]

Fenton mentions the 'general panic', the people deserting their houses and hiding in the 'rocks and thick furze' – expecting their homes to go up any minute in flames.[79] The town of Fishguard itself emptied as women and children and valuables were moved into the interior.[80] Fenton moves from his own people to the French, details their activities but declines to provide particulars of the more serious depredations such as killings and rape. He comments on the lengths that the French took to satiate their hunger and quench their thirsts: 'Not a fowl was left alive and the geese were literally boiled in butter'.[81] Fenton wraps his ornate prose around the 'veil of night' to conceal more serious atrocity. The French had appetites for more than goose boiled in butter, they: 'let loose to every brutal excess that pampered and inflamed appetites could prompt them to, but the veil of night was kindly drawn over their execrable orgies, disgraceful to nature and which humanity shudders to imagine.'[82] The French appetites were untamed and unchecked: 'Gluttony was followed by intoxication.'[83] Fenton provides new and additional detail from local knowledge. A smuggling vessel had been recently wrecked and there were copious supplies of wine and brandy available in local cellars. The availability of the wine was an act of divine providence that 'raised the men above the control of discipline, and sunk many of their officers below the power of command'.[84]

The French force posed a considerable threat to the region. Fenton's sense of relief over the disaster averted reflects his own position as a local and his own sense of personal salvation and escape from distress and disaster.[85] Employing an appropriate nautical analogy, Fenton writes that the 'French General', the pilot of the ship, faced a mutinous crew and took the first opportunity 'without consulting the dissatisfied crew, to run her ashore'. Late on Wednesday evening the general proposed a surrender 'by us accepted as absolute and unconditional' which the French soldiery acceded to, 'with a sort of sulky submission to the imperiousness of the terms'.[86] Fenton is the first to mention internal dissension as the reason for the surrender with the implication that the decision to surrender was not universally accepted by the French. Fenton paints a loyal, patriotic but patrician picture of the surrender from the British side, replete with romantic imagery that celebrated restoration and relief but also the inclusive nature of the opposition to the French. The troops together with the 'meanest' of the 'gallant peer's' followers had taken 'a judicious position and waited with firmness the motions of the enemy'.[87] The surrender was achieved 'without hazarding the precious blood of our brave defenders', the troops.[88] His description of the surrender is a reaffirmation of the social order.

Fenton was writing this account in his *Historical Tour* of a modern event comparable to the battles of the past, an event of national interest and significance. He was also writing about an event that involved himself and his family directly; he wrote of his child being nursed on the peninsula and he not knowing for two days whether his son was living or dead.[89] His relief was as a father and as a loyal subject.

In contrast to the loyalty that he had shown so far, Fenton ends his account on a controversial note. His treasonable aftermath was a defence of the patriotic and loyal integrity of the event against those who wished to diminish it.[90] Fenton did not wish to question the indictment of Samuel Griffith and Thomas John, but to vindicate 'the principles of the accused' who were 'poisoned, as by all accounts they probably were' by the 'seditious publications' disseminated from the 'corresponding societies in the capital'. His reservations about their guilt were more practical and to do with their lack of resources. His comments were also socially and linguistically biased reflecting his higher social status compared to the Baptist accused. He chooses not to name Tate or Cawdor, and he does not name the defendants, but he does choose to identify them as 'fanatics', and their sect as 'Baptists' even though Griffith was an Independent. What had brought the Baptist 'fanatics' behind enemy lines was not treason, not ideology, but 'that fool-hardy inquisitiveness, a prominent feature in the character of the low Welsh'.[91] They had neither the learning nor the language skills to do anything more. Not even the patrician Fenton would suppose that just being 'low Welsh' was a crime; their innate inquisitiveness was at fault, which also according to Lipscomb was why the red-mantled women ventured to reconnoitre the enemy from the hill side at Goodwick.[92] Fenton distanced himself from the 'low Welsh'. The extent to which Fenton could understand Welsh was a moot point in his own day.[93] Whether he had some Welsh for scholarly purposes or not, his attitude to ordinary Welsh speakers was patrician and disparaging.

Fenton's account does not mention the fury of the people, the array of rustic weapons. or the women in their red mantles. This did not go unnoticed. *The Eclectic Review* for September 1812, which is generally complimentary about Fenton's tour, welcomes his piece on Fishguard as a necessary correction of previous misinterpretations, one of which was 'a story of a regiment of Welsh amazons, of old women ... Our readers will be glad to see an account of the occurrence from the pen of an impartial eye witness.'[94]

The First Jemima

Other views emerged as the tourists visited Fishguard and talked to people affected directly by the invasion and probed their memories of the event. This is what Richard Ayton and William Daniell did in researching and drawing up *A Voyage round Great Britain undertaken in the Summer of 1813*, their *magnum opus*. The first volume appeared in 1814.

Ayton had read Fenton's *A Historical Tour through Pembrokeshire*. He combined the knowledge gained from Fenton with his own findings from his conversations and interaction with local inhabitants. It was not antiquity but 'an event of late occurrence' that recommended Fishguard 'more powerfully to the notice of the traveller'.[95] Ayton and Daniell learned about this event from the people who witnessed it, and went as far as getting involved in some sort of re-enactment.

Ayton and Daniell scrambled down the steep cliff at Carreg Wastad point, which the French had ascended sixteen years earlier. The exercise may have stimulated their powers of empathy and insight into the French motivation for such an arduous ascent.[96] The narrator tried to imagine the position from the French perspective. They had missed their opportunity; if they had marched directly to Fishguard they would have found the houses empty to receive them, nor 'was there anything to have prevented their penetrating much farther into the country'.[97] The French knew they would fail before they had left their ships and therefore cut their losses. The French priority was how to satisfy their hunger. They were taken to each of the cottages in Llanwnda, which the French had 'gutted' in 'proper order'.

The first house 'invaded' was the largest and most opulent in the village and 'furnished an extraordinary supply'. Among the articles consumed were eight geese and eight pounds of butter that 'the party boiled up together and several of them feasted on this mixture so intemperately that they died in consequence of their excess'. Ayton and Daniell were the first to make the connection between the consumption in haste and in excess of a mixture of butter and uncooked poultry and death through food poisoning.[98] This information concerning the food poisoning came not from Fenton or from any other third-party source, but from the people of the neighbourhood themselves, who gained their information 'by the confession of some of the party concerned who consumed this terrible stew'.[99] Apart from their reckless waste of the poultry the French 'did not commit any wanton barbarities', Ayton and Daniell did not mention the unnamed brutalities hinted at by Baker, no mention of the rapes recalled by Rutland and the invasion propaganda, no mention of the 'execrable orgies' alluded to by Fenton.

They were quick, though, to censure the French general for his inaction during that first night. Ayton criticised Tate for his dereliction of duty, this inaction prompting a renewed confidence and courage amongst the people of Fishguard. At this point in their narrative, Ayton and Daniell introduced for the first time an outline of a character that would be prominent in the narrative in later years: Jemima Nicholas. Her name does not appear, but it is clearly the proto-Jemima, the ur-Jemima on which later accounts drew in terms of recall from popular communal memory. This is how these first narrators introduce her:

> at this period of the transactions a feat of heroism is recorded which is still looked upon in the neighbourhood, and not unjustly, as the most signal that occurred in any stage of the invasion. It relates to an old woman, who imagining that she had little to fear from invaders, and impelled by a strong feeling of curiosity, wandered from the town, that she

might have a nearer view of the enemy, in about an hour she returned, and to the utter astonishment of the inhabitants, in company with a French soldier whom she had taken prisoner, and who had been found willing to exchange his liberty for a promise of food and shelter.[100]

There are elements in this extract that continued to be central to an enlarged version of the incident and character that took up a life of their own around the middle of the century. The details that are present at this embryonic stage are: first, that the story comes from the neighbourhood itself; second, the act of valour is performed by a woman, an 'old woman'; third, the woman had come from Fishguard town; and finally, she had captured a French soldier on her own without any male or military assistance of any kind. The other features of the story – the she-cobbler, her great strength and size, the pitchfork, the liking for beer and liquor, the inflated number of prisoners captured – were all to be added later.

Ayton and Daniell, using local information and remembrance, add to the male force of 700, a contingent of women. The surrender scene gives the women prominence, a central position in the denouement. Cawdor's force was followed: 'at a little distance by a large body of women, all anxiously trembling for their husbands, fathers and brothers.'[101] Instead of the anticipated bloody struggle, there was an unexpected and abrupt unconditional surrender. The reason for the surrender, 'the cause of their yielding to so inferior a force', was the crucial role of the women. This information had come from the people themselves, and not in any half measures or in passing but 'confidently asserted'. The women were in the rear in their red woollen shawls and these together with their black beaver hats 'gave them not only a masculine but a very martial appearance'. The French mistook them for troops and 'immediately gave up the contest in despair'.[102]

However, it was Fenton's account and interpretation, not that of Ayton, which dominated the reports of travel writers for the next thirty years, used indiscriminately and unquestioningly. In 1813, George Nicholson printed the second and enlarged edition of his *The Cambrian Travellers Guide*.[103] The description of the French Invasion contained in this popular guide was essentially a simplified version of Fenton's.[104] Fenton made much of the local alarm and panic, the gluttony and intoxication of the French, the bravery of the military and the threat posed to the area, but suppressed the role of the women despite its significant place in the local remembrance.

Endnotes

1. For the Irish remembrance, see Guy Beiner, *Forgetful Remembrance: Social Forgetting and Vernacular Historiography of a Rebellion in Ulster* (Oxford, 2018) pp. 195; footnotes 264, 250, 301, 478–9, 495.
2. Alistair Moffat, *Sea Kingdoms: The Story of Celtic Britain and Ireland* (London, 2001), p. 257
3. Catherine Charnell-White (ed.), *Welsh Poetry of the French Revolution 1789–1805* (Cardiff, 2012), pp. 28–9.
4. 'Anglesea Volunteer Song', *Chester Courant* (31 October 1797), 3. The poem is published in full in Elizabeth Edwards, *English Language Poetry from Wales 1789–1806* (Cardiff, 2013), pp. 221–3, notes to the text on pp. 303–4.
5. For the debate, see David Ceri Jones and Eryn Mant White, *The Elect Methodists: Calvinistic Methodism in England and Wales*, vol. 2 (Cardiff, 2011), pp. 221–3.
6. The song was republished in 1804: *Chester Courant* (3 July 1804), 4; in the *Hereford Journal* (11 July 1804), 2, it was retitled significantly as the 'Welsh Volunteer Song'.
7. *Ipswich Journal* (28 July 1798), 3; *Bath Journal* (30 July 1798), 3; *Chester Courant* (31 July 1798), 2; *Hereford Journal* (1 August 1798), 3.
8. 'On the Union by an inhabitant of Shrewsbury', *Salopian Journal* (4 February 1801).
9. Thomas Thomas, *Memoirs of Owen Glendower (Owain Glyndwr) With a Sketch of the History of the Ancient Britons* (Haverfordwest, 1822), p. 239.
10. Thomas Thomas, *Memoirs of Owen Glendower*, p. vi.

11 M. Philp, 'The British response to the threat of Invasion 1797–1815', in M. Philp (ed.), *Resisting Napoleon: The British Response to the Threat of Invasion 1797–1815* (Aldershot, 2006), p. 2.
12 *Sun (London)* (14 July1803), 1.
13 Stuart Semmel, *Napoleon and the British* (Yale CT, 2004), pp. 42–5.
14 For the translations of 1792–3, see Hywel M. Davies, 'Loyalism in Wales, 1792–1793', *The Welsh History Review*, 20/4 (December 2001), 687–716.
15 Association for the Preservation of Liberty and Property (APLP), *Important Considerations for the People of this Kingdom, published July 1803. And sent to the officiating Minister of every Parish in England* (London,1803).
16 Association for the Preservation of Liberty and Property (APLP), *Ystyriaethau Pwysfawr I Bobl y Deyrnas Hon, a gyhoeddwyd yn y Gorphenaf, 1803. Ac a ddanfonwyd at bob Gweinidog Eglwys trwy Loegr* (Liverpool, 1803).
17 Daniel Green, *The Great Cobbett: The Noblest Agitator* (Oxford, 1985), p. 232.
18 APLP, *Important Considerations*, p. 13.
19 APLP, *Ystyriaethau Pwysfawr*, p. 14.
20 Ian Dyck, *William Cobbett and Rural Popular Culture* (Cambridge, 1992), p. 25.
21 Stella Cottrell, 'English Views of France and the French 1789–1815' (unpublished DPhil thesis, Oxford University, 1990), p. 225; quoted in M. Philp, *The British Response*, p. 2.
22 Dyck, *William Cobbett and Rural Popular Culture*, p. 6
23 Association for the Preservation of Liberty and Property (APLP), *An Address to the People of the United Kingdom of Great Britain and Ireland on the Threatened Invasion* (London, 1803), p. 15.
24 Only the APLP sponsored edition had the Addendum, those with 'Printed by Order of the Association for preserving Liberty and Property at the Crown and Anchor, in the Strand etc', and printed by J. Downes, Temple-Bar, J. Spragg, King Street, Covent Garden, J. Asperne, Cornhill and J Hatchard, Piccadilly.
25 This advertising broadside appears in secondary literature; for example, in H. F. B. Wheeler and A. M. Broadley, *Napoleon and the Invasion of England: The Story of the Great Terror* (London, 1908), p. 73, and again in Trevor Herbert and Gareth Elwyn Jones (eds), *The Remaking of Wales in the Eighteenth Century* (Cardiff, 1988), p. 125, as 'A memento of Fishguard in 1797'.
26 APLP, *An Address to the People*, p. 15.
27 James Baker, *A Brief Narrative of the French Invasion* (Worcester, 1797). See also the version of the story that has the French soldier condemned to death, not the Welsh peasant from whom he stole: John Evans (ed.), *Remains of William Reed, late of Thornbury; including rambles in Ireland* (London, 1815), pp. 88–90.

28. Edward Davies, *Cyfarch i Bobl Prydain Fawr ar fygythion y Ffrangcod i ruthro i'w gwlad; wedi ei gyfiethu o'r Saesneg gan y Parchedig Edward Davies, Rector Llanarmon Dyffryn Ceiriog Argraphwyd trwy orchymym Cymdeithas a sefydlwyd yn Llundain er cadw a noddi Rhyddid ac Eiddo etc Gan H.Bryer, Bridewell-Hospital, Bridge Street* (London, 1804).
29. Davies, *Cyfarch i Bobl Prydain Fawr*, p. 9.
30. 'Specimens of French Ferocity and Brutality' appears in Welsh as *Esiamplau o ymddygiad creulon anifeilaidd y Ffrangcod y'Nghymru*, which may be translated freely as 'Examples of the animal like cruel behaviour of the French in Wales'. The Welsh translation is more graphic than the English.
31. APLP, *Important Considerations*, p. 13.
32. APLP, *An Address to the people*, p. 15.
33. Davies, *Cyfarch i Bobl Prydain Fawr*, p. 14.
34. *The Kentish Chronicle* (10 March 1797), 2; *Northampton Mercury* (11 March 1797), 1; *Ipswich Journal* (11 March 1797), 4; *Reading Mercury* (13 March 1797), 1.
35. *Saunders's Newsletter* (28 February 1797), 2.
36. *Leeds Intelligencer* (20 March 1797), 3.
37. British Library Add MS 25388 folio 4 10-11, John Reynolds to William Reynolds, 3 April 1797.
38. Baker, *A Brief Narrative*, p. 4.
39. For John Owen and his home, see E. H. Stuart Jones, *The Last Invasion* (Cardiff, 1950), p. 83. Pontiago is a mile or so from Caerlem.
40. Richard Fenton, *A Historical Tour through Pembrokeshire* (London, 1811), p. 12.
41. H. Mathias to Milford, 24 April 1797, in David Salmon, 'French Invasion of Pembrokeshire in 1797', *West Wales Historical Records*, 14 (1929), 170.
42. John Henry Manners, Duke of Rutland, *Journal of a Tour through North and South Wales, the Isle of Man, &c* (London, 1805) p. 132.
43. J. E. Thomas, *Britain's Last Invasion: Fishguard 1797* (Stroud, 2007), p. 189.
44. *Speech of the Duke of Rutland at the meeting on Statherne Hill near Belvoir Castle, 25 August 25 1803*, The Loyalist, 19 (November 1803), 16.
45. *Speech of the Duke of Rutland*, 16.
46. H. L. Ap Gwilym, *An Authentic Account of the Invasion by French Troops on Carrig Gwasted Point, near Fishguard, 1797* (Haverfordwest, 1842), p. 16.
47. Mathias to Milford 24 April 1797; Ap Gwilym, *An Authentic Account*, p. 16; David Salmon, *French Invasion of Pembrokeshire 1797* (Carmarthen, 1930), p. 42
48. Anon [David Meyler], 'Adgofion Tiriad y Ffrancod', *Y Traethodydd*, 12 (1856), 365.
49. For example, *Falkirk Herald* (6 October 1853), 4; *Worcestershire Chronicle* (28 September 1853), 3; *Sun (London)* (19 September 1853), 5.

50 Manners, Duke of Rutland, *Journal*, p. 132. See also footnote 48.
51 *The Times* (27 July 1799), 3.
52 *An Account of Tenby, containing An Historical Sketch of the place compiled from the best authorities and a description of its present state* (Pembroke, 1818), p. 182.
53 See Hywel M. Davies, 'Terror, Treason and Tourism: the French in Pembrokeshire 1797', in Mary-Ann Constantine and Dafydd Johnston (eds), *Footsteps of 'Liberty and Revolt': Essays on Wales and the French Revolution* (Cardiff, 2013), pp. 247–70.
54 Thomas Evans, *Cambrian Itinerary or Welsh Tourist* (London, 1801), pp. 152–3; Clement Cruttwell, *A Tour through the whole island of Great Britain divided into journeys, vol. 3: Wales* (London, 1801), p. 208.
55 [Theophilus Jones] Cymro, 'Cursory remarks on Welsh Tours or Travels', *Cambrian Register*, 1796 (London, 1799) p. 441.
56 Cymro, 'Cursory remarks', p. 440.
57 Thomas Rowlandson, 'A Welsh Landlady', in Henry Wigstead, *Remarks on a Tour to North and South Wales in the year 1797* (London, 1800), p. 77.
58 For example, Edward Pugh, *Cambria Depicta: A Tour through North Wales illustrated with Picturesque Views by a Native Artist* (London, 1816), p. 117; Ap Gwilym, *An Authentic Account*, p. 33.
59 'Review of Lipscomb, Journey into South Wales', *Monthly Review, or, Literary Journal* (1805), 205.
60 Cymro, *Cursory Remarks*, pp. 440–1.
61 *Bath Chronicle* (13 April 1797), 3; *Hereford Journal* (19 April 1797), 3.
62 George Lipscomb, *Journey into South Wales through the counties of Oxford, Warwick, Worcester, Hereford, Salop, Stafford, Buckingham, and Hertford; in the year 1799* (London, 1802), p. 169.
63 Benjamin Heath Malkin, *The Scenery, Antiquities and Biography of South Wales from Materials Collected During Two Excursions in the Year 1803* (London, 1804).
64 Malkin, *The Scenery, Antiquities and Biography*, p. 415.
65 Malkin, *The Scenery, Antiquities and Biography*, p. 432.
66 Malkin, *The Scenery, Antiquities and Biography*, pp. 455–6.
67 Malkin, *The Scenery, Antiquities and Biography*, p. 482. The 'whittle' related to the Englishries of Pembrokeshire and Gower. See Jacqueline Lewis, 'Passing Judgements – Welsh Dress and the English Tourist', *Folk Life: Journal of Ethnological Studies*, 33 (1994–5), 37.
68 Meyrick, *The History and Antiquities of the County of Cardigan* (London, 1808) p. ccii.
69 Ap Gwilym, *An Authentic Account*, p. 42.
70 See Dillwyn Miles, 'Richard Fenton, Pembrokeshire Historian 1747–1821', *Journal of the Pembrokeshire Historical Society*, 7 (1996–7), 51–65.
71 Richard Fenton, *Poems by Mr Fenton*, vol. 2 (London, 1790), Dedication.

72 'Review of Fenton, A Historical Tour through Pembrokeshire. Reprint. Brecknock 1903', *Archaeologia Cambrensis: the Journal of the Cambrian Archaeological Association*, 6/6 (1906), 71.
73 Richard Fenton, *A Historical Tour Through Pembrokeshire* (London, 1811), p. 10–15.
74 *Hereford Journal* (5 April 1797), 2. Richard Fenton, 'A POEM, Written at Fishguard by a Spectator to the French Invasion', in J. Baker, *Visions, A Poetic Essay; hastily sketched for the present juncture of danger, to assist in forming the national spirit in AN UNION OF LOYALTY AND PATRIOTISM, to which is added, A BRIEF AND FAITHFUL NARRATIVE OF THE RECENT FRENCH INVASION, UPON THE COAST OF WALES NEAR FISHGUARD* (Bath, 1803), pp. 10-12
75 Brynley F. Roberts (2004), 'Fenton, Richard (1747–1821), topographical writer and antiquary' in *Oxford Dictionary of National Biography*, www.oxforddnb.com/view/10.1093/ref:odnb/9780198614128.001.0001/odnb-9780198614128-e-9298 (last accessed 14 March 2024).
76 The dedication in the *Tour in Quest of Genealogy* is dated 20 November 1809, the dedication to Hoare in the *Historical Tour of Pembrokeshire* is dated 20 October 1810.
77 Fenton, *A Historical Tour*, p. 10.
78 Fenton, *A Historical Tour*, p. 10.
79 Fenton, *A Historical Tour*, p. 11.
80 Fenton, *A Historical Tour*, pp. 11–12.
81 Fenton, *A Historical Tour*, p. 12.
82 Fenton, *A Historical Tour*, p. 12.
83 Fenton, *A Historical Tour*, p. 12.
84 Fenton, *A Historical Tour*, p. 12.
85 Fenton, *A Historical Tour*, p. 12–13.
86 Fenton, *A Historical Tour*, p. 13.
87 Fenton, *A Historical* Tour, p. 13.
88 Fenton, *A Historical* Tour, p. 13.
89 Fenton, *A Historical* Tour, pp. 13–14.
90 Fenton, *A Historical* Tour, p. 14.
91 Fenton, *A Historical* Tour, p. 14.
92 'Review of New Publications, Journey into South Wales 1799', *The Gentleman's Magazine*, 74/2 (1804), 743.
93 Miles, 'Richard Fenton', 54.
94 Richard Fenton, 'A Historical Tour through Pembrokeshire', *The Eclectic Review*, 8/2 (September 1812), 869.
95 Richard Ayton and William Daniell, *A voyage round Great Britain: undertaken in the summer of the year 1813, and commencing from the Land's-End, Cornwall / by Richard Ayton; with a series of views, illustrative of the character and prominent features of the coast, drawn and engraved by William Daniell*, vol. 1 (London, 1814), p. 125.
96 Ayton and Danniell, *A voyage*, p. 126.

97 Ayton and Danniell, *A voyage*, p. 126.
98 On the night of the 'surrender', 24 February, Knox went to Trehowell where he found 'five French officers, their servants, two surgeons and twenty-three men who were sick'. Thomas Knox, *Some Account of the Proceedings that took place on the landing of the French near Fishguard in Pembrokeshire on the 22nd February, 1797* (London, 1800), p. 25.
99 Ayton and Danniell, *A voyage*, p. 126.
100 Ayton and Danniell, *A voyage*, p. 127.
101 Ayton and Danniell, *A voyage*, p. 127.
102 Ayton and Danniell, *A voyage*, p. 127.
103 George Nicholson (ed.), *The Cambrian Travellers' Guide in every direction containing remarks made during many excursions in the Principality of Wales and bordering districts, augmented by extracts from the best writers* (London, 1813).
104 Nicholson, *The Cambrian Travellers' Guide*, p. 506.

Chapter 4

Remembrance and Legacy, 1813–56

By the mid-nineteenth century, contemporaries and eyewitnesses of the invasion were ageing, and increasingly anxious to commit their stories to writing before the memories were lost. Participants of the invasion still active included Major Bowling of the Castlemartin Yeomanry, the last surviving officer to witness the 'surrender' on Goodwick Sands, Mary Williams of Caerlem (who was by then living in Fishguard), David Meyler the Methodist minister at Fishguard, and several of the Fishguard women themselves. An English government inspector was sent to the town in 1854 to inspect the old fort creating 'a great sensation in the town, especially among the old women who frightened the French with their red flannel shawls in February 1797'.[1] The 'old women' would have been in their seventies if they were girls at the time of the invasion. Witnesses were still around therefore to relive and authenticate the memories of the past, whether they were personal, collective or communal.

The annual anniversary services initiated by the Methodists in 1798 were still held on Goodwick Sands. These services lost their original purpose of thanksgiving over time and became a holiday, with only a few keeping up the religious services.[2] In the Old Testament, there is an account of a victory; the place where they stopped to give thanks, was the 'valley of blessing' or, in

Hebrew, *Beracah*.³ This was the name which the Methodists gave to the new chapel they built in Goodwick in 1830. This chapel was built in commemoration of the deliverance in 1797 and was to replace the annual anniversary on the Sands that had been taken over as a 'holiday of feasting and frolic'.⁴ The moveable pulpit that was used on the Sands was still available to use, but Beracah was a physical monument of permanent remembrance and thanksgiving, embodying the Methodist capture of the French invasion legacy. The Baptists revered the site of the surrender as earnestly as their Methodist brethren, but disapproved of popular frivolity with equal intensity. Religious services were not held on Goodwick Sands after 1830, but the Sands would continue to remain a sacred place and a place of pilgrimage for the Methodists and other Nonconformists of the area.

Theories of social remembering also refer to forgetting, reflecting society's need to eliminate segments of its social memory which interfere with its present functions.⁵ In the August of 1824, the Baptist periodical *Seren Gomer* published the obituary of John Reynolds, one of their ministers who had been implicated in the events of 1797, where they commented for the first time as a denomination on the unfairness and injustice of their treatment at the time, but without any particulars.⁶ In 1839, David Jones included new information concerning the ministers John Reynolds and Henry Davies in his final version of his *Hanes y Bedyddwyr yn Neheubarth Cymru*, the summation of a long-standing project.⁷ Nothing again was said about the case of Thomas John, the falsely accused and later acquitted Baptist preacher at Llangloffan, when Henry Davies was minister there at the time of the Invasion. The denominational history wanted to avoid any association between treason and traitors, however unjust, and the good civic name of the Baptists. For the time being at least, he was missing from the historiography: the Baptists had gone silent about him.

There was no diffidence in the military; the French Invasion was memorialised by the Pembrokeshire Yeomanry. The militia forces who had, with popular support and fury, defended their communities against the hostile French invaders now had the task to protect the people from themselves. The memory of the French Invasion and their involvement was celebrated by the militia alongside their role, and a local role at that, of maintaining civil obedience. The irony of men who had once fought, or rather nearly fought, the French now fighting the Welsh people who had recently stood with them against a common enemy, was not lost on commentators.

In February 1797, several separate local corps had been involved in encountering the French and it was to Cawdor's credit that he achieved a unity of command. However, after the landing, the forces reverted to their local roots or disappeared completely. The Pembrokeshire Militia became divided over Thomas Knox with the South Pembrokeshire officers all siding with Cawdor and the North Pembrokeshire men with Knox. The legacy of the landing was shared by several units but there was competition amongst them for the greatest recognition and after 1800, when the system was formalised, for the award of 'battle honours' by the government.

The earliest newspaper reference to plaudits received by a local force during the Fishguard Invasion was to the Cardiganshire Militia. When the Royal Cardiganshire regiment of Militia was reviewed in August 1808, the *Cambrian* reported that the Cardiganshire regiment was 'the only Militia regiment that ever faced the French on British ground. General Taite [*sic*] who landed at Fishguard last war surrendered to them'.[8]

A key aspect of what would become the Last Invasion hypothesis was present as early as 1808; namely, the highlighting of Fishguard as a unique encounter with the French, not due to any bravery or achievement, but because of its location. However, the reward of the official battle honours for the only defeat of an enemy force on British soil was won eventually by only the Pembrokeshire and not the Cardiganshire militia.

The Pembrokeshire Yeomanry Cavalry (also known as the Castlemartins) commemorated their part in the French Invasion on the anniversary of the landing annually from the end of the war with Napoleonic France onwards.[9] In the 1830s, the field days, parades, the patriotic male-bonding were 'interspersed with sterner duties'.[10] At the height of the Rebecca Riots in 1843, the Castlemartins were often out for days on end throughout west Wales. When Fishguard was involved in July 1843, the commentaries immediately reminded readers that Fishguard was where the French had landed, not always getting the date right.[11] The Militia, not only those from Pembrokeshire continued to ridicule the old story of the women. A remembrance from 1890 stated that:

> there were many old men living in 1842 members of the Cardiganshire Militia and were present at Fishguard, when the French surrendered; and they ridiculed the old story, which has been so often repeated, that the women, dressed in red whittles on a hill, frightened the French to surrender.[12]

The Jubilee in 1847 was celebrated 'with *eclat*' not as the 'invasion of Fishguard' but as the 'Jubilee of the Surrender of the French troops at Fishguard'.[13] Since it was the Jubilee, the Castlemartin officers entertained the old veterans residing in Pembroke who had volunteered their services at the time with a 'sumptuous dinner'. The twelve veterans, averaging seventy-eight years of age, marched through Pembroke in good order, exhilarated 'with the same chivalrous spirit which no doubt they felt fifty years ago when they made a foreign foe surrender'.[14] In October 1850, during Cavalry Week when the work of the Yeomanry Cavalry across Great Britain was celebrated, the Castlemartin regiment was singled out for praise.[15]

It was later in May 1853 that Palmerston conferred the honour to wear the word 'Fishguard' on their standard and appointments. The regiment was in the unique position of being the only one in the whole British Army, regular or territorial, that bore the name of an engagement on British soil, and it was the first battle honour to be awarded to any volunteer unit.[16] People were proud of the regiment all over Wales.[17]

Recollections and interpretations of the details might differ but in Wales the Invasion enjoyed a high profile as a significant national event. Richard Llwyd's *Topographical Note*s in the 1832 revision of Caradoc of Llancarfan's *History of Wales* mentioned the 'gentlemen volunteers and colliers and common people of all descriptions' and just one brief sentence describing the women running down to the seashore wearing their whittles and terrifying the French.[18] From this, Edward Parry, in his companion guide on the history of Wales for tourists, wrote 'how the women of Wales, without the aid of either husbands or brothers, overcame and made prisoners fifteen hundred of the French army!'[19] In *Hanes Cymru*, the most ambitious history of Wales attempted hitherto, Thomas Price (known by the Bardic name of Carnhuanawc) considers the invasion to be one of the few events in Wales worthy of note from the time of the Civil Wars to the present.[20] Carnhuanawc was a Francophile and a Celticist. There was no martial glory or ideological hatred towards the French in his account of the French invasion, unlike the history penned by that other Welsh Anglican cleric, Thomas Thomas.[21] Carnhuanawc's account was brief, just seven lines, in which he praised the readiness of the Welsh to protect their own, rising up against the enemy using whatever weapon they could find.[22] A few Frenchmen were killed by the country people in their acts of plunder but there was no fighting due to the sudden French surrender.[23] Carnhuanawc's account is noteworthy for its total focus on the acts of the people in repelling the French, not one mention of the military, but giving no mention of the women either. The histories of Richard Llwyd and Thomas Price would soon be overtaken by a ramshackle collection of memories from Haverfordwest.

Joseph Potter, of High Street, Haverfordwest, published *An Authentic Account of the Invasion by French Troops on Carrig Gwasted Point near Fishguard* in 1842, the first separately published narrative about the Invasion for a generation. The work prided itself on providing information that had 'never before been published', and that only 'authentic' stories were published in this packed account of forty-four pages. The author's pseudonym was H. L. Ap Gwilym, an appropriate name for an author who described himself as 'A Native of the Principality'.

A great deal of what is popularly known about the invasion comes from Ap Gwilym. Stuart Jones identifies the author as Henry Lewis Williams, the son of Peter Williams, a tenant farmer in 1797, of Carnachenllwyd Isha in Mathry parish.[24] Ap Gwilym was not an eyewitness to the invasion itself but he knew several who were and was extremely keen to demonstrate a direct link to the invasion, to attest to the authenticity of his account. The book was dedicated to Major Bowling of the Castlemartin Yeomanry Cavalry, the only surviving officer from the Invasion at the time Ap Gwilym was writing.[25] Ap Gwilym also received the approbation and signed testimony of two veterans (non-officers) and participants of the campaign who were respected and well known in Fishguard.[26] Ap Gwilym's account combined military memories with those of the wider community. Precedence is given to Knox over Cawdor in Ap Gwilym's dedication. Despite his fall from grace, Knox was still highly regarded in Fishguard.

Ap Gwilym's *Authentic Account* was responsible for shaping the development of the narrative significantly. As well as fixing the features of the fluid capitulation/surrender account, he also adds new details to existing descriptions of events. Ap Gwilym identifies characters involved in the story that would be known in the community. He gives their names. They are not fictitious characters of his creation. Mary Williams, Jemima Nicholas, Thomas Williams and others were real people.

Thomas Williams, for example was identified by Ap Gwilym as the actual person who recognised the ships as French even though they were flying English colours. Ap Gwilym gives Williams's full particulars: 'Thomas Williams, esquire of Trelethin, near St David's Head, in the county of Pembroke.'[27] Williams had been a sailor in his youth, but more to the point, he was then a magistrate of the county, owner of a large estate, Trelethin, in the extremity of the county and a former high sheriff. The family and the estate continued to enjoy a high profile in the 1840s. Williams had in fact written to the Mayor of Haverfordwest from Trelethin on that February day in 1797 and was the first eyewitness on record to inform the authorities of the news, and therefore deserved the plaudits as first sighter.[28]

Ap Gwilym's account of the surrender was totally new. Ap Gwilym tells of how two French officers arrived at Fishguard with a flag of truce asking for Col. Knox, under the escort of Thomas Williams whom Ap Gwilym identifies as the husband of the 'woman that was wounded', Mary Williams of Caerlem. It was Knox, not Cawdor, who issued the ultimatum that that secured the capitulation, which Ap Gwilym mentions as being signed by two French officers.[29] Ap Gwilym is the source that allowed the Royal Oak public house, in later years, to present the table on which the 'surrender treaty' was signed.[30] This statement was, unfortunately for the Royal Oak, incorrect. If there was a surrender document then it would have been signed by both commanders, Tate and Cawdor, but there is no evidence of such a document. As Stuart Jones concedes there is no trace of 'this important military document, no yellowing parchment with the signatures, "Wm Tate" and "Cawdor" in fading ink at the bottom, has ever been found in the archives on either side of the Channel'.[31] The claim for the existence of a document rests entirely on the evidence of *The Times* for 6 March 1797. *The Times* reference is fleeting and sparse, and incidentally identifies Tate as a Scotsman.[32] No other newspapers mention the 'articles of capitulation' and, significantly, Cawdor makes no mention of them in his correspondence or in any of his writings. The articles of capitulation do appear in the dispositions of the arrested, where they are mentioned as a work in progress.[33] These articles existed in Tate's mind only.

The Ap Gwilym account of the surrender then turns to noon, the next day. The British forces were drawn up in a line, in a field, on Windy Hill Farm, in sight of the enemy's advanced post. The officer given prominence by Ap Gwilym on this field day was Colonel Colby who is given words to say: 'let us be all ready, my boys; perhaps they may disappoint us after all'.[34] The Hon. Capt Edwardes is sent to offer terms to Tate. There is uncertainty even in Ap Gwilym's text as to whether the terms of the surrender would be met or not by the French at large. When the delegation arrives at Trehowel, the French General's headquarters, 600 of the enemy were 'drawn up in line' (fewer than half of the total contingent) and ordered to 'open pans, and shed priming'.[35]

At two o'clock, the enemy appeared on Goodwick Sands, marching down from the top of Goodwick Hill playing their music 'their brass drums echoing through the hills'. This reference to two o'clock is the only time Ap Gwilym's account agrees or coincides with any aspect of the Cawdor correspondence with the home secretary. The French troops, the privates, and the NCOs, marched up in front of the 'English'. Ap Gwilym, a Pencaer man, with Fishguard Fencible connections describes the armed militia as English, that is from south of the county. The French were organised in columns, laid down their arms peaceably and were marched off. Ap Gwilym describes the 'grand spectacle ... the surrounding hills, crowded with innumerable spectators of both sexes: the women in their scarlet mantles and round hats, appeared at a distance like so many soldiers'.[36]

Not all the French soldiers had laid down their arms on Goodwick Sands that afternoon, it was on 'Friday evening' that the 'drunken dispersed French soldiers returned to Trehowel', the French headquarters. The remaining part of the French army joined their comrades at Trehowel from their camp at the defensive position in Carnwnda, voluntarily or otherwise, 'leaving the whole of the ammunition and spare arms in the camp'.[37] The soldiers who had surrendered on Goodwick Sands had been marched to Haverfordwest on the Friday evening, but those rounded up later were marched to prison in Fishguard on Saturday, 'where the sick and hurt received the necessary medical assurance'.[38] Fishguard was the place where not only the ill soldiers (the victims of their own excesses – eating half-cooked poultry) were kept, but also the worst offenders.

This account of the surrender entered the popular narrative from Ap Gwilym. Some of the favourite anecdotes of the French invasion may have first seen light of day in his work.[39] But Ap Gwilym is not responsible for the story of the women influencing the French capitulation. There is no mention of 'judicious positioning' nor of any active female role in the engagement. In this respect, Ap Gwilym is closer to the military account than the popular versions and is the creator of the orderly, ceremonial surrender, replete with music.

Ap Gwilym reserves his praise for the resilience and resourcefulness of the Welsh, as well as their loyalty. He promotes the French Invasion in terms of Welsh patriotism, which makes his reference to the militia from south of the county as 'English' quite barbed, rather than British patriotism. The French expected to have been 'received as friends with open arms, they found nothing but brave opposition'.[40] But, at this point, Ap Gwilym had to account for the exceptions. It was said, by some at the time that a few had not been loyal. This was an 'authentic account' so there could be no whitewash. However, of the forty-four pages of his account, Ap Gwilym devotes only two paragraphs to the 'few farmers charged', which he dismisses as invalid charges. The episode is summarily dismissed but, significantly, not before referring to the bribery involved.[41]

The second half of his account is more disjointed than the first. Most of these stories were new in print, if not in oral tradition, and because of Ap Gwilym these events have become incorporated as historical truths into the writing about the invasion: the Brestgarn Clock (the French shot at the clock believing that a person was hiding inside, leaving the bullet holes), the woman in childbirth at the Cotts farm, the Spoons and Ann George (the maid Ann George stayed behind after the master had fled saving the silver spoons), the possible spy or traitor James Bowen and the literary birth of Jemima Nicholas. Other features covered were unrelated directly to the invasion story, but important to the general narrative, including the story of the Golden Prison at Pembroke. This tale of a group of French prisoners escaping from Pembroke Prison helped by two local girls and using Cawdor's yacht to escape featured in virtually every account of the invasion after 1842.[42]

Ann George also stays in the story as the woman who identified the local horse-thief and traitor, James Bowen, who had fled to France some years earlier in disgrace. Ap Gwilym had no doubt that he was the man 'who pointed out the spot on which the French landed'.[43] There were also other Welshmen, among the French, an observation corroborated by contemporary accounts.[44] They were Welsh speakers from the northern part of Pembrokeshire, prisoners of the French according to the Ap Gwilym narrative who were too afraid to leave in case they were shot.[45]

Another woman of ice-cool courage was the unnamed mother from the farm at Cotts, who had very recently given birth. Several of the French entered her house, and in defiant fear 'the poor woman took up the newly born infant in her arms'.[46] This is remarkable enough, but what was even more incredible was what followed: 'the enemy endeavoured to soothe the poor woman's fears and left the home without further molestation.'[47] The Cotts story is in direct contrast to the experience of Mary Williams of Caerlem, whom Ap Gwilym describes as being 'wounded and otherwise ill-treated'.[48] The ill-treated Mary Williams is named, while the 'poor woman' of Cotts is not. Ap Gwilym was very interested in the compensation Mary Williams had been awarded, and calculated that by the time of his writing in 1842, she had received 'eighteen hundred pounds sterling!'[49]

(his exclamation mark). 'She now lives in Fishguard', he adds. The Cotts woman became renowned in Welsh culture through the poetry of Ceiriog, who gave the newborn infant a precise age as *Y Baban Diwrnod Oed* ('The Day-Old Baby').[50] Mary Williams will reappear shortly.

Also immortalised by Ap Gwilym was Jemima Nicholas. Jemima Nicholas appeared in the story under her own heading, 'AN HEROIC SINGLE WOMAN'.[51] Ap Gwilym was the first to give this heroine who captured the French marauding party a name in public, but as we have already seen, Ayton and Daniell (1813) were the first to mention the incident in print.[52] Ayton's 'old woman' had become Jemima Nicholas. A note supplied by the Revd Samuel Fenton, the son of the historian Richard Fenton, in the Fishguard Parish Register on the death of Jemima Nicholas aged eighty-two in 1832 reads 'Jemima Vawr or Jemima the Great from her heroine acts' against the French in 1797 'and being of such personal powers as to be able to overcome most men in a fight'.[53] Fenton remembered her well; a shoemaker, she had made him shoes when he was a boy. Jemima lived in the Main Street, Fishguard. In 1820 her residence was sold by auction at the Angel Inn, Fishguard as a 'desirable freehold estate' in the Main Street: 'Lot 3. The Messuages or Dwelling Houses and part of the Garden together with the Blacksmith's Shop' belonging 'now or late in the several occupations of Elizabeth Philip, Rachael Roch, Jemima Nicholas, Henry David and William Barzey.'[54]

The memory of Jemima was alive in the neighbourhood. Ap Gwilym may not have known her personally as Fenton, the local Fishguard man, had, but as he had done in other cases, he identifies a participant who was known locally by naming them in print. Ap Gwilym's description of Jemima confirms, without replicating, the memories of the vicar of Fishguard. Samuel Fenton calls her 'Jemima Vawr', for her heroic acts and strength, Ap Gwilym describes her physical bulk: 'a tall, stout, masculine female'. Ap Gwilym does not call her Jemima Fawr, but is the first to describe her mannish appearance. Her heroism stemmed not from her masculinity, but in Ap Gwilym's words, because she was 'imbued with the noble and patriotic spirit of ancient Cambria'.[55] In 1842, the spirit and courage of the ancient Britons that had featured so strongly in earlier descriptions relating to the valour of men, has now become the 'spirit of ancient Cambria' and associated with a woman, albeit a woman with masculine characteristics. We also have, for the first time (although not the last), Jemima with her weapon of choice, a pitchfork. Jemima was not only armed with a pitchfork but with an element more feminine than masculine: her 'rhetoric'. Another new feature was the manner of Jemima's heroism itself, Ap Gwilym has Jemima marching boldly to Pencaer, whereas the earlier Ayton and Daniell account has her approaching the French out of curiosity. By 1842, Welsh female inquisitiveness had become Welsh female heroism, with marked masculine features. In 1813, the 'old woman' takes one French soldier captive, luring him with the promise of food and shelter. In 1842, Jemima Nicholas, marches boldly to Pencaer taking twelve French men captive and bringing them to confinement at Fishguard.

Ap Gwilym itemises the intensity of the devastation caused by the French incursion on that terrible day in 1797: twenty-three houses, substantial dwellings, were plundered, commencing with what became the French headquarters at Trehowel and ending with Llanwnda Church. Caerlem, the home of Thomas and Mary Williams, was number five. He also identifies the farms plundered by the French; nineteen in all. Cotts was fifteenth on the list, suggesting that the French did more than just enter and leave after the drama of the showing of the newborn infant, they also had the time to plunder. In addition, there were 'many small houses too numerous to be particularized'.[56]

Just after Ap Gwilym's first *An Authentic Account*, another retelling of the French invasion appeared, titled simply *The French at Fishguard in 1797*. This was a ten-page article, published anonymously, which appeared in the *United Service Magazine* for February 1843.[57] *The French at Fishguard in 1797* is an early source written at a time when contemporaries and eyewitnesses were still alive and their experiences drawn on. Ap Gwilym's work features largely in the historiography of the invasion, while this work, which appeared less than one year later, has been neglected. The main reason for this neglect is that David Salmon, the early twentieth-century authority on the Invasion and a standards setter, in his 1929 article and 1930 book dismissed the article as a 'fictious narrative' and thereby false.[58]

It would be a mistake to dismiss this work or to categorise it as 'historical fiction' in the same way as the Invasion was fictionalised and romanticised later the same century. It was neither fiction nor history, but a military memoir, a specific form of memory-production that appeared in a periodical that specialised in the genre, the *United Service Magazine*, a new title for the periodical previously titled *United Service Journal and Military Magazine*.[59] Its owner was Henry Colburn, one of the key figures for publishing the new professional military journals and gazettes that appeared in the late 1820s.[60] The military memoir emerged as a central element in the patriotic remembrance of wars, written by military authors.[61] The readership of the journal comprised men and women of the armed services but also the general reader particularly 'our accomplished countrywomen'.[62]

The *French at Fishguard* appeared a few months after that of Ap Gwilym, but it was completely different. Ap Gwilym's was a collection of local anecdotes connected quite randomly, written, or rather collated by a gentleman farmer, while this is metropolitan and English, an example of professional writing by a military journalist.[63] When reviewed, the *French at Fishguard* compared to the weighty paper titled 'The Balance of Military Power in Europe' was considered one of its 'lighter' articles, exemplifying the periodical's aim to be as 'entertaining as it is useful'.[64] To be entertaining to a general readership, embellishments were undoubtedly made, the dialogue was imagined and there were colourful additions; in addition, Welsh words were misunderstood and misspelt.

The article is presented as a product of two persons, the author as memoir writer, and then the author as journalist or reporter. The anonymous author begins in the first-person as narrator, both singular and plural, 'my remembrance' and 'we the country people' and also refers to the people of the area in the third person. The narrator sighted the French ships from near Llanwnda, had a wife named Mary, was a master of a farm with servants that he never left, even after the French occupied it, and guided the French officers to Fishguard. The features and activities of the narrator fit the profile of Thomas Williams, very closely recalling his experience from the landing to his escorting the French officers to Fishguard, but he is not named. We know that Thomas Williams was the owner of Caerlem farm, which was plundered by the French. Hugh Meyler, in his letter from the 'Fishguard guard house' dated 5 March 1797, refers to the man who accompanied the French officers as a 'Country Farmer' but does not name him.[65] We know too that Thomas Williams had stayed in Caerlem throughout the ordeal and that it was Thomas Williams who conducted the French officers to Fishguard to negotiate with the British forces. These particulars are known to us mainly from Ap Gwilym's *Account* where Thomas Williams is named for the first time and identified as the husband of the woman who was 'wounded'.[66] James Baker, for instance, only mentions that the French officers received the 'guidance of a peasant'.[67]

The 'Thomas Williams' narrator/memoirist in the *United Service Magazine* is a romanticised construct of the military author, but the memories to which he gives voice and the narrative that he shapes are rooted in the local community and authenticated by the direct experience of the living.[68] The author visited Fishguard and met:

> One poor woman, still alive, named Mary Williams, whom I visited at Fishguard, the mother of six children, and then pregnant with a seventh, had been brutally violated by a

drunken Frenchman and when she afterwards attempted to escape, was shot at, and desperately wounded in the thigh.[69]

The name of Mary Williams was at that point unknown in the public narrative, her name only appears publicly for the first time in Ap Gwilym in 1842, just eight months before the publication of *The French at Fishguard in 1797*.[70] There is no evidence of overlap or borrowing between these two very different versions of the same story, the first published in Haverfordwest, the other in London. Not one of the familiar Ap Gwilym anecdotes appear in *The French at Fishguard*. There is no Jemima and no mention of the treason trials. Ap Gwilym refers to Mary Williams from the farm at Caerlem trying to escape the French approaching their house who 'fired at her, wounded and otherwise ill-treated her'.[71] Otherwise, the details differ: the 'drunken Frenchman' and the pregnancy of the raped woman are not mentioned in Ap Gwilym. *The French at Fishguard* has 'brutally violated', which is nearer the truth than Ap Gwilym's 'otherwise ill-treated her'. The author of the 1843 work knew that Mary Williams was pregnant when she was raped, ten years before it became publicly known; it was only on her death in 1853 at the age of eighty-eight, when she was described as 'the last living relic of the French invasion', that the fact that she was 'maltreated by one of the soldiers, being then far advanced in pregnancy' widely reported.[72] The only possible conclusion was that he knew this intimate detail because Mary Williams had told him.

The narrator/memoirist describes the scene at Llanwnda as one of confusion, fear and flight as carts and waggons were drawn up and loaded with 'their most valuable property'. The chaos and hurried removal of property accords with other accounts. The author explains the different roles of the women, pointing out to the readers that these women know no other language than Welsh, and putting their experience into historical context.[73] The narrator, hastened to his own dwelling, which 'lay about two miles from the scene of burning and distress', well within

French-occupied Pembrokeshire on the Pencaer peninsula near to the point of embarkation in Llanwnda parish, in other words (but not stated) Caerlem.

The locals were busy preparing for the French: fixing weapons onto poles, hiding their valuable feather beds in the furze, or gorse, which grew so abundantly in that part of Pembrokeshire and was often used as an animal feed (reduced in furze mills for that purpose). The narrator hid his wife and child together with his best feather beds in a furze brake and the French, because there was no wood, burnt the furze to cook their stolen provisions of livestock and poultry. The focus on the terrified and their concealment in the furze is also a prominent feature that does not appear frequently in accounts other than those of the local eyewitnesses such as Richard Fenton.[74] The narrator of *The French at Fishguard* recalls terrified people hiding themselves in a brake on 'Treleaze'.[75] 'Treleaze' is Tre-llys, in the parish of St Nicholas, a vantage place of safety mentioned by Samuel Griffith in his deposition to the assizes.[76]

The narrator was taken to Trehowel to conduct two of Tate's officers to the quarters of the British commander. He describes the chaotic and frantic scene there that Samuel Griffith also described as 'two officers at the Door and the French Army about the House'.[77] The two officers are described by the narrator; their ages and appearances fit their known identities. This section of the narrative ends with the narrator taking the French officers to meet Knox in Fishguard with the famous letter of surrender from Tate. At this point, this half line is inserted in the text as if to close the section. The voice of the narrator becomes silent, and the author as reporter takes over entirely. 'Thomas Williams' disappears from the story. The author is more matter of fact, and the text becomes a well-informed commentary rather than the memories of a participant. The author presents the famous Tate letter of the 5th Ventose, but without the republican date. The Tate letter is followed by Cawdor's reply in full. Both letters had been released into the public domain just days after the invasion and quoted extensively in newspapers and periodicals at the time, but their appearance here in 1843 was the first opportunity for them to be read by a new generation.

What we have next in the *French at Fishguard in 1797* is an exposition of the landscape and the disposition of forces, including the peasantry, the colliers and the women, along the cliffs, a description of the 'judicious positioning' described by newspapers in March 1797 (discussed in Chapter 2 of this volume). The accurate topographical details demonstrate local knowledge. In this account we encounter the first detailed and sustained appearance in the narrative of the positioning and impact of the women 'attired in the scarlet whittle and round beaver hat, the common costume of the female Welsh peasantry'.[78] The author gives the women a key role in affecting the French surrender.[79] In the telling of this aspect of the story, the author gives the source of his information. In a footnote, he said that during a tour in Wales, he met a lady at Llanelli who had gone with her uncle in a gig to see the French surrender; she told him about the rush of women onto the Sands and the brave words uttered by the dashing Colby. People travelled long distances to witness the surrender, a congregation of Methodists from Carmarthen, according to one early account, followed the charismatic preacher David Jones to Goodwick and may have been with Jones at the surrender.[80] This is another instance of the female testimony that underpinned the account.

An entirely new theme is also introduced: the presence of French women, who joined in even greater rage, including the woman whom the author described as the 'wife or mistress' of General Tate. She rushed upon him, tore the hair from 'his grey head' and then, 'with a gesture of the hands resembling that of Lady Macbeth in her dream and in the most ferocious language, regretted the lost opportunity of bathing their hands in the Welshmen's blood'.[81] These bloody histrionics do not appear elsewhere and are probably fictional reconstructions for the entertainment of its female readers: French women punishing the French soldiers for being weak and forced to surrender by the Welsh women. We do know that there were four French women in their midst, two wives of officers and two wives of privates, but no Madame Tate.[82]

The author, the military journalist, as opposed to his narrator, can stand back and identify with the suffering of the invaded. The attack on Mary Williams, and other similar 'brutal outrages', unheard of in a peaceful religious community 'like the agricultural Welsh', produced 'at the time a deep and solemn impression, which half a century has failed to remove'.[83] Many of the inhabitants of Llanwnda, the author notes, emigrated to America soon after, and any stranger seen 'in their villages' was mistaken as a Frenchman. These observations are well attested, the fear of strangers by Benjamin Malkin, for instance, and the emigration to the United States by the Baptist Gymanfa (southwest) of 1801.[84]

The *Weekly Dispatch (London)* published an extract from the *United Service Magazine* on the role of the women at Fishguard, giving it the dramatic title 'The Welch Amazons', enjoying the 'ludicrous manner in which we captured a body of men that might have been so formidable'.[85] The *Monmouthshire Merlin*, a week later, published the 'Welsh Amazons' extract and also thought it 'ludicrous' because of the way the women overcame the men.[86] But as the *Weekly Dispatch* put it, the women 'with their clubs and pitchforks, [they] would have been most formidable to a broken and dispersed enemy'.[87] The *Pembrokeshire Herald*, a newspaper read by and large by the people of Pembrokeshire, published the entire piece in August 1844 without comment.[88] To contemporaries, *The French at Fishguard in 1797* was exactly what it said it was, an account of the French at Fishguard in 1797.

Of the two works – Ap Gwilym's and that which appeared in the *United Service Magazine* – Ap Gwilym's had the most impact and influence in the longer term in Wales, but the *French at Fishguard in 1797* won a new readership both in Wales and beyond when a reworked and enlarged version of the piece appeared in the popular *Chambers's Journal* in 1860, written by 'A Native'.[89] It was also republished in the *Red Dragon* much later.[90] It is a neglected classic presentation of the French Invasion, and in it the women, as 'Welsh Amazons', are prominent as active participants, not only as spectators, although Jemima does not feature.

The anniversary of the French Invasion of 1797 in February 1848 provided an occasion to use the memory of 1797 to avoid a new invasion that year. A piece titled *The first invasion of Britain by the French* ran in several newspapers in England and Wales; it was a brief commentary heading an abridged version of Ap Gwilym's *An Authentic Account*. The commentary warned people in 1848 to heed the experience of the past: another invasion could happen again, therefore 'it may not be out of season to give a few reminiscences of it'.[91] The second edition of *An Authentic Account*, published in 1853 under the author's own name, Henry Lewis Williams, had a much greater impact than the first edition and influenced the work of others.[92] A new Welsh-language version of the story with content based largely on Ap Gwilym's (or Williams's) second edition appeared as an additional chapter in a new edition of Titus Lewis's *Hanes Prydain Fawr*.[93] Lewis's *Hanes* lived long after him and was issued and updated as a second edition by John Emlyn Jones, Ebbw Vale, in 1857, an example of the explosion of 'Information Texts' in Nonconformist Wales in the mid-century.[94]

As well as becoming the fifth chapter of the new edition of *Hanes Prydain Fawr*, this version was also published separately as a twopenny pamphlet of fifteen pages (*Hanes Tiriad y Ffrancod* ('History of the French Landing')), which came out before the parent volume in 1856.[95] Ap Gwilym's account was a random collection of anecdotes, whereas this Welsh adaptation was a coherent, chronological narrative and received positive reviews in the denominational press.[96]

Hanes Tiriad y Ffrancod has an exclusive preface to the Jemima Nicholas story.[97] When Jemima is introduced, instead of the long English-language description in Ap Gwilym of her being 'imbued with the noble and patriotic spirit of ancient Cambria', there is just one Welsh word, and that a very fitting one: *Buddug* ('Boudica'). The Welsh version has Jemima as a latter-day warrior-queen: Boudica, a term that was also used by the Welsh poets to describe Queen Victoria.[98]

The new contribution to this Welsh-language narrative came from the Revd Henry Davies, Llangloffan, who supplied information about his father, whom he was named after and, also, in his time, minister at Llangloffan. Henry Davies the elder was a major figure among the Welsh Baptists in the early nineteenth century; he has been called a patriarch and one of the Baptist greats not only in Pembrokeshire but in Wales as a whole.[99] In parallel, and separate to the work of a man of high moral stature as evidenced by his achievements and his effects on others, there is this alter ego, a ghostly fabrication of a traitor, who colluded with the French.

Suspicion and allegations of connivance with wrongdoers continued to be levelled at Dissenters, now more commonly known as Nonconformists; the Rebecca Riots brought the Pembroke Yeomanry and the local people of south-west Wales into focus, but this time on opposing sides. A letter in *Seren Gomer* in 1843 addressed *At Yr Ymneillduwyr* ('to the Nonconformists') protested that the Nonconformists were again targets of baseless allegations of disloyalty made by High Churchmen, in the same way as they had been after the French invaded in 1797.[100] The lawlessness of the Welsh, the Welsh language and Nonconformity made its way into official and popular rhetoric. It was in this tacit climate of misapprehension and suspicion that the memory of the invasion and the impact on the Baptists was kept alive in family and chapel memory.

Henry Davies, the elder, of Llangloffan had committed no wrong; in fact, he was lauded for his patriotism in thwarting the French by refusing to relinquish his cart to them. Nonetheless, a black cloud hung over the reputation of this respectable and popular Baptist minister. It was believed that he had stood on a rock to show the French where to land. This statement had no basis in fact other than malicious gossip preserved by oral tradition.

Henry Davies the younger used the *Authentic Account* of H. L. Ap Gwilym as republished in 1853, to exonerate the Baptists who had been traduced.[101] Ap Gwilym's work, Davies argued, referred to Welsh men and women already operating in the French camp; James Bowen was one, as spotted by Ann George, but there were others too. There may have been four Welsh people among the French. Why was no attempt made to question these four for treason instead of harrying and persecuting the innocent?[102] The new material supplied exonerated his father explicitly and publicly. He was 12 miles away when the French landed and he knew nothing about them until the Thursday. How could he therefore have been on a rock showing the enemy where to land?

The assistant preacher belonging to Llangloffan tried in the 1797 trial had been burnt in effigy at the Fishguard fair in 1798. Thomas John was still not named.[103] The preacher was described as 'very unpopular' ('yn ammhoblogaidd iawn'). A respectable friend had written to Davies to say he remembered an effigy of the preacher being burnt at the fair in Fishguard on the 5 February 1798.[104] The people must have been enraged against him for his 'spirit to be burned' as 'people in the country say' ('cyn eu bod yn "llosgi ei ysbryd" ys dywed llafar gwlad').[105] The quiet acceptance of the effigy burning, a generation later, without comment or demur, showed a studied indifference even among Baptists of his own church at Llangloffan. Thomas John continued to be hated in the area, complicit in the popular mind with the invasion of the French.

Revd David Meyler (1789–1865), the Calvinistic Methodist minister at Fishguard, was regarded as one of the most prominent Calvinistic Methodist ministers of his day in south Wales and a 'household word in his own county'.[106] He was active in the Fishguard Bible Society, and unusually for the normally anti-papal Methodists, was a supporter of a fund to help the 'distressed Irish'.[107] He died in 1865.[108] In 1856, by then in his later years, he published, anonymously, his own *Adgofion Tiriad y Ffrancod yn Sir Benfro* ('Memories of the Landing of the French in Pembrokeshire').[109] Meyler was seven or eight years old when the French invaded.[110] He regretted not having published his *Memories* earlier, but the alliance between Britain and France in the Crimea made the international situation more favourable to bring memories alive of a time when Britain and France were at war.[111] Interwoven with his own memories are elements from Ap Gwilym's account, some translated and not developed, others taken and adapted, and some details that are completely new.

His account of the Jemima Nicholas story constitutes a deviation from Ap Gwilym as well as an expansion. In Ap Gwilym, Jemima single handedly captures twelve French men.[112] Meyler downgrades the achievement from twelve French men to one. Jemima was from Fishguard and she was commonly known as Jemima Fawr ('*gelwir hi yn gyffredin Jemima Fawr*') even before the Invasion, a term not used by Ap Gwilym but used by the local vicar Samuel Fenton, possibly demonstrating a local Fishguard and Welsh tradition of attaching descriptors to names on account of her size, as well as signifying greatness. Meyler follows Ap Gwilym in describing her as 'dynes gref, wrywaidd ei gwedd' ('a strong woman, with masculine features').[113] He provides a new character trait that would be picked up by later writers in the temperance movement: 'she received as much beer as she could drink that afternoon in the town, a drink she was very fond of throughout her life'.[114]

His closeness to the experience of the Invasion is illustrated in several ways. His language is more passionate, more involved, than the restrained, more military composure of Ap Gwilym. Meyler knew the participants and had seen the aftermath. He remembers a particularly bloody encounter between Welsh men armed with straightened scythes on poles against French troops with firearms in front of their advanced station on Carn Wnda, during which a Welsh blacksmith was killed in the unequal confrontation.[115] The Frenchman was shot by the friend of the blacksmith. Meyler was not a witness to the killing, but to the sight of the bloody corpse being carried to the town and was deeply affected by it.[116] He tells of the fear and panic in the port of Fishguard on hearing the news of the invasion in nearby Pencaer and how the terrible news spread through the entire countryside like wildfire.[117] Later, Meyler highlights and commends the heroism of the people of Fishguard who throughout that Wednesday night, deterred the French from attacking them, by beating the drums and firing the guns of their fort. The 'trigolion cynhyrfus' ('alarmed people') stood their ground in Fishguard, armed and defiant against the enemy.[118]

To Ap Gwilym the French are the 'enemy', to Meyler they are 'lladron' ('thieves').[119] Meyler quotes directly from the people who were there at the time and adds commentaries of his own.[120] Mortimer, the master of Trehowel before and after Tate, became a Methodist elder in 1799 and was one of the elders in Meyler's chapel in Fishguard when he started preaching there in 1814.[121] Mortimer was the source of some of the details that Meyler published in his *Adgofion* with regard to Trehowel and Tate.

Between Meyler, the narrator of eyewitness experience, and Meyler the older, more reflective commentator and Methodist minister, lies a creative tension and a pacifist strand which owes more to 1856 than 1797. Meyler was active in the Bible Society in Fishguard, an anti-war and, if not pacifist, pro-peace and peacefulness movement. He tended to seek the good in human affairs, even in the French enemy, hence his assertion that Mary Williams (he did not name her) was not ill-treated as some people had said. As narrator of direct experience, however, the details he recalled were both bloody and dramatic. As an advocate of peacefulness, he deplored the bloodlust, 'yr ysbryd baeddu' ('the spirit of despoliation') that had descended on the country people in 1797.[122] Throughout his *Adgofion*, Meyler is at pains not to glorify military valour. Meyler was the first of any narrative account of the invasion to mention a Welsh fatality caused by 'friendly fire'.[123] On the day of the surrender a woman in the Plough in Fishguard was shot accidentally by one of the yeomanry who was emptying his musket. She was treated by a French doctor who was there to look after the French who were sick from food poisoning, despite his best efforts, the woman died.

Meyler was critical of many of the stories that had circulated relating to the Invasion. One of the more dubious stories, in his opinion, was that of the women and girls in their red flannels. The women in red were there as spectators in a crowd of uneasy mood and tense expectation, fearing the worst, not understanding the significance of the absence of the banner and the sound of the band, a detail from Ap Gwilym, as the French marched down from the heights onto the Sands.

In 1868, the *English Encyclopedia* reviewed *Y Traethodydd* and explained for its English readers that many of the Welsh-language articles merited translation, including 'a curious account of the French invasion at Fishguard, much fuller, we believe, than any that has yet appeared in English'.[124]

Endnotes

1 *Pembrokeshire Herald and General Advertiser* (7 April 1854), 4.
2 'Commemoration of the landing of the French at Fishguard', *The Cambrian* (14 September 1883), 6.
3 2 Chronicles 20 v 26.
4 *The Cardiff Times* (22 February 1908), 10.
5 Barbara A. Misztal, 'Collective Memory in a Global Age: Learning How and When to Remember', *Current Sociology*, 58/1 (January 2010), 24–44, quoted in Guy Beiner, *Forgetful Remembrance: Social Forgetting and Vernacular Historiography of a Rebellion in Ulster* (Oxford, 2018), p. 24.
6 *Seren Gomer*, 7/107 (Awst 1824/August 1824), 3–6.
7 David Jones, *Hanes y Bedyddwyr yn Neheubarth Cymru* (Carmarthen, 1839), pp.186–7, 196–7.

8   *The Cambrian* (27 August 1808), 3.
9   *Carmarthen Journal* (6 February 1829), 3.
10 E. H. Stuart Jones, *The Last Invasion of Britain* (Cardiff, 1950), p. 286.
11 *Derbyshire Courier* (15 July 1843), 4.
12 'Landing of the French at Fishguard', *The Welshman* (17 October 1890), 7.
13 *The Pembrokeshire Herald and General Advertiser* (5 March 1847), 2.
14 *The Pembrokeshire Herald and General Advertiser* (5 March 1847), 2.
15 *The Yorkshire Gazette* (5 October 1850), 7.
16 Stuart Jones, *The Last Invasion*, p. 289.
17 *The Welshman* (23 June 1854), 3
18 Richard Llwyd, 'Topographical Notes', in Caradoc of Llancarfan's *History of Wales*, (Shrewsbury, 1832), p. 126. For Richard Llwyd and his 'dissonant qualities of a forgotten and marginalised past', see Elizabeth Edwards, *Richard Llwyd, Beaumaris Bay and other Poems* (Nottingham, 2015), p. xx.
19 Edward Parry, *Cambrian Mirror or A New Tourist Companion Through North Wales*, 2nd edn (1846), p. xxxiv.
20 Y Parch Thomas Price, Carnhuanawc, *Hanes Cymru a Chenedl y Cymry, o'r Cynoesoedd hyd at farwolaeth Llewelyn Ap Gruffydd* (Crickhowell, 1842).
21 Thomas Thomas, *Memoirs of Owen Glendower (Owain Glyndwr) With a sketch of the History of the Ancient Britons* (Haverfordwest, 1822). For Thomas, see Huw Pryce, *Writing Welsh History: From the Early Middle Ages to the Twenty-First Century* (Oxford, 2022), pp. 245–6; Dafydd Glyn Jones, *Agoriad yr Oes: erthyglau ar len, hanes a gwleidyddiaeth Cymru* (Talybont, 2001), pp. 206–9.
22 Price, Carnhuanawc, *Hanes Cymru*, p. 792.
23 Price, Carnhuanawc, *Hanes Cymru*, p. 792.
24 Stuart Jones, *The Last Invasion of Britain*, p. 275. See also *The Cardiff Times* (27 February 1897), 6.
25 H. L. Ap Gwilym, *An Authentic Account of the Invasion by French Troops on Carrig Gwasted Point near Fishguard* (Haverfordwest, 1842), dedication page. Bowling was a young cornet (lowest grade of commissioned officer) with the Castlemartins, see Stuart Jones *The Last Invasion*, p. 190.
26 Ap Gwilym, *An Authentic Account*, p. 4.
27 Ap Gwilym, *An Authentic Account*, p. 5.
28 Carmarthenshire Record Office, Cawdor Collection Box 223, Thomas Williams to the Mayor of Haverfordwest (Francis Edwardes), Trelethin, 22 February 1797.
29 Ap Gwilym, *An Authentic Account*, p. 18.
30 There are numerous references, for one example, see Ron Thomas, *Childhood Reminiscences of Fishguard* (privately printed, no date,), p. 27.
31 Stuart Jones, *The Last Invasion*, p. 122.
32 *The Times* (6 March 1797), 2.

33 David Salmon, 'A Sequel to the French Invasion of Pembrokeshire', *Y Cymmrodor*, 43 (1932), 80–1, 88–9.
34 Ap Gwilym, *An Authentic Account*, p. 19.
35 Ap Gwilym, *An Authentic Account*, p. 20.
36 Ap Gwilym, *An Authentic Account*, p. 21.
37 Ap Gwilym, *An Authentic Account*, p. 20.
38 Ap Gwilym, *An Authentic Account*, p. 21.
39 Richard Rose, 'The French at Fishguard: Fact, Fiction and Folklore', *Transactions of the Honourable Society of Cymmrodorion* 2002 new series, 9 (2003), 85.
40 Ap Gwilym, *An Authentic Account*, p. 24.
41 Ap Gwilym, *An Authentic Account*, pp. 24–5.
42 Rose, 'The French at Fishguard', 92.
43 Ap Gwilym, *An Authentic Account*, pp. 32–3.
44 John Lloyd to J. G. Philipps 1 March 1797, 'The Cwmgwili Manuscripts (continued)', *Transactions of the Carmarthenshire Antiquarian Society*, 29 (1939), 19.
45 Ap Gwilym, An Authentic Account, pp. 29–30.
46 Ap Gwilym, *An Authentic Account*, p. 25.
47 Ap Gwilym, *An Authentic Account*, p. 25.
48 Ap Gwilym, *An Authentic Account*, p. 16.
49 Ap Gwilym, *An Authentic Account*, p. 16.
50 Ceiriog (John Ceiriog Hughes 1832–87) wrote a popular poem on this incident, *Y Baban Diwrnod Oed*, in 1859, as discussed further in Chapter 5 of this volume.
51 Ap Gwilym, *An Authentic Account*, p. 33.
52 Richard Ayton and William Daniell, *A voyage round Great Britain: undertaken in the summer of the year 1813, and commencing from the Land's-End, Cornwall / by Richard Ayton; with a series of views, illustrative of the character and prominent features of the coast, drawn and engraved by William Daniell*, vol. 1 (London, 1814), p. 127.
53 Pembrokeshire Archives, handwritten note by the vicar Samuel Fenton, 6 July 1832, Fishguard Parish Burial Register. In 2006, the BBC and media covered the exciting discovery by a descendant of Jemima of her baptism date, 2 March 1755 in Mathry, daughter of William and Elinor Nicholas from Llanrhian. BBC News 'Invasion heroine's records find' *www.bbc.co.uk/1/hi/wales/south_west/4874226.stm* (last accessed 2 August 2024). The memorial stone and parish record showing her age at death in 1832 as eighty-two seems to be five years out.
54 Advertisement in *The Cambrian* (11 and 18 March, 22 April 1820). William Barzey was also a real person mentioned by Ap Gwilym, a horse dealer by trade, see Ap Gwilym, *An Authentic Account*, pp. 9–10.
55 Ap Gwilym, *An Authentic Account*, p. 33
56 Ap Gwilym, *An Authentic Account*, pp. 39-40

57 'The French at Fishguard in 1797', *The United Service Magazine and Naval and Military Journal*, 41/171 (February 1843), 202–13.
58 David Salmon, 'The French Invasion of Pembrokeshire in 1797', *West Wales Historical Records*, 14 (1929), 205; David Salmon, *The Descent of the French on Pembrokeshire* (Carmarthen, 1930), p. 77
59 Laurel Brake and Marysa Demoor (eds) *Dictionary of 19th Century Journalism in Great Britain* (London, 2009), p. 131
60 Neil Ramsey, *The Military Memoir and Romantic Literary Culture 1780–1835* (London, 2011), p. 69.
61 Ramsey, *The Military Memoir*, p. 76.
62 Address of the Editor, *The United Service Journal*, Part 1 (1829), 1–2.
63 The example *par excellence* of the military journalist was Thomas Henry Shadwell Clerke (1792–1849), the editor of the magazine from January 1829 to July 1842, who wrote many of the articles.
64 *Saunders's News-letter* (31 January 1843), 2.
65 *Bath Herald* (11 March 1797), 2.
66 Ap Gwilym, *An Authentic Account*, p. 17.
67 James Baker, *A Brief Narrative of the French Invasion Near Fishguard Bay. Including a Perfect Description of that Part of the Coast of Pembrokeshire, on which was effected the landing of the French forces, on the 22nd of February, 1797, and of their surrender to the Welch Provincial Troops, HEADED BY LORD CAWDOR* (Worcester, 1797) p. 7.
68 Note Beiner's 'communal body of cultural knowledge relating to the past'; *Remembering the Year of the French: Irish Folk History and Social Memory* (Madison WI, 2007), p. 28.
69 'The French at Fishguard in 1797', 213. In 1851, Mary Williams was living in Hottipass Street, Fishguard, with her daughter Anne who was baptised April 1786 in Llanwnda parish (Pembrokeshire Record Office).
70 The dedication in Ap Gwilym's *An Authentic Account* was dated 28 August 1842; 'The French at Fishguard' appeared in the *United Service Magazine* in February 1843.
71 Ap Gwilym, *An Authentic Account*, p. 16.
72 For example, *Falkirk Herald* (6 October 1853), 4; *Worcestershire Chronicle* (28 September 1853), 3; *Sun (London)* (19 September 1853), 5.
73 'The French at Fishguard in 1797', 203.
74 Richard Fenton, *A Historical Tour Through Pembrokeshire* (London, 1811), p. 11.
75 'The French at Fishguard in 1797', 204.
76 Salmon, 'A Sequel', 86.
77 Salmon, 'A Sequel', 88.
78 'The French at Fishguard in 1797', 211–12.
79 'The French at Fishguard in 1797', 212.
80 *Leeds Intelligencer* (20 March 1797), 3. Gomer M. Roberts, 'The Year 1797 in the life of the Rev David Jones, Llangan', *Cylchgrawn Cymdeithas Hanes y Methodistiaid Calfinaidd*, 23 (1938), 101.

81 'The French at Fishguard in 1797', 211.
82 Rose, 'The French at Fishguard', 92–3.
83 'The French at Fishguard in 1797', 213.
84 Benjamin Heath Malkin, *The Scenery, Antiquities and Biography of South Wales* (London, 1804), p. 456; Richard Edwards, *Hanes Llangloffan* (Solva, 1932), p. 66.
85 'The Welch Amazons' *The Weekly Dispatch* (London) (12 February 1843), 10.
86 'The Welsh Amazons', *Monmouthshire Merlin* (18 February 1843), 4.
87 *The Weekly Dispatch* (London) (12 February 1843), 10.
88 *Pembrokeshire Herald* (23 August 1844), 2; (30 August 1844), 2.
89 'A Native', 'How the French Fared at Fishguard, 1797 A.D.', *Chambers's Journal of Popular Literature January*, 14 (1860), 17–21.
90 'How the French Fared at Fishguard [By a Native]', *The Red Dragon*, 7 (1885), 235–45.
91 *Monmouthshire Beacon* (19 February 1848), 4; *Eddowe's Shrewsbury Journal* (23 February 1848), 2; *Hereford Journal* (16 February 1848), 3; *The Monmouthshire Merlin* (19 February 1848), 2.
92 An early appearance of Jemima based on H. L. Williams appears in the account of the invasion from a Tenby perspective in *Tales and Traditions of Tenby* (Tenby, 1858), pp. 71–2.
93 'Pennod 5: Tiriad y Ffrancod', *Hanes Prydain Fawr yn wladol a chrefyddol gan y diweddar Barch Titus Lewis wedi ei ddiwygio a'i helaethu gan John Emlyn Jones* (Carmarthen, 1857), pp. 633–43.
94 T. Robin Chapman, 'The Turn of the Tide Melancholy and Modernity in Mid-Victorian Wales', *Welsh History Review*, 27/3 (2015), 519.
95 *Hanes Tiriad y Ffrancod yn Mhencaer yn agos i Abergwaen, swydd Benfro, ar ddydd Mercher, Chwefror 22, 1797* (Carmarthen, 1856).
96 For example, 'Adolygiad y Wasg', *Y Bedyddiwr*, 15/175 (July 1856), 205–8.
97 *Hanes Tiriad y Ffrancod*, p. 5.
98 See, for example, Carolyn D. Williams, *Boudica and Her Stories: Narrative transformations of a Warrior Queen* (Cranbury NJ, 2009), p. 46.
99 Carl Williams, 'Ein Treftadaeth Fedyddiedig: De-orllewin Penfro', *Trafodion Cymdeithas Hanes Bedyddwyr Cymru* (1998), pp 11,18; Edwards, *Hanes Llangloffan*, p. 24.
100 'At yr Ymneillduwyr', *Seren Gomer*, 26/336 (September 1843), 285.
101 *Hanes Tiriad y Ffrancod*, p.10.
102 *Hanes Tiriad y Ffrancod*, p. 11.
103 *Hanes Tiriad y Ffrancod*, p. 12.
104 *Hanes Tiriad y Ffrancod*, p. 12.
105 *Hanes Tiriad y Ffrancod*, p. 12.
106 Obituary of his grandson Revd Eleazer Meyler, *Haverfordwest and Milford Haven Telegraph and General* (22 December 1897), 3.
107 *The Welshman* (5 March 1847), 2.

108 Obituary, *The Treasury*, 26 (February 1866), 66.
109 'Adgofion Tiriad y Ffrancod yn Swydd Benfro', *Y Traethodydd*, 12 (1856), 362–81.
110 He was from one of several Meyler families in Pembrokeshire and not related to the owner of the house which later became the Royal Oak or the other Meylers in the story.
111 'Adgofion Tiriad y Ffrancod', 362–3.
112 Ap Gwilym, *An Authentic Account*, p. 33.
113 'Adgofion Tiriad y Ffrancod', 368.
114 'Adgofion Tiriad y Ffrancod', 368.
115 This contest was also mentioned in Thomas John's deposition; Salmon, 'A Sequel', p. 73.
116 'Adgofion Tiriad y Ffrancod', 368.
117 'Adgofion Tiriad y Ffrancod', 364–5.
118 'Adgofion Tiriad y Ffrancod', 367.
119 For example, Ap Gwilym *An Authentic Account*, p, 8; 'Adgofion Tiriad y Ffrancod', 365.
120 'Adgofion Tiriad y Ffrancod', 366.
121 John Hughes, *Methodistiaeth Cymru Sef Hanes Blaenorol a Gwedd Bresenol y Methodistiaid Calfinaidd*, vol. 2 (Wrexham, 1854), p. 329.
122 'Adgofion Tiriad y Ffrancod', 369.
123 'Adgofion Tiriad y Ffrancod', 371, footnote. Hugh Meyler mentioned this fatality in his letter from the Fishguard guard house of 5 March 1797, *Bath Herald* (11 March 1797), 2.
124 *Arts and Sciences: or, Fourth Division of the English Encyclopedia*, vol. 8 (1868), p. 877.

Chapter 5

The French Invasion in Popular History and Culture, 1847–85

The role of Welsh women in general in society and in the family, both present and past, was tested by the 1847 Report into the State of Education in Wales – the infamous Blue Books. Many elements of Welsh life and the people, particularly the women, were heavily criticised, and customs such as bundling – *caru yn y gwely* (a courting tradition that also drew the attention and criticism of early English tourists) – were described as immoral, reflecting a Welsh civilisation that was essentially barbaric.[1] Welsh women were for the first time encouraged by their men folk after 1847 to raise their voices in public and in writing to defend themselves from these slurs.[2] In response to the report, a number of journals aiming to raise religious, moral and educational standards among the women were established. In 1850–1, one of these, *Y Gymraes* ('The Welsh Woman') ran a series of prize essay competitions on the status of women in various Welsh localities. One of the earliest was for an essay on *Cyflwr Cymdeithasol a Moesol Merched Penfro* ('The Social and Moral Condition of Pembrokeshire Women').[3] The winner (after some debate) was a writer using the name *Sylwedydd* ('Observer').

Sylwedydd's essay was published in the October 1851 issue and opened with the achievements of the *rhyw fenywaidd* ('female sex') in the events that took place near Fishguard nearly '53 years ago': 'frail old women and frightened young girls, causing armed French soldiers to tremble like leaves and fold like reeds in the face of a terrible storm.'[4] The author states that this might have been fun for the 'female sex' but was not the type of behaviour endorsed by *Y Gymraes* for women.

The modern Pembrokeshire girl was different from their grandmothers fifty-three years ago, but still fell short of the more civilised behaviour expected by the contributors to *Y Gymraes*. For instance, the women of the coastal communities of Pembrokeshire – Newport (Trefdraeth), Fishguard, Solva, Tenby and Haverfordwest – were deemed to be too fond of sailors, and when their husbands were away at sea it was said that they behaved immorally. The comments of *Sylwedydd*, in fact a man, were those of an external observer, looking in on the women of Pembrokeshire. His was as external a voice – albeit more benign and written in a language that they could understand – as those of the young, male English undergraduates who visited picturesque Wales in the 1790s and after. As a result of the Blue Books, and the responses to them, the Welsh Nonconformists sought a particular literary construction of an ideal Welsh woman that would in time affect and contest aspects of the French Invasion narrative in Welsh.[5]

The French Invasion story was written and controlled by men (in both English and Welsh), even when the oral traditions and memories were those of women and the readers were women. It wasn't only Welsh and English men, but also American men writing about the women of Fishguard. By 1852, the story of the Fishguard women had crossed the Atlantic to New York through Thomas Richard Whitney's *The Republic: A Monthly magazine of American Literature*, which published 'An Historical Anecdote for the Ladies – Red Shawls and French Invaders'.[6] Women readers of New York were among the first to read about the women's walk around the Bigney and the effect on the French of the 'Welsh whittle, being no other than the red shawl now so fashionable in our city'.[7]

The Fishguard women had acquired a reputation and were mentioned even in Parliament. John Lloyd Davies, who represented the Cardigan boroughs raised the issue of a harbour of refuge for shipping in Cardigan Bay.[8] His proposal was mocked. Sir Charles Wood, the First Lord of the Admiralty, reminded him that when the French attempted to land in Wales some fifty or sixty years ago, the Principality was indebted for its security not to its harbours of refuge 'but to the bravery of Welsh women' who, robed in their customary 'red petticoat', scared the enemy, and made him sheer off.[9] There was 'much laughter'. This episode is significant, not because of the way the invasion and the women involved were used to comedic effect, as had often been the case from 1797 onwards, but for the fact that a senior British politician mentioned the Welsh women and their red undergarments in the House of Commons, in a very early public reference, cementing the image further.

The red petticoat represented a far more erotically charged male view of the Fishguard women than the previously used image of the red mantle, shawl or whittle. Clothes carried social meaning, and the Victorians were particularly sensitive to that. Fashionable dress articulated the wearer's identity, in terms of age, class and wealth. The language of clothes was also a moral and a sexual language. The figure of the woman in red was frequently associated with the nineteenth-century fallen woman or sex worker, and repeated so often that even today we have inherited a mythic image of the Victorian prostitute.[10] However, the colour red had another association in the context of the remembrance of 1797. Thomas Stephens, Merthyr chemist and historian, explained the significance of the colour in *The Literature of the Kymry* in 1849. In this account, the wearing of the colour red by women was justified by Welsh history. Red was a military colour, but in Wales it was not confined to the men, for red was also in 'favour with the fair sex': the army of 'red whittled old women' who frightened the French into submission in Fishguard, the red stripe was the exclusive wear of the women of Pembrokeshire and Carmarthenshire and in the Swansea Valley. The 'taste of modern females' was 'inherited from their ancestors'.[11]

The endorsement of Welsh history notwithstanding, the red petticoat and the women who wore it became, in what is perhaps one of the most remarkable turns in the remembrance of the French Invasion, the subject of one of the great English-language novelists and imaginary creators of the nineteenth century, Wilkie Collins. Collins is acknowledged as the master of sensation novels and literature. Aspects of his life were also sensational; he ran two illicit households and had a penchant for the grotesque.[12] His novel, *The Woman in White* first serialised in his friend Charles Dickens's journal *All the Year Round*, starting in November 1859, made him a fortune and secured his reputation.

By 1859–60 invasion fever had returned, following the conclusion of the Crimean War.[13] Collins's 'The Great (Forgotten) Invasion' appeared in Dickens's *Household Words* on 12 March 1859, a satirical piece on the French Invasion addressing pressing contemporary concerns about invasion, the role of volunteers – both men and women – and a Collins touch, the clothes they wore.[14] The work was republished with modifications in *My Miscellanies* in 1863.[15]

The story of the women in red petticoats would have appealed to Collins's taste for the unusual, the unexpected, unfettered by the restrictive stereotyping and literary conventions of the day that he both subverts and reinvents.[16] Collins not only demonstrates his considerable skills as a story teller and wit, but it also allows him to vent his own political opinion about the state of British defences in 1859. In the 'Preamble', Collins connects the current 1859 threat of invasion, 'that *may* come' with 'the French invasion that *did* come'.[17] He says that although there must be thousands of people alive at that moment who remember it well, the 'new generation knows nothing about it'. There was a gap in the modern history of 'England' that had to be filled, since it was a matter of national security.

The introduction of the women in their red petticoats was Collins's initiative alone. The red petticoats were the clothing of the wives of Welsh labourers but were now worn by 'wives of all classes of the community'. The petticoat was an under garment, the epitome of femininity. Following the development of the first synthetic dyes in 1856, vibrant new colours became available for dress fabrics, including the bold scarlet. Fashion continued to emphasise the contemporary ideal of womanhood stressing females' ornamental role and their dependent status, yet dress was simultaneously growing bolder and more diverse, giving women a more confident, assertive appearance.[18] It was Cawdor's idea, according to Collins, for the women to take off their red petticoats and put them over their husbands' shoulders. Collins developed his own taste for unconventional clothes. His hatred of formality extended to evening dress and he was known in later life to appear at evening engagements in a tweed suit, with a pink or blue striped shirt and a red tie.[19] It was with a similar rejection of convention that Collins imagined the use of the red petticoats as a garment to turn 'colliers into military men'. Collins employed his creative imagination to turn a historical incident into a recruitment drive, encouraging all classes and both sexes to get involved in the militia movement of 1859. He applauded the transformation from 'wives' and 'women' to 'patriot-matrons'. Wives, however, even patriot matrons, were subservient to their husbands. Collins has his men dressed by their women in women's clothing, thereby making the men, not the women, the saviours or heroes of the moment and achieving at the same time an erotic charge; since in the process of donning the women's undergarments, the men had 'the tenderest memento … of home and beauty', both on mind and body. The women were left shivering, while every collier was turned into a soldier. Colliers were among the lowest of the working class and were thus enhanced in status, which was far more acceptable to patriarchal values than women subverting their domestic roles by taking over the military duties of their men folk. By so doing, Collins was upending the system, through giving men the appearance of women but at the time supporting it, enabling the men to achieve a very masculine objective – success in war – while denying the women the opportunity to become free agents, not even mere spectators, just going home *to bed on their own*. The moral of the story, according to Collins: 'If we are invaded again, and on a rather larger scale, let us not be so ill-prepared this next time as to be obliged to take refuge in our wives' red petticoats.'[20]

As soon as Collins's account was published, it also appeared in several newspapers.[21] Shortly afterwards, a critique appeared from a man with connections to Fishguard. He provided a commentary on what he described as 'the excellently written and amusing account by the writer of the descent in Fishguard in 1797' in *Household Words*. 'Excellently written and amusing' it might have been, but the correspondent writing in the *Bicester Advertiser* thought it rather incorrect.[22] The commentator, it turned out, was a man from the Fishguard area who knew several farmers who as 'young men had ridden with the yeomanry that day'. The Bicester account reshaped memories from local eyewitnesses and participants to answer aspects of Collins's *Great (Forgotten) Invasion* article, which he had interpreted as historical writing rather than satire. The Bicester correspondent addresses Collins directly and unambiguously over the issue of the petticoats: 'how could men with red petticoats on their shoulders pass for troops in a soldier's eye? No, it was not the petticoat which conquered Clarke [Clarke is the name given to Tate] but the hat and whittle.'[23] He then explained what these garments were and how they were made. The author of the *Great (Forgotten) Invasion* is addressed, or rather dressed down, in the second person as if he is in front of him. Collins had referred to the death of two Welshmen; it was nothing of the sort: 'Blood was shed, but it was French blood'. Cawdor, the Castlemartin Yeomanry and the Welsh women had caused the French surrender, and 'we may well give three cheers for the warlike dames of the Cymro'.[24] The 'warlike dames of the Cymro' sums up the paternalistic ownership of the story of the women who were increasingly attired in red petticoats, whereas the Cymro knew they were red whittles.

The 1850s and 1860s were formative decades in Wales for the cultivation of the belief that war was necessary in defence, but not in defiance. This rested on a view that the Welsh were not a militaristic people but rather had through the years exercised restraint and taken up arms only in defence against the attacks of aggressors.[25] The story of the Fishguard women was one of stout defence against unwanted enemy aggression, and was used in a number of ways as part of the role of women in defence of their country, an aspect of a new preoccupation with civilian participation in military life.[26] But more often than not it was used to mock either the French or their own men for their reluctance to fight.[27] References were made to the Fishguard women in the recruitment drives in a disparaging, jocular way by men at the expense of women, and against men.

The creation of a volunteer force, by concentrating on a common enemy that united the different peoples of Britain, was a contributory factor to the different peoples' integration into British institutions.[28] The French Invasion of 1797 played a small part in this process as a failed attempt to invade Britain and undermine the British state, that happened to take place in Wales. This was of relevance to the defence of Britain as a whole and became directly connected to the London of 1859 when the Hon. George Denman, MP for Tiverton, referenced the French Invasion to promote the formation of a Rifle Corps in a speech to the inhabitants of Pimlico.[29] He described the French pillaging and plundering the neighbourhood before being dispersed by about 600 volunteers, 'and the sight of the red petticoats of the Welsh women who assembled on the adjacent hills', which drew a laugh.[30]

Denman's allusion to the defeat of the French and the cause of this defeat aroused the attention and raised the hackles of a certain Monsieur Edouard Tate who claimed to be a descendant of Colonel Tate and wrote as a proud Frenchman from Leicester Square in London. If Edouard was a French descendant of Colonel Tate, who was the 'Madame Tate', the mother to Tate's French offspring? The connection isn't clear or recorded.[31] Edouard Tate wrote to the editor of *The Times*, and corrected Denman to get the record straight, to rescue, if not restore, the reputation of his ancestor ('a respected relative') and that of his 'gallant countrymen'.[32] Edouard Tate denied categorically that the Welsh women, or the 'charming Welshes' as he calls them, had any part in the proceedings. The debate intensified over the Christmas period of 1859 when both *The Times* and *The Evening Mail* published a letter from another correspondent whose ancestor was involved in the French Invasion, but on the other side was Alexander Ridgway, the grandson of Second Lieutenant Thomas Ridgway of the Pembroke Volunteers.[33] Alexander Ridgway corrected the corrector and Tate's denial that the 'charming Welshes' were involved in the proceedings.[34]

Tate's and Ridgway's recall of family memories were of course different. Ridgway had unrestricted access to family memories and memorabilia; Tate, in contrast, would not have known his ancestors, since Tate left France in 1809. His only source of knowledge was the 'English Official Account', the official correspondence that had appeared in the *London Gazette* and *The Times* shortly after the surrender, which he called the 'justicative pieces attached to that account with which it entirely agrees'.[35]

At this stage in the newspaper battle of the ancestors, another family involved stepped forward: none other than the Earl of Cawdor, the son of John Campbell, Baron Cawdor, to give a definitive judgement, as his father had done at the time. The earl's account tended to side with Tate's since it was also based on the official narrative, to which his father had contributed. He denied that the 'charming Welshes' were marshalled in their red whittles by Lord Cawdor, who would neither have had the time, opportunity nor 'inclination, to form at such a moment, a regiment of old women'.[36]

Implicit in this debate between families on a long-ago event was a political point relevant to the volunteers of their own day: latent military capacity had to be developed again in 1859 as it had been in 1797.[37] Multiple newspapers entered the debate with their own accounts and contributions.[38] At around the same time as the *Times* controversy, just after Christmas 1859, the poet John Ceiriog Hughes (1832–87) composed a poignant lyrical poem based on an occurrence during the French invasion: 'Y Baban Diwrnod Oed' ('The Day-Old Baby'). Ap Gwilym in 1842 had first told the story of a woman at the farm called Cotts, who used her newborn baby to soothe the fury and avoid the molestation of the French.[39] Ceiriog was inspired by this story to compose his poem, which later appeared in his first anthology of poems, titled *Oriau'r Hwyr* (1860). The poem was first published in the Welsh religious press in the last days of 1859, preceded by a prose preamble giving the background to the incident.[40] Ceiriog's introduction has the French landing not in Abergwaun (Fishguard) but in Aberdaugleddyf (Milford Haven). The poem describes the Frenchmen fast approaching, and the husband trying to persuade her to flee but she was far too weak. The suspense is in the penultimate verse with the slow opening of the door, the terror-ridden expectation, the noisy entrance of swearing beasts crowding round her pillow, the petrified wife, the maternal gesture of holding up the newborn baby saving the day.[41] This simple gesture appeased the French who left the chamber immediately without causing any harm or trouble. Ceiriog concluded his brief history by saying that although these Frenchmen had committed many cruelties and atrocities, the way that they behaved on this occasion spoke strongly in their favour ('y mae yr amgylchiad hwn yn dadlu yn gryf trostynt'). Ceiriog maintained that their behaviour on this occasion was perfectly consistent with the natural disposition of the people of France ('yn berffaith gydweddol a nodweddiad naturiol pobl Ffrainc'). At a time of anti-French sentiment and fear of invasion, and when extensive efforts were being made across the country to recruit to the Rifle Corps, Ceiriog was praising the French for their 'natural' compassion and humanity.[42]

In the same anthology, *Oriau'r Hwyr*, appeared a pro Rifle Corps poem (*Y Rheiffl Gorau*) that has been seen as a straightforward, militaristic, anti-French, pro Rifle Corps poetic statement.[43] Ceiriog, like so many of the Welsh of his day, was a proud imperialist, but there were sometimes moments of doubt, moments of satirical resistance, of possible revolt against the oppressive weight of England and English culture.[44] Ceiriog was more complex and nuanced than commentators have imagined, and we can see this in his political views in late 1859 and early 1860. In his introduction to 'Y Baban Diwrnod Oed', he shows a totally different aspect of the French Invasion story, the obverse of the Mary Williams experience, the French men as instruments of mercy and not the brutes of the 1803 propaganda. The Cotts story as portrayed by Ceiriog is also another example of a Welsh woman triumphing over French male brutality, not through red cloaks or petticoats this time, but through the feminine virtue of Motherhood. The unnamed mother of the Cotts drama is as much a potent symbol of Welsh womanhood in the aftermath of 1847 as his other creations such as Myfanwy Fychan, the feminine counterpart of Alun Mabon, the paragon shepherd living in harmony with the natural world. As Saunders Lewis, writing much later, put it, Ceiriog was his mother's son, he understood the maternal heart, its inclination and its ambition.[45] The poem was published around Christmas time and when it appeared it was sub-titled 'Adroddiad y Nadolig'. There is a clear Christmas message in 'The Day Old Baby', as a grey-haired minister, the baby in his old age displays the 'Burdens of the Baby born to Us' in his arms.[46] More than 20,000 copies of *Oriau'r Hwyr* were sold,⁴⁷ and it had reached its fifth edition by 1872. Thousands of Welsh-speaking people came to know of the French Invasion through Ceiriog's poem 'Y Baban Diwrnod Oed', not only through the written poem itself, but also through recitation and song. John 'Ceulanydd' Williams was a Baptist minister, poet and writer.⁴⁸ His popular fame, however, lay as a singer; he possessed a 'sweet, pathetic voice' and it was a special treat to hear him sing 'Y Baban Diwrnod Oed'.⁴⁹ No trip to Fishguard by any organised group was complete without a rendition of the song.⁵⁰

In 1863, an even stronger Nonconformist female role model was introduced to the narrative of the French Invasion: Nansi Jones, the Nonconformist counterpart to Jemima Nicholas. There was no English-language equivalent. This new character first appeared in the periodical *Y Diwygiwr* ('The Reformer'). The journal was founded in 1835 as a monthly, serving the Independents of south Wales in counterpoint to *Yr Haul*, which represented opposite political and religious standpoints. Its editor-in-chief was David Rees, the radical Independent minister of Capel Als, Llanelli. David Rees opposed Volunteering and the militia generally and welcomed peace with France ('y mae y ddwy wlad wedi rhyfela digon a mwy na digon o lawer'; 'the two countries have been in war for far too long').⁵¹ In a meeting in Llanelli Town Hall in late 1859, he stood up to say that there were not sixty men in Wales who would stand before a cannon. *Yr Haul*, an Anglican periodical, denounced him for calling Welsh men cowards. It would have been acceptable for him to have denied that France was an invasion threat but not to scandalise the nation; 'canys pa scandal mwy a ellir ei roddi ar genedl o ddynion ,na'u cyhoeddi yn gowardiaid?'⁵² *Yr Haul* categorised Wales as a 'nation of men' ('*cenedl o ddynion*'), and those opposing volunteering were attacking the masculine virtues of Welsh men.⁵³ A Welsh-language version of the Invasion story was published in *Yr Haul* in November and December 1860, a sequential narrative based on Ap Gwilym and on the

Carmarthen publication of 1856, featuring Jemima. This was the first time for Jemima to appear in the Welsh denominational press.[54]

In October 1863, in an article in *Y Diwygiwr* on the benefits of hymn singing in terms of worship penned most probably by David Rees himself, Nansi emerged as a new character in the story of the French Invasion. She was not a fictitious character, but rather the established Revival figure of Nansi Jones, a contemporary of the great Methodist Revivalists of the eighteenth century. Nansi Jones was from Godre'r Mynydd near Crug-y-Bar in north Carmarthenshire and was famous in her time for her religious fervour; she was also often credited as the composer of the popular tune 'Crug-y-Bar'. The Independent church of Crug-y-Bar had become noted for the fiery sermons of its minister Isaac Price and the fervent singing and praying led by Nansi Jones. To Nansi there was no such thing as peaceful worship; to be effective, worshippers had to throw themselves boldly into an emotional frenzy.[55]

The account in *Y Diwygiwr* gave her prominence in a major service, a quarterly service, held in Rhydybont near Llanybydder in 1797, as the news of the invasion reached the chapel precisely when the service was being held. The preacher (a man) had introduced the text, when a latecomer who had learnt on his way to chapel that the French were in Fishguard, entered and sat down. This latecomer whispered the news to the one next to him who groaned out loud. Soon the news had circulated the entire congregation. The preacher noticed the commotion in the congregation and was told the terrible news. The chapel goers exclaimed in terror as one, then sat petrified. The 'dear angel' ('yr hen angyles') Nansi Crug-y-bar, got up and said, 'Let us sing, little children'. But nobody responded. She shouted at the preacher 'Give the Word out, Man', but he just stood there, half conscious, nobody remembered a word, and could do nothing but moan and weep. Nansi started to sing:

Duw os wyt am ddybenu'r byd
Cyflawna'n gynta'th air i gyd[56]

God, if thou wilt end the world,
Fulfil first all thy word[57]

Her heavenly voice reached the purest heights; she forgot the invasion and sang until others around her also sang.[58] The hymn that Nansi Jones sang and with which she conquered their collective fear of the French was very appropriate, having been written by the renowned hymn-writer and preacher William Williams, Pantycelyn at the time of the Lisbon earthquake in 1755 when there was widespread apocalyptic despair concerning the end of the world. Welsh Nonconformists found their answer to Jemima in Nansi Jones of Godre'r Mynydd, a combination of sacred womanhood and bravery in a Nonconformist Revival setting, providing the story of Fishguard with another dominant female character, who was bravely vocal when the men around her were struck dumb, but one who was sober, seemly and devout. Nansi Jones was not only more assertive in her response to news of the invasion but more godly than the men, the ministers and deacons around her who were superior to her in the chapel hierarchy. Nansi Jones represented far more acceptable Nonconformist values than those of the masculine, beer-drinking, pitchfork-wielding, Anglican Jemima.

By the 1860s, public awareness and knowledge of the French Invasion of 1797 had grown enormously. Few other incidents in the modern history of Wales were as well-known in Wales (to both Welsh and English speakers) and beyond. The demand and appetite for more information was heightened by an awareness that the generation who had suffered these terrifying events was gone.[59]

The popular history of the Invasion relied on certain texts, Ap Gwilym in particular, but also on personal knowledge and shared memory and a creative process that saw a deep relationship between the present and the past. Not all memories reached the printed page. The memories of one local historian, a member of the community who collected and chronicled oral traditions and memories, the Pembrokeshire antiquarian Henry Vincent, have survived in manuscript form. [60] Henry James Vincent was born in Fishguard in June 1799. His father was the local saddler, and he grew up amid the constant repetition and embroidering of accounts of the landing, and the elaboration of their experiences by those who had lived and shared in the events leading up to the actual surrender at Goodwick Sands. In 1825, Vincent became vicar of St Dogmael's and stayed there for the next forty years until his death in 1865.

Antiquarian studies occupied him increasingly and he accumulated a large collection of papers. One of the subjects which interested him was the French Invasion. His biographer, Margaret Walker, was disappointed, however, to find that he did not have much to add to the 'well-known story of the invasion', by which she meant the Ap Gwilym account. One reason was that, to his regret, he did not start writing his memories down earlier, since forty years earlier the event was 'quite fresh in the recollections of the inhabitants of the district'.[61] Vincent's memories and stories and those of Ap Gwilym resembled each other closely because they were recalling the same events. Vincent did not refer to *An Authentic Account*, there was no need for him to do so. Vincent did, however, describe the mechanism by which the local people generated and shared the knowledge concerning the events of 1797:

> In those days hundreds were wont to crowd to the spot [not specified but probably Goodwick Sands] every summer when the natives had the opportunity of refreshing their memories, fighting their battles over again and spinning long yarns which they turned to a more speedy and in a pecuniary point of view, to a more profitable account then the web of Penelope. All the places specified are familiar to me and I

either knew by sight or was personally acquainted with a vast number of the actors in the above affair.[62]

Vincent may have confused this annual event with the Methodists' day of thanksgiving that became secularised over time. Some commentators have used this extract to question the reliability of local oral traditions. The more pertinent point is that these memories were authentic; discussed, shared and disseminated, and even sold for money by local people themselves. The formation of these memories accords with Guy Beiner's definition of social memory.[63]

Jemima Nicholas was a person Vincent remembered clearly. She had lived for many years near his mother's home: 'Jemima Fawr, a tall stout powerful Amazon, a cobbler by trade and altogether the most muscular my eyes ever beheld.'[64] His description of Jemima as being 'tall and stout' is the same as the adjectives used by Ap Gwilym, although Ap Gwilym also referred to her in 1842 as 'masculine'.[65] Vincent's use of 'Jemima Fawr' relates to her size, not 'Jemima the Great' as Samuel Fenton had described her. He supplied additional details of his own not shared with or derived from Ap Gwilym. Her reputed feat of capturing twelve Frenchmen was, he felt, an exaggeration, but one for which 'she was rewarded by the inhabitants with as much ale as she could drink, and that not a little, it being a beverage to which she displayed no dislike all her lifetime'.[66] Vincent was also sceptical about the red-shawled women, not about their presence but about their role in inducing the French to submit so speedily. Other stories about the French Invasion, current when Vincent was a child, remained in his memory.[67]

Vincent was not just collecting this material for the sake of it, he intended to analyse it and put it to good use, possibly to publish, and certainly as a topic of lectures to fellow enthusiasts about antiquarian matters. He wrote of his intention of analysing the event for its 'salient points in the history of the three important days'.[68] But in the event Henry Vincent never published the lecture for which he had done so much preparatory work.

Others, however, did manage to publish to meet the demand for stories about the invasion and in turn to revive the invasion in popular culture in Pembrokeshire, in Wales and beyond. *Welsh Patriotism* was written and published by John Harries in 1875.[69] We know little about John Harries other than his Eisteddfodic triumphs as a poet, and the fact that he was a printer/publisher and stationer at Haverfordwest. It seems that military knowledge and partialities ran in the family since John Harries was well informed about military matters and may even have been a member of the volunteer force himself. He mentioned with pride the honour given to the Castlemartins, rewarded with having 'Fishguard' as their regimental motto, and he supplied a line drawing of the flag of 'white silk richly emboldened with silver', adding that it was 'rather surprising' that the Cardigan Militia did not receive the same honour since they were 'on the ground as early as any; and without doubt acquitted themselves gallantly'.[70] As a Pembrokeshire man he was familiar with the terrain, and advanced the opinion that the French used the natural outcrops of the Carnau, the Cairns, to their strategic advantage. They made Carn-Fawr near the place where they disembarked an encampment and Carn Wnda an advanced position. Working from these two centres 'the invaders succeeded in pillaging every cottage and farm in the neighbourhood'.[71]

The book was written in English, giving the work a wider geographical audience than the Welsh-language accounts. English would also have been the preferred language in Haverfordwest and south Pembrokeshire and the language of popular communication. Pembrokeshire pride as much as Welsh Patriotism bursts through this little book of twenty-four pages. It was dedicated, in capitals, to the 'Women of Pembrokeshire' (see Figure 7).

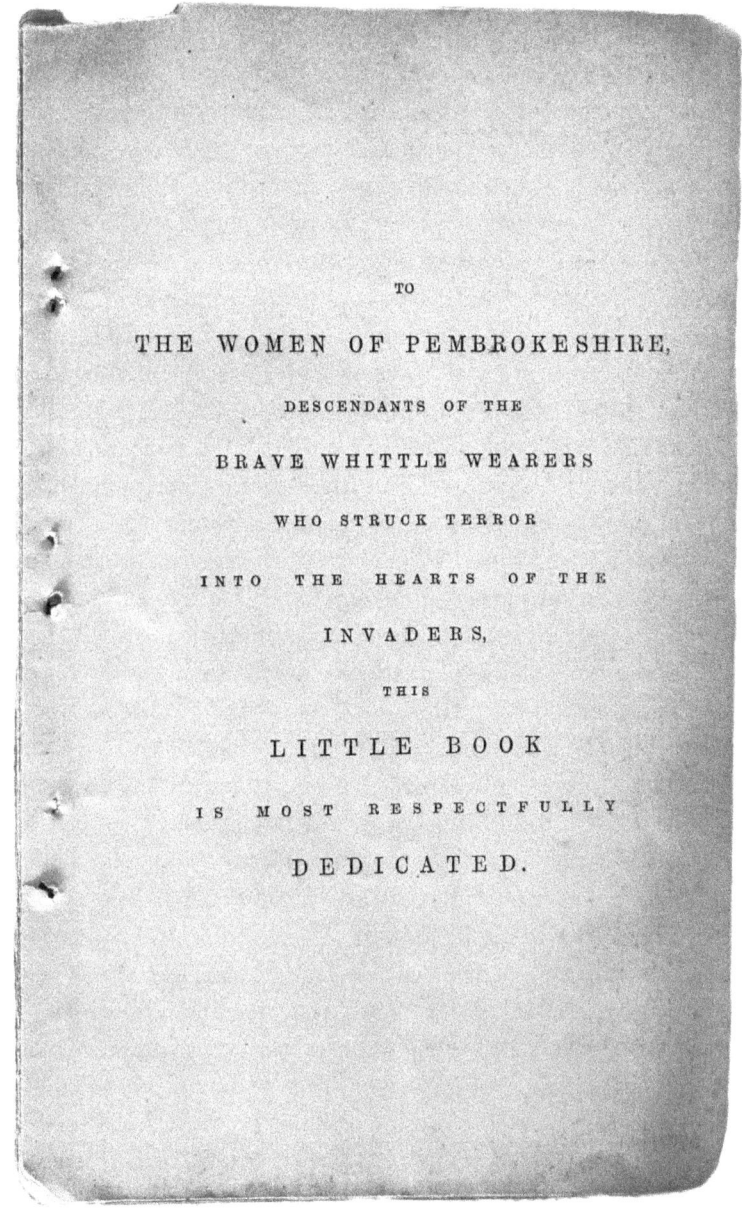

Figure 7: Dedication of *Welsh Patriotism* by John Harries to the women of Pembrokeshire

On the very last page of the book (Harries made the most of each side of paper in his own work) he printed a poem of his own composition, 'The Land of the Leek'. The Pencaer (not Fishguard) women had become emblems of Pembrokeshire and Welsh pride, celebrated in the same poem as the Prince of Wales and the Welsh language.[72] They came from their homes in Mathry, Letterston and Puncheston, and then went up to Fishguard and Dinas.[73] Jemima is mentioned as a 'native of Fishguard, noted for her great strength and commanding appearance', her heroic exploit of capturing a number of Frenchmen 'some accounts say ten, others twelve', far more accomplished 'and that too by a woman' than those of an Irish soldier who took only three of the enemy prisoner in the Crimean war.[74] Harries, however, has far more to say about the men and the military, recognising and responding to the living Women of Pembrokeshire as the linear descendants of the women of Pencaer in 1797, rather than involving the women of the time in the story.

His account of the surrender is conventional, based on the official correspondence, the Tate-Cawdor-Portland letters of 24 February 1797, which he reproduced in full. He also had access to contemporary newspapers. He quotes *Sarah Farley's Bristol Journal* of 4 March 1797 to address whether the men arrested and then acquitted were guilty or not, concluding that the Dissenters and Methodists, although not friendly to the administration, gave ample evidence of 'their aversion of Frenchmen and attachment to their country'.[75] There was no lack of people in those days who wanted 'to vilify the Welsh'. Harries also quotes Fenton on the issue of treason, where he criticises the attempts made to 'tarnish the lustre of this event'; he was the first commentator on the French invasion to quote the Pembrokeshire historian in a generation. Harries combined local knowledge and pride with elements of the official version and contemporary evidence not previously seen. Popular accounts could as easily accommodate the official version as reject it. Harries's account was proud of its military, its people and the women of Pencaer and had a

Pembrokeshire English-speaking readership very firmly in mind. The task of bringing the French Invasion back to life in Welsh-speaking Nonconformist Wales, giving prominence to Nansi Jones and less attention to the Castlemartin Yeomanry, fell to T. Cunllo Griffiths.

T. Cunllo Griffiths came from Newcastle Emlyn, and after being educated at the grammar school there, he was ordained as a Congregationalist minister in Nazareth, Pontlottyn in the Rhymni Valley in October 1868.[76] He moved to several chapels in south Wales and eventually become a Baptist. An active Eisteddfod adjudicator, in 1879 he published an anthology of poems by several south Wales poets.[77] Griffiths was a radical Nonconformist, against state intervention in the teaching of religion in schools, shocked by the Bulgarian atrocities of 1876, and standing later with fellow Protestants in Ireland against Irish Home Rule. The Irish were 'y genedl fwyaf anfoddog ac aflonydd ar wyneb y ddaear' ('the most disturbed and restless country on the face of the earth').[78]

Griffiths was not only a minister and Eisteddfodwr, he was also active on the lecture circuit. His subjects were both secular and religious, popular and well received.[79] Griffiths wrote in Welsh, an indication that he wished to communicate with a popular readership for whom Welsh was their first language and to many their only language.[80] One of his lectures was on the French Invasion. This lecture was revised regularly, since it was a technique of his to incorporate into his lecture the oral traditions of the people he met concerning this traumatic event. Griffiths travelled the country and listened to the oral history of the Invasion, adding new details from local sources to the basic content adapted from Ap Gwilym's work. When he gave the lecture to the Independents at Pontgynon, Crosswell in Pembrokeshire in 1882, several members of the audience came up to him after the lecture to say that their mothers had been among the women in the red flannels.[81] Oral tradition continued to both curate and celebrate the French Invasion alongside the printed word.[82]

Griffiths was eventually persuaded to publish, and the lecture appeared in 1885 as *Glaniad y Ffrancod yn Abergwaun*. The lecture material was much older and dated to the early 1870s. His friends had told him to publish it many times, but he did not want to do so if he would be out of pocket, but he now had hundreds of names as purchasers before he went to press.[83] In the preface to this work he said that he had been lecturing on this topic for fifteen years to tens of audiences throughout Wales.

Others had written on this subject before him, he said, so he would not tread old ground, he would only give the main facts. Griffiths was writing as an Independent minister and, as with David Meyler, his account reflected his Nonconformist values. He too was at pains not to glorify violence. Earlier accounts had stressed the bloodlust of the Welsh; Griffiths acknowledged the bravery of the common people but in introducing two new characters in brave 'Dai a Wil', introduced to appraise and question that bravery and with comedic impact. Griffiths posed the question in capital letters *GWROLDEB POBL Y WLAD* ('THE BRAVERY OF THE COUNTRY PEOPLE'). How wise was it for common people to stand up against regular soldiers, wouldn't their sacrifice have been excessive? He thought that the conduct of the people would have been more like that of Dai and Wil, two lads from Cardiganshire, their parents' only sons who went to Fishguard but whose doubts and fears increased as they got nearer. When they reached Dinas Cross ('y Dinas') just outside Fishguard, Dai said to Wil 'we could get killed, you know'. Wil agreed, and said 'will you turn back, Dai'. He agreed. They asked an old lady for some water, and she told them when they were quenching their thirst: 'Boys, you have come to defend your country, you can go back, the French have laid down their arms this morning and are all prisoners.' Dai jumped about a yard into the air and waved his scythe in the air in his joy. Dai and Wil were thought of as the bravest lads in the country. Griffiths thought that thousands of like-minded people had gone to Fishguard.[84] As well as Wil and Dai, Griffiths detailed other men's behaviour in war.[85]

Quoting oral tradition from several local communities ('mewn gwahanol gymydogaethau oddiar lafar gwlad') he provided testimony from social memory that, some men, head of households ('penau teuluoedd') hid in the forests during the day, only returning to their homes late at night. Their women folk would bring them food and drink. They were not hiding from the French, but from their neighbours, to avoid being pressurised by them to face the enemy. One day they heard a huntsman's shotgun: their terror knew no bounds and they flew from the forest like wild things ('fel gwylltiaid'). It was said that when they heard that the enemies had been made prisoners their joy was as intense as their fears had been.[86] No contemporary record exists of this story, but there is no reason why families should recall the terror or cowardice of their menfolk at the time unless the experience was authentic. The story of men, heads of the household, hiding in the forests fits in well with the testimony of terror recorded by contemporaries, as well as aligning with the author's honesty about the behaviour of ordinary people in war.

Contemporary Nonconformist values, those of respect for the godly woman and the dangers of drink, were evident in Griffiths's treatment of Jemima Nicholas and the new heroine of Fishguard, the leader of the hymn singing at Rhydybont, the saint, Nansi Jones. They were both old ladies, according to Griffiths, but that is where the similarity ended. Griffiths makes a conscious comparison between the two (who he brackets together, giving Jemima an extra 'H' since it was more bibilical):

JEMIMAH NICHOLAS, Abergwaun, a
NANSI JONES, o Godre'r Mynydd[87]

One could admire the bravery of Jemimah Nicholas in capturing fourteen enemy soldiers, she achieved something that only one in 10,000 women of her age could have achieved.[88] Her name could be compared with that of Boudica and Joan of Arc. She fought like a 'she-bear protecting her cubs' ('fel arthes wedi colli ei chenawon') but what fortified her was beer, she drank two quarts on capturing the French, and this fondness for beer stayed with her throughout her life.[89] Griffiths, like several others, thought that Jemima received a pension for her services that paid for a lifetime of drink.[90] But how different was Nansi Jones! Griffiths created a new trope of Nansi Jones linked to the French Invasion story and imbued her with Nonconformist values of piety, godliness and worship of God. Jemimah and Nansi represent different values, but both women were superior to the men around them. Jemima was physically strong and brave, but with a fondness for tobacco and an over fondness for drink. Nansi was clearly his preferred female role model, sharing his denominational affiliations and his spirituality. The story was told and retold in the Nonconformist press and becomes part of Nonconformist popular culture in Welsh-speaking Wales in a similar way to Ceiriog's poem.

As we have seen, T. Cunllo Griffiths gave more attention and space to Nansi than Jemima. He paid far less attention to Mary Williams, and, other than repeating the Ap Gwilym line that they were present with their rustic weapons on the sands at Goodwick, the red-cloaked women are also ignored. Welsh Nonconformists such as Griffiths referred to red cloaks or mantles ('mentyll cochion') and only very rarely mentioned the less respectable, English (and more erotic), red petticoat.[91]

Griffiths used the invasion story to make a case for Welsh patriotism, to counteract the allegations of disloyalty made against Nonconformists in the past, evidenced by the spontaneous bravery of ordinary Welsh men and women who rose against the enemy to defend their country. There is hardly any recognition of the militia or the military in Griffiths's account. When he does list the forces assembled against the French he gives pride of place to the thousands of country people of both sexes and their weaponry before proceeding to name the various bodies of military.[92] Griffiths, like Harries before him, stands up for the Welsh, responding to the commentators who had argued that the French had chosen to land in Wales because they had received correspondence from the Welsh of a seditious nature, denouncing them as 'ein gelynion Seisnig' ('our English enemies').[93] He does not name the Baptist preacher from Llangloffan who was tried for treason. Griffiths's stance is decidedly ambiguous, the unnamed preacher had gone to the French headquarters at Trehowel for a purpose that was still unknown. Griffiths seemed to be suggesting, like Henry Davies before him, that the preacher was deserving of this hostility.[94]

The greatest defence against this 'Pack o Frenchmen' was not the force of physical arms but the spiritual force of Nansi Jones, even though she was nowhere near Fishguard. If Napoleon thought the Welsh would rise in support of republican France, then he was mistaken.[95] Other nations would have fled but not the Welsh.[96] Wales had always been a loyal country and the Fishguard landing was proof of this.[97] Loyalty to what is not clearly detailed, to the Empire presumably, but primarily to Welsh Nonconformist values: 'hen grefydd anwyl ein tadau' ('the old religion of our fathers'). He ends (in capital letters) with 'CYMRU, CYMRO, A CHYMRAEG AM BYTH!' ('Wales, Welshmen, and the Welsh Language For Ever!').[98]

By the 1870s, the French Invasion story or stories were popular in Welsh and in English, as well as in different contexts, in poetry, history, politics and satire. It had featured in the correspondence columns of the *Times*. The leading London literary magazine the *Athenaeum* reviewed *Welsh Patriotism* and judged that the 'Welsh, military and civil' should be proud, even if the French were a gang of cowardly ruffians.[99] Two very powerful female characters had emerged to dominate the popular narrative, Jemima Nicholas, in both languages, and Nansi Jones, in Welsh. However, the credibility of the story that now enjoyed some standing and the rather outsized characters that refracted popular culture faced an imminent threat.

The French Invasion narratives from about 1869 onwards had to accommodate a growing scepticism of folk history and oral tradition from a more 'scientific' historical method, which cast doubt on evidential grounds of the role of the Fishguard women. The women were defended by an unfamiliar source: George Jabet, a retired Birmingham solicitor, who provided the Mathias letter of February 1797 describing the women in 'red flannels', previously unknown in print, as contemporary evidence. Jabet wrote in the *Birmingham Daily Post*, after a doubting piece appeared in a local *Notes and Queries*, that it was 'the approved fashion of modern historical critics to deny well established facts, and, with an air of profound wisdom, call for evidence'. He had in his possession a copy of the February 1797 letter from John and Mary Mathias in Narberth to their sister in Swansea giving contemporary evidence of the 'four hundred women in red flannels'. The original letter was in the possession of a 'Miss Powell' in Glamorgan Street, Brecon.[100] Jabet went on to say that some modern histories of England omitted the women in red cloaks as 'apocryphal, or not flattering to our gallant neighbours'. Wilkie Collins, however, in his *'Historical Notes* says Lord Cawdor dressed the colliers in red petticoats, to give them the appearance of soldiers'.[101] The *Pembrokeshire Herald* picked up the story and in presenting the Mathias letter to its readers, exclaimed that working-class men wanted to know 'were they colliers in red or women in red to whom the French capitulated when they invaded Wales in 1797?'[102]

Endnotes

1. Gwyneth Tyson Roberts, *The Language of the Blue Books: The Perfect Instrument of Empire* (1998), p. 166
2. Jane Aaron, *The Welsh Survival Gene: The 'Despite Culture' in the Two Language Communities of Wales*, Institute of Welsh Affairs National Eisteddfod Lecture, Meifod 2003 (Cardiff, 2003), p. 7.
3. For *Y Gymraes* and the images of women generally in Welsh periodicals, see Sian Rhiannon Williams, 'The True "Cymraes": Images of Women in Women's Nineteenth-Century Welsh Periodicals', in Angela V. John (ed.) *Our Mother's Land: Chapters in Welsh Women's History 1830–1939*, revised edn (Cardiff, 2011), pp. 73–94.
4. *Y Gymraes*, 2/10 (Hydref, 1851), 297.
5. Jane Aaron, *Nineteenth-Century Women's Writing in Wales: Nation, Gender and Identity* (Cardiff, 2007), pp. 80, 192–3.
6. 'Red Shawls and French Invaders. An Historical Anecdote for the Ladies', *The Republic: A Monthly Magazine of American Literature*, 3/3 (March 1852), 146.
7. 'Red Shawls and French Invaders', 146.
8. Nansi Ceridwen Jones, (1959). 'DAVIES, JOHN LLOYD (1801–1860), Blaendyffryn and Alltyrodyn, Llandysul, Cardiganshire, M.P.', *Dictionary of Welsh Biography* from *https://biography.wales/article/s-DAVI-LLO-1801* (last accessed 3 August 2024).
9. 'Harbour of Refuge, Cardigan Bay', *The Morning Advertiser* (13 February 1856), 3.
10. Lynda Nead, 'Fashion and Visual Culture in the 19th Century: Women in Red', (2014) lecture available online, *www.gresham.ac.uk/watch-now/women-red* (last accessed 3 August 2024).
11. Thomas Stephens, *The Literature of the Kymry: Being a Critical Essay on the History of the Language and Literature of Wales* (Llandovery, 1849), p. 33.
12. For a biography of Collins, see William Clarke, *The Secret Life of Wilkie Collins* (London, 1988), and for his relationship to women, Philip O'Neill, *Wilkie Collins: Women, Property and Propriety* (London, 1988).
13. Terry Jenkins, 'The Orsini Affair and the Crisis of 1858', *History Today*, 58/2 (February 2008).
14. Wilkie Collins, 'The Great (Forgotten) Invasion', *Household Words*, 29 (12 March 1859), 337–41. Only Dickens's name as 'conductor' appeared, so some believed that Charles Dickens was the author of the Invasion piece. The historical narrative also appeared later in Collins's first collection of short pieces in 1863, when the identity of the author became generally known.
15. Wilkie Collins, 'The Great (Forgotten) Invasion', *My Miscellanies*, vol. 1 (London, 1863) pp. 151–67.
16. O'Neil, *Wilkie Collins* p. 186.

17 Collins, 'The Great (Forgotten) Invasion', all quotations from *www.online-literature.com* (last accessed 3 August 2024).
18 Jayne Shrimpton, *Victorian Fashion* (London, 2016) pp. 14–15.
19 Catherine Peters (2011), 'Collins, (William) Wilkie (1824–1889), writer', *Oxford Dictionary of National Biography*.
20 Wilkie Collins, 'The Great (Forgotten) Invasion', 341.
21 For example, *Illustrated Berwick Journal* (19 March 1859), 3.
22 'Fishguard or it is 60 years since', *Bicester Advertiser* (2 April 1859), 4.
23 'Fishguard or it is 60 years since', 4.
24 'Fishguard or it is 60 years since', 4.
25 Paul O'Leary, 'Arming the Citizens: The Volunteer Force in Nineteenth-Century Wales', in Matthew Cragoe and Chris Williams (eds), *Wales and War: Society, Politics and Religion in the late Nineteenth and Twentieth Centuries* (Cardiff, 2007) p. 63.
26 Stephen Shapiro, 'The British Army in Home Defense, 1844–1871: Militia and Volunteers in a Liberal Era' (PhD thesis, Ohio State University, 2011), p. 201.
27 For examples, see, *Baner ac Amserau Cymru* (21 December 1859); *Hereford Times* (4 February 1860), 15; 'Cwmafon,Morganwg', *Seren Cymru* (25 November 1864), 382.
28 O'Leary, 'Arming the Citizens', p. 66.
29 For George Denman, see William Carr and Hugh Mooney (2004), 'Denman, George (1819–1896), judge and politician', *Oxford Dictionary of National Biography*.
30 *Evening Mail* (16 December 1859), 7; *Edinburgh Evening Courant* (17 December 1859), 3.
31 Stuart Jones notes that Tate in 1809 did have a 'lady friend of extravagant habits' named Genselle, but there is no mention of French offspring. E. H. Stuart Jones, *The Last Invasion* (Cardiff, 1950), p. 138.
32 'The French in Wales', *The Times* (19 December 1859), 10. He also wrote to the Editor of the *Evening Mail* (19 December 1859), 4; the text also appeared in other newspapers for example, *Bury and Norwich Post* (3 January 1860), 4; *Cardiff and Merthyr Guardian* (24 December 1859), 8.
33 'The French in Wales. To the Editor of the Times', *The Times* (24 December 1859), 5; 'The French in Wales. To the Editor of the Evening Mail', *Evening Mail* (26 December 1859), 4.
34 *Evening Mail* (26 December 1859), 4.
35 'The French in Wales', *The Times* (27 December 1859), 4.
36 The debate and correspondence are reproduced in 'The Welch Invasion Controversy', *Volunteer Service Gazette* (31 December 1859), 7.
37 'Letter to the Editor' of the *Evening Mail* (23 December 1859) and *Evening Mail* (26 December 1859).
38 *Bury and Norwich Post* (3 January 1860), 4.

39 H. L. Ap Gwilym, *An Authentic Account of the Invasion by the French Troops on Carrig Gwasted Point, near Fishguard, 1797* (Haverfordwest, 1842), p. 25.
40 *Charles o'r Bala, sef cyhoeddiad pythefnosol at wasanaeth crefydd, llenyddiaeth ac addysg*, 1/27 (29 Rhagfyr 1859), 369.
41 John Ceiriog Hughes, 'Y Baban Diwrnod Oed', *Oriau'r Hwyr: sef Gweithiau Barddonol* (1860); p. 57, lines 48–55.
42 'Y Baban Diwrnod oed (Adroddiad Nadolig)', 369.
43 John Ceiriog Hughes, *Oriau'r Hwyr* (Ruthin, 1860) p. 103. The poem was used as a literary recruitment tool in the Great War, see for example, 'Oddiar Llechwedd Penrhys', *Y Darian* (3 June 1915), 3.
44 Branwen Jarvis detects occasional small signs of resistance in Ceiriog's work that he was anxious to quash. 'Ceiriog a Chymru', *Transactions of the Honourable Society of Cymmrodorion* (1987), 92–94. See also Bethan Angharad Huws, 'Gwell Cymro, Cymro oddi cartref? Cymhlethdod meddwl a Gwaith John Ceiriog Hughes' (MPhil thesis, Cardiff University, 2015), p. 137.
45 Saunders Lewis, *Yr Artist yn Philistia 1: Ceiriog* (Aberystwyth, 1929), p. 31.
46 'Y Baban Diwrnod Oed', lines 62–4.
47 *The Welsh Academy Encyclopaedia of Wales* (Cardiff, 2008), p. 383.
48 Benjamin George Owens. 'WILLIAMS, JOHN CEULANYDD (Ceulanydd; 1847?–1899), Baptist minister, poet, and writer'. *Dictionary of Welsh Biography*, https://biography.wales/article/s-WILL-CEU-1847 (last accessed 4 March 2021).
49 *Evening Express* (13 September 1899), 4.
50 'Gwibdaith y Cymmrodorion i Abergwaun, Canu Baban Diwrnod Oed', *The Llanelly Mercury and South Wales Advertiser* (15 July 1909).
51 'Codi Milisia', *Y Diwygiwr* (September 1852), 'Trem ar 1855 ar ddydd ei therfyniad', *Y Diwygiwr* (February 1856).
52 *Yr Haul* 4/39 (Mawrth, 1860), 93.
53 The biographer of David Rees does not think that the account of Rees's speech in *Yr Haul* should be believed, 'O'r braidd y gellir dibynnu ar eirwiredd y ffynhonell'. Iorwerth Jones, *David Rees y Cynhyrfwr* (Swansea, 1971) p. 251
54 'Y Ffrancod yn Abergwaun', *Yr Haul* (*Cyfres Caerfyrddin*), 48/4 (December 1860), 354.
55 Geraint H. Jenkins, *The Foundations of Modern Wales 1642–1780* (Cardiff, 1987), p. 384; R. Tudor Jones, *Congregationalism in Wales* (Cardiff, 2004), p. 156. The information otherwise about this major Independent figure is scant. She is not in the *Dictionary of Welsh Biography*. What little there is on her life and career is in the denominational press of the nineteenth century in which *Y Diwygiwr* played a lead. See the informative blog https://daibach-welldigger.blogspot.com/ (last accessed 3 August 2024) and Maggie Humphreys and Robert C. Evans (eds), *Dictionary of Composers for the Church in Great Britain and Ireland* (London, 1997), p. 191.

56 William Williams, 'Am y ddaeargryn a ddygwyddodd mewn amryw o deyrnasoedd helaeth yn y fwyddyn 1755 a 1756', *Gweithiau Williams Pantycelyn* (Holywell, 1887), p. 238 verse 8.
57 tr. 2015 Richard B Gillion.
58 'Caniadaeth y Cysegr', *Y Diwygiwr* (Hydref 1863), 302.
59 *Potter's Electric News* (6 February 1861), 2.
60 Margaret S. Walker, 'The Reverend Henry Vincent, 1793–1865, a neglected Pembrokeshire antiquarian', *Journal of the Pembrokeshire Historical Society*, 6 (1994/5), 69–78.
61 Walker, 'The Reverend Henry Vincent', 70.
62 Walker, 'The Reverend Henry Vincent', 70.
63 Guy Beiner, *Remembering the Year of the French: Irish Folk History and Social Memory* (Madison WI, 2007), p. 28.
64 Walker, 'The Reverend Henry Vincent', 71.
65 Ap Gwilym, *An Authentic Account*, p. 33.
66 Walker, 'The Reverend Henry Vincent', 71.
67 Walker, 'The Reverend Henry Vincent', 72.
68 Walker, 'The Reverend Henry Vincent', 72.
69 John Harries (Cymro Sir Benfro), *Welsh Patriotism: Or ,The Landing of the French at Fishguard on the 22nd of February, 1797 compiled from authentic sources* (Haverfordwest, 1875).
70 *Welsh Patriotism*, p. 23.
71 *Welsh Patriotism*, p. 7.
72 *Welsh Patriotism*, p. 24.
73 *Welsh Patriotism*, pp. 11–12.
74 *Welsh Patriotism*, pp 14–15.
75 *Welsh Patriotism*, p. 18.
76 *Y Tyst Cymreig* (30 October 1868), 3.
77 T. Cunllo Griffiths, *Lloffion y Beirdd* (Wrexham, 1879).
78 T. Cunllo Griffiths, 'At Etholwyr Ceredigion', *Ye Brython Cymreig* (17 June 1892), 1.
79 *Y Tyst a'r Dydd* (16 February 1872), 5; *Merthyr Telegraph* (9 October 1869), 2; *Y Tyst Cymreig* (5 August 1870), 7.
80 Huw Pryce, *Writing Welsh History: From the Early Middle Ages to the Twenty-First Century* (Oxford, 2022), p. 300.
81 *Y Tyst a'r Dydd* (21 April 1882), 8.
82 For example, Robert Herbert Williams (Corfanydd),'Adgofion am Gymry Liverpool, Glaniad y Ffrangcod yn Nghymru', *Y Tyst Cymreig* (18 March 1870), 10.
83 T. Cunllo Griffiths, *Glaniad y Ffrancod yn Abergwaun: Darlith*, (1885), Rhaglith.
84 Griffiths, *Glaniad y Ffrancod yn Abergwaun*, pp. 21–2.
85 Griffiths, *Glaniad y Ffrancod yn Abergwaun*, p. 42.
86 Griffiths, *Glaniad y Ffrancod yn Abergwaun*, p. 42.
87 Griffiths, *Glaniad y Ffrancod yn Abergwaun*, p. 26.

88 Griffiths, *Glaniad y Ffrancod yn Abergwaun*, pp. 28–9.
89 Griffiths, *Glaniad y Ffrancod yn Abergwaun*, p. 26.
90 Griffiths, *Glaniad y Ffrancod yn Abergwaun*, p. 27.
91 Griffiths, *Glaniad y Ffrancod yn Abergwaun*, p. 34.
92 Griffiths, *Glaniad y Ffrancod yn Abergwaun*, p. 39.
93 Griffiths, *Glaniad y Ffrancod yn Abergwaun*, p. 13.
94 Griffiths, *Glaniad y Ffrancod yn Abergwaun*, p. 46.
95 Griffiths, *Glaniad y Ffrancod yn Abergwaun*, p. 34.
96 Griffiths, *Glaniad y Ffrancod yn Abergwaun*, pp. 33–4.
97 Griffiths, *Glaniad y Ffrancod yn Abergwaun*, p. 33.
98 Griffiths, *Glaniad y Ffrancod yn Abergwaun*, p. 35.
99 *The Athenaeum*, 2498 (11 September 1875), 336.
100 George Jabet, 'The French Invasion of Wales in 1797', *Birmingham Daily Post* (11 September 1869), 7. The original letter was donated to the National Library of Wales in 1950 by Captain Hugh Vivian who stated that the letter had been preserved by 'his wife's maternal ancestors, the Illtid Thomas family of Glan Môr, Sketty' (National Library of Wales MS 14005C). E. D. Jones, 'The French Landing at Fishguard, 1797', *National Library of Wales Journal*, 6/3 (Summer 1950), 303.
101 George Jabet, *Birmingham Daily Post* (11 September 1869), 7. Jabet had compiled a catalogue for Birmingham Library, and in so doing came across this otherwise obscure reference in a Local Notes and Queries column in a Birmingham newspaper, probably the *Birmingham Journal*.
102 *The Pembrokeshire Herald and General Advertiser* (24 September 1869), 2.

Chapter 6

A Laddo a Leddir: Who Slays Shall Be Slain, 1885 to the 1897 Centenary

From the early 1870s, Jemima begins to become more prominent in the narratives. Her story usurped the masculine, military order and attempts were made to neutralise this threat. Ap Gwilym had called her 'An Heroic Single Woman', but this had been misreported by *The Cambrian* newspaper as 'A Single Woman'.[1] To Ap Gwilym her heroism came from her bravery in single-handedly capturing twelve Frenchmen, whereas the newspaper had a different interpretation. To them, Jemima was literally a single woman, in other words unmarried.[2] This situation could not be allowed to continue, it challenged Welsh manhood, she should have become the wife of a noble husband and produced progeny like herself. Her rhetoric and her 'arch look or roguish smile' were more powerful weapons than her pitchfork, as formidable as that may have been. It was men like Sir Thomas Picton who were responsible for the 'sharp fighting' that defeated the French, not the women.[3] Despite challenges of this kind, Jemima's heroism was acquiring a following and an appreciation that even crossed the Atlantic. Thomas Morgan, originally from Maesteg but ministering to the Independents in Hyde Park, Scranton, (Pennsylvania) mentioned the women of Fishguard but particularly Jemima ('yn neillduol Jemima') in his 1876 lecture on Welsh historical heroines. Jemima belonged in the same company as Boudica, Ann Griffiths and Sarah Jane Rees (Cranogwen), among others.[4]

By the 1880s, the Invasion generation had now almost all passed away; a frequent arena for the settling of old scores was the obituary. Old tensions were brought to the surface by the obituary of one veteran that mentioned that the French had been defeated by the 'historical red flannel whittles and conical hats of the tall Welsh women' so that when the Castlemartin Yeomanry appeared on the scene the battle had already been won.[5] This drew a furious response from a military man who begged 'most respectfully and emphatically' to state that the red whittles were not the cause of the French surrender. The pride and honour of the Pembroke Yeomanry Cavalry had to be protected because 'they were a Regiment of importance so far back as the year 1797' and the ultimate surrender of the French was 'due mainly to the Yeomanry'.[6] Matters were more balanced between the sexes in another obituary of a native of Fishguard, whose mother had been one of women who had donned 'scarlet petticoats', while his father had been one of Knox's Fishguard Fencibles.[7]

This reference to scarlet petticoats reignited another hot topic of debate. The *Western Mail* published an article titled 'Red Petticoats or Scarlet Mantles?'[8] The author was Owen Morgan, also known by his Bardic name Morien, from Pen-y-Graig in the Rhondda, *Western Mail* journalist and miscellaneous writer. He was a supporter of Iolo Morganwg and his works were heavily influenced by his Druidism but they also contained a vision of Wales that fitted in with the *Welsh Patriotism* of John Harries.[9] Morien not only wrote about Druids, he also wrote a history of Pontypridd and the Rhondda Valleys. He was a Welsh cultural nationalist who ascribed a leading historical role to Welsh women. He wrote against the 'scarlet petticoats' because they were both historically inaccurate and implausible in their historical context. Morien was, however, prepared to alter the historical record to suit his needs.[10] Two Welsh classes frightened the English authorities in ancient times, he claimed: 'the Cambrian dames and the Cambrian bards.'[11] After mentioning historical cases of Welsh women's success and brutality in battle, he thought 'gallant Frenchmen would have been far more likely to do the reverse of running away at sight of red petticoats', evidently recognising the erotic allure of the petticoat. But it was more in 'the interest of historic truth and the credit of the sons of ancient Gaul' to assert positively 'that it was scarlet mantles that Welshwomen wore on that occasion'. The proof he had were the dispatches from Knox to the Duke of Portland, he had evidently come across Knox's apologia of 1800 in which he documented his innocence of the allegations of cowardice, and the 'printed report of eye-witnesses of the whole affair'.[12]

In this, and in other instances, Morien manipulated the text. There were no references to red-cloaked women in Knox's communications with Portland.[13] The eye witness report he ostensibly produced was from Ap Gwilym's 1842 *An Authentic Account*, an account he composed of six separate extracts from Ap Gwilym, cobbled together to make one whole, to make a more convincing case for the central role of the women in red mantles.[14] He reordered text from a single page of Ap Gwilym to make a stronger point about the women's agency in the surrender, and substituted Ap Gwilym's 'English' for his 'Welshmen', all the while reshaping the past to fit his interpretation in the present.[15]

A more scientific approach towards historical evidence was on display when the Cambrian Archaeological Association visited Fishguard for its annual meeting in 1883. The Association was interested in examining, preserving and illustrating the ancient monuments and remains of Wales. When they visited Fishguard in August of that year, its significance as the spot where the French invaded was a major attraction. These men were among the leading intellectuals of their day, they looked forward to visiting the sites where the 'the warriors of France laid down their arms at the appalling sight of the red cloaks of the women of Pembrokeshire'.[16] To a large number of those present, the French invasion 'was of greater interest than archaeology, than crosses, forts or inscribed stones'.[17] The day's proceedings were closed with the delivery of what the *Western Mail* called an 'able paper' by a Mr Laws on 'The French Invasion of Pembrokeshire'.[18] This paper was published in the 1883 volume of the Association's learned journal, *Archaeologia Cambrensis*.[19]

The author of the paper, Edward Laws, was born in Lamphey Court in 1837, the home of the Mathias family.[20] His mother was Mary Mathias, his father John Milligan Laws, an English Admiral. After a short military career with the Royal Sussex Regiment, he returned to Pembrokeshire and devoted the rest of his life to the study of the archaeology, history and antiquities of the county. The prime mover in the establishment of a local museum for Tenby, he immersed himself in the activities of the town, being variously a member of the Borough Council, Mayor, Justice of the Peace and Sheriff of Pembrokeshire.

Laws set himself the task of telling the story of Pembrokeshire from start to finish. In *A History of Little England Beyond Wales*, he gave the early history of Pembrokeshire, from the earliest prehistoric evidence to the end of the Civil War.[21] Laws was the first since Richard Fenton to have the leisure and means to research and write history unencumbered by the necessity of having to earn a living. Laws wrote in English, he knew no Welsh, and his history was not imbued with the values of Nonconformist ministers, nor with the Welsh Patriotism of John Harries. Laws had his own prejudices and assumptions, like all historians, but his overriding focus was his love of the county of Pembrokeshire, especially the 'non-Kymric colony settled in Pembrokeshire': the Pembrokeshire south of the Landsker, or Little England, beyond Wales. Laws also had no time for the republican ideologies of France, either past or present. His history was full of stock French stereotypes of 'frog-eating

Mounseers' coupled with counter-revolutionary stories of the excesses of the French Revolution.[22] This first scholarly version of the Invasion story, replete with four footnotes, was still firmly based on the Ap Gwilym's *An Authentic Account* of 1842. The non-Ap Gwilym components came from his reading of Fenton and oral tradition, particularly the stories disseminated by John Mortimer, the master of Trehowel. A new component is his reference to William Davies, a veteran of Bunker Hill, who orchestrated the positioning of the troops: it was the 'ill natured' who declared that it was the women in their high hats and red whittles who helped him by their resemblance to regiments of the line. [23] 'William Davies' was actually a composite character based on John Colby. Laws preferred to believe that Cawdor achieved his objectives through the assistance of men, not women.

Despite his hatred of French republican ideology, Laws was quite tolerant of French behaviour and, as in the early accounts of the invasion, played down the violence of the French. It was this leniency that one newspaper called a 'singular absence of outrage' and 'the most wonderful feature of the invasion'.[24] Laws cites the 'Day Old Baby' story as evidence of French leniency and was more critical of the 'cowardly husband' who had abandoned his wife and child than he was of the French.[25] Mary Williams was the 'worst case'; she had been wounded with a gunshot and then 'maltreated, probably by drunken men'. But he said, as others had frequently, she received a pension of £40 a year so 'did not make a bad bargain'.[26]

Laws, a Tenby man, preferred to believe the Castlemartin men rather than the Fishguard women. The traditions of male military prowess centring on the Pembrokeshire Yeomanry and their traditions in the south had at times been in creative conflict with the women at Fishguard in the north, and this could be seen as a south-English versus north-Welsh Pembrokeshire tussle. It was, however, more a military and masculine disdain of the role of women, a fear of ridicule, rather than a show of south Pembrokeshire English hauteur against the Welsh of the north. The story belonged to all of Pembrokeshire, and it was even claimed that the French Invasion reconciled differences and united the people of Pembrokeshire. Writing in 1885, Twm ap Iorwerth discussed the historic differences between south and north Pembrokeshire in a piece on 'Some Pembrokeshire Worthies' in the *Herald of Wales*.[27] He wrote from an evangelical perspective: the people in the south were without religion compared to the godly *Kymru* of the north. There were deep grudges between the different peoples, the high Tory 'Thanes of Cawdor' in the south and the Baptists in the north. What healed the wounds was the French Invasion: 'the combined efforts of the Castlemartin Yeomanry and the Welsh women in their scarlet whittles ... united the Welsh and English speaking peoples together in bonds of amity, and links of friendly concord.'[28]

As well as Twm ap Iorwerth, other attempts were made by Pembrokeshire men to bridge the divides between north and south, represented in terms of the French invasion by the male yeomanry of Pembroke and the red shawled women of Fishguard. At a dinner to coincide with the Fishguard Show in August 1884, Charles Philipps of Picton Castle, the Lord Lieutenant of Haverfordwest and a senior officer in the Yeomanry, said there was no better place in the county, where an officer of the Pembrokeshire Yeomanry could more fitly toast thanks to than Fishguard. The 'good women' of Fishguard had shown pluck when the French invaded but so too had 'the men of Pembrokeshire – the men of the Pembrokeshire Yeomanry and the men of the Pembrokeshire Militia'.[29] To which the male gathering gave 'Loud Applause'. Philipps urged more men from Fishguard to join the Yeomanry since they had 'few members from that part of the county'.[30] Local tensions between south and north would remain, but when Laws came to write about the French invasion in his *History of Little England beyond Wales* in 1888, he did so from a whole Pembrokeshire perspective.[31] The invasion may have taken place in north Pembrokeshire but men from all parts of Pembrokeshire contributed to the defeat of the French.

Evan Jones (1840–1903), known by his bardic name of Gurnos, one of the chief public lecturers of his day and, for the last twenty years of his life the leading Welsh eisteddfod conductor, popularised the invasion story in south Wales.[32] At the age of twenty he began to preach at Gurnos chapel and took the name as his own. He won several eisteddfod chairs. He was renowned in Victorian Wales, but was also known as an 'odd' man who ploughed his own furrow. It was Gurnos who dismantled Morien's claims for Druidism at the Gorsedd Circle at the Eisteddfod in Swansea in 1891.[33] His lectures drew huge crowds and one of his lecture topics was on the landing of the French at Fishguard. His approach was unique and radical. Gurnos's lecture was never published, but we can get a flavour of what he said from the response to his lecture at Bethania Chapel, Dowlais in November 1893 from the report in the *Merthyr Times*:

> [h]e sought to make his hearers believe that Bounaparte was one of the best friends of democracy that ever lived and that he warred only for the benefit of mankind - that he sought only to establish a republic in Britain which would have made us all ever so much better than we are.[34]

The *Merthyr Times* admired Gurnos very much but 'when he seeks to glorify the gory spawn of French blood guillotines we must raise our voice in protest'. Gurnos was not a political creature, but it is evident where his sympathies lay; the proceeds of his Fishguard invasion lecture at Pontycymmer in October 1891 went 'to assist a working man in the district'.[35] He was a splendid orator, and, so the newspapers said, a great advocate of the Fishguard women. He waxed 'so eloquent[ly] on the platform over their resourcefulness and pluck that immense audiences were in a white heat of enthusiasm as a consequence'.³⁶ The story of the French Invasion could be used to advance radical programmes, as well as celebrate the defeat of the French Revolution and its ideas in Wales.

Attitudes to the past shift from the historical to the remembered and from the remembered to the commemorative.³⁷ The people of Pembrokeshire were not slow to cash in on one aspect of their commemoration; the fame of the scarlet shawls. Messrs Jones of Newport (Trefdraeth) manufactured soft red shawls that were sold at Tenby and elsewhere. The actual trademark or logo used for the marketing of the shawls by Messrs Jones was a rough, rocky headland with women in high crowned hats and red shawls walking to and fro.³⁸ It prompted more interest and enquiries. Tourists visiting Fishguard were proudly shown the whittles that had been worn on the occasion.³⁹ In a similar vein, Mr Williams of Brestgarn farm was proud to show his clock to visitors, the clock with bullet holes caused by the French who thought there was someone hiding there. When Ap Gwilym wrote about the clock in 1842, the hole in the clock and the clock itself had already been seen 'by hundreds of curious strangers'.⁴⁰ In the 1880s, Mr Williams hit upon the idea of asking visitors for contributions that he then passed on to the secretary of the Pembrokeshire and Haverfordwest Infirmary.⁴¹ In 1887, at a public meeting in Fishguard to decide on how best to commemorate Queen Victoria's Golden Jubilee, it was agreed that the memorial should take the form of a town clock, but that any surplus should be used to commemorate the landing of the French at Fishguard; a statue representing a Welsh matron in native costume and giving prominence to the 'red flannel shawl' was suggested.⁴² Two years later when the design for the Pembrokeshire county seal was being considered, one proposal had the figure of a girl in Welsh costume with the motto 'Fishguard 1797' in English, and opposite it, in Welsh, 'The land of my birth'. The Tenby people had a different opinion to that of Fishguard. The *Tenby Observer* would have preferred to see a figure of Lord Cawdor on his charger with 'the Welsh girl in the background'.⁴³ The Parish Council of Fishguard finally adopted as its motto *Dewrion ferched Abergwaun* ('Brave Women of Fishguard') in February 1895.⁴⁴

The first novel with an historical introduction of the French Invasion was initially published in 1892.⁴⁵ The unnamed author was later revealed to be Miss Margaret Ellen James from Tenby. From the first lines of her introduction, James is at pains to provide authenticity for the 'facts mentioned in the story' because 'the whole affair reads like fiction – and very improbable and imaginative fiction'.⁴⁶ James, significantly, gives priority in the introduction to social memory, to 'the evidence of persons who had witnessed the landing and who have told the story to me'.⁴⁷ She had talked to many of them herself during her life as her home 'was within sight of Fishguard Head'. One of these she names as the last survivor: Eleanor Phillips (Nelly Phillips) who had just died at the age of 103.⁴⁸ The *Introduction* is a work of original historical research, in which she lists her sources: eye witness accounts and published histories such as those of Ap Gwilym, Laws, the official correspondence between Cawdor, Milford and Portland and others, but also new sources including verbatim extracts in French from the biography of Hoche by Emile de Bonnechose.⁴⁹ She had undertaken substantial research to make her imagined account of the lives and loves of the people who witnessed the landing and experienced the French during the three days of occupation as vivid and as realistic as her plot demanded. The framework is Ap Gwilym and the events are from Ap Gwilym, but the romance and plot are James's own, including a fictional eyewitness narrator, a young clerk, later to become the Revd Daniel Rowland of the title: *The Fishguard Invasion of 1797. Some Passages taken from the Diary of the Reverend Daniel Rowlands, sometime Vicar of Llanfihangelpenybont*. The plot is one of the thrills of concealment from the enemy, hiding in a cave, reminiscent of the past, together with the romance of Nell, the Pembroke girl, who later marries a Frenchman and becomes Madame Roux. James is careful to distinguish her 'facts' from fiction; for instance, when Jemima is introduced surrounded by twelve Frenchmen there is a footnote which reads simply 'A fact'.[50] James makes room in her plot for Madame Tate, and includes a confrontation between Jemima and Madame Tate, on the sands at Goodwick, a fictional consummation of the tension between French and Welsh women reminiscent of earlier periodical narratives. The focus is on the plot but James is never shy of making her opinions known: of the wretched horse stealer James Bowen, the heroine Nancy says 'Cursed for ever and throughout all ages be the traitor'.[51]

The female characters are young, dynamic and strong, in contrast to the frequently negative representations of Welsh women in Victorian and Edwardian fiction as morally deviant and physically and mentally degenerate.[52] James follows Ap Gwilym writing in 1842, before the publication of the Blue Books, who also depicted his female characters as strong, resourceful and brave.[53] The book was well received and caused a sensation in some quarters. It was widely reviewed by the press across the kingdom.[54] This was the first account of the invasion to be written by a woman, although others would follow.[55] Fiction or semi-fiction about the French Invasion has invariably been written by women, while the historians of the invasion have, until recently, been exclusively male.

The French Invasion resonated in both languages and in both linguistic cultures of Wales. As Robin Chapman has noted, Welsh literature exists in an ambivalent but inescapable relationship with English as a paradigm of cultural comparison.[56] Developments in both language cultures occurred at different times, but often separately and in parallel, sometimes with cross cultural borrowing but often in different worlds. There were no English language equivalents to the *Day-Old Baby* or to Nansi Jones as they were both developed within the Welsh language Nonconformist domain, but there would be popular historical fiction renditions of the story in both languages. At about the same time as the French Invasion was made popular in English though the work of M. E. James, a Welsh-language account appeared in *Papur Pawb* in the summer and autumn of 1894, totally separate from James's English version. *Papur Pawb* was a relatively new breed of Welsh-language newspaper, a weekly publication with its main contents being humorous in nature, as well as including literary extracts and short stories. The French Invasion story that appeared every week from July to November 1894 was titled *Peryglon Pencaer* ('Dangers of Pencaer'), authored by the editor Dan Rhys (1851–1914). Rhys gave his biography in the pages of his own newspaper. Born in Llandeilo in 1851, it was from his grandmother that he heard the story he was to relate about *Peryglon Pencaer*. His grandmother was one of the 'red shawled regiment' ('Catrawd y shawls cochion').[57] The story was pan-Celtic (the French were as Celtic as the Welsh), anti-English and, albeit reluctantly, pro-British.

His was a Gothic tale of wreckers and shipwrecked captains, mistaken identity and multiple capture. Rhys asked questions that were of direct relevance to his own day. What kind of Wales would it have been had the French succeeded in 1797? Rhys had seen the instructions to Tate, his main objectives, he wrote, were to free the Welsh from their English yoke. The French believed that they were the blood brothers of the Welsh, part of an old Celtic family, and thought quite naturally that the Welsh would flock to the banner of their fellow Celts. There was significant room for doubt; first, whether they would have successfully ended English rule in Wales; and second, whether the fate of Wales as a nation would have been better than it was now. Was it not true that a man's worst enemies are often his family? ('Onid gelynion gwaethaf dyn yn aml yw tylwyth ei dy ei hun').[58] The lesson from history of the past 100 years or so was that Wales was far better off even as one of the weakest of the British 'partners' ('as Lord Salisbury had said' 'ys dywed Arglwydd Salisbury') rather than as a partner of their fellow Celts in France.[59] Wales had rendered great service to England by repelling the French invaders but had received not even one word of thanks.[60]

Rhys continued in this vein, he mentioned a Jemima figure and her capture of the twelve Frenchmen, achieved to popular applause and acclaim, but her name in his story was Sali, not Jemima.[61] Chapter Nine was titled 'Mae Swn Magnelau yn y Gwynt a Swn Tabyrddau'n Curo', the familiar words from Ceiriog's *Y Baban Diwrnod Oed*. However, the most resonant aspect for the Welsh readership was the treatment of Captain Huws. Captain Huws was the rich shipowner and the main love interest who had been captured by Niclas Pencaer, the Wrecker (a 'Fleming' from 'waelod y sir', bottom of the county, not an Englishman), and then by the French. He thus appeared from the ranks of the French after the surrender and was immediately accused of treason through the recrimination of two of the Wrecker's henchmen.[62] It was only after a great deal of trouble and a full trial in Haverfordwest that he was cleared of the charges of treason. The testimony of the two henchmen was undermined by the criminal conduct of one and the flight of the other. The parallel with the historical treatment of Thomas John is unmistakable. Uncomfortable historical truths could be told at times in the form of fiction.

M. E. James looked forward, as she noted in her introduction to her work, to the centenary of the invasion in 1897.[63] That year, her novel was republished by the *Western Mail* as a 1 shilling Centenary Edition and promoted by the newspaper, pleased that the 'ladies' were entering into the spirt of the occasion.[64] 'This age of centenaries', James called it at the time. Centenaries had been celebrated since the late eighteenth century but the years after about 1880 saw a great surge in their incidence and popularity.[65] Particularly well celebrated in Wales were two centenaries for the Sunday School movement, depending on denominational affiliation, in 1880 and 1885.The French Invasion had been in a constant state of recall and memory as well as forgetfulness since 1797, but this fashion for celebrating centenaries brought it to prominence again. In the arrangements for the centenary that commenced in early 1896, we see a movement from history to heritage. Heritage, a selective use of the past for contemporary purposes, was and is a highly political process, malleable, depending on the needs of power and often subject to contestation.[66] Political tensions were evident from the first meetings, a complex connection of history, memory and identity, and a power game of local politics, gender and culture played out in Pembrokeshire and across West Wales but with implications for London and the Empire. The practical preparations for the 1897 centenary commenced as early as 1895, if not earlier.[67] From the start tensions existed between Haverfordwest and Fishguard. A Fishguard correspondent noted in January 1896 that the centenary would be celebrated at Haverfordwest by a grand banquet and hoped that the inhabitants of Fishguard would not be 'backward on such an important and interesting occasion'.[68] Leaders of the Fishguard cause did emerge, such as the Revd Morlais Davies, minister at Tabernacl, the Independent chapel in Fishguard, and the doctor and local Fishguard Councillor Englishman Dr H. Lawton Swete. Councillor Swete was keen to involve the military and invite the Castlemartin Yeomanry to hold their annual review and inspection at Fishguard in the summer of 1897. Others wanted a statue to Jemima Nicholas, 'the bravest of her sex'.[69] The planning committee was held at Fishguard Town Hall on 24 February 1896 and concluded with the establishment of an organising committee of fifteen men. Dr Swete was its joint secretary and would prove to be the most influential member of the committee.[70]

The proposed centenary celebration reignited interest in the invasion. The story of the invasion, the London-Welsh press noted, was on the lips ('ar wefus') of every mother and daughter in the counties of Pembrokeshire and Cardiganshire while Ceiriog's poem *The Day-Old Baby* had made the details of the invasion known throughout the whole of Wales.[71] Out of respect to their mothers and to keep the story alive, the London-Welsh newspaper recommended that all young girls ('ein merched ieuainc') should bring the red shawl back to fashion and make the 24 February a day to remember Jemima, mothers and the red-shawled women throughout Wales.[72]

In October 1896, a public meeting was held.[73] It was now not a proposed celebration, but a 'movement' that had received several letters of support.[74] A letter from the solicitor of the North Pembrokeshire and Fishguard railway was read out by the chairman, it supported the scheme of a new promenade, would grant it the necessary land (Windy Hill Farm) and would undertake to construct the walk over that part. This promenade was to be known as the 'French Walk'.[75] There were dissenting voices, but not in public. The following conversation was heard in Newport (Trefdraeth) in November 1896 and recorded:

> Churchman: I should like to see the channel fleet in action in Fishguard Bay on the celebration day of the landing of the French.
> Baptist: I would rather have an association preaching service and the texts of the preachers to be 'Thou shalt not bear false witness against thy neighbour'.[76]

Notwithstanding the few pockets of resistance, the centenary celebrations were highly popular. Various ways of commemoration often worked together in a multimedia layering of text, music and image. The French Invasion story in popular culture made the most of its Welsh and French characters and occurred not only in Fishguard but in places throughout south Wales. This came to the fore in the musical presentations of the story. The operetta *Glaniad y Ffrancod*, or *Madam Dumas*, was particularly popular with church and chapel operatic ensembles in the Amman and Swansea Valleys, and then spread across the south Wales coalfield. It had already been performed thirteen times in June 1896 when it was performed in Cwmllynfell by the Cwmllynfell Operatic Society led by the composer of the music D. W. Rowlands from Upper Cwmtwrch. They intended taking it to Fishguard itself in the next summer in time for the centenary celebrations.[77] *The Stage*, however, warned that if the libretto score was only in Welsh, it would not 'travel very far beyond gallant little Wales'.[78]

Public awareness of the French invasion increased as 1897 approached but the *South Wales Daily Post* was concerned that there continued to be 'confusion in the public mind as to the precise character of the event itself'.[79] In particular it would be interesting to know what foundation there was, if any, for 'the popular version which attributes the surrender of the French to the fear produced by a body of Welsh women in red cloaks marching around a hill'.[80] During the centenary, serious attempts were being made by the *South Wales Daily Post*, *The Western Mail* and *Y Geninen* to position the French Invasion within the historical complexities of Ireland, Hoche and Napoleon. The *South Wales Daily Post* was very doubtful concerning the historicity of the event and its historical importance, the resemblance of the women marching around the hill so much of a Gilbert and Sullivan comic opera that 'standard historians' could be forgiven for ignoring it. The idea that this was a serious expeditionary force the newspaper thought absurd.[81] *Y Geninen* précised Laws in Welsh, criticised Ceiriog for his lack of historical accuracy in his famous poem, and gave a full account, including a reference to Mary Williams ('chamdriniwyd hi' ('she was maltreated')) who they mistakenly thought was receiving her pension from the French Government not the British.[82] The *South Wales Daily Post* and *Y Geninen* concluded that the invasion, despite the popular attention, was not worthy of serious historical attention. 'Standard historians' seemed to take no notice of it. But there was another reason why the *South Wales Daily Post* was not taking the invasion seriously: its rivalry with the more liberal *Cardiff Times*.

The Welsh press was divided over the centenary. The *Cardiff Times and South Wales Weekly News* produced an impressive Centenary Anniversary Special on 27 February 1897 – 8,000 words of commentary and history and coverage of the centenary celebrations. In its introduction it noted the consensus among Welsh and English writers that the instantaneous uprising of the Welsh in the three south-west Wales counties was a patriotic exploit well worth celebrating; however, 'a limited section' – for reasons best known to themselves – thought only to disparage or sneer at this 'grand outburst and effort of Welsh patriotism'. This was 'a bad survival of the old English Tory spirit a hundred years ago'.[83] The newspaper that the *Cardiff Times* had in its sights was its Tory rival, the *South Wales Daily Post*. The *South Wales Daily Post* had questioned the historical authenticity of the invasion and its standing in January 1897; this was the only article, apart from a letter in the 'Post Bag' in August that it published on the Fishguard Invasion commemoration that entire centenary year. It seemed that there were political reasons for this silence as well as uncertainty over the history. Other newspapers in Wales printed pages on the celebrations and on the historical background. *The Western Mail* tended to believe this was an event of primary importance to west Wales but not to Wales as a whole.[84] But it did have its own investment in the centenary; namely, the centenary edition of M. E. James's historical novel *The Fishguard Invasion or Three days in 1797*, which the *Western Mail* was promoting. Its competitor, the *Cardiff Times*, was simultaneously serialising another Fishguard Invasion historical romance, advertised as '*GWENNY VAUGHAN: or THE FRENCH INVASION. A Pembrokeshire Story of Pirates and Smugglers*'.[85] Written by Gwyn Meredith, it was serialised in both the *Cardiff Times* and the *South Wales Weekly News* as a story of all Wales significance.[86] *Gwenny Vaughan* was advertised as a story of a 'happily frustrated invasion' involving local actors 'whose names are now the traditional heritage of the Welsh people'.[87] It was described 'as a contribution, and a very true and exact one, towards the national fiction which we are often told has not yet been written for Wales'.[88] There was far more involved than commemoration of an event 100 years previously.

The *tour de force* of newspaper coverage of the February centenary events was undoubtedly that of the *Cardiff Times*. After criticising the limited section that wished to belittle the grand outpouring of patriotism that the event represented, the *Cardiff Times* went to the trouble of commissioning a new history of the invasion from an unnamed Pembrokeshire writer, who may very well have been M. E. James. This writer did not claim to 'possess special qualifications for narrating this story of Welsh patriotism and manhood' but was acquainted with Peter Davies who during the later part of his life was landlord of the Castle Hotel Fishguard and who served as colour-sergeant in the Fishguard Fencibles under Knox. The writer had received the story on several occasions from Peter Davies himself and furthermore was 'well acquainted' with Henry Lewis Williams (H. L. Ap Gwilym) who had also taken part in resisting the invaders, but was at the time of the invasion a 'gentleman farmer residing near Mathry'. As if this pedigree was not enough, the writer's grandfather and father were living in Pencaer at the time of the invasion and, like so many others, had to flee.

The new version of the story follows the established Ap Gwilym narrative quite closely, with additions that suggest recourse to other oral traditions and written sources.[89] This new account expressed the patriotism of the local people (men and women), a Welsh patriotism that aligned more closely with notions of patriotism and national pride in the assertive times of the 1890s, when Welsh institutions such as the University of Wales and the National Museum were coming into being or becoming more established and when the Cymru Fydd movement was at its most aspirational. Cymru Fydd was a patriotic movement, literally 'Wales of the future', known in English as 'Young Wales', formed in London in 1886, primarily by emigré Welshmen, on the model of Young Ireland. Initially a cultural and educative movement, Cymru Fydd became, under the influence of T. E. Ellis and Lloyd George, a political campaign, Ellis underlining 'the necessity of declaring for self-government'.[90] This new account of the Invasion story was popular Welshness in action.[91] It was also at this time that the red cloaks of the women became associated with Welsh national costume, culminating in the almost complete takeover of local dress by national costume during the Great War.

The *Cardiff Times*, as well as the history, gave an account of the celebrations. The Revd Parry Davies who took charge of the procession and the service on the Sands, proclaimed this as an event 'of which we, as a Welsh nation, need not be ashamed'. He trusted that the descendants would not be behind their ancestors 'in patriotism in love of home and country'.[92] *Tarian y Gweithiwr*, in a pointed rejoinder to the *Cardiff Times*, complained that their Centenary Special had omitted the 'name of a hero who should not be forgotten: Jemima Nicholas'.[93]

Where the local press saw neighbours, friends, and families, contested and uncontested, but patriotic, the English Press by and large saw 'Gallant Little Wales'. The parameters of the concept of 'Gallant Little Wales' as a brave martial country were set as much by the French Invasion as by other Welsh military encounters past, present or future. Gallant Little Wales showed that she was not to be caught napping, and what she was made of.[94] The worst effect of the invasion according to the *Worthing Gazette* was 'the alarm occasioned in London'.[95] *The Penny Illustrated Paper* recalled the work of the late Wilkie Collins who corrected the impression that England had last been invaded in the dim and distant past by narrating the story of the 'Welsh wives, in their red shawls'. These incidents had now been forgotten, 'notwithstanding the eminent novelist's recital of them' but were still cherished in 'the locality of their happening'. The newspaper looked forward to the summer and the full celebrations and gave an illustration of Fishguard: 'a prettily situated, quaint little place' well worth seeing in the summer 'with many of the feminine inhabitants attired in the same old garments as those which caused the French to imagine them a body of infantry'.[96]

The local press focused on the February celebrations and avoided the extremes of the English male gaze.[97] *The Welshman* ran a piece titled 'How England was saved by the Women of Pembrokeshire', an irreverent, half comical-half serious use of the Fishguard women story for political purposes. The French Invasion had conferred a lasting renown on the women of Pembrokeshire 'to whom England is under an untold obligation to which she has never responded'.[98]

The *Western Mail*, on the other hand, adopted the opposite political position. Some of the English press had reported that both the Welsh and English national anthems were sung in Fishguard on the 24 February.[99] The *Western Mail* was having none of it: it was perfectly wrong to 'invest "Hen Wlad fy Nhadau"' with the dignity of a Welsh national anthem. This it has never been, and never, it was to be hoped, would be: it had no poetry, little reason and rhyme and was nothing more than a song that belonged more in 'wild Saxon times' expressing disloyalty and revenge and opening old sores that should have healed. Wales, 'a peace-loving and law-abiding people under the beneficent rule of the best of sovereigns' deserved better, 'an anthem worthy of Wales and of the occasion'.[100] *The Western Mail* did not cover the summer celebrations.

There was no doubting the local pride in the role of the Fishguard women, even if their role in the February centenary celebrations had been limited to the banquet in the evening of the 24 February. At the banquet, the High Sheriff of Pembrokeshire was flanked by his wife and by Miss James of Tenby of the *Fishguard Invasion or Three days in 1797* fame. At the head table was a Welsh motto tribute to 'The Brave Women of 1797' and the toast of the evening was 'The Heroes and Heroines of 1797', which met with an enthusiastic reception when proposed by the chair.[101] The women of Fishguard also figured prominently on the commemoration medal that had been struck and was selling well (see Figures 8 and 9).[102]

Figure 8: Commemorative medal. Text reads: '1897 Centenary of the last foreign invasion of Britain 1797. In commemoration of the surrender of the French on Carreg Wastad Point Pencaer Feby 24th 1797'

Figure 9: Reverse side of the commemorative medal, with an image of the Welsh women on Carreg Wastad Point. Text reads: '*A laddo a leddir*', and '1797 *Fishguard* 1897'

The commemoration medal is a visual and tangible embodiment of what the Invasion meant to the people of Fishguard and district who commissioned it. First, the people of 1897 were clear what they were celebrating – the surrender of the French – even though they were not sure where it had taken place (the reference to Carreg Gwastad as the point of surrender when it was in fact just the landing place). Second, they were aware and proud of the 'Last Foreign Invasion of Britain' claim, at the same time framing it in the context of Welsh patriotism with leeks circling the edges of the medal. Third, the people of 1897 gave prominence to the role of the women with their pitchforks, there is no mention of Cawdor or any male military figure on the medal. Lastly, '*A Laddo a Leddir*' ('Who slays shall be slain') is a stark reminder that the people of 1897 were commemorating not a picturesque romantic farce (although there were elements of that) but a bloody reciprocal encounter where people on both sides were the killers and the killed.

Not for public consumption or celebration were the familial memories of the trauma experienced by ancestors long dead. At the centenary, a writer recalled the very vivid accounts given by members of his own family in his youth, of the panic that the landing of the French caused throughout the counties of Pembroke, Cardigan and even as far as Carmarthen, and the devices adopted by some to escape the necessity of serving that the invasion demanded, even to the extent of personal maiming.[103] The *Herald of Peace* gave opportunities for the public expression of painful memory for an anti-war cause. But there is no reason to doubt these memories, the memory of fear persisted within families and communities and a lasting sense of trauma.[104]

The prominent positioning of the women was always contested, and the challenge in April 1897 came from the usual source: Pembrokeshire men. The Pembroke County Club was the London club for the gentlemen from Pembrokeshire. In April 1897 it met for its fourth anniversary at the Holborn restaurant, London. The great and the good of Pembrokeshire in London and London Welsh society were there. The second toast was to 'The Memory of Lord Cawdor and the County Forces in 1797' and was entrusted to Mr Edward Laws who admitted that 'the legend about the heroic conduct of the Fishguard ladies, which he trusted they all believed implicitly, had, however, no foundation in fact'.[105]

Laws had never been an enthusiast for the story of the Fishguard women. In an article of 1883, he had mentioned that only the 'ill natured' declared that the women in their high hats and red whittles had assisted Cawdor by their resemblance to regiments of the line. Laws preferred to believe that Cawdor defeated the French with the assistance of men and not women.[106] Laws was now explicitly and publicly (but only to selected Pembrokeshire men) denying that the story had a basis in fact. However, he did provide a reasoned case for his assertion.[107] The availability of the Cawdor diary from the Cawdor family changed the terms of the historical enquiry. Cawdor had nothing to say about the women of Fishguard, the absence of any reference by Cawdor was, by inference, the reason for Laws' assertion that there was no factual basis to the story of the 'Fishguard ladies'. The account of Laws's toast at the Pembrokeshire Dinner in the *Cardiff Times* was slightly different to that in the *Western Mail*. Mr Laws, 'Tenby historian': 'in his care for historical accuracy, demolished the pretty story (*which, however he desired his hearers to continue to believe*) of the part played by the women of Fishguard in defeating the invaders'[108] [my italics].

The story of the women of Fishguard was a matter of belief, more important than historical accuracy. Edward Laws was a consummate politician and public Pembrokeshire figure as well as historian. In 1899, Laws would become High Sheriff of Pembrokeshire. He was a military man, and the Castlemartin Yeomanry were, as he mentioned as they were departing for South Africa, his 'dear old friends, in whom he took a real, deep and personal interest'.[109] There was a tension between his loyalty to the reputation of the military, his historical care and the requirement not to upset communities like Fishguard. Fishguard had made the 'Brave Women of Fishguard' its parish motto and would give the women prominence in their memorabilia such as the commemorative medal and in their celebratory processions in 1897. He may have realised the damage to his popular standing in Pembrokeshire that the public debunking of the story would do.

The centenary events in Fishguard in February had been the focus for local celebrations, the main events for people from near and far were to take place with the better weather in July 1897. The Great Western Railway would be offering cheap return tickets from many stations in south Wales for the duration of the festivities. Several hundreds of people were expected from Aberdare alone.[110] One commentator observed: 'Never in the memory of anyone now living has there been seen in any part of Pembrokeshire, so many people thronged together.'[111] The whole town was metamorphosed in the space of a few hours, commemorative medals were distributed and the Royal Oak emblazoned with the Cawdor crest. It was from The Royal Oak that the procession started for Pencaer.

Dr Swete used a numbering on cards system to get the order of the processions together and off they went, the first out the Pembroke Dock Volunteer Band. The second out were 100 ladies all young, robed in Welsh costume, thought to be true to that of 1797.

Figure 10: Photograph showing women of the area in traditional dress posing for a photograph before the parade[112]

The numbers on cards can be seen in a photograph of the time (see Figure 10). Some of the hats that they wore were heirlooms again, with imagined if not real connection to 1797. With the young ladies were 'two gentlemen with distinctly feminine features, neatly attired in the orthodox dress'.[113] The Cardiff based, Tory supporting *Evening Express* suggested, with sarcasm, that the procession of the ladies in Welsh costume was 'a sight for a Cymru Fyddite'.[114] The drum major used a rusty musket that had been used at the time. It was nearly a two-mile pageant and 'many a snapshot was taken'. The 'point, in which the interest centred' was the spot where the stone ('a boulder of native igneous rock from Trehowel mountain', 7-foot long, 3.5-foot wide and about 2.25 tons in weight) was unveiled (see Figure 11). Both languages recall the simple fact of the landing (not an invasion) and the date, but the Welsh comes first, as it should:

> 1897
> CARREG GOFFA
> GLANIAD Y FFRANCOD
> CHWEFROR 22 1797
> —
> MEMORIAL STONE
> OF THE
> LANDING OF THE FRENCH
> FEBRUARY 22 1797

Local MPs and other significant political figures such as Mabon (William Abraham, MP for Rhondda) and David Lloyd George did not make an appearance. The Revd Dr Parry Davies, a local Anglican, took charge and made much of the absence of the local MPs, saying that 'thereby England has declared that she must cry "Halt" to our proceedings'.[115] He guessed that the reasons for their absence was nervousness about upsetting France in the informal *Entente Cordiale* of the late 1890s, but as Dr Parry Davies noted: 'we are not here today to abuse the French people – (Hear, Hear) – nor are we here today to slander the French nation (Hear Hear).'[116] They were there simply to unveil this memorial stone (the *garreg goffa*) in memory of their ancestors, men and women, in defence of their hearths and home. Carreg Wastad was the 'scene and place of the last invasion of Great Britain by a foreign foe'.[117] The presence of 7,000 Welsh people was a celebration of a democratic folk movement that,

Figure 11: Postcard early 1900s showing the large memorial stone placed at Carreg Wastad to commemorate the centenary of the French Invasion

with its heroes and heroines, had captured the imagination of a nation, without any support from the British state. Poetry both in English and Welsh was recited, old ballads of the period were rediscovered and Thomas Propert's map of 1798, depicting the main sites on Pencaer affected by the invasion and the positions of the opposing sides, republished as 'one of the most interesting souvenirs of the centenary celebrations'.[118] Memories were rekindled and new claims made about who precisely made the first sighting.[119] Queen Victoria's Diamond Jubilee was also in 1897, but it was overshadowed by the Centenary of the French Invasion in Fishguard that year.

The past provided tangible and intangible assets. The hats and costumes worn by the young girls in the procession were in many cases family heirlooms passed down from mother to daughter, even if they were not as old as the invasion itself. Their stories about Jemima were important intangible assets passed down and retold through oral tradition, as the *Evening Express* put it: 'the Welsh people of the neighbourhood still nurse a vivid recollection of the thrilling stories which they had heard of the terrible anxieties of their grandfathers and grandmothers during the stay of the 1500 foreigners.'[120]

We have a rare example of one such family oral tradition set down, for the first time, in writing, and coincidentally in 1897. The author was Ferrar Fenton (1832–1920), the grandson of the historic tourist Richard Fenton. Ferrar Fenton was an antiquarian in his own right, linguist and biblical scholar. He writes of the traditions about the landing told by his own family and by the local people. One of the community memories that he records for the first time was of 'a powerful old giantess of six feet high', who had been one of the 'defenders of the walls'.[121] The French were captured in twos and threes, the giantess captured two while they were drinking from a *pistyll* ('spring'). This entire account was, Ferrar claimed, taken entirely from traditions and wholly without consulting any written or printed record.[122]

Endnotes

1 *The Cambrian* (25 September 1874), 3.
2 This was true, Jemima had two brothers and nephews and nieces, but no children of her own.
3 *The Cambrian* (25 September 1874), 3.
4 'Arwresau Cymru', *Y Gwladgarwr* (17 November 1876), 2.
5 *Weekly Mail* (3 February 1883), 2.

6   'The Pembroke Yeomanry Cavalry', *The Tenby Observer* (28 June 1883), 3.
7   *Western Mail* (30 November 1883), 3.
8   *Western Mail* (4 December 1883), 4.
9   Robert Thomas Jenkins, 'MORGAN, OWEN (Morien; 1836?–1921), journalist and miscellaneous writer', *Dictionary of Welsh Biography*, https://biography.wales/article/s1-MORG-OWE-1836 (last accessed 18 December 2020). For Morien and his bardo-druidism and his intellectual context, see Marion Löffler, *The Literary and Historical Legacy of Iolo Morganwg 1826–1926* (Cardiff, 2007), pp. 37, 85, 94, 115, 127.
10 *Western Mail* (4 December 1883), 4.
11 *Western Mail* (4 December 1883), 4.
12 Thomas Knox, *Some account of the proceedings that took place on the landing of the French near Fishguard* (London, 1800).
13 There was only one letter from Knox to Portland during the time of the landing, dated 24 February 1797, no. 9 in the appendix to his *Some account of the proceedings*, pp. 45–7. There is no mention of any women.
14 H. L. Ap Gwilym, *An Authentic Account of the Invasion by French Troops on Carrig Gwasted Point near Fishguard* (Haverfordwest, 1842), p. 21.
15 Ap Gwilym, *An Authentic Account*, p. 21.
16 'The Cambrian Archaeological Association Meetings at Fishguard', *Western Mail* (18 August 1883), 2.
17 *Western Mail* (18 August 1883), 2.
18 *Western Mail* (18 August 1883), 2.
19 Edward Laws, 'The French Landing at Fishguard', *Archaeologia Cambrensis*, 4th ser., 14/56 (October 1883), 311–24.
20 Ann Sayer, 'Review of The History of Little England Beyond Wales by Edward Laws (1837–1913)', www.pembrokeshirehistoricalsociety.co.uk/papers-from-the-past-2// (last accessed 4 August 2024).
21 Edward Laws, *The History of Little England Beyond Wales, the Non-Kymric Colony Settled in Pembrokeshire* (London, 1888).
22 Laws, 'The French Landing at Fishguard', 311.
23 Laws, 'The French Landing at Fishguard', 316.
24 'Cambrian Archaeological Association', *South Wales Daily News* (17 August 1883), 2.
25 Laws, 'The French Landing at Fishguard', 314.
26 Laws, 'The French Landing at Fishguard', 315.
27 Twm ap Iorwerth, 'Some Pembrokeshire Worthies', *Herald of Wales* (14 February 1885), 4.
28 Twm ap Iorwerth, 'Some Pembrokeshire Worthies', 4.
29 Twm ap Iorwerth, 'Some Pembrokeshire Worthies', 4.
30 Twm ap Iorwerth, 'Some Pembrokeshire Worthies', 4.
31 Laws, *The History of Little England beyond Wales*, pp. 368–74.
32 Evan David Jones, 'JONES, EVAN (Gurnos; 1840–1903), Congregational and Baptist minister, poet, critic, lecturer, and eisteddfod conductor',

Dictionary of Welsh Biography. https://biography.wales/article/s-JONE-EVA-1840 (last accessed 22 December 2020).

33 See, for example, *South Wales Daily News* (22 August 1891), 4, 6.
34 *Merthyr Times* and *Dowlais Times* and *Aberdare Echo* (3 November 1893), 5.
35 *South Wales Daily News* (16 October 1891), 7.
36 *Evening Express* (22 June 1901), 2.
37 Tessa Morris-Suzuki, quoting Pierre Nora, in *The Past Within Us: Media, Memory, History* (London, 2005), p. 22.
38 'Red Shawls', *Notes and Queries*, 4/10 (October 1872), 331.
39 Article from *Blackwood's Magazine*, republished in several newspapers, for example, *South Wales Daily News* (31 August 1875), 2, 5.
40 Ap Gwilym, *An Authentic Account*, p. 2.
41 'Infirmary Collections', *The Pembrokeshire Herald* (30 November 1883), 3.
42 'Memorial of the "Red Flannel Shawl Brigade" at Fishguard', *Weekly Mail* (5 February 1887), 7.
43 *The Tenby Observer Weekly List* (25 April 1889), 5.
44 *The London Kelt* (16 February 1895), 3.
45 Anon [Margaret Ellen James], *The Fishguard Invasion of 1797. Some Passages taken from the Diary of the Reverend Daniel Rowlands, sometime Vicar of Llanfihangelpenybont* (London, 1892). See also Rita Singer, *Some Thoughts on Margaret Ellen James: The Fishguard Invasion by the French in 1792 (1892)*, https://bydbach.hcommons.org/some-thoughts-on-margaret-ellen-james-the-fishguard-invasion-by-the-french-in-1797-1892/ (last accessed 4 August 2024).
46 All citations are from the centenary edition of 1897, titled *The Fishguard Invasion by the French in 1797*. M. E. James, *The Fishguard Invasion by the French in 1797*, centenary edn (London, 1897), p. 9.
47 James, *The Fishguard Invasion by the French in 1797*, p. 9.
48 James, *The Fishguard Invasion by the French in 1797*, pp. 9–10. The death of the famous Pembrokeshire centenarian was widely reported in the press; for example, *Pembrokeshire Herald* (13 February 1891), 3; *Baner ac Amserau Cymru* (18 February 1891), 10.
49 Emile De Bonnechose, *Lazare Hoche: General de Chef ... sous la Convention et le Directoire 1793–1797* (Paris, 1867).
50 James, *The Fishguard Invasion by the French in 1797*, p. 129.
51 James, *The Fishguard Invasion by the French in* 1797, p. 188.
52 J. Aaron, 'Hoydens of Wild Wales: Representations of Welsh Women in Victorian and Edwardian Fiction', *Welsh Writing in English: A Yearbook of Critical Essays* (1995), p. 29. See also Rita Singer, https://bydbach.hcommons.org/some-thoughts-on-margaret-ellen-james-the-fishguard-invasion-by-the-french-in-1797-1892/ (last accessed 4 August 2024).
53 James, *The Fishguard Invasion by the French in 1797*, p. 147.
54 For example, *Glasgow Herald* (15 December 1892), 9.
55 For example, D. K. Broster, *Ships in the Bay!* (London, 1931), Charlotte Grey, *The Last Invasion* (London, 1982).

56 T. Robin Chapman, *The Oxford Literary History of Wales, vol. 2: Writing in Welsh 1740–2010: A Troubled Heritage* (Oxford, 2020), p.11
57 'Mae son amdanynt', *Papur Pawb* (22 September 1894), 4; 'Catrawd y shawls cochion', *Papur Pawb* (22 September 1894), 9.
58 'Peryglon Pencaer. NEU FFWDAN Y FFRANCOD YN ABERGWAUN PENNOD XI AMCAN Y FFRANCOD YN DOD', *Papur Pawb* (22 September 1894), 9.
59 See Glenn Dymond and Hugo Deadman, 'The Salisbury Doctrine', *House of Lords Library Note*, LLN 2006/006 (2006), p. 12.
60 'Peryglon Pencaer', Pennod XV, *Papur Pawb* (20 October 1894), 9.
61 'Peryglon Pencaer, Pennod XVI', *Papur Pawb* (27 October 1894), 9–10; 'Pennod XV11', *Papur Pawb* (3 November 1894), 6.
62 'Peryglon Pencaer, Pennod XVII', *Papur Pawb* (3 November 1894), 6.
63 James, *The Fishguard Invasion by the French in 1797*, pp. 38–9.
64 20 February 1897. The binder's title was *The Fishguard Invasion or Three Days in 1797* and it was printed at the Tudor Printing Works in Cardiff, published by the *Western Mail* of Fleet Street, London. The name of the author appeared only on the centenary edition, not on the 1892 first edition, and simply as 'M. E. James', with no recognition of gender.
65 R. Quinault, 'The Cult of the Centenary *c*.1784-1914', *Historical Research*, 7/176 (1998), 303–23.
66 Sara McDowell, 'Heritage, Memory and Identity', in Brian Graham and Peter Howard (eds), *The Ashgate Research Companion to Heritage and Identity* (Aldershot, 2008), pp. 37–54.
67 The first reference to what should be done in the centenary and the first use of the term itself *'chan'mlwyddiant'* (centenary), 'At Olygydd y County Echo. Glaniad y Ffrancod', *The County Echo* (26 December 1895), 2.
68 *The County Echo* (16 January 1896), 2.
69 *The County Echo* (30 January 1896), 2.
70 *Cardiff Times and South Wales Weekly News* (29 February 1896), 7.
71 *London Kelt* (29 February 1896), 6.
72 *London Kelt* (29 February 1896), 6.
73 Accounts of this meeting appear in several newspapers; see, for example, *South Wales Daily News* (26 October 1896), 5; (9 November 1896), 6.
74 *South Wales Daily News* (9 November 1896), 6.
75 *South Wales Daily News* (9 November 1896), 6; 'Can'mlwyddiaeth Tiriad y Ffrancod yn Mhencaer, ger Aber-gwaun', *Tarian y Gweithiwr* (26 November 1896), 3.
76 *The County Echo* (19 November 1896), 3.
77 'Glaniad y Ffrancod yn Abergwaun', *Tarian y Gweithiwr* (2 July 1896), 3; see also *The Musical Herald* (1 June 1896), 188.
78 *The Stage* quoted in *The County Echo* (16 July 1896), 3. The score was eventually published in both English and Welsh in 1908. It continued to

be popular into the 1930s and was published again by Snell of Swansea in around 1934.
79 *South Wales Daily Post* (5 January 1897), 2.
80 *South Wales Daily Post* (5 January 1897), 2.
81 *South Wales Daily Post* (5 January 1897), 2.
82 *Y Geninen*, 15/1 (Ionawr 1897), 64.
83 'French in Pembrokeshire: Centenary Anniversary. Story of the Landing Retold', *Cardiff Times and South Wales Weekly News* (27 February 1897), 6.
84 'An Abortive Invasion', *Western Mail* (20 February 1897), 4.
85 *Cardiff Times* (19 December 1896), 4.
86 Serialised in the *Cardiff Times* each week from 19 December 1896 to 17 April 1897 as 'Gwenny Vaughan, or the Fishguard Invasion'. This novel was never published as a book.
87 *Cardiff Times* (28 November 1896), 3.
88 *South Wales Echo* (15 December 1896), 2.
89 *Cardiff Times* (27 February 1897), 6.
90 J. Graham Jones, 'Review of Dewi Rowland Hughes, *Cymru Fydd* (Cardiff, 2006)', *Journal of Liberal History*, 57 (Winter 2007–8), 50.
91 See Martin Johnes, *Wales: England's Colony* (Cardigan, 2019), pp. 126–42.
92 *Cardiff Times* (27 February 1897), 6.
93 *Tarian y Gweithiwr* (4 March 1897), 5.
94 *Globe* (25 February 1897), 7; *Worthing Gazette* (3 March 1897), 8.
95 *Worthing Gazette* (3 March 1897), 8.
96 'The Latest Invasion of "Gallant Little Wales"', *The Penny Illustrated Paper* (27 February 1897), 6.
97 *The Cardigan Observer and General Advertiser* (27 February 1897), 1.
98 *The Welshman* (12 March 1897), 6.
99 For example, *London Evening Standard* (25 February 1897), 3.
100 *Western Mail* (26 February 1897), 4.
101 *Cardiff Times* (27 February 1897), 6.
102 *Cardiff Times* (27 February 1897), 6.
103 'The French Invasion of 1797', *The Herald of Peace and International Arbitration* (1 December 1897), 335.
104 For the importance of trauma in folk history with reference to remembrance of the 1798 Rebellion in Ireland, see Radvan Markus, *Echoes of the Rebellion: The Year 1798 in Twentieth-Century Irish Fiction and Drama* (Bern and Oxford, 2015), p. 56.
105 'Pembrokeshire Men in London', *Weekly Mail* (3 April 1897), 8.
106 Laws, 'The French Landing at Fishguard', p. 316.
107 'Pembrokeshire Men in London', *Weekly Mail* (3 April 1897), 8.
108 'Pembrokeshire Dinner in London', *Cardiff Times* (3 April 1897), 3.
109 'Feted at Tenby, Pembroke and Haverfordwest', *Haverfordwest and Milford Haven Telegraph* (28 February 1900), 2. The Pembrokeshire Yeomanry fought in the Second South African War, at the dinner given at Tenby in their honour, Laws gave details of his family's extensive

military connections: his son, his nephew and two of his cousins had been involved in the Second South African War.
110 *South Wales Daily News* (3 July 1897), 6.
111 J. W. Maurice, *History of the French Invasion of Fishguard in 1797* (Fishguard, no date but approx. 1910), p. 45.
112 'Welsh Ladies in the French Centenary Procession at Fishguard in 1897', NLW, Album 1048, PB 7441.
113 'Centenary Rejoicings', *South Wales Daily News* (7 July 1897), 6.
114 'French Invasion. Fishguard Celebrations', *Evening Express* (7 July 1897), 4.
115 *Evening Express* (7 July 1897), 4.
116 *Evening Express* (7 July 1897), 4.
117 *Evening Express* (7 July 1897), 4.
118 Thomas Propert's map, reprinted as a 'centenary' souvenir can be seen in E. H. Stuart Jones, *The Last Invasion* (Cardiff, 1950), p. 101. The centenary map is mentioned in the *South Wales Daily News* (6 July 1897), 4; Ebenezer Richards's ballad of the time is transcribed in full in *The London Kelt* on 20 March 1897, p. 3, and 3 April 1897, p. 4. A new poem by N. Neander Richards on 'Canmlwyddiant Glaniad y Ffrancod yn Abergwaun,' appeared in the *Glamorgan Free Press* (24 July 1897), 7.
119 *Cardiff Times* (27 February 1897), 6.
120 *Evening Express* (7 July 1897), 4.
121 Ferrar Fenton, 'Landing of the French at Fishguard in 1797', *Pembrokeshire Antiquities* (Solva, 1897), p. 66.
122 Fenton, 'Landing of the French at Fishguard in 1797', pp. 63–7.

Chapter 7

New Prosperity, New History, an Old Story, 1897–1913

The French Invasion played a special role in the history and identity of the Pembrokeshire Yeomanry. The word 'Fishguard' itself was emblazoned on their cap badges. Their memories of the past deepened through their own long history of service, as the longest surviving Yeomanry regiment in Wales. They were popular, especially in the south of the county. Shortly after the outbreak of the South African War in 1899, the regiment became known as the Pembrokeshire (Castlemartin) Imperial Yeomanry.[1] In February 1900, the regiment volunteered for the Second South African War. Before departure, they were given the freedom of Tenby. At the ceremony, weapons taken from the French at Fishguard were on view, a ceremonial and symbolic link between the present and the past.[2] Memories of Fishguard and of the Fishguard women were recalled, symbolically at least, as ordinary Welsh men and women celebrated their men's bravery for going to the South African War. The red shawl became a symbol in some quarters for imperial success. Red shawls were hung out of the windows in the mining community of Llansamlet near Swansea by the women in celebration of the relief of Ladysmith and anti-Boer songs sung to the tune of '*Hen Wlad fy Nhadau*'.[3] As Kenneth Morgan has observed at the high noon of Anglo-Saxon imperialism, some

Welshmen, too, sought to claim their place in the sun.[4] Also some Welsh women.

Rowlands's Welsh language operetta about the Invasion, *Glaniad y Ffrancod* continued to be popular throughout the Edwardian period. Many of the inhabitants of the coalfield communities had come from rural Welsh-speaking west Wales, and the operetta was culturally and emotionally relevant and offered much-needed comic relief based on their memories and oral history, without threatening Nonconformist scruples. In February 1901 the Blaenrhondda Dramatic Society gave 'two good character performances of the "French Invasion at Fishguard"' at the Public Hall, Pentre and also at the Public Hall, Treherbert.[5] It was played to a crowded house and made a great impression later in Pontardawe in the Swansea Valley in May 1903.[6]

The popularity of the operetta rested on the comic interplay between genders and caricatures of local Welsh and national identities. The comic highlight was the performance of the two Cardigan farmers, based on the T. Cunllo Griffiths characters 'Dai a Wil', full of bravery and bravado and bluster, who 'each time they appeared, elicited roars of laughter'.[7] However, the dramatic highlight was the scene where 'the Welsh women marched round with red shawls'. Each national group was introduced with their own musical accompaniment; the Welsh farmers, including the two 'bold' Cardiganshire farmers, were led in to the familiar and patriotic strains of *Hen Wlad fy Nhadau*.[8] The story of the French Invasion rendered this way proved a popular form of entertainment, interplaying comedy, drama and humour, performed by local amateur music and drama groups and artistes.[9]

During this period Fishguard prospered, largely through its connections with Ireland. Its prospects were celebrated in the Irish newspapers as well as in the Welsh.[10] The advent of the railway to Fishguard developed its commerce and made it a great power in Wales;[11] a parallel development at Rosslare completed the railway connection to Waterford. After legal wrangling between various railway companies, the Great Western Railway (GWR) effectively took over control of the developments at both the harbour and railway in 1900. The chairman of the GWR was a great grandson of Lord Cawdor and this family link was not lost on commentators and observers in narrating the story of the new harbour and the new route between Wales and Ireland. The *Cambrian News*, a newspaper that covered mid-Wales, was impressed by the scale of the investment and the engineering works that involved blasting tons of rock from the cliff. This was also the place where the French had landed it recounted: 'Immortal story! Would that the French had landed at Aberayron'.[12]

New prosperity brought in new people. A Catholic mission was established in Fishguard in 1899. The following decade saw a great influx of Irish labourers and their families in connection with the construction of Fishguard port by the GWR. A new town was built in Goodwick, Harbour Village, prompting one newspaper to comment that such 'a hasty construction of stone and mortar' had never been known before in Wales.[13] Bethany English Congregational chapel in Goodwick opened in 1905, and Bethel Baptist chapel was built in 1908 in Fishguard for the English-speaking Nonconformists. The old stories may have given comfort and reassurance to those who felt threatened by the changes brought about by the new prosperity, not least the influx of new people (see Figures 12–14).

An explicit connection was made by the GWR in promoting the coming of the new route to Ireland and the story of the French invasion. The GWR were experts in linking their routes with the history and heritage of the places where they had invested their resources. They were promoting more than holiday opportunities for the growing numbers of middle classes who could afford to take holidays, they were also promoting romance, mystery and nostalgia, and a rich sense of place. This sense of place was,

Figure 12: Postcard of Harbour Village

Figure 13: Postcard of Goodwick Harbour

Figure 14: Postcard of Fishguard Harbour

however, artificial, ahistorical, misogynistic and ideologically driven, Anglo-centric and imperial.[14] These aims came together and suited the romance of a 'Little England beyond Wales' perfectly, as did the story of the French Invasion, striking a patriotic chord of English victory over the foreign enemy and celebrating the site of the Last Invasion. An implicit confidence underpins the work that there would not be another invasion of British soil under any circumstances. This made Fishguard and the other places in their literature politically subservient to a conservative political creed as well as commercially dependent, but the corporate imagery brought in visitors seduced by the lure of personal encounter with a special place. The GWR drew a direct connection between 1797 and 1905, a prosthetic memory to affect behaviour in the present, to invite customers to enjoy an encounter between the present and the past in their experience of present day Fishguard. Fishguard was significant ground. Modern-day tourism has dulled us to lose sight of the complex cultural mesh that lies behind the act of treading on significant ground.[15]

In June 1905 the GWR produced its highly influential and popular travel compendium *South Wales: The Country of Castles*.[16] This booklet, with fare information, photographs, maps and short descriptions of places on the GWR network, became essential reading for GWR travellers. It was very popular over the next twenty years and was reissued four times. The smart buff card cover with bold red lettering had 'South Wales' in red at the top right hand corner and the GWR company crest in the top left. 'South Wales' had become partnered with the corporate identity of the GWR. What strikes the modern reader of this work immediately is how literate and researched it is. About half of the introduction is focused on Pembrokeshire, a county that was evidently dear to GWR's corporate heart. Edward Laws's 'Little Britain [sic] Beyond Wales' was singled out for praise.[17] The misprint of 'Britain' for 'England' in the title of Laws's history sums up the political bias of the GWR series.

Tate was not invading Wales, but England, and for England, read Britain.[18] Pembrokeshire was 'the playground *par excellence* of the Principality'. It was on Pembrokeshire soil that the 'the last invasion of British territory was successfully repelled'.[19] But Cawdor, even though his great grandson was chairman of the GWR, did not defeat the French invaders unaided. He had useful allies in the 'comely and stout hearted dames' whose descendants still lived in this 'Paradise' to which the GWR invited the holiday-maker as well as the 'seeker for change, health or sunshine'.[20]

The 1905 guidebook compendium commences the journey into Wales following the GWR railway line. Chapter 14 is titled 'Fishguard and Goodwick, Past, Present and Future. The French Invasion of 1797'.[21] The story of the invasion is told, focusing on the men who participated: pitmen, miners, peasants and the gentlemen; the labouring classes were 'armed in the most primitive style'. The male involvement continues with the tale of the 'dissenting clergyman named Jones' armed with his double-barrelled fowling piece 'at the head of his entire male congregation', leading them on to meet the French. Meanwhile, Cawdor and a small party of his Castlemartin cavalry went to survey the French, to within half a mile of their camp, deceiving the French who mistook them for 'the English General and his staff' because of the look of their 'splendid chargers and handsome uniforms' and that they must belong to a far larger body.[22] Thus the male version of the female, red-cloaked stratagem was repeated. The guidebook states that the popular story of the brave women on the other hand was a 'misconception' and 'still more ludicrous which, even to the present hour, is a subject of merriment to the Welsh'.[23]

The guidebook then becomes a cutting-edge treatise, showing the easy interchange between academic and amateur history at this time, reproducing in facsimile the first and fourth pages of an original letter from Cawdor to Portland. The letter, found in a Birmingham curiosity shop, was Cawdor's detailed report of the event to the Home Office.[24] This despatch from Cawdor –

dated 5 March 1797, Oxford Street – had been found by A. M. Broadley who would, in three years' time with his co-author H. F. B. Wheeler, publish a ground-breaking work, *Napoleon and the Invasion of England*, which would have more to say about the French Invasion.[25] This newly discovered Cawdor letter (now in the National Library of Wales) was published (but not discussed) in this 1905 GWR guidebook. An original document, previously unseen, the GWR used it first as promotional material to encourage holidaymakers. Assured by the past and confident of the future: 'In a short time Fishguard will be one of the best known and most popular starting points for Ireland.'[26] Things had changed dramatically since 1797, when Fishguard was invaded by La Hoche and the descent on Fishguard planned by Tate, an Irishman. The GWR travel books were highly influential and put Fishguard and the route to Ireland on the popular tourist holiday map.

Other guidebooks too gave Fishguard and its history full coverage. In 1905, the prolific and enigmatic West Country folklorist, antiquarian and Anglican priest Sabine Baring-Gould, author of the hymn 'Onward Christian Soldiers', wrote his *Book of South Wales*,[27] the companion to his *Book of North Wales*, which had been published in 1903. Not since Willkie Collins in 1859 had an Englishman of such popular, literary stature written on the French Invasion. Sabine Baring-Gould's oeuvre is immense, but he also wrote with sympathy, erudition and speed. With speed, however, came mistakes. Baring-Gould had fifteen children, and he needed to write to feed them. He turned his hand to fiction, travel books, sermons, religious tracts and hymns. He was also an archaeologist and a hagiographer with a particular interest in Saints. A year before the *Book of South Wales* was published, Baring-Gould wrote a work of historical fiction *In Dewisland* set at the time of the Rebecca Riots in south Wales. In his immense range of interests, the proud Devonian had a special place for Pembrokeshire and Wales. As *Young Wales* put it, Baring-Gould was a 'lover of our nation'.[28]

Figure 15: James Baker engraving of Goodwick Sands

Figure 16: James Baker engraving of 'Carngwastad'

Baring-Gould's account uses Thomas Knox's *Some Account of Proceedings* for the first time, and all of Baker's engravings, not only the two that had been used previously by M. E. James (see Figures 15 and 16). He also claimed that he had an exclusive: the letter from Cawdor to his wife, dated 13 March 1797, Oxford Street.[29] This is the letter that gave the details of their journey from Carmarthen with the high-ranking French prisoners. His claim, however, was not true, as the letter had already been published previously by Miss James in her book *The Fishguard Invasion by the French in 1797*, published initially in 1892, and reissued in 1897 as a centenary edition by the *Western Mail*. James clearly acknowledged the assistance of Edward Laws who had provided her with this letter.[30] There is no mention of Jemima in Baring-Gould's work, the extent of the destruction is played down, there is no mention of intoxication or gluttony and the French force are again discredited as criminals.[31] Tate was an Irishman pretending to be an American.[32] The Welsh are portrayed as victims of their own stupidity and aggression. The '1000 petticoated, scarlet-hatted Welshwomen, armed with broomsticks' was a story 'told and generally believed'. The 'sole result of this absurd invasion was to raise a laugh through England'.[33]

The new sea route from Fishguard to Ireland was opened officially on 30 August 1906,[34] bringing prosperity to Fishguard.[35] The *Westminster Gazette*, published at the heart of imperial power, saw the connection between Fishguard's past and its future. In 1797 Fishguard had shaped one invasion, in the early twentieth century it had brought about 'a peaceful invasion of a very different nature' by opening up new parts of Ireland to tourists.[36] The original invasion continued to be recalled in different ways along different gender and geographic lines. In 1904, at the annual dinner of the Cardiganshire squadron of the Pembrokeshire Imperial Yeomanry, at the Talbot Hotel in Aberystwyth, a toast was proposed to the Regiment as one of the oldest corps in the country, having been formed shortly after the landing of the French at Fishguard. Therefore 'they could claim the famous women of Fishguard with their red shawls as ancestors but he did not mean to say that the Pembrokeshires were a lot of old women (laughter)'.[37] A Cardiganshire man could get away with that joke in Aberystwyth but not in Tenby.

The Pembrokeshire Yeomanry were both proud and aware of their regimental history. An article on their history appeared in the *Pembroke County Guardian* in June 1905.[38] The commanders of the Pembrokeshire Yeomanry were carefully and respectfully listed in chronological order, culminating with the then commander, Col. F. C. Meyrick CB of Bush, Pembroke, who had seen service in South Africa. Meyrick was to liaise with Engineer Lieutenant B. F. M. Freeman of the Royal Navy to compile a formal history of the Pembrokeshires, one of a series of regimental histories that would form the history of all the Yeomanry regiments. The stimulus for this concerted effort was the disappearance of the Yeomanry as historically constituted and their absorption from April 1908 into the Territorial Force. The Prospectus for the series mentioned only one Yeomanry regiment and that was the Pembrokeshires, who were in the 'enviable position of having surrendered and captured the last foreign invaders who dared to violate the soil of these islands'.[39]

Work had already started on compiling the *History*; in 1905 a series of articles appeared in *The Welshman*, published by permission of Meyrick.[40] Although the work was still publicised as 'being written' in May 1907, financial support was not forthcoming and it was announced in February 1908 that the work in volume form with colour plates would not appear 'due to there being an insufficient number of subscribers'.[41] There were two reasons for this; the volume was advertised in a handsome prospectus with engravings from Baker, a portrait of Cawdor and an order form; the price for subscribers was one guinea, and for non-subscribers it was one-and-a-half guineas.[42] This price was prohibitive for ordinary members of the Pembrokeshire public. The second reason was that readers of *The Welshman* and *The Volunteer Service Gazette* had already seen most of the content.

The book was available as a press copy, and the manuscript was kept in the Meyrick family, but never published in volume form with the colour plates as so lavishly advertised.⁴³

Figure 17: Title page of 'History of the Pembroke Imperial Yeomanry'

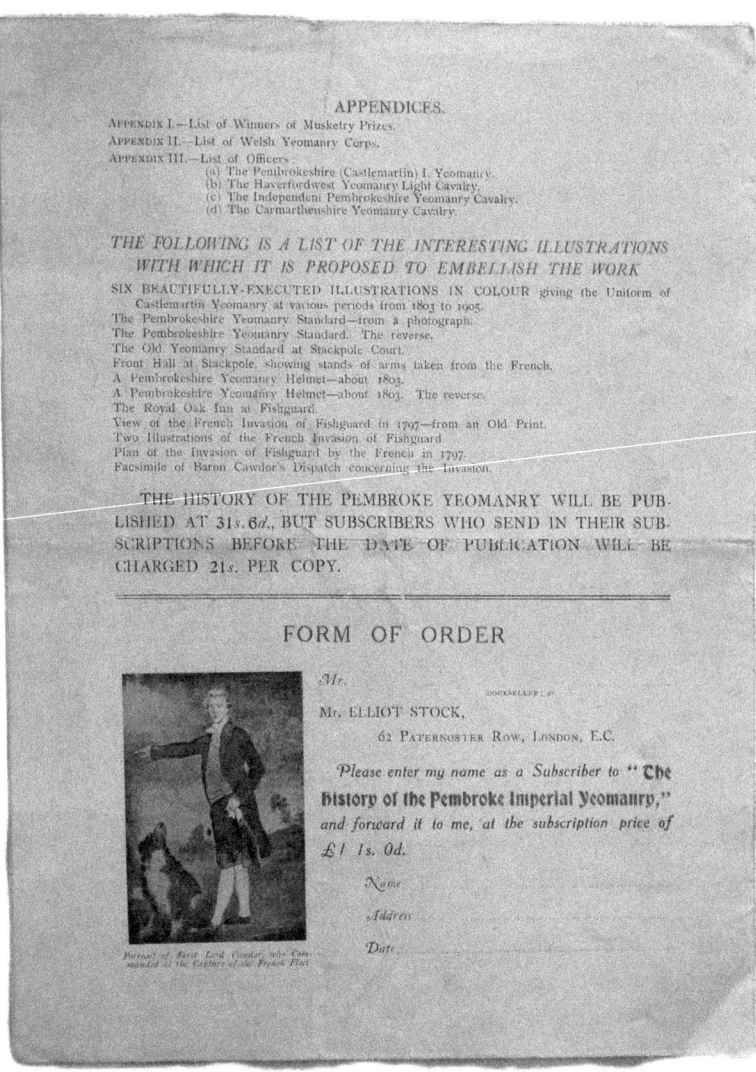

Figure 18: Order Form for 'History of the Pembroke Imperial Yeomanry'

The account of the French invasion that would have appeared in Meyrick's book was detailed in the press in 1905 and again in 1907.⁴⁴ Some of the content is similar to the GWR *The Country of Castles* guidebook, and Meyrick also pays tribute to M. E. James's book, which he treated as a work of history rather than as the work of historical fiction. However, there were aspects to the narrative that were new, and these were crafted, not unexpectedly perhaps, to shed the best light on Cawdor and his Castlemartin cavalry, the predecessors of the Pembrokeshire (Castlemartin) Imperial Yeomanry. The Yeomanry were compared to King Arthur's knights. Meyrick's *History* had a distinct male and martial bias, not unexpectedly since this was an official history of a regiment. Given the popular currency of the story of the women in their red shawls, it was a feat of intellectual courage and loyalty to his regiment not to mention or even acknowledge the existence of this story. Meyrick did not challenge its historical authenticity; he simply ignored it and in so doing he was adhering to a regimental tradition. It did not belong in his military, male-orientated account of a famous regiment that set such great score by the men defeating the French in 1797 under the leadership of their commander Lord Cawdor. The Pembrokeshires were not a lot of old women. The press copy[45] had been made available for reviews anticipating publication; one reviewer, a female journalist named Sabrina, writing in *The Wellington Journal* (the Meyrick family of Bush, Pembroke had links to Shropshire), made sure that the Fishguard women were mentioned.[46]

The story of the Fishguard women was under strain: first, from traditional male military and regimental histories that tended to ignore the story of the red shawls completely; and second, from the changing political climate of the *Entente Cordiale*, which made it less fashionable to criticise the French openly. While ridiculing the French was welcome at a time when an invasion was feared, it did not make for friendly relations at a time of rapprochement. The primary threat, however, came from the growing historical criticism that questioned the authenticity of the story on evidential grounds, all of which would meet with resistance from the people of Fishguard and Pembrokeshire generally, who were proud of their history and the invasion especially. Growing prosperity emboldened them to defend the integrity of the invasion narrative, including the role of the women in their red shawls. The turn of the century traveller to south Wales would have been fully aware of the events of 1797 at Fishguard and Pencaer. At no other time would people be more aware of the story than the period between the centenary and the outbreak of the Great War, such was its impact on popular culture, assisted largely by the opening of south Wales as a tourist and holiday destination, a feature of the booming economy of south Wales at this time.[47] New primary sources were being identified by historians that would both bolster and challenge these memories and sense of place.

Alexander Meyrick Broadley was a collector of Napoleonic letters and a prolific autograph hunter. He had acquired some notoriety in his younger years as the lawyer who defended the Egyptian nationalist known as Aribi Pasha, for which he was paid the enormous sum of 10,000 guineas. After a tumultuous career, he settled down in his later years to a life of autograph collection and study of Napoleonic literature. Harold Wheeler, much younger, was a much quieter and more scholarly character. He was the historian of the pair, who later wrote biographies of Napoleon and a work on the French Revolution.[48] When advance copies of their *Napoleon and the Invasion of England: The Story of the Great Terror* were available in the autumn of 1907 the critical response was overwhelmingly positive.[49] The strength of their work was the diverse range of contemporary evidence that they had gathered (including satirical prints, engravings, facsimiles of correspondence and poetry) to illustrate their theme, which fitted neatly into the contemporary interest in invasion, albeit with the threat at this time not from France but from Germany. Wheeler and Broadley were 'scientific' historians engaged in archival research in the primary sources, adopting a critical approach towards the evidence. They were the first historians of this type to engage with the French Invasion of 1797. The interest in the Fishguard Invasion was apparent from the dedication of their book to a Bristol baronet, the city the historians noted, against which 'the attack of the 'Black Legion' was originally directed.[50]

Their research introduced new evidence and allowed new interpretations of the events of 1797. A facsimile of the 1803 broadside *An Address to the People of the United Kingdom of Great Britain and Ireland on the Threatened Invasion* that contained the infamous *Specimens of French Ferocity and Brutality in Wales* (see figure 6, page 85) first appeared here.[51] In their expressions of gratitude they thanked, among others 'Mr Edward Laws, the historian of Pembrokeshire, for the communication of several new facts concerning the Fishguard episode of February 1797.'[52]

Chapter two of the book was titled 'A three days' war – The invasion of Wales by Hoche's Black Legion under Colonel Tate, February 22nd, 23rd and 24th 1797'.[53] The title is a conscious imitation of M. E. James's binder's title *The Fishguard Invasion or Three Days in 1797*.[54] The authors quote from James several times in their chapter. They regarded the work as 'entertaining'.[55] Wheeler and Broadley did not know the name of the author; they had evidently only seen the 1892 first edition. They treated it as a work of 'fiction or semi fiction' mixed up with perfectly authentic documents.[56]

Wheeler and Broadley's work was a landmark in the development of the French Invasion story, providing a new evidential base which would frame the narrative for the next twenty years, and it was on their base that David Salmon later built his reconstruction of the story. Wheeler and Broadley provided new evidence that would have been beyond the reach of the popular historians and remembrancers of the past, enterprising, imaginative and gifted as they were.

The work to which the authors were most indebted was not those of the well-established military historians Hozier or Creasy, but to the more recent, five-volume French-language work of Captain Edouard Desbrière: *Projets et Tentatives de Debarquement aux Isles Britanniques* (Paris, 1900–2).[57] One of their achievements was to bring the work of Captain Desbrière to the attention of an English-speaking audience. Desbrière's work was a French-government approved army project under the direction of *la section historique de l'etat-major de l'armee* to detail the invasion arrangements against Britain of the Napoleonic era and had involved archival work in both London and Paris. Wheeler and Broadley, inevitably, spotted a few mistakes.[58] Nonetheless, they noted that Captain Desbrière always wrote of England 'in a spirit of courtesy and conciliation'.

Desbrière describes the French Invasion (or as Wheeler and Broadley put it, 'a piratical attempt') as 'a singular expedition of jail birds'.[59] The French Invasion was a melodrama providing 'comic relief' after the failure in Bantry Bay.[60] The authors had done their homework citing James Baker, J. Wright's pamphlet of 1798 of Tate's *Instructions*, and also 'a narrative by Mr Williams of Crachenliwyd [sic] near St David's, the farmer who sent his servant to give the alarm'.[61] They had mixed up their Williamses, Williams the author of *An Authentic Account*, and Thomas Williams of Trelethin, the first sighter. Most of these early publications, the authors said, could be found in the Cardiff Free Library. Their list of works cited is very close to the source list in James. They then come to the primary story, the 'Fishguard romance'.[62] There was a charm about the story that was 'almost irresistible'; it fascinated its hearers and 'will probably continue to do so for all time, although it is never even faintly alluded to in the first contemporary accounts'.[63] Even the 'practical and matter-of-fact mind' of Captain Desbrière was taken in by it. Desbrière' gave a laconic note on the subject', which the authors thought would be lost in translation.[64] What Desbrière did say was that the filibuster Tate and his bandits were capable of anything: *'de la part de ce filibuster et de ses bandits, tout est possible'*.[65] The authors noted James's oral source, Eleanor or Nelly Phillips, whom they described as the last survivor of the 'alleged Amazons'. They concluded that the 'romance of Fishguard rests upon very questionable grounds'. What clinched it for them was that Edward Laws did not mention any contemporary source that demonstrated that 'the occurrence had any shadow of foundation in fact'.[66] Broadley and Wheeler had been charmed by the story. They did not come down forcibly on the side of rejection, neither did they say or impute that Nelly Philipps, the last survivor of the alleged Amazons, had denied its veracity as one of the later reviews would claim.[67] For the time being, the doubts and denials remained a matter for further consideration, a matter for historians to deliberate and not the stuff for popular debate in the correspondence columns of newspapers and periodical columns. The seeds of academic doubt had been sown though, and other historians took the statements made by Wheeler and Broadley, who had in their turn taken what Edward Laws had said, to harden and embellish.

After casting doubt on, but not denying, the story of the women, the authors moved on to document the history of the invasion from original documents used by Desbrière from the French National Archives. It was a process of knowledge sharing and exchange between the Frenchman and the English (with contributions from the Welshman, Laws). Desbrière had a document 'of considerable interest' that the authors summarised for their English-speaking readers: the journal of Commodore Castagnier. The journal of Castagnier, Commander of the frigate *Vengeance* and having under his orders the other ships, established clearly that Castagnier's departure with the ships was not a sudden act of abandonment but an agreed decision between Tate, his officers and Castagnier.[68]

Much of the content in Broadley and Wheeler consisted of copies of original documentation, but the authors did venture some commentary. They transcribed the familiar official letters published in the *London Gazette* and the provincial press at the time.[69] The authors also transcribed the letters between Milford and Portland (the Home Office correspondence) giving Milford's change of mind between Friday and Sunday concerning the full nature of the surrender.

Before finishing their treatment of the French Invasion, remarkable for the number of new original documents made available, the authors commented in conclusion that 'the recollection of the event itself has been kept green in Pembrokeshire by several ballads'. These were English-language ballads supplied to the authors by their Pembrokeshire collaborator Edward Laws. The first is titled 'The French Invasion' and comes from a Tenby oral tradition, the second is untitled and came directly from Earl Cawdor in 1891, passed down orally in Corston, a village on the Cawdor estate near Castlemartin.[70] The English ballads, fewer than the Welsh, although somewhat similar in content, are distinctively different in that they were not published at the time or circulated in manuscript form, but retained as part of an oral tradition, transcribed later by family or neighbours.[71] The English-language ballads, like the Welsh, also show the interaction between the military and civilians and challenges to the orthodox surrender account. Unlike the Welsh though, the English-language ballads do not portray the depredations suffered by the invaded: no mention is made of loss of property, livestock or personal harm. These ballad writers were not local to northern Pembrokeshire, the area most affected, and sang only of their own experience, which was that of going to war.

Broadley and Wheeler were not quite done with Fishguard. In their footnotes they paid full homage to the present Earl Cawdor, for many years the chairman of the GWR and, for a brief period, First Lord of the Admiralty.[72] Broadley and Wheeler's work was widely reviewed and the French Invasion section received prominent attention.[73] The press did not go into the detail of the Invasion but repeated the conclusion of the authors that the story of the women in their red shawls appeared to 'rest, however, upon very slender grounds'.[74] The Pembrokeshire press did not take this scepticism lightly and defended their story: 'One by one our pet traditions are being taken from us. Now it is the story connected with the scarlet-cloaked women of Pencaer who struck terror into the French in 1797 that is subjected to the sledge-hammer of modern historical criticism.'[75] It was not Wheeler and Broadley's book that roused their ire so much but the review of that book which appeared in *The Athenaeum*. It was a complimentary review overall, the authors had conferred a benefit on historical scholarship by 'rounding off in a satisfactory manner a subject which has hitherto received scant justice in these islands'.[76] Although Wheeler and Broadley were unable to throw any light on the expedition to Bantry Bay in 1796, 'more interesting' were their details on the invasion at Fishguard in February 1797. Hoche's *Instructions* to Tate and his *Legion Noire* of gaol birds drew their attention but what was especially noteworthy was the 'well known story of the Welsh women in their scarlet cloaks' was not mentioned in contemporary sources: 'We must therefore, with some reluctance, consign it to the limbo of patriotic legend.'[77]

The *Pembroke County Guardian* stood its ground, claiming that 'The *Guardian* would not be true to its name if it did not attempt to discredit this view'.[78] It was not therefore a matter of accepting or not accepting the *Athenaeum* view; the *Guardian* intended to discredit it. They appealed to their readers 'familiar with the literature of the event' to 'favour us with the facts'. The Pembrokeshire newspaper thought, quite sensibly, that the story of the ruse would have been kept out of the official reports at the time, but was it true, they asked, that it was not mentioned in contemporary ballads?[79]

Memories of the invasion troubled the Baptists into the twentieth century and were also under-represented in print. In 1907, the French invasion was recalled by the *Pembrokeshire Herald* as so many 'interesting reminiscences'; the fact that the Pembrokeshire Yeomanry bore 'Fishguard' on their head gear badge was one, another was the need to celebrate the role of the red-whittled dames of Fishguard in future pageants connected with Empire Day. But there was a discordant note, and not all reminiscences were positive, particularly that the north Pembrokeshire Baptists were suspected of complicity in the invasion: 'No proof of such treason was discovered, but the bitterness then engendered by the Government's aspersions on the loyalty of a patriotic body of the King's subjects, *has not even yet disappeared*'[80] (my italics).

In 1908 a by-election was held in Pembrokeshire caused by the elevation to the peerage of the incumbent Liberal MP John Wynford Philipps. Emmeline Pankhurst and the leading suffragettes canvassed in the by-election. They had come to campaign against the Liberal candidate Walter Roch because Asquith, the Liberal prime minister at the time, was against the enfranchisement of women. They failed, but their campaigns were popular and they were treated courteously by the Pembrokeshire people who turned out to see the famous English suffragettes when they toured the county in July. Rosamund Massy (1870–1947) visited Fishguard, which she noted was 'a Liberal stronghold near Mr Lloyd George's birthplace'.[81] When Emmeline Pankhurst was in Haverfordwest she was specifically asked 'if women would fight if they had the vote'. She replied 'that Haverfordwest had its own Joan of Arc, who captured twelve French soldiers single-handed when they sought to invade these shores'.[82]

Jemima, it seems, had been conscripted as a suffragette. Both candidates mentioned the women in their red shawls in their speeches. The Liberal mixed up the ladies of Llangwm with the ladies of Fishguard.[83] The Tory retorted, the Radicals (by which he meant the Liberals) had done 'a very unkind thing to the Fishguard ladies': it was not the ladies of Llangwm who had frightened the French invaders but the ladies of Fishguard.[84] This was not mere light-hearted banter: 'They must learn a little more about their own country and little more about politics before they addressed the electors.'[85]

The remembrance of the Fishguard women of 1797 was nuanced with multiple possible meanings and implications and could be used against women by men. In an eisteddfod held in the Jewin Street Welsh chapel in London in December 1908, a man shouted out in Welsh: 'who beat the French a century ago? Pembrokeshire girls, the suffragettes of their day. Suffragettes have been a bit rough in every age!' ('merched Sir Benfro-suffragettes yr oes honno. Rhai garw yw'r Suffragettes ym mhob oes!').[86] The witticism worked because the story was so well known and understood.

However, the story was not as highly regarded as some would have liked. A young Oxford don from Llanuwchllyn, O. M. Edwards (1858–1920), in 1901 published in Thomas Fisher Unwin's book series *Story of the Nations* his history of Wales, titled simply *Wales*, written for people who knew little about the history of their own country.[87] There was no mention of the French Invasion. A Fishguard solicitor wrote to him to complain, and this complaint was noted in the local press together with O. M. Edwards's response. He would include it, he said, in any larger work.[88] Another reader, based in Llanelli, investigated *Wales* to find out more about the invasion and was also surprised that there was no mention of it. He then wondered whether there was any historical basis to Ceiriog's poem about the Day-Old Baby. He had to turn to older works such as that by Carnhuanawc to find out, but did not find it much there either.[89] In contrast, the younger generation of Welsh speakers would have been much better informed; they could read about the invasion and the Day-Old Baby in the innovative, inter disciplinary textbook *Ein Gwlad* by David James (Defynnog),where it featured alongside episodes as significant as Chartism and Rebecca.[90]

Historians and works of historical reference in Wales still came down firmly on the side of the historicity of the 'red-cloak heroines' of 1797. This phrase was used to describe Jemima Nicholas in a new work of historical reference for Wales, T. Mardy Rees's *Notable Welshmen* published in October 1908. In this work, which became highly influential with time, but evidently not immediately, Jemima Nicholas was given her own biographical entry as 'JEMIMA NICHOLAS, FISHGUARD (1750–1832): THE

REDCLOAK HEROINE' (capitalisation as published).[91] Rees, using text supplied by Gurnos Jones, elevates Jemima from a solitary figure capturing a clutch of Frenchmen on her own, into the 'leader of the Welsh heroines'. She is the *chief* red-cloaked heroine. The focus of the biographical article was on the Welsh women in their red garb ascending and descending the nearby hill to give the impression to the French of their being red coats. Jemima was given the respect of her own identity, which she shared with eminent Welsh men: judges, bishops, preachers, MPs and others. The inscription on the memorial stone in her honour in Fishguard church that was erected because of the centenary banquet in 1897 was transcribed in full as part of the entry.

The legacies of Fishguard in 1797 were more than just memories in some instances, it was part of their DNA – or so it was claimed. At around the same time as the boom in prosperity in Fishguard, the 'descendants' of the great Jemima Nicholas began to make themselves known, writing to the newspapers to celebrate their ancestry. A 'grandson' lived in St Clears, Carmarthenshire, and a 'granddaughter' lived at Jeffreston, near Tenby in Pembrokeshire. The Jeffreston 'granddaughter', it was claimed, still possessed her red shawl.[92] The historic Jemima had, in fact, never married, therefore these were not direct descendants; M. E. James's character of 'Aunt Jemima' is nearer the mark.[93] Direct ancestry was not relevant to claim ideological descent. Jane Jones, in a letter to the *Barry Dock News* about the Barry Territorials, claimed such a descent. She was, she claimed, 'only a woman, descended from one of the brave Fishguard women', but the Fishguard women in their red shawls and hats had had to defend their country from invasion despite the lack of preparation. Invasion was not only possible but probable whenever 'we are at war with a European nation'. Her son had joined the Barry Territorials, and she urged other women to persuade their male family members to do the same.[94]

The red flannels that were so strongly associated with the women of Fishguard were not just confined to the past; the shawls and hats were carefully preserved and passed down from grandmother to mother to daughter. They were, when the occasion demanded, brought down from the attic, taken out carefully from their preserving paper and worn proudly again. These clothes were Sunday finery and would not have been worn to fight the French even if they had survived for over a century.[95] The connection with the past and the symbolic respect was as important as the clothing associated with it. The centenary celebration of 1897 was one such occasion when they were worn and the opening of the new sea route to Ireland in 1906 another. The next big occasion was the coming of the pride of the Cunard Line, the SS *Mauretania*, and the opening of the transatlantic crossing between Fishguard and New York. The new transatlantic ocean mail route was opened on Fishguard harbour's third anniversary in August 1909, and the shawls and hats 'actually worn in 1797 by the gallant Welsh women' were brought out from storage to celebrate the occasion of the coming of the *Mauretania*. The women in their red cloaks and hats were described as the 'lineal descendants' of the brave women of 1797.[96] The *Mauretania*, a majestic, world-record beating liner, sailed into Fishguard on 31 August 1909.

The arrival of the *Mauretania* caused another surge in coverage about Fishguard and its past across the entire press network, both in England and Ireland.[97] However the picture of harmony, of a community celebrating together, was not all it seemed to be. Local tensions and jealousies could not be concealed. The *Tenby Observer* wrote a scathing review of the occasion, saying it was a very underwhelming experience, and the reporter went so far as to question the story (or 'yarn' as he called it) of the women of Fishguard.[98]

The Welsh-speaking communities in north Pembrokeshire, on the other hand, were enlivened by the occasion, the honour that it gave to their county and the memories it revived. The arrival of the *Mauretania* was proof, if proof was required that Pembrokeshire was the premier county in Wales.[99]

One writer in the *Llan* (the newspaper of the Anglicans in Wales) regretted not being there when the *Mauretania* docked in Fishguard on the last day of August 1909, but asked if anyone else from the 'fraternity' had attended to let him know.[100] A reply came from a Maenclochog woman. She had wanted to visit Fishguard since she was a child, having heard so much about the landing of the French and read so much about it. On the train from Maenclochog, the first verse from Ceiriog's famous poem, *Y Baban Diwrnod Oed*, which recaptured the horror so deliciously in verse, drummed in her mind. She then went into a reverie about the number of stories that she had heard from the old people as she helped with the harvest. She remembered one of Jaci Pwllcorn's stories, in which the battle was getting hot between 'y Cymru a'r French'. Heads were being cut off like apples falling from a tree but there was a 'clever' man in their midst who was able to put the heads back onto the bodies so well that nobody knew any differently. But one time he made a mistake and put the head of a Frenchman onto the body of a Welshman and ever since that man was known as 'Dai Ben Frenchman'. This was Welsh humour and folklore, as exemplified by Shemi Wad, the notorious storyteller from Goodwick, whose white lies were so popular in Welsh oral tradition.[101]

There was something else the Maenclochog woman remembered that made Fishguard famous. She remembered her mother wearing a red whittle and a silk 'sugar loaf' hat on special Sundays in the summer to go to chapel; something she was proud to wear. She asked her mother why she was so proud to wear these garments, and was told it was because they were a memorial of the victory of the Welsh over the French at Fishguard in 1797. So, when, as the *Mauretania* docked, she saw two dozen Fishguard girls dressed in their red whittles, a tear came to her eyes since she saw herself again as a young girl going to chapel hand in hand with her mother.

On arrival in Fishguard, the passengers of the *Mauretania* were presented with a GWR guidebook, *Historic Sites and*

New Prosperity, New History, an Old Story

Scenes of England, which had been recently published.[102] Subtle differences between the Fishguard Invasion story in the GWR publication of 1905 and GWR publication five years later demonstrate the growth in historical criticism. The chapter on Fishguard in 1910 was expanded from that of 1905 to include more information on Fishguard as a port of departure outlining its advantages especially for American travellers.[103] The content on the Invasion was virtually identical to the 1905 account, but there were differences reflecting the changes in the cultural and historical environment. In 1905 the picture on the opening page of the Fishguard chapter showed the women in their red cloaks or shawls, titled 'THE REDCOATS OF 1797'.[104] In the 1910 *Historic Sites and Scenes of England* the same picture was used (see Figure 19), but with the title 'THE HISTORIC RED CLOAKS OF WALES, CONNECTED BY TRADITION WITH THE FRENCH ATTACK ON FISHGUARD IN 1797'.[105]

THE HISTORIC RED CLOAKS OF WALES, CONNECTED BY TRADITION WITH THE FRENCH ATTACK ON FISHGUARD IN 1797.

Figure 19: Opening page of the Fishguard chapter in the GWR publication *Historic Sites and Scenes of England*

The text in 1905, which read 'the heroines of the red cloaks remained heroines till the end of their days', had become 'the heroines of the red cloaks, *who were supposed to have played an important part in the defeat of the French*, remained heroines till the end of their days' [the new text is shown in my italics], a much more circumspect and cautious description.[106] The caution of the GWR guidebooks was replicated in academic history. John Holland Rose, a Cambridge historian and prolific writer on the period, dismissed the story of the women in their high hats and scarlet cloaks as a legend that appeared only in later accounts. His authority for this assertion was that 'Wheeler and Broadley, Napoleon and the Invasion of England have proved this'.[107]

Debate in England about the issue spilled over into Wales. The discussions were reignited, as had happened previously, by a newspaper obituary. In November 1912 the *Pall Mall Gazette* reported the death of a centenarian, whose mother took part in repelling the French invasion.[108] Among the learned contributions were those from Wheeler and Broadley.[109] 'H. F. B' (Wheeler) concluded from the authorities mentioned and 'from other sources which I will not inflict on you' that the women 'did play a useful part on this occasion, although not at the instigation of Lord Cawdor. The speedy surrender of the invaders was largely due to bluff on our side, for they numbered twice as many as the attacking force'.[110] Broadley came down on the side of the argument that the story was a myth.

The 'picturesque legend' would not be killed off so easily; J. H. Seabrooke provided the Mends correspondence that he had from John Mends's grandson himself, the late Col. Herbert Mends.[111] The *Pall Mall Gazette* printed this letter with evidence of the '400 poor women with red flannel over their shoulders' (a direct quotation from the original letter of 27 February 1797 from John Mends). As Seabrooke concluded, this was 'strong contemporary evidence for the substantial truth of the story of the red-cloaked Welshwomen'.[112]

The editor ruled on 10 December to publish no further letters on this subject.[113] However, one further letter was published, and it was a Welshman who had the last word. Llewellin Davies, MA Oxon of Cardigan agreed that there were no references to red-cloaked Welsh women in the historical evidence, but – and this was a very large but – he had spoken to 'several old persons, who stoutly maintained that their grandmothers contributed to the surrender of the French troops by means of their "red shawls and petticoats"'.[114]

Historical enquiry tends to mediate the memories and experiences of the women of Pembrokeshire and west Wales. For them though, this was not a legend or a myth but a story that connected them to their mothers and grandmothers, and to the places where they lived or where they were from.

Endnotes

1. E. H. Stuart Jones, *The Last Invasion of Britain* (Cardiff, 1950), p. 288.
2. 'Tenby Honours. Presentation of the Freedom', *South Wales Daily News* (23 February 1900), 4; 'Enthusiastic Proceedings. Entertained by the Mayor of Tenby', *Haverfordwest and Milford Haven Telegraph* (28 February 1900), 2.
3. 'Llansamlet Rhyddhad Ladysmith', *The Cambrian* (9 March 1900), 8.
4. K. O. Morgan, 'Wales and the Boer War – A Reply', *Welsh History Review*, 4/1–4 (1968–9), 380.
5. *The Rhondda Leader* (16 February 1901), 5.
6. 'The French Invasion in Fishguard', *The County Echo* (21 May 1903), 3.
7. For 'Dai a Wil dau fachgen o Aberteifi unig fechgyn eu rhieni', see T. Cunllo Griffiths *Glaniad y Ffrancod yn Abergwaun: Darlith* (1885), pp. 21–2.
8. Griffiths, *Glaniad y Ffrancod yn Abergwaun*, pp. 21-22
9. 'Cwmaman, 'Glaniad y Ffrancod yn Abergwaun'', *Tarian y Gweithiwr* (23 March 1899), 5.
10. 'The Fishguard Pier and Railway. What the Project is Like', Supplement to the *Wicklow People* (3 April 1897), 5.
11. *Wicklow People* (3 April 1897), 5.
12. 'More Graves and Other Inspiring Spots', *Cambrian News* (21 September 1900), 8.

13 'Welsh Rock Town. The Growth of Fishguard. Invasion by the Builder', *South Wales Daily News* (11 September 1909), 4.
14 For a general description of the GWR's approach towards place advertising, see A. D. Bennett, 'The Great Western Railway and the Celebration of Englishness' (DPhil thesis, University of York, Institute of Railway Studies, October 2000).
15 Mary-Ann Constantine, 'Celts and Romans on Tour: Visions of Early Britain in Eighteenth-Century Travel Literature', in Francesca Kaminski-Jones (ed.), *Celts, Romans and Britons: Classical and Celtic Influence in the Construction of British Identities* (Oxford, 2020), p. 139.
16 Great Western Railway (GWR), *South Wales: The Country of Castles* (London, 1905).
17 GWR, *South Wales: The Country of Castles*, p. 6.
18 GWR, *South Wales: The Country of Castles*, p. 7.
19 GWR, *South Wales: The Country of Castles*, p. 7.
20 GWR, *South Wales: The Country of Castles*, p. 7.
21 GWR, *South Wales: The Country of Castles*, pp. 67–75. This chapter was reproduced as a separate booklet by the GWR in 1906 and given as a memento to passengers on the new route to Ireland, titled *Fishguard 1797–1906: The story of the last invasion of England, as told from the original MSS with a note on modern Fishguard*, see *Army and Navy Gazette* (17 November 1906), 7. It was reissued again in 1908, with the updated title *Fishguard 1797–1908*, see *Pembroke County Guardian* (29 May 1908), 6.
22 GWR, *South Wales: The Country of Castles*, pp. 72–3.
23 GWR, *South Wales: The Country of Castles*, p. 73.
24 GWR, *South Wales: The Country of Castles*, p. 74. For the find, see A. M. Broadley, *Chats on Autographs* (London, 1910), p. 51.
25 H. F. B. Wheeler and A. M. Broadley, *Napoleon and the Invasion of England* (London, 1908).
26 GWR, *South Wales: The Country of Castles*, p. 75.
27 S. Baring-Gould, *A Book of South Wales* (London, 1905); for more on the remarkable Baring-Gould, see J. E. Thomas, *Sabine Baring-Gould: The Life and Work of a Complete Victorian* (Stroud, 2015).
28 *Young Wales*, 9/104 (August 1903), 177.
29 Baring-Gould, *A Book of South Wales*, pp. 230–1.
30 Anon [M. E. James], *The Fishguard Invasion of 1797. Some Passages taken from the Diary of the Reverend Daniel Rowlands, sometime Vicar of Llanfihangelpenybont* (London, 1892), pp. 22–3.
31 James, *The Fishguard Invasion of 1797*, p. 228.
32 James, *The Fishguard Invasion of 1797*, p. 227.
33 Baring-Gould, *A Book of South Wales*, p. 229.
34 'Fishguard and Rosslare New Route. Splendid Turbine Steamers', *London Evening Standard* (25 August 1906), 6.
35 Peter M. Solar, 'Shipping and Economic Development in Nineteenth Century Ireland', *The Economic History Review*, 59/4 (November 2006),

Table 3: 'Destinations of Irish coastal shipping: steamship tonnage entered at British ports 1871–1911 (%)', 731.
36 'Irish Invasion of Fishguard', *The Kilkenny Moderator* (16 September 1908), 2.
37 'Annual Dinner at the Talbot Hotel', *Cambrian News* (13 May 1904), 8.
38 'The Pembrokeshire Imperial Yeomanry. History of the Regiment,' *Pembroke County Guardian* (1 June 1905), 2.
39 National Library of Wales Minor Deposits 1145 B, Prospectus: Historical Records of the Yeomanry Regiments (1908).
40 'Historical Records of the Pembrokeshire (Castlemartin) Regiment of Imperial Yeomanry', *The Welshman* (15 September 1905), 3. Also in *The Welshman* every week until the end of December 1905: 22 September 1905, 3; 29 September 1905, 3 and 6; 6 October 1905, 3; 13 October 1905, 6; 27 October 1905, 3; 3 November 1905, 3; 10 November 1905, 6; 17 November 1905, 3; 24 November 1905, 3; 1 December 1905, 6; 8 December 1905, 8; 15 December 1905, 6; 22 December 1905, 6; 29 December 1905, 3.
41 'Publication of a New History', *Pembrokeshire Herald* (17 May 1907), 4; it was also announced for 'publication shortly' by *The Army and Naval Gazette* (8 June 1907), 8; the *Daily Mail* referred to it as a work in progress ('Meyrick and Freeman are writing A History of the Pembrokeshire Imperial Yeomanry'), 'Literary Notes and News', *Daily Mail* (8 June 1907), 3. The *Pembroke County Guardian* (28 February 1908, p. 8) announced that it would not appear because of the lack of subscribers.
42 See illustration for the Advert and Order Form.
43 E. H, Stuart Jones saw a copy in the possession of the author's son Sir T. F. Meyrick, *The Last Invasion of Britain*, p. 296; The press copy and cuttings from the newspapers where the History had appeared in advance of publication arranged in chronological order with handwritten additions and deletions are at National Library of Wales Minor Deposits 1145B.
44 The Fishguard Invasion account from Meyrick's history appeared in *The Welshman* on 15, 22 and 29 September 1905, and the same text later appears in *The Volunteer Service Gazette* on the 6 November 1907 (p. 4) and 20 November 1907 (p. 4).
45 NLW Minor Deposits 1145B, Press Copy of F. C. Meyrick and B. F. M. Freeman, History of the Pembroke or Castlemartin Regiment of Imperial Yeomanry 1794–1907. Sabrina's account is very similar to that which appears in GWR, *Country of Castles* (1905), including the reference to the story of the women as a 'subject of merriment to the Welsh', p. 73.
46 *The Wellington Journal and Shrewsbury News* (5 June 1909), 3.
47 It was covered in full, for example, in A. G. Bradley, *Highways and Byways in South Wales* (London, 1903), pp. 297–300.

48 H. F. B. Wheeler, *The Story of Napoleon* (London, 1910); H. F. B. Wheeler, *The French Revolution from the Age of Louis XIV to the Coming of Napoleon* (London, 1913); H. F. B. Wheeler, *Napoleon 1769–1821* (London, 1921).
49 'Napoleon Once Again: A Great Book', *The Tatler* (2 October 1907), 22; 'A Literary Letter: Two Good Books on Napoleon', *The Sphere* (19 October 1907), 22.
50 H. F. B Wheeler and A. M. Broadley, *Napoleon and the Invasion of England: The Story of the Great Terror* (London, 1908), dedication page.
51 Wheeler and Broadley, *Napoleon and the Invasion of England*, p. 73.
52 Wheeler and Broadley, *Napoleon and the Invasion of England*, p. 27.
53 Wheeler and Broadley, *Napoleon and the Invasion of England*, pp. 31-73
54 The colophon title of the centenary edition of her work was 'The Fishguard Invasion by the French in 1797' (1897). Her name was given as the androgynous M. E. James.
55 Wheeler and Broadley, *Napoleon and the Invasion of England*, p. 36.
56 Wheeler and Broadley, *Napoleon and the Invasion of England*, p. 37. James's historical fiction continued to be treated as history until the 1930s; see J. M. N. Jeffries, 'The Truant Caught in an Invasion', *Daily Mail* (8 June 1931), 4.
57 E. S. Creasy, *The Invasions and the Projected Invasions of England from the Saxon Time with Remarks on the present Emergencies* (London, 1852); H. M. Hozier, *The Invasions of England: A History of the Past with Lessons for the Future* (London, 1876).
58 Wheeler and Broadley, *Napoleon and the Invasion of England*, pp. x–xi.
59 Wheeler and Broadley, *Napoleon and the Invasion of England*, p. 32.
60 Wheeler and Broadley, *Napoleon and the Invasion of England*, p. 33.
61 Wheeler and Broadley, *Napoleon and the Invasion of England*, p. 34.
62 Wheeler and Broadley, *Napoleon and the Invasion of England*, pp. 35–73.
63 Wheeler and Broadley, *Napoleon and the Invasion of England*, p. 36.
64 Wheeler and Broadley, *Napoleon and the Invasion of England*, p. 36.
65 Wheeler and Broadley, *Napoleon and the Invasion of England*, p.36, footnote 1.
66 Wheeler and Broadley, *Napoleon and the Invasion of England*, p. 36.
67 *The Athenaeum* (5 October 1907), 396.
68 Wheeler and Broadley, *Napoleon and the Invasion of England*, pp. 50–1.
69 For example, *Kentish Chronicle* (28 February 1797), 3–4.
70 Wheeler and Broadley, *Napoleon and the Invasion of England*, pp. 66–71. Both ballads appeared again in Stuart Jones's work in 1950 in an Appendix, but were not used by him in his telling of the story of the Invasion. Stuart Jones, *The Last Invasion of Britain*, Appendix I, pp. 269–74
71 For the Welsh-language balladry publishing businesses, see Ffion M. Jones, *Welsh Ballads of the French Revolution 1793–1815* (Cardiff, 2012), pp 3–7.
72 Wheeler and Broadley, *Napoleon and the Invasion of England*, p. 55, footnote 1.

73 For example, 'Napoleon and the Invasion of England. Bristol and the Great Terror', *Western Daily Press* (16 September 1907), 7; 'Toujours-Napoleon', *Yorkshire Post* (26 December 1907), 4.
74 'Napoleon and the Invasion of England', *Army and Naval Gazette* (28 September 1907), 8.
75 'On the Square', *The Pembroke County Guardian and Cardigan Reporter* (5 June 1908), 4.
76 Review of Wheeler and Broadley, *The Athenaeum* (5 October 1907), 396.
77 Review of Wheeler and Broadley, *The Athenaeum* (5 October 1907), 396.
78 'On the Square', *Pembroke County Guardian* (5 June 1908), 4.
79 The role of the women is mentioned in Anne Brigstocke's ballad *'God and Gideon'*, 1797 lines 53–5. See Chapter 1.
80 'French Invasion at Fishguard. How the Women Repelled the Invaders. Interesting Reminiscences', *The Pembrokeshire Herald* (21 June 1907), 2.
81 Rosamund Massy, 'Pembroke By-Election', *Votes for Women* (9 July 1908), 293.
82 *'The Welshman* (10 July 1908); *Votes for Women* (16 July 1908), 11.
83 'Pembrokeshire Election. Llangwm Women to the Front. Red Shawls give way to Blue', *Cardiff Times* (14 July 1908), 83.
84 'Mr Lort-Williams at Fishguard', *The County Echo* (9 July 1908), 3.
85 'Mr Lort-Williams at Fishguard' *The County Echo* (9 July 1908), 3.
86 'Am Gymry Llundain', *Cymro a'r Celt Llundain* (5 December 1908), 5.
87 O. M. Edwards, *Wales: The Story of the Nations* (London, 1901).
88 'Fishguard', *The County Echo* (1 May 1902), 2; 'Goodwick Notes', *The Pembroke County Guardian* (3 May 1902), 9.
89 'Glaniad y Ffrancod yn Abergwaen', *The Llanelly Mercury and South Wales Advertiser* (29 July 1909), 7.
90 *Ein Gwlad neu Cymru – Ei Daear, Ei Hanes, A'i Llen,* 3rd edn (Newport, 1911), pp. 124–130. First published in 1905.
91 T. Mardy Rees, *Notable Welshmen 1700–1900* (Caernarfon, 1908), p. 175.
92 'Snap=Shots', *Barry Herald* (10 September 1909), 3.
93 In James's *The Fishguard Invasion or Three Days in 1797* (1897), Jemima is Ann George's 'Aunt', for example, p. 69.
94 'The Territorial Movement', *Barry Dock News* (26 February 1909), 5.
95 The material of the surviving shawls and hats is not earlier than 1830. See https://welshhat.wordpress.com/chronological-survey/1790s/the-fishguard-invasion/ (last accessed 5 August 2024).
96 'A Record Voyage (from our special correspondent)', *Irish Times* (31 August 1909), 7.
97 All British and Irish newspapers covered the event; for example, see *Liverpool Echo* (28 August 1909), 5; *The Daily Telegraph* (30 August 1909), 9; *Gloucester Journal* (4 September 1909), 3; *South Wales Daily News* (31 August 1909), 5.
98 'Local Notes', *The Tenby Observer* (2 September 1909), 3.
99 'Parliament y Crefftwyr (gan Colman)', *Y Llan* (10 September 1909) 2.

100 'Parliament y Crefftwyr (gan Colman)', *Y Llan* (10 September 1909), 2.
101 See R. Gwyndaf, 'The Welsh Folk Narrative Tradition: Continuation and Adaptation', *Folk Life*, 26 (1987–8), 84; and the work by Brian John, *Pembrokeshire Folk Tales Compendium* (1991–6), *www.peoplescollection.wales/collections/2058491* (last accessed 5 August 2024).
102 GWR, *Historic Sites and Scenes of England* (London, 1909).
103 The chapter heading in *South Wales: The Country of Castles* (1905) was 'Fishguard and Goodwick, Past, Present and Future. The French Invasion of 1797', pp. 67–75. The chapter heading in *Historic Sites and Scenes of England* (1910) was 'Fishguard, the Great Western Railway Company's new Port of Call: its Past, Present and Future', pp. 133–46.
104 GWR, *South Wales: The Country of Castles* (1905), p. 67.
105 GWR, *Historic Sites and Scenes of England* (1910), p. 135 .The fact that the picture showed Caernarfon castle was irrelevant, it was a Welsh scene with a Welsh castle.
106 GWR, *South Wales: The Country of Castles*, p. 69; GWR, *Historic Sites*, pp. 134–5.
107 J. Holland Rose, *Pitt and the Great War* (London, 1911), p. 309, footnote 453.
108 'Talk of the Town', *The Pall Mall Gazette* (28 November 1912), 2. The centenarian was Mary Hughes of Nine Wells, near Solva, who died at the age of 104; she was brought up in Llanychaer in the Gwaun valley. She was a splendid conversationalist (in her native tongue, she spoke no English) and delighted in talking about her youth, 'Pembrokeshire lady aged 104 years', *Cardigan and Tivy-side Advertiser* (10 November 1911), 3.
109 'The Fishguard "Invasion"', *Pall Mall Gazette* (30 November 1912), 8.
110 'The Fishguard "Invasion"', *Pall Mall Gazette* (30 November 1912), 8.
111 Sir James Herbert Seabrooke (1852–1933), a Gloucester man, had few connections with Wales but was a prominent civil servant in the India Office and was the Joint Military Secretary from 1915–19. His son was named Lawrence *Mends* Seabrooke; *Gloucester Journal* (9 September 1933). For the Mends family, see L. Phillips, 'The Naval Family Mends of Haverfordwest', *Dyfed Family History Journal*, 10/7 (December 2010), 26–7.
112 'The Fishguard Invasion', *Pall Mall Gazette* (10 December 1912), 4.
113 'The Fishguard Invasion', *Pall Mall Gazette* (10 December 1912), 4.
114 'The Fishguard Invasion', *Pall Mall Gazette* (17 December 1912), 4.

Chapter 8

The First World War and the Legend of the Women, 1914–36

Memories of the historic invasion intensified when a new invasion became a present and real danger during the early years of the Great War. Questions about aspects of the Fishguard story, or the legends as many were now describing them, continued in the early months of the war but there was no appetite to question national heroes, heroines or legends at a time of such uncertainty. It would have been unpatriotic to do so. Scrutiny revived in the 1920s with the development of academic Welsh history, when serious attempts would be made again to purge the national story of its legendary accounts.

David Salmon first wrote on the French Invasion in the early months of the war in October 1914. He was the historian who, by the early 1930s, made the story of the women of Fishguard in 1797 intellectually unfashionable. Salmon was a Pembrokeshire man, through and through: born in the parish of Newport in 1852, his forbears on both sides had for generations been farmers in the parish of Nevern. Salmon was a dedicated teacher, who had risen from a pupil-teacher in Haverfordwest from 1865 to 1869, to then become a student, headmaster and teacher trainer. In 1891, he became Principal of Swansea Training College for Women where he remained until 1922.[1]

His first incursion into the history of the French Invasion was in the academic correspondence journal *Notes and Queries*. The magazine has been likened to a nineteenth-century version of a moderated Internet chat room or news group, where interested parties could ask questions and share information. A question was asked on 16 October 1914 about Jemima Nicholas. The questioner wanted to know if anyone could verify the story about Jemima capturing twelve Frenchmen, or state where it occurred and whether anything further was known about 'this heroine'.[2]

Salmon answered the query in the next issue.[3] There were two forms of the 'legend', he explained, from the outset working on the premise that the story was a myth, that is to say not factually true. The first form presented Jemima as the heroine who single handedly captured ten or twelve French soldiers in a field armed only with her pitchfork.[4] The second form of the story had Jemima involved with, or leading the red-shawled women, on the cliff top to deceive the French, taking text verbatim from T. Mardy Rees's *Notable Welshmen*.[5] This was Salmon's verdict on the two forms: 'I disbelieve the first form of the legend and doubt the second. I should disbelieve that *also if my mother's description of the part played by her mother as a private in the stage army were not one of my earliest recollections*'[6] (author's italics).

Salmon observed shrewdly that contemporaries had not mentioned the 'Welsh Heroine', but this was not proof in itself that the writers had not heard of her.[7] The questions relating to authenticity went unanswered. This first foray into the debate was a curious blend of aggression and ambivalence, his scholarly conclusions seemingly restrained by the memories of the women in his family.

Unlike the previous debate triggered by the review of Wheeler and Broadley in 1908–9, which had generated a great deal of heat in the London and Pembrokeshire papers, on this occasion, the only newspaper to comment on Salmon's piece was *The Western Mail* in November 1914. *The Western Mail* took what Salmon said about the absence of contemporary reference to

Jemima as regret on Salmon's part that 'no really full account has come down to us'.[8] Jemima Nicholas was, as stated in Salmon's account, but not by Salmon, 'a powerful woman' who 'seized a pitchfork, marched to the enemy's camp and took a dozen Frenchmen prisoners'.[9] Jemima was a national heroine. At a time of war, there was no appetite to question whether national heroines were authentic or not. What had brought the article to the *Western Mail*'s attention in the first place was not historical enquiry, but the 'problem of the invasion of England'.[10]

In imagining and fearing invasion, as a real occurrence at this time of war, the threat of the present was compared to the experience of the past. In the early years of the war in particular there were several articles from across Britain remembering the French Invasion of 1797 in order to draw lessons, reassurance and emotional succour for the present. As early as August 1914, two articles appeared in *The Scotsman*.[11] There were interesting historical parallels. 'In the present crisis' history might repeat itself by some attempts at invasion but it was safe to say that no deception or manoeuvring could succeed 'while our watchdogs guard the coast'.[12] This confidence was shared by other newspapers who wished to commend the 'utter failure' of the Fishguard Invasion to 'the notice of Germany'.[13] Other newspapers were just as confident, but imagined different invasion scenarios; it was conceivable that the Germans might be able to land a small force so as to enact a repetition of the Fishguard Invasion. It would be too much to expect the Navy to protect against small 'raids'. There may be a 'sporting chance' of a small German force landing in England, but if this did happen, 'there would not even be a sporting chance of them getting out again'.[14]

Welsh newspapers focused on the specific threats to their coasts and the U-boat threat in particular. The German submarines were launched into St George's Channel and the Irish Sea from 1915 (after the British blockade of Germany) to conduct unrestricted warfare against British vessels – effectively making the triangle of Cornwall-Ireland-Pembrokeshire as dangerous as the French trenches. Over a two-day period in March 1915, *U-28* sank several ships off the Pembrokeshire coast, including the SS *Aguila*, with considerable loss of life – with survivors coming ashore at Milford Haven and Fishguard.[15] The Welsh Anglican newspaper *Y Llan* had anticipated danger from this quarter in February 1915. The Germans were following the example of the French at the time of Bonaparte and were eyeing Fishguard. One hundred and twenty years previously, the whole of south Wales and particularly Pembrokeshire was consumed with fear; then 'the French have come' was on every tongue, now the Germans had their sights on Fishguard and had 'sent their submarine machines to the neighbourhood there' ('yn anfon y peirianau tan-forawl yma i'r gymydogaeth').[16] The sighting of a German submarine off Fishguard 'brought home to many the scare caused over a century ago'.[17] *The Aberdare Leader*'s assessment of the state of readiness was gloomy: 'if the Germans succeeded in invading the Welsh coast, would they be as easily frightened and as efficiently repelled as were Bonaparte's "Party". Hardly.'[18]

On the anniversary of the Fishguard invasion in February 1915, several newspapers republished an article from the *Westminster Gazette* of that month that simply told the story of 1797, with no embellishments or lessons for the present. The telling of the story was enough, the utter defeat and humiliation of an invading force without a shot fired or a blow struck.[19] The components of the story were stinging instruments of propaganda in no need for additional commentary. In May 1916, *The People* described the victory in 1797 as a 'Petticoat Victory', that these 'last invaders' of England met with the 'bitterest humiliation' that could fall to the lot of any soldiers; namely, 'to be scared by petticoats into surrendering'.[20] That spring, Germany entered unrestricted submarine warfare.

The French Invasion narrative was used for propaganda purposes, making use of well-established sources such as the *Chambers* journal article of 1860, read as history rather than fiction, or, more frequently, the information in the Great Western Railway (GWR) travel guides. In September 1916 two Zeppelins were shot down over Essex. All the crew members of one of the airships were killed, but the other crew survived and were arrested by the local police walking along a road. Parallels were drawn with Fishguard in 1797 where the French surrendered 'almost as tamely as the Zeppelin crew the other night did to the Essex "special"'.[21] The journalist in the London newspaper was assured 'by several correspondents' that the event in Fishguard was celebrated in a diamond jubilee year as 'the last invasion of England'.[22]

Invasion scares, spies, rumours and the like fed the fears and imaginations of civilians. The details of the story of Fishguard in 1797 were misremembered to such an extent that the historic French behaviour was cast in new atrocious ways that reflected contemporary fear of Germans. An example of this came not from the coastal communities of Pembrokeshire faced by an unseen U-Boat threat, but from the industrial city of Leeds menaced by the threat of death from the air by Zeppelins.

This background and fear of loss may explain why the reporter in the *Leeds Mercury*, the main newspaper in Leeds, covered the Fishguard Invasion twice in October 1914 and again with similar but amended text in April 1917.[23] Reports of the French Invasion of 1797 in newspapers during the war were usually positive and regarded the humiliation of the French in 1797 as a lesson for the Germans in 1914 and later. Unlike most other press accounts though, this story was not a brief account based on other sources, but the research and interpretation of its own reporters. Most of the detail of the newspaper accounts referencing the Fishguard Invasion during this period came from recently published and readily available material such as the GWR publications. The *Leeds Mercury* articles of 1914 and 1917 are totally different in this respect. They are distinguished by the absence of reference to women and by their exaggeration of the extent of the French destruction.

In 1797 the havoc of the French was confined to the farms and houses on the Pencaer peninsula, the French did not approach let alone enter the town. However, according to the *Leeds Mercury*, writing in 1914 and again in 1917, 'the French men set fire to Fishguard' and 'soon the town was a blazing mess'.[24] The effects of the 'burning' of Fishguard are worse in the 1917 account than in the 1914. This exaggeration was due more to the fears of the First World War than evidence from any source of what did or did not take place in 1797. The total absence of reference to women, when other newspapers were lauding the 'Petticoat Victory' of 1797 makes this reportage unique as well as disturbing. The accounts are very masculine, bleak and terror-laden, with the ludicrous surrender being the necessary anti-climax in both accounts.

With peace came a return to business, but recovery from the First World War was to be slow. It was not just the dislocation of the war; the uncertain political situation in Ireland had 'an adverse effect on the Fishguard-Rosslare route'.[25] The main sea link of the port and the reason for its new prosperity and fame, it did not reopen until 1 January 1920, when the three 'Saints' – GWR vessels that had been repurposed as hospital ships during the war – returned to regular service.[26] With the reopening of the sea routes came a renewal of tourist promotion and the story of 1797 was rehearsed for a new post-war generation.

The atrocities and terrors of more recent wars far eclipsed the horror of the three-day war in 1797, but the romance, the mystery and, above all, the legends persisted after the First World War and would be tested and challenged by a new professional cadre of scholars, before a new audience and readership, who were also middle class and educated. This was an aspect of a growing awareness of the importance of Europe in Welsh culture and history, sharpened by the impact of the war that had seen so many Welsh deaths; it was an awareness that was shared by thinkers of different and contrasting political and religious opinions.[27] The French Revolution was considered as a historical source for modern Wales, both for good and ill, freed from the State and Church and open to new values. This was in contrast to the European reactionism from the early nineteenth century onwards that viewed the French Revolution of 1789 as the fount of all evil.[28] The notion of a French influence on Wales assumed a direct relationship between Wales and France without any other intermediary such as England, Britain, America or even Ireland. The Revd David Davies of Penarth positioned the French Revolution positively within a social and cultural history of Wales (although he would not have used or recognised these terms) in his work *The Influence of the French Revolution on Welsh Life and Literature*.[29]

David Davies is one of those writers whose reputation and achievements may have diminished over time but his writing on the French Revolution in Wales is still widely cited if not widely read.[30] Throughout his life, Davies was a committed Welsh Baptist and British imperialist. His last and longest ministry was at Penarth, where he stayed from 1909 until his death in 1926, and it is with Penarth that his name is commonly associated. Davies was a master at the essay-writing competition of the National Eisteddfod. Although a Welsh speaker from Carmarthenshire, his periods spent outside Wales meant that he was not confident or prepared to write in Welsh.[31] He wrote several essays for the eisteddfod's English-language essay writing competitions and won very lucrative prizes.[32] These essays were generally not published, the exception being his successful essay at the 1925 eisteddfod at Pwllheli, titled 'The Influence of the French Revolution on Welsh Life and Literature', which was published by William Evans, Carmarthen in 1926.

Davies displayed his knowledge and familiarity with the major characters of the French Revolution in Wales, and his observations were invariably astute. His distaste for Roman Catholicism comes out clearly in his description of France in 1789. To the people in this country who had 'caught the fervent evangelism of the Methodist revival', the French Revolution soon became synonymous with anarchy and godlessness.[33] Those who took the most prominent part in the early days of the French Revolution, he argued, were not associated with the orthodox religious denominations but were either irreligious or were Unitarians.[34]

Towards the end of this work, Davies begins his discussion of the landing of the French at Fishguard. His treatment preceded Salmon's by three years. The 'romantic character of the story', repeated by one generation to another, for nearly 130 years, had led many to view it 'as more or less legendary' and not of historical significance.[35] He would prove otherwise and regarded it as a proper subject for historical investigation. He quoted at length from Tate's *Instructions* (from the 1798 pamphlet), which showed the potential seriousness of the planned devastation and the tactics to be employed. From this, Davies argued that the landing (he did not call it an invasion) was far more significant than the dramatic story that had been repeated from mouth to mouth in eest Wales.[36] Davies stood up for the historical integrity of the story, even its 'most romantic' aspects, against recent detractors, who qualified or doubted the story of the landing. Despite his intentions to defend the story from those who dismissed it as mythical, he included the story of the women based on local tradition but added a footnote to give historical credibility to their tall hats, supporting the 'local tradition' with historical evidence.[37]

Nearly half of Davies's essay on the landing at Fishguard was an account and assessment of the trial of Thomas John and Samuel Griffith. Davies was a Baptist; his interest was deep and personal, his coverage extensive. The allegations made against local Dissenters were concealed and forgotten particularly at a time of war. The Welsh Baptists, however, had retained the sense of injustice in their denominational memory, and in writing about the landing of the French at Fishguard in 1926 Davies brought the wrongful persecution back into the public domain. It was Churchmen who suspected Nonconformists of disloyalty and some even of treason. Davies repeats the baseless allegation that Henry Davies, it was whispered far and wide, had stood on a rock to instruct the French how to land.[38]

The French Invasion was not only a topic for academic debate and historical investigation, but it also continued to be well known in popular culture. The male gaze continued to be one such aspect. At the Cardiff and District Pembrokeshire Society dinner in February 1927, one man thought 'that the fact about the French invasion of Fishguard was not that the French soldiery were frightened by a show of lovely shawls but by the petticoats they wore'.[39] The Pembrokeshire men in Cardiff exile laughed. A Welsh-language London-Welsh Cabaret was held at the Hotel Russell in London on New Year's Eve 1929, at which the revellers were delighted to view the *piece de resistance*: 'Merched Abergwaun', a dance by a bevy of pretty girls dressed in white satin with scarlet cloaks and tall Welsh hats purporting to portray the deception of the French at Fishguard in 1797.[40]

As well as male jocularity, half-truths and misremembering were commonplace. There was still a gap between academic and popular knowledge. One correspondent wrote to the *Western Mail* that the French Invasion never happened, the French were turned back by the sight of the 'red coats' on the headland. The person writing could vouch for this fact as 'my great grandmother was numbered among these women'.[41] What was remarkable about the columns of the *Western Mail* was that people were quick to write to correct mistakes and in so doing added misconceptions of their own. A Tenby correspondent confirmed the French Invasion as fact, there were stacks of arms in Tenby museum, captured cannon at Stackpole Court, and M. E. James of Tenby's very interesting novel. It was not, however, red shawls, but '*red flannel petticoats* which they wore over their shoulders but the prudery of Victorian days converted these into *shawls i*n the histories!'[42] In fact, it was the opposite that had taken place, the original shawls had become mid-Victorian petticoats and then had returned to being shawls under the influence of Nonconformist Wales. The Tenby correspondent had been reading his Baring-Gould as well as his Wilkie Collins: in his telling, the women also shouldered broomsticks as well as wearing tall hats.

The anniversary of the Invasion had been frequently marked by correspondence and reminiscence, it seemed in the late 1920s that Jemima Nicholas would have her day, on 6 July, the date of her death. The *Western Mail* published articles on Jemima on 6 July 1927 and 1928, and in September 1927 it was recalled that when Emmeline Pankhurst was in Pembrokeshire, Mr Frederick Warren, the borough accountant, had written a literary tribute to Jemima that had appeared in the organ of the Women's Suffrage movement at that time. They thought that Jemima deserved a better memorial than the one she had: 'Perhaps Fishguard will provide one!'[43] The next month, they reported that Jemima's great granddaughter (*sic*) Mrs Parry from Trelewis still retained her 'historic red cloak' among her 'cherished possessions'.[44] In 1929 the Swansea Pembrokeshire Society visited Fishguard and other places on their 'Day Out' and a Miss Evans laid a bunch of flowers on the memorial stone of 'the heroine of the French invasion at Fishguard'.[45]

Jemima Nicholas also appeared in an new work of scholarship produced by John James Evans (known by his initials as J. J.) in 1928, with a similar Welsh-language title to that of the Revd David Davies, *Dylanwad y Chwyldro Ffrengig ar Lenyddiaeth Cymru*. The title is where the similarity ends; this was an academic dissertation rather than a prize eisteddfod essay, however learned. Evans was born in rural Cardiganshire in the Unitarian 'Black Spot', in Cwrtnewydd.[46] Evans went in 1912 from Llandysul County School to the University College at Bangor, where he graduated with honours in Welsh in 1915. He fought with the Royal Welch Fusiliers and then with the Hood Battalion Royal Naval Defence Force. In 1920 he was appointed Welsh teacher at Fishguard County School where he remained until 1935, when he became headmaster of St David's County

School. At the same time, he continued his studies at Bangor and in 1926 was awarded an MA for his thesis, which was then published in 1928.[47]

The *Dylanwad* is scholarly, carefully researched and written. It set down the parameters on which the French Revolution in Wales was to be studied for at least a generation. Evans divides his book into chronological sections on forerunners, influencers, advocates, opponents and counter-revolutionaries. This approach made for a succession of groupings to be discussed together, often giving the people discussed a commonality that they did not have. Nonetheless, the depth and application of knowledge was impressive, as was its academic apparatus, a footnote in the *Dylanwad* evidenced the comment in the text associated with it and after each chapter he included a detailed list of works read that had contributed to the writing of that chapter.

The French landing is discussed in his chapter 'Adwaith a Gwrthchwyldro (1796–1805)' ('Reaction and Counter-Revolution 1796–1805').[48] Evans gives the story of Bantry Bay as background and then proceeds to Hoche's *Instructions* to Tate (which unfortunately he credits in a footnote to Ap Gwilym, 1797). His description of what took place is brief: they landed 'yn y Garreg Wastad gerllaw Abergwaun', 1,400 in all, 1,400 of them regular soldiers and the rest sweepings from French prisons. Evans the schoolmaster came to the fore, he gave the reasons for their sudden failure in point form (translated by the author):

    1. the drunken excesses of the soldiers
    2. mistaking the levels of rebellion in Wales to be as strong as it was in Ireland
    3. the cunning of Jemima Nicholas and the ladies of the three counties who progressed in red petticoats around the hill 'Y Bigni' tricking the French into thinking that Lord Cawdor had a new army behind him.[49]

His scholarship bestowed on the story of the women academic respectability. In his account, they regained their red petticoats ('peisiau cochion') and lost their red shawls. He adds the anti-Jemima of Nansi Jones, a story more readily available through Welsh-language sources than English, then proceeds to the treason trials and lists those who had been accused of treason.

The story of the trial could be read in full in the history supplied by Dr William Richards in his *Cwyn y Cystuddiedig* and published in English under the title *Triumphs of Innocency*.[50] Evans picked up the anti-Nonconformist prejudices of the local gentry and churchmen from Richards, but also the alliance between Methodists and Churchmen and the impact of the Philip Dafydd quatrain in his ballad that had caused Richards such upset. Evans fell into the trap of conflating the assistant preacher (Thomas John) with the minister of Llangloffan (Henry Dafydd) and claimed that Henry Dafydd was burnt in effigy at the Fishguard fair on 5 February 1798.[51] This in turn influenced the much-loved Baptist minister at Harmony, Fishguard, William Rees (Arianglawdd), who wrote in 1933 of the injustice suffered by Henry Davies and John Reynolds. 'Henry Dafi' had been burnt in effigy at the fair in Fishguard on 5 February 1798, according to Arianglawdd, because the enemies of Nonconformity had encouraged the 'gwerin ffôl' ('foolish people') to do so.[52] It was as a direct result of J. J. Evans that the burning of the wrong Baptist in effigy became an accepted part of the narrative in the twentieth century.[53]

Evans's *Dylanwad* was reviewed by R. T. Jenkins.[54] Jenkins is one of the greats of the writing of the history of Wales, his contribution and standing is, as his biographer in the *Dictionary of Welsh Biography* put it (a work that he helped to edit), truly unique.[55] He was both a Francophile and an authority on eighteenth-century Wales.[56] No great admirer of Liberal sentiments or the polemics of nationalists, he defended vigorously the 'independence of the past' and saw dispassionate objectivity as the mark of a good historian.[57] The French Revolution had hindered the development of the 'political mind' ('y meddwl gwleidyddol') in Wales.[58] The Welsh militia in Ireland in 1798, he condemned as wild and undisciplined detritus.[59] No other Welsh historian before or since has done so. He appealed for historical empathy, for ideological context and noted the particular interest the Welsh had in the American Revolution. The American Revolution brought ideas home to Wales, and that is what happened for a second time when the French landed in Fishguard in 1797: it struck a direct nerve, and the Revolution could now no longer be ignored by ordinary Welshmen who knew nothing and cared even less about Burke or Priestley.[60]

Jenkins had an extremely productive year in 1930, it was the year in which he published *Yr Apêl at Hanes* ('The Appeal to History'), as well as an article in which he had the most he ever had to say about the French landing, while actually writing about the career of the iconoclastic Baptist, William Richards, Lynn.[61] After providing a masterly biographical overview of William Richards, Jenkins turned to discuss the French landing as the backdrop to Richards's *Cwyn y Cystuddiedig*.[62] He introduced a rare biographical note into his history, saying that people should not be surprised by the trial of the falsely accused; those who remembered the war of 1914–18 would realise how easy it was for any of us to fall into such unreasonable behaviour in an emergency. Jenkins had never forgiven Aberystwyth for its disgraceful mob treatment of his friend the German scholar Herman Ethé, and this is reflected in his work here.[63] His discussion of the landing was brief, he took it for granted that people knew the details ('fel y gŵyr pawb'). Jenkins did not want to step on the toes of other historians who had written on the landing, most recently a long article by former Principal David Salmon a year previously.[64]

Salmon's article in the *West Wales Historical Records* was the culmination of years of research on the subject, pursued in tandem with his professional commitments as Principal of Swansea Training College for Women, from where he had recently retired. Salmon's achievement is immense, like that of Professor J. E. Lloyd at Bangor, but on a smaller canvas; Salmon brought the full glare of modern historical method to bear on the French Invasion.[65] Salmon was the main driver as secretary behind the *West Wales Historical Records*, the journal of the Historical Society of West Wales that flourished for a relatively short period from 1913 to 1929. The history of the French Invasion became fully subject to methods of archival research practised by a professional academic. Other Welsh historians, including David Davies and J. J. Evans, had not questioned the historicity of the women in their red cloaks nor Jemima, but this changed with David Salmon.

Salmon's project in 1929 was to reproduce primary sources to tell the story, a method also employed by Wheeler and Broadley. Salmon, likewise, presented several types of evidence: diaries, correspondence, official documents, maps and plans.[66] His article was heavily reliant on the Library of Sir Evan Jones, which Sir Evan, Treasurer of the National Library of Wales, subsequently donated to the Library, with the exception of the gem in the collection, the caricature of the Fishguard Fencible, which was described but not included.[67]

Salmon brought new evidence and new sources to the fore. The use of the Theobald Wolfe Tone diary, for example, was new. Salmon was providing primary sources with a commentary, not a historical account as such. The narrative flow is to be found in the footnotes; Tate, the man appointed to lead the expedition, for example, was, according to Hoche, a 'man of brains and experience', but according to Salmon, the 'Irish-American Col Tate ... proved conspicuously wanting in ability'.[68] Also in a footnote to a statement from Hoche that the Second Legion of France would be 'well armed and equipped and will wear jackets from Quiberon', Salmon mentions, for the first time, that one of the motivations for the Fishguard Invasion was revenge for the British raid on Quiberon in 1795. In his footnote Salmon presents the story showing, without any doubt, the horror of what happened in suppressing the counter-revolution in Brittany.

Salmon did not give vent to his own voice other than in the introduction, in footnotes and occasional commentaries as in the section on 'The Traitors'. Salmon had failed to find any official record of the trial in the Record Office, but fortunately there was quite a full account of it in *Cwyn Y Cystuddiedig*. Unbeknown to Salmon, Edward Arthur Lewis, working with Henry Owen on the Calendar of Public Records for Pembrokeshire, had transcribed the documents sometime between 1911 and 1914.[69]

Salmon reproduced several pages of the *Cwyn*, the proceedings in court, which he translated himself, proving that he maintained a mastery of his native tongue even though he did not publish or write in Welsh.[70] He concluded that all Thomas John had done to trigger his arrest and imprisonment was to have a short discussion with the American Charles Prudhomme.

He gave a full account of the Knox affair, documents and commentary, and was the first to use the Duke of Rutland's *Journal of a Tour through Wales*, which he titled misleadingly *Lord Cawdor's own Narrative*. Readers in Wales now had the opportunity to see English aristocratic prejudice against the Baptists and their ambivalent attitude towards the peasantry. They could also read about St Leger who 'ravished a virgin 60 years old' as well as Manners's unstinting praise for Cawdor who had saved the day by taking the command from the 'infirm' Lord Milford.[71]

The women of Fishguard only get a mention towards the end of the book. Jemima Nicholas's name did not enter his account at all, not even in his separate section on what he termed 'The Legend of the Women'.[72] Salmon concedes that the letters of Mathias and Mends proved that the 'myth of the red cloaked women sprang up very early, and few picturesque accounts of the invasion are considered complete without it'.[73] Salmon does not doubt the authenticity of the letters that he reproduces in full without comment. The Mends letter was communicated to him by Sir James Seabrooke.[74] The letters are authentic eyewitness accounts concerning the active role of women and what they wore did not persuade Salmon that the account of the women was anything other than mythical. He gives no reason or rationale to support his supposition. The fact that 'picturesque accounts' refer to the red-cloaked women demonstrates their status in Salmon's mind as nothing more than a myth.

As an illustration of what he meant by 'picturesque account', which varied with the fancy of the writer, he gave a long extract from Ferrar Fenton's record of local memories published for the first time in 1897.[75] Salmon did not mention that Fenton's authority for the story was that of his own family tradition endorsed by the memory of the community. Salmon chose not to transcribe the extract fully, omitting that Fenton had written that he *'was assured by my father, uncle and the old Fishguardians'* that the story was authentic. Salmon himself had heard at an early age from his mother that his own grandmother had been one of the red-shawled ladies, but had decided to subordinate his own family memories to his own historian's craft and decided to do the same with Fenton's own familial memories. In a footnote, he criticises Ferrar Fenton personally and his grandfather, the great Richard Fenton, the 'historical tourist'.[76] 'Not one word of this story is true', he states. However, by this he did not mean that the story of the red-cloaked women was untrue. His own grandmother had been one of the red-cloaked women and it was true that 'on the fateful Friday' a 'good many red-cloaked women were on the hills around Goodwick'. He believed it utterly false, however, 'that they were formed into a line or that their presence contributed to the surrender'. What Salmon regarded as mythical or untrue was not that the women had a role in the engagement, but the nature of that role. The version of the legend he was disputing was that of the women contributing to the French surrender and this thesis rested on Salmon's view of the surrender itself.

Salmon regarded the surrender as a reasonably smooth transition from Tate's decision to capitulate made on the

Thursday night to the laying down of arms on Goodwick Sands on Friday afternoon, 'the fateful Friday', as he called it. This transition was, in reality, far from smooth, the position was tense, unpredictable and with no certainty of outcome as evidenced by the nervousness of the local commanders and contemporary evidence generally. It can be illustrated by the sources that Salmon himself presented in his 1929 work, which also allow his presuppositions to be examined.

Salmon reproduced letters from the Public Record Office, some of which had also appeared in Wheeler and Broadley, including the letter from Milford to Portland on 24 February, dated Friday morning, six o'clock. A close reading of the original letter shows a misreading by Salmon of the crucial figure of the number of men left behind by the ships who then 'surrendered themselves Prisoners'. This letter also appeared in Broadley and Wheeler, who transcribed from it the following sentence: 'I received information of the French ships having sailed and left *300 men* behind, who have surrendered themselves prisoners'[77] (author's italics). This is Salmon's transcription: 'I received information of the French ships having sailed and left three *[thirteen]* hundred men behind, who have surrendered themselves prisoners' (author's italics).[78] The original in the Public Record Office has 'three hundred' written clearly.[79] Wheeler and Broadley are correct, Salmon is not. Salmon seems to have corrected the original by putting the larger number 'thirteen' in square brackets. That conveyed that most of the French troops had surrendered, thus aligning with the later official account but not Milford's own uncertainties and worries that morning, reflected in the correspondence that Salmon knew and reproduced in his article. It suited Salmon's argument that the surrender was agreed the night before and that the surrender was orderly and without incident, and not subject to any popular influence or pressure.

After his annotated bibliography, where, like a school master, he evaluates the historical sources and works of the past,

Salmon reproduces three valuable illustrations. The first was Propert's map from a copy in the British Museum that formerly belonged to George III. The size of the original map, according to Salmon, was 29 inches by 26 inches.[80] The second was the Plan of Fishguard Bay and the third a picture of the surrender 'from what seems to be a contemporary painting by an amateur'.[81] This painting is a good imaginative recreation of several themes of the invasion that happened at different times located together in one space, and making the surrender a moment of military ceremony, for which there was no contemporary evidence.[82]

David Salmon's influence on the understanding of the story and on further historical enquiry was substantial. His 1929 article was clear, he was not proposing 'to produce a history of the invasion' only 'to garner all the materials for such a history'.[83] His research findings in the Public Record Office and the National Library of Wales aided by direct contact with people such as Sir Evan Jones laid the basis for the history writing of others, notably E. H. Stuart Jones and the generation that followed. There were less favourable outcomes, a consequence of his 'scientific' archival approach, which prioritised written and official accounts. Salmon effectively killed the legend of the women; even though he may have had only one version of it in his sights, his language was extreme, and it was only by going beyond the headlines of 'the myth of the red-cloaked women' that the limited nature of his critique could be appreciated. Salmon's long article, essentially a compilation of primary and secondary sources, formed the substance of the book *Fishguard Invasion 1797: The Descent of the French on Pembrokeshire*, which he published the following year.[84] He prepared a short introduction, but of the remainder of the book, more than two-thirds of the content was the 1929 article.

The red-cloaked women do not appear in Salmon's narrative, only in the footnotes. His scepticism about Jemima meant that he did not take the role of the women seriously, despite his family memories. He explained where he stood on Jemima Nicholas, but was quite reluctant to do so, and when he did he merely gave her description from Ap Gwilym. His only observation in relation to Jemima was: 'modest doubt is called the beacon of the wise'.[85] Nansi Jones is simply not mentioned. Salmon is more sympathetic to the men than the women. The raiders seemed to have 'refrained from wanton attacks on unarmed and unresisting men, but two women were violated'. He mentions St Leger as the violator of one ('he only came for that amusement') from the Rutland journal. The 'other' might have escaped had she not been shot in the leg as she was running; Mary Williams is not named.[86] The article was reviewed favourably in a masterly retelling of the story from the Salmon documents by Professor John Young Evans of the Theological College Aberystwyth.[87]

When the anniversary of the landing was marked in February 1931, an extensive extract from Salmon's newly published book on the Invasion appeared (narrative only) in the *Western Mail* on 21 February with a photograph of Principal David Salmon.[88] All the sections up to the 'surrender' were included, plus a new section written especially for the *Western Mail* on 'The Legend of the Women'. This is a more muted, even nuanced, version of what Salmon had in his book in 1930. It makes no mention of his family tradition nor his footnoted scepticism about Jemima; nonetheless, it remains a forthright refutation of one version of the story and its supposed effects.

A few days later there was a positive response to the article from the Vicar of Blaenavon who congratulated Principal Salmon for supplying more information about the Fishguard Invasion than he had read elsewhere. He looked forward to future and further articles. The Vicar in the next sentence sums up what was unformed, unsaid, but had been on the minds of generations of male observers and commentators particularly the military: 'I am glad that the picturesque narrative of the Welsh women is not wholly true for it belittles the valour of the local militia and yeomanry in checking what might have been a much more serious invasion.'[89] But not everyone was pleased. The landlady of the

Royal Oak complained that Salmon's account of the surrender was incomplete, no mention of the 'terms of capitulation' that were dictated there. If Salmon was to write again on the subject in the press, she asked him politely to mention the 'historic association of the Royal Oak with the invasion'.[90]

Salmon's next article on the French Invasion did not appear until July; the reason for the delay being that he had been provided with new information about the Haverfordwest Trial. The July 1931 article in the *Western Mail* was not the next instalment from his book but totally new information. He had been looking for the original court records on the trial in the Public Record Office but had looked in vain. As a result of the *Western Mail* piece in February a previously unknown correspondent, a Mr G. H. Warlow from Sevenoaks, informed him that he had been more successful.[91] These documents were then published in full by Salmon, giving due recognition to Warlow, in *Y Cymmrodor* for 1932.[92] These legal texts are a rich, unique and under-used resource that give insight into the invasion as seen by the active participants and in their own words. Anyone who encountered the French fell under suspicion. For his part, Salmon did not have much time for Thomas John: 'John was evidently one of those prying persons who will push in whenever there is anything doing and he had only his own curiosity to thank for the trouble into which it got him.'[93]

The legend of the women was remarkably resilient. The 'Women of Fishguard' earned a chapter for themselves in the *Women of Wales*, an innovative work from the early folklorist, social historian and active participant in Welsh public life, Leonard Twiston Davies, and Averil Edwards.[94] *Women of Wales* had a pretty eclectic mix of Welsh women divided into two sections: one historical arranged in chronological order, the other legendary. The Women of Fishguard appeared in the historical section together with women such as the Ladies of Llangollen, Hester Thrale Piozzi and the present-day Mary Davies, the musician and Welsh folksong collector. Twiston

Davies and Edwards were sure that the women of Fishguard merited inclusion in their historical section but recognised that 'critics are divided as to whether it should be treated as a serious incident or an absurd episode'.[95] They took the former view and sympathised with the people of Pembrokeshire who would have been in 1797 'in a considerable state of alarm'. Queen Victoria had conferred battle honours on the Castle Martin Yeomanry. The authors regretted that there was 'no record of any favour having been accorded to the red whittled women who so distinguished themselves upon that notable occasion!'[96]

It was to refute conclusions like this that David Salmon returned to the argument again in the columns of the *Western Mail* in February 1936. February, as the anniversary month of the Fishguard Invasion, was a popular choice for both remembering and debating the subject. On this occasion, his title was only to do with the legend of the women: '*What did Women of Fishguard do when French came? Had Nothing to do with the Capitulation.*'[97] The title could not have been clearer. The 1936 article was a far more explicit refutation. Salmon's contention was that people believed, as a matter of faith almost, that the women had caused the French to surrender because of their deception. He added a new example of the form of the legend of which he specifically disapproved; a 'recent book of travels' had said that the 'Frenchman's terror was increased when they saw the marching and counter marching of redcoats'. The offending work was H. V. Morton's *In Search of Wales* published in 1932.[98] Salmon continued his familiar but now much more focused argument. Like most legends this one had a grain of truth, he conceded that women were present when the invaders laid down their arms and 'among them my mother's mother from Llanychaer, three miles away'. The French coming down the hill to Goodwick saw the red mantles of the women and took them, mistakenly, to be soldiers, but – and this was the crux of his argument – the mistake had nothing to do with the capitulation, because in his account of the surrender, 'the offer to capitulate was made by their commander on Thursday night before he had seen either a red coat or a red mantle'.[99] He introduced new material on women's fashion from Mrs Mary Morgan and her *Tour to Milford Haven* (1795) to confirm that their appearance would have made it easy for them to be mistaken as soldiers. That is where Salmon's article ended, but it was not the end of the treatment of the Fishguard invasion, the *Western Mail* presented a counter-argument on the same page.

Concurrent with Salmon's article in parallel columns was a feature titled 'Record in Diary of Rector of Llangan. By a Correspondent'. This was an extract from the Rector's diary with an introduction from the unnamed correspondent stating that it was not generally known that one of those who witnessed the surrender of the French at Fishguard in 1797 was the renowned David Jones. From this information, never published, the correspondent proceeded to give a brief history of the Invasion allowing the impression to be made that the women in their red costume, which 'at a distance impressed the spectators with the idea of a numerous body of soldiery', came from the diary, where there is no evidence of women, whether red- attired, or not.[100]

Between these articles, almost wrestling to keep them apart, was a drawing of 'THE WOMEN'S COSTUME' from one of the images on a commemorative jug made for Lord Cawdor, then owned by Mr A. G. O. Mathias, with the note that there was an account of the jug in the *Western Mail* of January 1936.[101] Cawdor had had two jugs made by John Johnson of Liverpool, it was said, to commemorate his victory at Fishguard, but there is no evidence for this. On one side of the jug is a portrait of Cawdor leaning against a pedestal with a background of trees with a fort in the distance, believed to represent Fishguard Fort and soldiers on the march are also to be seen. On the other side of the jug there is a soldier and his lass standing in front of a thatched cottage with latticed windows. Nearby is a company of fencibles, with a mounted officer in charge. By the side of the soldier is a woman wearing a hat and draped with a large shawl.[102] This is the only contemporary material evidence of the partnership between women and male soldiery, but it is not a visual presentation of the red-attired women in 1797, which the *Western Mail* article of 22 February 1936 seems to suggest. It is more subtle and subversive than this. The image of the women in the shadows, standing shoulder to shoulder with the men of the Cawdor militia, suggests strongly that the Liverpool potter knew the story. The jug commissioned by Cawdor, probably without his knowing, represents the soldiers and their lasses together, not only as courting couples, but also as partners in war.[103]

Figures 20a and 20b: Cawdor jug, and detail showing a woman in the midst of militia

Endnotes

1. David Williams, (2001), 'SALMON, DAVID (1852–1944), training college principal', in, *Dictionary of Welsh Biography*, https://biography.wales/article/s2-SALM-DAV-1852/ (last accessed 21 January 2021).
2. *Notes and Queries*, 11th ser., 10 (16 October 1914), p. 290.
3. *Notes and Queries*, 11th ser., 10 (31 October 1914) p. 350.
4. Salmon provides a verbatim extract from John Harries, *Welsh Patriotism: Or, The Landing of the French at Fishguard on the 22nd of February, 1797* (Haverfordwest, 1875), pp. 14–15 to illustrate this aspect of the 'legend'.
5. T. Mardy Rees, *Notable Welshmen* (Caernarfon, 1908), p. 175.
6. Salmon, *Notes and Queries* (31 October 1914), p. 351.
7. Salmon, *Notes and Queries* (31 October 1914), p. 351.
8. 'Wales Day by Day', *The Western Mail* (11 November 1914), 17.
9. *The Western Mail* (11 November 1914), 17.
10. *The Western Mail* (11 November 1914), 17.
11. 'Invasion 117 Years Ago', *The Scotsman* (22 August 1914), 11; 'Invasion of Great Britain', *The Scotsman* (25 August 1914), 6.
12. *The Scotsman* (22 August 1914), 11.
13. 'The Last Invasion of England', *The Yorkshire Evening Post* (30 November 1914), 2. *The Yorkshire Evening Post* is here repeating and endorsing what the *Daily Chronicle* had recently reported.
14. 'The Passing Week', *The Carmarthen Weekly Reporter* (4 December 1914), 4.
15. Simon Hancock, 'The Great War at Sea' (2019), www.stdavidshistoricalsociety.org.uk/Great%20War%20at%20Sea.pdf (last accessed 6 August 2024). For the U-Boat threat generally, see Royal Commission on Ancient and Historical Monuments 'U-Boat Project Wales 1914–1918: Commemorating the War at Sea', https://uboatproject.wales/blog/ (last accessed 6 August 2024).
16. 'Parliament y Crefftwyr', *Y Llan* (5 February 1915), 2.
17. 'Scraps', *The Aberdare Leader* (6 February 1915), 2.
18. *The Aberdare Leader* (6 February 1915), 2.
19. 'Under False Colours', *The Westminster Gazette* (22 February 1915), 3; 'Personal and Incidental', *The Northern Whig* (24 February 1915), 7; 'The Last Invasion', *The Birmingham Daily Post* (26 February 1915), 10.
20. 'A Petticoat Victory', *The People* (7 May 1916), 2.
21. 'Historic Record, Zeppelin Crew the First Invaders since French landed at Fishguard', *Haverfordwest and Milford Haven Telegraph* (4 October 1916), 2; 'The Last Invasion', *Daily News (London)* (4 October 1916), 4.
22. *The Daily News (London)* (4 October 1916), 4.
23. 'When Britain was Invaded: The Last Descent upon our Shores', *Leeds Mercury* (14 October 1914), 2; Mark Potter, 'The Last Invasion of Britian: 1400 Prisoners taken-all the men who landed', *Leeds Mercury* (23 April 1917), 4.
24. *Leeds Mercury* (14 October 1914), 2; *Leeds Mercury* (23 April 1917), 4.

25 Miles Cowsill, *Fishguard Rosslare* (Kilgetty, 1990), p. 10.
26 Cowsill, *Fishguard Rosslare*, p. 10.
27 See M. Wynn Thomas, *Eutopia: Studies in Cultural Euro-Welshness 1850–1980* (Cardiff, 2021) for the several models of Euro-Welshness including the Cultural Right.
28 Emlyn Sherrington, 'Welsh Nationalism, the French Revolution and the Influence of the French Right 1880–1930', in D. Smith (ed.), *A People and a Proletariat: Essays in the History of Wales 1780–1980* (London, 1980), p. 142.
29 David Davies, *The Influence of the French Revolution on Welsh Life and Literature* (Carmarthen, 1926).
30 John Williams Hughes (1959), 'DAVIES, DAVID (1849–1926), Baptist minister and author', *Dictionary of Welsh Biography*, https://biography.wales/article/s-DAVI-DAV-1849 (last accessed 27 January 2021).
31 Review of 'David Davies, The Ancient Celtic Church of Wales', *Y Goleuad* (20 April 1910), 9.
32 'National Eistddfod', *The Cambrian News* (15 August 1919), 6; 'Chairing the Bard', *The Yorkshire Post* (11 August 1922), 9.
33 Davies, *The Influence of the French Revolution on Welsh Life and Literature*, p. 7.
34 Davies, *The Influence of the French Revolution on Welsh Life and Literature*, p. 20.
35 Davies, *The Influence of the French Revolution on Welsh Life and Literature*, p. 224.
36 Davies, *The Influence of the French Revolution on Welsh Life and Literature*, p. 226.
37 Davies, *The Influence of the French Revolution on Welsh Life and Literature*, p. 228. Michael Freeman on his indispensable website for the history of fashion in Wales has identified a ballad published in Trefriw (near Bala in north Wales), which refers to the 'ffasiwn hyll': *https://welshhat.wordpress.com/elements-of-welsh-costumes/hats/early-tall-hats/* (last accessed 6 August 2024). The first three parts of this ballad were written by Ellis Roberts, the fourth by J. W. and E. Owens. Ballad printed by David Jones, Trefriw, 1778; J. H. Davies, 'Bibliography of Welsh Ballads', *Transactions of the Honourable Society of Cymmrodorion*, 304 (1908–11), 111.
38 Davies, *The Influence of the French Revolution on Welsh Life and Literature*, p. 235.
39 'Pembroke's Great Men. Cardiff Dinner. Sir David Hughes-Morgan as Guest', *Western Mail* (17 February 1927), 7.
40 'London Welsh Cabaret. Bardic Welcome for 1930. Native Folk-Songs and Dances', *Western Mail* (1 January 1930), 8.
41 'Links with the Past. Why the French did not land at Fishguard', *Western Mail* (9 March 1927), 9.
42 'Wales Day by Day', *Western Mail* (17 March 1927), 8.
43 'Wales Day by Day', *Western Mail* (20 September 1927), 6.

44 'Historic Red Cloak. Relic of Jemima Nicholas as Keepsake', *Western Mail* (1 October 1927), 10.
45 'Swansea Pembrokeshire Society's Day Out', *Western Mail* (2 July 1929), 10.
46 An area of Unitarian concentration in Cardiganshire collectively known to a hostile Methodist historiography as the 'Black Spot' ('Y Smotyn Du'). Evan David Jones (2001), 'EVANS, JOHN JAMES (1894–1965), teacher and writer', in *Dictionary of Welsh Biography*, https://biography.wales/article/s2-EVAN-JAM-1894 (last accessed 28 January 2021).
47 John James Evans MA, *Dylanwad y Chwyldro Ffrengig ar Lenyddiaeth Cymru* (Liverpool, 1928), Preface.
48 Evans, *Dylanwad y Chwyldro Ffrengig*, pp. 175–8.
49 Evans, *Dylanwad y Chwyldro Ffrengig*, p. 176.
50 Richards wrote to Samuel Jones, Pennepek, Philadelphia to say that he had been warned off publishing an English version of his incendiary pamphlet.
51 Evans, *Dylanwad y Chwyldro Ffrengig*, p. 178.
52 W. Rees (Arianglawdd), 'Bedyddwyr Penfro: Glaniad Y Ffrancod 1797', *Trafodion Cymdeithas Hanes Bedyddwyr Cymry* (1933), 1; the wrongly attributed effigy burning does not appear in the entry on Henry Davies in R. Edwards, *Hanes Llangloffan* (Solva, 1932), pp. 24–6.
53 R. T. Jenkins (1959). DAVIES, HENRY I, (1753–1825), Baptist minister in, *Dictionary of Welsh Biography*, https://biography.wales/article/s-DAVI-HEN-1753 (last accessed 26 March 2024). Evans may have mentioned this misconception to others too; Syd Walters, for example, was convinced that Davies was burnt in effigy. Evans was his Welsh teacher.
54 R. T. Jenkins, 'J. J. Evans, Dylanwad y Chwyldro Ffrengig', *Y Llenor*, 8/1–4 (1929), 126–8.
55 John Gwynn Williams (2001). 'JENKINS, ROBERT THOMAS (1881–1969), historian, man of letters, editor of *Y Bywgraffiadur Cymreig* and the *Dictionary of Welsh Biography*', in *Dictionary of Welsh Biography*, https://biography.wales/article/s2-JENK-THO-1881 (last accessed 29 January 2021).
56 For R. T. Jenkins and France and his disagreement with Saunders Lewis over France, see Thomas, *Eutopia*, pp. 134–6.
57 Geraint H. Jenkins, '"Taphy-land historians" and the Union of England and Wales 1536–2007', *Journal of Irish and Scottish Studies*, 1/2 (2008), 19–20.
58 R. T. Jenkins, *Hanes Cymru yn y Bedwaredd Ganrif ar Bymtheg* (Cardiff, 1933; repr. 1972), p. 29.
59 Jenkins, *Hanes Cymru*, p. 32.
60 Jenkins, *Hanes Cymru*, p. 127.
61 R. T. Jenkins, 'William Richards o Lynn', *Trafodion Cymdeithas Hanes Bedyddwyr Cymry* (1930), 17–72.
62 Jenkins, 'William Richards o Lynn', 30.

63 E. L. Ellis, *The University College of Wales, Aberystwyth 1872–1972* (Cardiff, 1972), p. 234.
64 Jenkins, 'William Richards o Lynn', 30; David Salmon, 'The French Invasion of Pembrokeshire in 1797', *West Wales Historical Records*, 14 (1929), 133–207.
65 For J. E. Lloyd see Huw Pryce, *J. E. Lloyd and the Creation of Welsh History: Renewing a Nation's Past* (Cardiff, 2011). See also Geraint Jenkins, 'Clio and Wales: Welsh Remembrancers and Historical Writing', *Transactions of the Honourable Society of Cymmrodorion*, 2001 new ser., 8 (2002), 119–36.
66 Salmon, 'The French Invasion of Pembrokeshire in 1797', 136–209.
67 List of Books in Evan Jones Library, National Library of Wales ex 1780. For the influence on Salmon see NLW Salmon Correspondence 7351C, letters dated 16 and 17 September 1929. Sir Evan Jones had bought manuscripts also from Broadley's Collection. Undated David Salmon letter, NLW MS 19439B.
68 Salmon, 'The French Invasion of Pembrokeshire in 1797', 135 note 2.
69 National Library of Wales, Henry Owen Papers 1419 C and endnote 101, chapter two.
70 Salmon, 'The French Invasion of Pembrokeshire in 1797', 172–4. For the section translated by Salmon see Marion Löffler with Bethan Jenkins, *Political Pamphlets and Sermons from Wales 1790–1806* (Cardiff, 2014), pp. 281–4.
71 Salmon, 'The French Invasion of Pembrokeshire in 1797', 187.
72 Salmon, 'The French Invasion of Pembrokeshire in 1797', 194–5.
73 Salmon, 'The French Invasion of Pembrokeshire in 1797', 194.
74 For Sir James Seabrooke and the Mends letter, see Chapter 7, footnote 111.
75 Salmon, 'The French Invasion of Pembrokeshire in 1797', 194. The extract quoted by Salmon is from Ferrar Fenton, 'Landing of the French at Fishguard in 1797', in *Pembrokeshire Antiquities* (Solva, 1887), 65–6; see Chapter 6, footnote 113.
76 Salmon, 'The French Invasion of Pembrokeshire in 1797', 194.
77 H. F. B. Wheeler and A. M. Broadley, *Napoleon and the Invasion of England*, (London, 1908), p. 65.
78 Salmon, 'The French Invasion of Pembrokeshire in 1797', 151.
79 National Archives, PRO 42-40-3 no. 240.
80 Propert's 1798 map of the Pencaer peninsula with the key invasion sites marked was reproduced and reduced as a souvenir for the 1897 centenary and again for the bicentenary in 1997; it has also been reproduced in several books, for example E. H. Stuart Jones, *The Last Invasion* (Cardiff, 1950), as well as Salmon. See also D. W. Davies, 'Mapping Invasion: Cartography, Caricature, Frames of Reading', in Sally Bushell and Julia S. Carlson and Damian Walford Davies (eds), *Romantic Cartographies: Mapping, Literature, Culture 1789–1832* (Cambridge, 2020), pp. 101–21.
81 Salmon, 'The French Invasion of Pembrokeshire in 1797', 206.

82 This painting is reproduced in Stuart Jones, *The Last Invasion*, p. 128, and is the cover of J. E. Thomas, *Britain's Last Invasion: Fishguard 1797* (Stroud, 2007). It was formerly in the Middleton Hall collection and was presented to Carmarthenshire Museum by Major W. J. Hughes in 1926.
83 Salmon, 'The French Invasion of Pembrokeshire in 1797', 131.
84 David Salmon, *Fishguard Invasion 1797: The Descent of the French on Pembrokeshire* (Carmarthen, 1930).
85 Salmon, *Fishguard Invasion 1797: The Descent of the French*, p. 23 footnote.
86 Salmon, *Fishguard Invasion 1797: The Descent of the French*, p. 11.
87 J. Young Evans, 'The French Freebooters at Fishguard', *Pembroke County and West Wales Guardian* (3 October 1930).
88 'Last Invasion. The French came to Pembrokeshire', *Western Mail* (21 February 1931), 11.
89 'Fishguard Invasion. Was it Seriously Regarded by the French?', *Western Mail* (25 February 1931), 4.
90 Pembrokeshire Archives, D/Sal/169, Mrs M. Thomas to David Salmon, 24 February 1931.
91 David Salmon, 'When the French landed in Wales. Hunt for the traitors followed by Treason Trial', *Western Mail* (28 July 1931), 6.
92 David Salmon, 'A Sequel to the French Invasion of Pembrokeshire', *Y Cymmrodor*, 43 (1932), 62–92.
93 David Salmon, 'When the French landed in Wales. Hunt for the traitors followed by Treason Trial', *Western Mail* (28 July 1931), 6.
94 L. Twiston Davies and Averil Edwards, *Women of Wales* (London, 1935), pp. 184–93.
95 Davies and Edwards, *Women of Wales*, p. 184.
96 Davies and Edwards, *Women of Wales*, p.193.
97 'What did Women of Fishguard do when French Came? Had Nothing to Do with the Capitulation', *Western Mail* (22 February 1936), 11.
98 H. V. Morton, *In Search of Wales* (London, 1932), p. 199.
99 *Western Mail* (22 February 1936), 11.
100 For the diary, see Gomer M. Roberts, 'The Year 1797 in the life of the Rev David Jones Llangan', *Cylchgawn Cymdeithas Hanes y Methodistiaid Calfinaidd*, 23 (1938), 101.
101 *Western Mail* (22 February 1936), 11
102 'Jug Memento of Famous Invasion, French Landing at Fishguard', *Western Mail* (27 January 1936), 13.
103 Information about the jug provided by A. G. O. Mathias in correspondence with David Salmon, January 1936, see Pembrokeshire Archives D/Sal/169. The jug was donated by A. G. O. Mathias to the National Museum of Wales . See Jug - Collections Online *https://museum.wales/collections/online/object/3531f0c9-f210-3113-8309-360645e93a54/Jug/?field0=string&value0=40.463&field1=with_images&value1=1&index=0* (accessed 8 January 2025).

Chapter 9

The Second World War and the Last Invasion, 1936–50

Memories of the French Invasion for Pembrokeshire people or people with Pembrokeshire connections had a personal quality. The troubled but brilliant poet and journalist, lapsed preacher, drunk and sometimes tramp, David Emrys James, *Dewi Emrys*, wrote of his memories in the *Western Mail* in his distinctive folk-erudite Welsh on the Fishguard landing and the heroines of Pencaer, the land of his youth.[1] He recalled the memorial stone erected at Carreg Wastad, the stone with the unassuming inscription. It was erected there in 1897, when, he says, he was a dreamy youth among the old inhabitants who had never seen a train. His paean of praise to the 'Heroines of the Land of his Boyhood' ('Arweresau Bro fy Mebyd') commenced with Ann George, the maid at Trehowel who saved the silver spoons after being left in charge when the squire Mortimer had galloped away, another embodiment of superior female behaviour compared to the men of the time. But the crowning representatives of the women at that time were the brave Jemima Nicholas, Fishguard and Nansi Jones, Llanybydder, two very different women in temper, work and behaviour. When Jemima heard there were invaders in their midst she first turned in to the Royal Oak for a drink and then went towards Pencaer with a pitchfork on her shoulders. 'This story was not a legend' ('Nid chwedl mo'r hanes hwnnw').

Nansi Jones's heroism was different; to seek a memorial stone for Nansi would be in vain, but one day she would be remembered in the 'minute book of Heaven'. Through her the spirit of the Pentecost had cast out fear. To Dewi Emrys these were not stories but memories. Jemima was not a mythical figure but a heroine from the land of his boyhood. Principal David Salmon had had his doubts, but Dewi Emrys had none.

Interest about the Invasion was not restricted to Pembrokeshire or Wales. In 1935, John Gore wrote an influential article for the *Quarterly Review* titled 'The Last Invasion of Britain', the first major work to have 'Last Invasion' in its title.[2] John Gore was the then the earl of Cawdor's son-in-law, he had married Lady Janet Helena Campbell, daughter of Hugh Frederick Vaughan Campbell, fourth Earl Cawdor of Castlemartin, in 1926. He was entitled to practise as a barrister but spent most of his time as a writer, a journalist and author, dying in 1983.[3]

The social and cultural extremes of interest and involvement in remembering the French Invasion are represented clearly by Dewi Emrys and John Gore: the frequently impoverished, lapsed preacher and brilliant poet Dewi Emrys on the one hand, writing in Welsh; the Radley-educated, Cawdor son-in-law John Gore, upper-class aristocrat on the other hand, writing in English. The social and cultural divides were as wide in 1935 as they had been in 1797. Gore's lasting contribution was to frame the French Invasion as the Last Invasion.[4]

Gore wrote as an English gentleman-scholar and patronised the natives. Pembrokeshire was one of the 'outlying corners of England' and could not just await 'instructions from headquarters'.[5] The handful of volunteers, however, had a 'greater destiny' awaiting them than the 'browbeating of disgruntled yokels'. Gore, as is to be expected, was extremely respectful of his wife's ancestor, Lord Cawdor, and had access to the Cawdor diary. He was the first to publish extracts from the diary, Salmon had not seen it, but Laws had. He published the entry of the first day of the landing, which he prefaced with the comment that 'There is something of the Drake touch in the entry in his diary for this day of fate':

> Feb. 22, 1797: A fine day. Major Ackland & Minhouse called. Walked to the garden with them. After rode with Car [Lady Cawdor, daughter of the fifth Earl of Carlisle] & Minhouse to the Warren, back by Freeman's Quarry. At 11 o'clock, received Mathias' express respecting the French.[6]

This was the only extract from the diary that Gore reproduced, probably because Cawdor's diary actually had very little to say about the invasion. Why did Tate land only to kick his heels for a few hours and 'ignominiously surrender to a force of half his number?' Gore asked.[7] The majority of his men were gaolbirds over whom he had little command, but there remained 'the picturesque explanation of the Welsh wives and their red and white whittles. This, indeed, was no romantic legend which grew up after the event'.[8] The denial of the 'romantic legend' was a direct challenge to the unidentified doubters, primarily Wheeler and Broadley, and Salmon. At the end of the article, he reproduced the Mathias letter ('written by a local woman, in the red-heat of excitement to her sister in domestic service in Swansea'), a 'gem', he said, which proved the 'substance' of the legend.[9] The credit for 'the successful defeat of the last invasion of Britain' could be 'fairly divided between Lord Cawdor and his officers, the local volunteers, the peasantry, and their womenfolk, in just proportion'.[10]

Gore's influential piece, disconnected as it was, was a very 'English' example of the narrative with a focus on military movements, his own Cawdor family connections, Cawdor and the militia, and with very little reference to the victims. There was no mention of the treason trials and total ignorance of stories that Welsh speakers identified so closely with elements of the invasion.

These elements came into their own when the first National Eisteddfod to be held in Pembrokeshire took place in Fishguard in 1936. Through the influence of Lloyd George, Fishguard beat Cardiff in the application to host the National Eisteddfod that year.[11] Like the opening of the new sea route to Ireland in 1906 and the coming of the *Mauretania* to Fishguard in 1909, this would bring fame, although perhaps less fortune, to Fishguard. The run up to the Eisteddfod in 1936 started early, memories of 1797 were prevalent and affected the competition planning. Visitors came to Fishguard for the proclamation ceremony in June 1935 and wanted to be told again the story of the 'Fishguard women who repelled the French invader in 1797' even though the *Western Mail* conceded that 'perhaps the story is more legend than fact, but it serves to epitomize the courage of Pembrokeshire people'.[12]

The *Western Mail* sent a reporter, 'The Wanderer', to Fishguard in July 1936 to see how the town was preparing for the National Eisteddfod, which was less than a month away. A number of Pembrokeshire young women were preparing to wear the national costume and at the same time commemorate the victory over the invaders. The story of the women in their red cloaks came up, everyone knew it even 'though stern historians disbelieve it'. 'The Wanderer' knew a dear old woman at St Clears who jealously retained the garments worn by her ancestors at the time of the French Invasion and 'to her intimate friends she relates the story of the brave women of Fishguard as it has been handed down to her from generation to generation'.[13] The *Western Mail* covered the event thoroughly and issued a special National Eisteddfod Supplement including a survey of what people thought of when they first heard 'Fishguard': 'To nine people out of ten the name "Fishguard" will immediately be associated with the "French Invasion" ... but all will this year find "national Eisteddfod" also coming into mind.'[14]

Given the recent coverage in their columns and the high profile of the 'legend of the women' discussion the *Western Mail* had to give an opinion on what it called the 'Red Cloak legend' as part of this National Eisteddfod Supplement: 'Recent researches into the occurrences of those February days tend to refute the colourful tale; yet to support it there is the tomb of Jemima Nicholas who led the "red army" bearing witness in front of the Parish Church.'[15] The *Western Mail*'s reporter Llewellyn Evans retold the story about the deception played by the red-cloaked women on the French, that they were regular reinforcements. But a 'more cogent reason for the decision to treat for surrender' was the intoxication of the troops and their mutinous behaviour, abandoned by the ships. By 'recent researches', he meant the work of Principal Salmon.

The speakers on the Eisteddfod stage made frequent mention of the events of 1797, and many Eisteddfod visitors went to see the memorial stone at Carreg Wastad for themselves. There was gossip and good conversation aplenty. Sitting next to the *Western Mail* reporter in the pavilion was Canon David Davies of Fishguard. In response to a remark by a 'local orator-historian', possibly David Salmon himself, the Canon turned to the reporter and whispered: 'I can show you an entry in the burial roll about Jemima Nicholas … which destroys the insinuations of cynics that much of the story concerning her is a pretty fiction.'[16]

As usual the Eisteddfod drew the leading politicians both in and from Wales. There was no greater draw than the 'Welsh Wizard' himself, David Lloyd George. Lloyd George was a frequent Eisteddfodwr and had made speeches at several. The first National Eisteddfod to be held in Pembrokeshire was special, his son was an MP there and his family had Pembrokeshire roots: William George, Lloyd George's father was from Trefwrdan (Jordanston).

Lloyd George's connections with the French Invasion lay with his great grandparents on his father's side. When his career was in the ascendancy, his great grandmother was referred to as one of the red-cloaked ladies, and his great grandfather's farm, Tresinen or Tresinwen, was listed by Ap Gwilym as being one of the houses looted by the French.[17] According to Lloyd

George's son, his father enjoyed telling the story of how his great grandmother had dressed a 'party of housewives in scarlet cloaks' and paraded them to deceive the French into thinking they were British Redcoats. This camouflage technique appealed to Lloyd George as an indication of 'the early manifestation of Lloyd Georgian tactical skill', according to his son.[18] Lloyd George saw no political advantage in recalling this family memory, but this did not deter public imaginings that his 'grandmother' had been one of the red-shawled women. In 1935 the *Western Mail* imagined Lloyd George's grandmother (*sic*) marching around the Bigny in her red shawl 'if only the story were not a bright legend'.[19] Lloyd George was at the Fishguard Eisteddfod and gave a speech at the chairing ceremony on lessons from Welsh and Pembrokeshire history.[20] It was a plea for English-speaking and Welsh-speaking Welshmen and women to unite as one people in common devotion to their native land. He would have gone on to proclaim a modern Pembrokeshire hero who embraced both cultures, the painter Augustus John, but the microphones failed and his speech was cut short.[21]

Sir John Simon, whose father was from Stackpole Elidor, Castlemartin, was also at the Eisteddfod and was not reluctant to include his great grandmother as one of the red-cloaked ladies. Sir John Simon has been called one of the most intellectually distinguished politicians of the twentieth century.[22] Like Lloyd George, he was born in Manchester, but he held a strong fondness for his father's land and he and his sister returned to 'Little England beyond Wales' for four weeks every summer during his boyhood years.[23] When Sir John Simon was elevated to the Lords on becoming Lord Chancellor in 1940, the Cawdor family consented to the name of his father's village, which was on their estate, being associated with his viscountcy, so he became Viscount Simon of Stackpole Elidor.[24] At the National Eisteddfod, Sir John Simon spoke from the stage of the landing of the French near Fishguard and of the 'tradition' that the 'peasant women' in marching round the hill were mistaken for a regiment of soldiers; 'I should like to think', added Sir John, 'that my great grandmother was one of those who thus helped to repulse the last of the invaders'.[25]

The 'Legend of the Women' still simmered. David Salmon took issue with the piece in the Eisteddfod Supplement and took the journalist, Llewellyn Evans, to task for quoting from sources that had no basis in fact.[26] Salmon was then in turn challenged by a correspondent who disagreed, 'I have just spoken to a schoolmaster near Narberth whose great grandmother was an eyewitness of this stratagem of Lord Cawdor's'.[27] David Salmon's last published work was a bibliographical article on the histories of the French Invasion.[28] In this article he classified the various histories by one of three categories: original, derivative and fictitious – each was then described and a brief assessment provided. It reads almost as a school report, with some works needing to do much better than others. This article was an expanded, sharper version of the bibliography in his 1929 compilation, with the addition of his classifications. Salmon had become very critical of the works of previous historians and this article showed him at his most didactic.

John Gore's term, the 'Last Invasion', grew in relevance in the period 1939–45. The French Invasion was incorporated into the war effort, a component of the propaganda of the period that positioned the historic campaign against Napoleon with the new campaign against the threat of invasion from Hitler's Germany. Mark Rawlinson has suggested that Napoleonic scares became doubly distanced from the realm of 'empirical' war by the non-occurrence of occupation and by their association with the 'wrong' war, a war that predated the Germano-British (and American) conflicts of the twentieth century.[29] Although the French in 1939–45 were the 'wrong' enemy, there were still some similarities between the war of 1939–45 and that against Napoleon. Britain had avoided invasion and had prevailed against Napoleon; the French Invasion of Pembrokeshire was of relevance to the present as a statement of defiance that this was the 'last' invasion of Britain, there would be no other. There were two angles to this definition: historical fact and patriotic aspiration. The prospect of invaders suffering a similar fate to those in Pembrokeshire in 1797 in another major war was a psychological comfort. The ignominious surrender of Tate was recalled in the anxious days of July 1940. His 'Nazi imitators' would do us more harm but would, like Tate, end up in the Admiralty for examination.[30] This reconnection between present and past was particularly strong in those areas that suffered most from German aerial bombardment and that also had a strong historical link with the French Invasion and Fishguard, Liverpool in particular.

The histories of Liverpool and Fishguard were inextricably linked by the 1797 Invasion. Liverpool was one of the original destinations of the French expedition, and the news of the Invasion prompted rapid and successful reinforcements to the port of Liverpool and demonstrations of loyalty organised and led by the Mayor George Dunbar. Richard Brooke's *Liverpool as it was during the last quarter of the eighteenth century 1775–1800* published in 1853 gave detailed coverage of the events at Fishguard in 1797. The readers of this Liverpool history were better informed about Fishguard in 1797 than any other group of English readers. Brooke used Ap Gwilym's new edition of 1853 in the *Additions and Corrections* to his Liverpool history. Brooke was impressed by the Welsh and believed that their response to French hostility had probably been underreported.[31] Brooke had also picked up the newspaper reports regarding the death of Mary Williams, or 'Matty Carham' as she was known (Matty from Mary, Carham from Caerlem).

Liverpool was the most heavily bombed area of the country outside London, due to the city having, along with Birkenhead, the largest port on the west coast and being of significant importance to the British war effort. Descriptions of damage were kept vague to hide information from the Germans, and downplayed in the newspapers for propaganda purposes;

this led to many Liverpudlians feeling that their suffering was overlooked compared to other places. Around 4,000 people were killed in the Merseyside area during the Blitz which commenced in Liverpool in August 1940.

Between 1 and 6 September 1939, the evacuations, organised by Liverpool Corporation, saw 8,500 children, parents and teachers moved from the city to rural areas and small towns in the Liverpool hinterland. As months went by with no signs of an air raid by the Luftwaffe, many parents brought their children back to Liverpool and, by January 1940, 40 per cent of the evacuated children were back in the city.[32] This uneasy complacency features in a scene in Liverpool discussed by the *Liverpool Echo* in January 1940. Liverpudlians sat over their 'morning coffee' and discussed the war and its manifestations. It was almost unanimously agreed that all talk of an invasion of their shores, apart from air raids, was ridiculous. But when this belief was probed it was found to be based on the belief that Britain had not been invaded since 1066. 'Precisely the same belief prevailed at the end of the eighteenth century' when the inhabitants of Liverpool received a rude shock that the French had landed at Fishguard and were to march to Liverpool.[33] The *Liverpool Echo* then told the story of Mayor Dunbar and the efforts made by the people of Liverpool to fortify themselves from attack. The French had surrendered so the people of Liverpool had been preparing anxiously and excitedly to combat a peril that had ceased to exist. But the threat had been made and Liverpool acted promptly and expeditiously.[34] On 17 June 1940 the leading article in the *Liverpool Echo* was 'FRANCE LEAVES THE WAR', but the paper also included an article that day on the 'Liverpool Volunteers' in February 1797. The events of 1797 had proved to be a false alarm 'but Liverpool was ready'.[35] This earlier threat was again recalled in May 1941, a time when Liverpool was experiencing terrible air raids: 'The threat of invasion which now hangs over our heads in addition to monthly air raids, recalls that in 1797 there was a threat of invasion of Liverpool.'[36] Liverpool was prepared and the people were relieved that the French surrendered in 1797; would the same thing happen in 1941?

There was a scientific historical basis to the comparisons between past invasions and strategies to protect the country from the prospect of a new invasion. As in the First World War, the history of invasions and how England had succeeded to evade and avoid invasion for such a long period had a practical application. Historical context was of strategic significance. In 1941 the foremost naval intellectual, retired Navy officer and distinguished historian committed himself to the task. Admiral Sir Herbert William Richmond, KCB, FBA (1871–1946) published a history of the invasions of Britain since 1586.[37] It was a technical treatise on naval tactics based on historical research on how Britain, through offensive and defensive measures, could reduce the risk of invasion.[38] As part of the larger campaign in Ireland, Richmond discussed Fishguard. Its objectives were to interrupt or hinder commerce, to start a rising in Wales and to facilitate a landing elsewhere. He drew parallels with the present.[39] Tate landed 12,000 of his *Legion Noire* in Fishguard and surrendered to a body of militia of less than half their strength. No mention, of course, was made of the red-cloaked women in this military account. Richmond dismissed the raid as a 'trivial affair'. This view was not, however, shared by the popular media. It was the role of the women that had the popular appeal, even more so in the Second World War than the First.

In February 1940, the same piece appeared in the *Liverpool Echo*, the *Midland Daily Telegraph* and elsewhere. The story carried different headlines; the one in the *Midland Daily Telegraph*, for example, was 'Welsh Women Scared Britain's Last Invaders. French Mistook them for Troops'.[40] The purpose of the stories was clearly in all cases to associate a present and real danger with one from the past that not only failed but failed ridiculously. Napoleon, the papers commented, had envisaged the invasion of England by means of balloons and there was talk of German parachutes landing at remote spots for sabotage purposes, how to negate this threat? 'The last actual attempt at an invasion of Britain ended in inglorious failure'.⁴¹ Local stories such as the Crawshays organising militia forces from their iron workers in Merthyr Tydfil in 1797 were used by Edgar Chappell to respond to the German threat of June 1940.⁴² *The Sphere* the same month presented a popular historical survey of all the invasions of England and concluded that only small and quickly suppressed landings had taken place since 1066. Fishguard was described as a 'fiasco', a prelude to the more serious threats of 1803–5.⁴³

The early months of 1940 drew a new enthusiast of the Fishguard Invasion into the debate, the established and well-respected journalist, Derek Hudson. A member of the editorial staff of *The Times* from 1939 to 1949, Hudson was an accomplished and fluent writer, able to turn his hand successfully to a variety of literary forms; a man of letters. He had written and would come to write well-received biographies such as one on Lewis Carroll, but in early 1940 his attention fell on Fishguard. His first article on the Fishguard Invasion in the February edition of the *Spectator* in 1940, began with a reflection on the times: 'within the past few months the thoughts of most of us must have turned however reluctantly and sceptically to the possibility of an enemy invasion.'⁴⁴

Hudson had visited Pencaer for himself. In January 1940 he stood by the memorial stone above Carreg Wastad, called in at the farmhouse at Trehowel and paid sixpence to see the famous bullet hole in the Brestgarn clock. He sat in the parlour at the Royal Oak and saw a musket provided by one of its habitues whose great-grandmother had picked it up on Pencaer, and 'which he treasures more than all his possessions'.

Hudson drew parallels with modern Britain and the current war with Hitler. Like the 1797 expedition, Hitler's expeditionary force to Britain would be equally ambitious in its aim and in the unscrupulousness in which it would be executed. Hoche's instructions to Tate are given in some detail, the burning of Bristol and the devastation intended for Chester and Liverpool would have touched more than a nerve in 1940. 'John Bull' prevailed and Colonel Tate and his marauders didn't advance more than 2 miles from the cliff edge. Fortune favoured the Fishguard Fencibles, the second-oldest volunteer corps in the country; the invaders made themselves ill through eating half-cooked mutton or drunk from ship-wrecked wine. There was also the legend of the women in their red cloaks 'whatever the actual facts, the episode from the military standpoint, could hardly have been briefer or more successful'. A few men on both sides were killed but several hours before the actual surrender the French were selling their cutlasses to all comers for 6d each. David Salmon 'who knows more about the Fishguard invasion than anyone else' sent him a document from the Pembrokeshire county archives that gave the overall cost of the expedition in terms of compensation at the time: £890 19s. 9 1/2d; this was no small sum, and in 1940 the costs would be proportionately and alarmingly increased. The concluding lesson for 1940 was heartening, the modern volunteer, the air-raid warden, could take courage 'from the example of his predecessor, the Fishguard Fencible, and, like him, may find the reality less evil than his expectation'.[45] This remark was particularly heartening to readers in February 1940 given the grim realities of the war in Norway, France and Poland.

A short debate ensued in subsequent editions under the title of 'Invaded Britain' concerning the role of the women. A correspondent from East Grinstead raised the issue of the role of women and supplied Hudson with an exact copy of the Mathias letter suggesting that what Hudson had termed a 'legend' was not so, and incidentally suggesting 'what a fine film might be made of this remarkable affair'.[46] Derek Hudson responded in the next edition again under the title of 'Invaded Britain'.[47] He used the research of David Salmon and the letter from John Mends, which was equally explicit concerning the role of the women, but he agreed with Salmon that it was utterly false that their presence contributed to the surrender of the enemy. And yet, Hudson also had some doubts of his own. He had obviously been researching the invasion and had seen Salmon's compilation of court documents in *Y Cymmrodor* in 1932. He had noticed Prudhomme's reference to Thomas John's alleged statement that 'half were women with red Flannels', although he acknowledges that this recollection may well have been coloured 'by six months of gossip in a local gaol'.[48] Hudson and Salmon were in amicable correspondence over these *Spectator* articles, Salmon impressing on Hudson that the 'English-speaking Prudhomme had been carefully coached' by the gentry to implicate John.[49] Hudson agreed with Salmon that the women 'can hardly be said' to have contributed to the surrender. The responsibility for the capitulation lay entirely with the French, dumped on the Welsh coast with no prospect of assistance; they had eaten too little and had drunk too much, and 'were only too pleased to get out of their miserable adventure'.[50]

David Salmon himself was the next to contribute to the public exchange.[51] 'The legend of the doings of the red mantled women at Fishguard seems immortal', he exclaimed. Since Hudson agreed with him, his task was to confirm not dispute. He used his well-rehearsed argument that the women were there, but not the cause of surrender. The capitulation had been agreed on the Thursday night before Tate 'had seen either a red coat or red mantle'. The editor of the *Spectator* stepped in to declare that this correspondence had now come to an end.

John Gore returned to his French invasion research in August 1940 as a 'Brief Escape from this War'.[52] The revival of interest in the events of 1797 in Wales was prompted by a general hope and prayer that Fishguard was indeed 'the last invasion of England'. Gore presented a summary of his 1935 article that addressed the psychological needs of the summer of 1940. As reassurance he quoted the Mathias letter in full as documentary evidence that the legend of the watching old women in their red whittles or 'flanes' was not a legend at all. He was still trying to find out what happened to Colonel Tate. Perhaps he was 'the ancestor of one of Petain's Government'.[53]

Sir Charles Grant Robertson, distinguished establishment historian, re-elected as president of the Historical Association on 3 January 1941, had frequently been asked for specific information of historical attempts made to invade the British Isles. He thought that if the Association prepared the facts, the Ministry of Information and the British Council might be interested: 'the publication would have a tremendous reception at present.' The data, he suggested, might include details of 'why the two attempts to invade Ireland failed and why the small expedition which landed in Pembrokeshire proved equally futile'. He recommended that the preparation of such a publication might be entrusted to Sir Herbert Richmond.[54]

Derek Hudson rushed to reply. He did not 'wish to put a damper on what might well be an interesting publication' but he felt that Sir Charles might be making too much 'of the one or two rather feeble and half-hearted episodes at his disposal'. There was nothing in the story of the 'Three days' War' that would be likely to 'encourage us at a time when we are preparing to meet a very different kind of assault'.[55] These reservations did not deter the popular press from using the story, focusing on the farcical nature of the failure and its contemporary appeal, and what Hudson had studiously avoided, the role of the women. In February 1941 when the invasion threat was perceived to have receded but still constituted a real possibility and the Blitz was at its height, an article on 'Britain's Last Invasion' was syndicated across the provincial press. The story was retold as part of a concerted anti-invasion publicity campaign across the local and national press, the main point and purpose of the Fishguard story being to show the farcical nature of the Last Invasion with plenty of contemporary meaning to reassure readers that this too would be the fate of any future attempt.[56]

The women of Fishguard in 1797 afforded several examples of equality to Welsh working-class women in the 1940s, not only fighting prowess and patriotism but also compensation rights. These specific lessons were drawn by Elizabeth Andrews (1882–1960), born into a mining family at Hirwaun in the Cynon Valley. Andrews was a central figure in the building of the Labour party in Wales after the First World War. In 1918, when women's suffrage was won, the Labour party needed to revise its structure to include the new female voter. Consequently, a Women's Department was established, and female organisers appointed; Andrews was one of the first. She was also secretary of the first branch of the Women's Co-operative Guild in Wales, and responsible for the formation of several other local branches. In what was traditionally a male-dominated political arena, Andrews highlighted subjects that previously went unspoken, such as maternity and childbirth.[57] It was the focus on women that drew her to the French Invasion story in her articles in May and October 1941.[58] The May 1941 piece also appeared in the *Flintshire County Herald* but with a different heading than the *Glamorgan Gazette*, this title summed up the contents of the article more succinctly: 'When Wales was Invaded Dafydd and the Minister were Dumb But Nancy's Faith and Trust were Equal to the occasion, Ale-Loving Jemima, armed with Pitchfork brings in prisoners. And the Welsh Women of To-day are just as Courageous.'[59]

It was a matter of record that the 'during those critical days the women did better than the men'.[60] Lessons for 1941 could be drawn from the women of Fishguard ('merched Abergwaun') and both Jemima and Nancy (as Andrews spelled it) Jones were cited as examples. Their 'courage and faith' carried them though their experience; 'the same qualities will carry us through these days'. The call to action was: 'to stand fast behind our men, in factory and forces, cheering them, encouraging them, helping them and giving of our best in service of any kind to win this war and afterwards to win a lasting peace.'[61] Elizabeth Andrews turned to historical precedents. The predecessors of the Home Guard were the hundreds of country folk who helped the small British

Army in 1797 to keep the French from penetrating inland. They were untrained and armed themselves with all sorts of weapons. The only difference with today's Home Guard was that the new equipment was much better. Neither was 'modern war legislation altogether new'; Andrews compared the compensation received by Mary Williams in 1797 to the Personal Injuries (Civilians) Act 1941. During the French Invasion, a Frenchman fired at her and wounded her in the foot and 'subsequently ill-treating her': 'Mrs Williams was granted an indemnity of £40 a year for the remainder of her life. No question of sex arose ... she received it in her own right. Taking the relative values of the money factor we cannot do much better today.'[62]

The French had shown some gallantry against which Hitler's 'savage sadism' stood in stark contrast, mercy was shown to the mother and the Day-Old Baby, but in contrast, 'the finer qualities of mercy, gallantry or justice do not enter into Hitler's regime'. The women of modern-day Wales could defeat the invaders in more direct ways through using the role models of their history. Boudica, Princess Gwenllian and Queen Elizabeth, these were all Welsh women according to Elsie Towyn Jones of New Quay, Cardiganshire writing in the *Western Mail* in May 1942 but, in more modern days, so too was Jemima Nicholas who led her friends in red shawls to give the impression that a 'crack regiment had arrived'. The women of 1942 had their own weapons, including 'our native speech to impede the invaders': 'May we recall the past and imagine that posterity depends on each of us.'[63]

The Welsh defiance of Hitler would be a repeat of the humiliation meted out to Napoleon. Hitler would prove a more formidable threat, but it would be met with the same indomitable spirit. In 1942 Wales was more ready and infinitely better equipped than in 1797 to repel an invasion.[64] In 1943 an entire book of anti-Napoleonic propaganda from authentic documents of the time was compiled for present day anti-invasion purposes.[65]

Figure 21: 'We Laughed at Boney': a humorous anti-Napoleonic work published in 1943

The compiler was Jack Werner, an Oxford musician and journalist. The dust wrapper introduced and summarised the purpose of the book succinctly. The author was not concerned with the historical or strategical aspects of Boney's threat but with the contemporary Briton's reaction to it. Werner's data – songs, cartoons, verses and documents and jokes of the day – all emphasised the 'British unfailing sense of humour', an attribute that 'stands us in good stead at this very moment'. The specific parallels were noted, triggered by the very recent developments in 1943, between Napoleon's Russian adventure and Hitler's march on Moscow. History was repeating itself.

The French Invasion was featured twice in the compilation. The first was on the map of Britain that showed the various sites of invasion since 1066, and then later in the section of the book titled 'What the People Sang' (which includes music), with a song called 'The Victory of Fishguard'. The first verse was given with the music by Highmore Skeats, and the fourth verse in the explanatory text. The author of the words was a 'certain Rev Dr Morgan' 'whose countrymen' as the inscription on the cover of the song said, according to Werner, 'went forward to repel the French Invaders, who very lately made a Descent on Wales'.[66] Elizabeth Edwards has identified Revd Dr Morgan as Caesar Morgan and reproduced the song in full.[67] Educated at Haverfordwest Grammar School, he was the nephew of Caesar Mathias of Hook who was High Sheriff of Pembrokeshire in 1774. Caesar Morgan, a disciple of William Paley, later became a theologian of some note and chaplain to the Bishop of Ely, but is probably one of the few eighteenth-century men to be overshadowed by their wives. His wife was Mary Morgan who published her 1791 *Tour to Milford Haven* in 1795.[68] A song from 1797 celebrating a victory over the French aggressor, obscure and long forgotten, was resurrected as propaganda in 1943 in the fight against Hitler.

The inheritance of the French Invasion played an active part in the identity and morale of the men from Pembrokeshire who fought in the Second World War. The collar badge of the 405th and 406th (the Pembrokeshire batteries) of the 102nd (Pembroke and Cardigan) Army Field Brigade continued the tradition of the Castlemartin troop and proudly bore the Prince of Wales plume with the word 'Fishguard'.[69] The Pembrokeshire men took part in the North Africa Corps in Algiers and after landing in Italy in December 1943 they were involved in the terrible fighting up to and including Monte Cassino. As Stuart Jones concluded: 'Another World War was over in which the Pembroke Yeomanry – under another name – had played a noble part.'[70]

The Borough of the Town and County of Haverfordwest conferred the freedom of the borough upon the 102nd (Pembrokeshire Yeomanry) on Victory Day on 8 June 1946.[71] A short history of the regiment appeared in the programme. The entitlement to wear 'Fishguard' on their badges was mentioned but nothing said about the role of the women. The 150th anniversary of the Fishguard Invasion in 1947 was not celebrated to any noticeable extent, partly because of post-war austerity and fatigue, but also because what went on at a meeting at the local council meeting early that year. When a proposal was introduced to celebrate the anniversary, several members expressed doubt about the authenticity of the story concerning Jemima Nicholas. The *Western Mail* rushed to defend her historicity, including a reference to Samuel Fenton's personal note in the burial register.[72] The 150th celebrations were low key, and when a plaque was eventually unveiled on Goodwick beach in 1952, it focused exclusively on the contribution of the military. The narrative was as contested as it had ever been. The *Western Mail* noted that the Castlemartin Yeomanry had permission from Queen Victoria to bear the word Fishguard on their accoutrements but there was 'no record of any honour being awarded to the women who distinguished themselves upon that notable occasion'.[73]

The work that transformed the historiography of the French Invasion and is still the authoritative work to this day was published in 1950 by Edwyn Henry Stuart Jones.[74] Commander

Stuart Jones R. N. had served with distinction in two world wars. His experience of naval service helped to shape his work, which was a classic of its type. He was aware of the importance of military tradition and military history and wrote it expertly. The book was titled *The Last Invasion of Britain* and it was dedicated 'In memory of my father', Henry Stuart Jones, the Principal of Aberystwyth from 1927 to 1934.[75]

Edwyn, the only child, might have been expected to follow his father's scholarly career but instead turned to the armed forces, specifically the Royal Navy.[76] He saw service in the Great War, and achieved fame in naval circles as the first person in the Grand Fleet to sight the German High Seas Fleet as it crossed the North Sea to surrender. After the war he qualified in gunnery, and this became his speciality. He retired from the Navy in 1922 and spent several years 'in business' in Rhodesia, returning in 1929; he then married Suzanne Long-Price of Talley, Carmarthenshire and settled in Wales. In 1938 he is described as a 'manufacturer's agent of the Dell, Milton Lane, Wells' (Somerset) and he remained a resident of Wells throughout the rest of his life.[77]

Stuart Jones had a 'good war'. He joined the Royal Naval barracks at Davenport as Lieutenant Commander where he oversaw training of seamen of the Allied Navies. In recognition of this service, he received medals of honour from Belgium and Denmark. In 1946 he returned to business, retiring in 1957. Stuart Jones was not a full time nor a professional historian, but this did not deter him from researching and writing two substantial works. Both books were published in 1950 – the first in order of both publication and historical chronology was *An Invasion that Failed: The French Expedition to Ireland 1796*, published by Basil Blackwell, Oxford; the second, *The Last Invasion of Britain*, published by the University of Wales Press.

The subject matter of Stuart Jones's research and of both publications were closely aligned, not only were they both failed invasions, but the 1797 Fishguard and the 1796 Bantry Bay expeditions were strategically linked. There was also an overlap of people: Wolfe Tone and Hoche. The reasons for the failure of both expeditions could be linked to Hoche. What Stuart Jones said about the failure of the Bantry Bay expedition could be said with equal validity of the failure of the Fishguard: the lack of communication between Hoche and his subordinates.[78]

Stuart Jones's work is impressive for the extent of his contacts with other historians, and for his emotional sympathy and passion for the subject coupled with the depth and reach of his research. The blurb on the jacket said that it 'is probably a definitive account of the landing in Pembrokeshire, its purposes and consequences'. As far as any work of history writing can be definitive, Stuart Jones's work gets near that mark. His acknowledgements outlined his considerable networking, which must have been made difficult at a time of war. He commences, fittingly, with his immense debt of gratitude to the late Principal Salmon whose research had proved invaluable as 'a basis for study of this event'.[79]

Salmon's major achievement was his research and his compilation of original letters and documents. Salmon tended to write in isolation; he thanked institutions, libraries and individuals for permission to research material and documentation, rather than fellow historians for the sharing of ideas. Stuart Jones, on the other hand, had contacts and collaborators in France in the *Archives Nationales* and the *Archives de la Guerre*, including a young researcher there who gave him information from the personal dossiers of Macheret (a terrorist of somewhat 'unsavoury reputation', as Stuart Jones called him, who at one time was regarded as a likely contender for leading the *Legion Noire*), and Lebrun, Tate's second-in-command. This young researcher was Richard Cobb, just starting a career that would see him become the most gifted English-speaking historian of the French Revolution.

Although Stuart Jones's Welsh was limited, he knew of J. J. Evans's book on the *Dylanwad* and had been in correspondence with him. Stuart Jones saw the effects of the French Revolution on Welsh literature, but from a practical, revolutionary, point of view the effect of the Revolution was nil and 'in this sense there was no parallel between Wales and Ireland'.[80] Stuart Jones was as at ease using tried and tested sources such as Ap Gwilym's *Authentic Account* (which he utilised uncritically recognising it for the valuable source it was), as he was in using new sources such as Castagnier's despatches.[81]

In his third chapter, 'Fishguard', he used Thomas Knox's *Some Account* and new French archival material from *Archives de la Guerre* on the correspondence between ministers of the French Directory commenting on Tate's actions. A new source gave additional credence to the role of women. In the *Proces Verbal* (7 Ventose, An 2), which the French officers drew up and Tate signed after the surrender, for the attention of their superiors in France, reference was made to the enemy rising *en masse* 'with troops of the line to the number of several thousand'.[82] Stuart Jones realised the importance of this evidence; it seemed 'to lend colour, and literally too, to the well known tradition that it was the Welsh women, arrayed in their red cloaks, who deceived the French'.[83]

Stuart Jones's foray into the legend of the women debate was fairly neutral.[84] He was respectful of Jemima, whom he calls a 'tall and masculine woman who followed the trade of cobbler in Fishguard', but adds carefully that she was 'reported' to have marched out to Llanwnda armed with a pitchfork.[85] Stuart Jones was a naval man, a supporter of the Pembrokeshire Yeomanry in the past and present, and it is tribute to his even handedness and skills that he gave the 'legend of the women' the attention that it deserved in a history that gave military men prominence.

Stuart Jones's work was primarily a military history, excellent on military and naval movements and issues, but not a social history. He did not use any of the ballads either in English or Welsh to supplement his narrative. It was not simply because his Welsh was inadequate for the purpose, but also that he was just not interested in ballads as source material for his military history. His bibliography contains only one Welsh-language work and that is *Cwyn y Cystuddiedig*, but the only mention of William Richards and the *Cwyn* in an entire chapter on the 'Treason Trials' is in the footnotes, and then in translation.[86]

The key influence on Stuart Jones was not another historian or writer or a desire to please his dead father, but that of war. It was the Second World War that made the component title of the work *The Last Invasion* prominent. The caricature of the cherubic Fishguard Fencible is described as a 'Home Guard of the eighteenth century'.[87] His line of continuity was the Pembroke Yeomanry who were as present in the Second World War as they were in the events of 1797. Writing at the start of the Cold War, the threat of a Third World War was already there, but he is confident that should a foe again emerge 'the same spirit which animated Lord Cawdor and his men as they rode to Fishguard one hundred and fifty years ago will spur on their descendants of today'.[88]

The reception given to Stuart Jones's book was almost overwhelmingly favourable. The new *Dock Leaves* magazine founded by Roland Mathias in Pembroke Dock doubted whether the book was as definitive as its title suggested it would be,[89] but the *Western Mail* in September 1950 was not ambivalent at all and accepted Stuart Jones's account as 'what is probably the definitive account of the Fishguard invasion of February 1797'.[90] This was praise indeed since the writer of the review was none other than the Principal of University College Cardiff, Milford Haven-born social and economic historian Sir Frederick Rees.[91] Rees welcomed the work unreservedly; he knew and appreciated the research of his antecedent, the late David Salmon, on whose research this work was built, enhanced by discovering new evidence in the French archives. A substantial part of the review is given over to the aspect that the readers of the *Western Mail* were really interested in – the 'Women in Red'. Rees was impressed by the new evidence from the *Archives de la Guerre* and noted that Stuart Jones was 'inclined to accept' the story of the women and gave the reasons. Always astute, Sir Frederick Rees commented on the Prudhomme deposition against Thomas John that had been concocted for him: 'Would they have put into the mouth of Thomas John a statement known to the public to be absurd?'[92]

It was generally accepted that the last word had been said about the French Invasion. What was left was to understand and interpret it in the context of a new history of modern Wales, and this is what David Williams did in 1950 in his *A History of Modern Wales*.[93] In his Preface, Williams, who had been Professor of Welsh History at Aberystwyth since 1945 and the most influential Welsh historian of his generation, acknowledged the 'imprint' of the man who influenced his writing on the eighteenth century, R. T. Jenkins. But David Williams had also been reading J. J. Evans and the influence of the latter seems to be the most marked on his writing on the French Invasion. J. J. Evans structured his analysis into specific compartments: Welsh writing in English, the writings of London Welshmen and so on, and into separate periods of 'Support' or 'Reaction'.[94] David Williams put the French Invasion into the 'Reaction' category and judged that 'such sympathy as the French Revolution had gained in Wales was quickly dispelled by the attempt to land in Pembrokeshire'.[95] After a full description of the events of the invasion, including a description of Jemima, Williams concluded that 'the shock cured the Welsh people of their vague radicalism. The reaction fell heavily on the dissenters'.[96] David Williams assumed the defeat of the French on Welsh soil also meant the defeat of *French principles* in Wales.

The widespread fear among the elites in Wales during the 1790s was that the 'Cymry uniaith' ('monoglot Welsh') the 'gwerinos tlodion' ('poor peasants') were thinking for themselves and reading Tom Paine in translation, hence the urgency that adaptations of English-language works into Welsh should be available to enable them to become loyal and modern Britons. A short lived Welsh cultural and patriotic renaissance, when modern Anglophone ideas of all kinds could be read in Welsh, came to an end long before the French Invasion.

Only one person is known to have changed his view on the French Revolution because of the French Invasion of Pembrokeshire and that was William Richards. Before the Invasion, Richards respected the religiosity of the Jacobins, which he contrasted with the atheism of the Gallican Church, after the Invasion Richards damned the French republican invaders as godless men whose oaths could not be trusted since they did not believe in an afterlife. This change of view did not mean that Richards had become less radical, there can be no more radical a document than *Cwyn y Cystuddiedig*, a pamphlet that, single-handed, took on the local state establishment and that, if it had been in English, would have got him into serious trouble.

David Williams's claim that the French Invasion cured the Welsh of their vague radicalism became influential and was shared to a greater or lesser extent by other historians and writers.[97] It also became embedded in the minds of pupils and learners in 1960 through the school text book edited by A. J. Roderick, based on a series of broadcast talks given in the Welsh Home Service of the BBC during the winter of 1959–60 on *Wales Through the Ages*, which included David Williams's essay on 'Wales and the French Revolution'.[98] The country people who vented their fury against the invaders did so in defence of their families, their lives and their properties, not to defend the Constitution, even though the authorities in London and Pembrokeshire spoke of their loyalty as if this were the case. The enemy was French violence, as it affected them directly, not *French principles*, their overwhelming response was the defence of their homes and homeland and the giving of thanks to God for their deliverance.[99]

Endnotes

1 'Rhamant y Glanio yn Abergwaun. Hanes Rhai o Arwresau Bro fy Mebyd', *Western Mail* (21 November 1934).
2 'The Last Invasion of Great Britain' as a title was first used to head a newspaper article on the French invasion of Pembrokeshire in the *Newcastle Courant* (21 February 1879), 7.

3 John Francis Gore (person page 2861), *www.thepeerage.com/p2861.htm* (last accessed 6 August 2024). A genealogical survey of the peerage of Britain as well as the royal families of Europe.
4 John Gore, 'The Last Invasion of Britain', *The Quarterly Review* (also called *The London Quarterly Review*), 160 (1935), 270–83.
5 Gore, 'The Last Invasion of Britain', 272.
6 Gore, 'The Last Invasion of Britain', 275. The Cawdor diary seems to have disappeared from the archives.
7 Gore, 'The Last Invasion of Britain', 278.
8 Gore, 'The Last Invasion of Britain', 278.
9 Gore, 'The Last Invasion of Britain', 283. First 'discovered' by Jabet in 1869.
10 Gore, 'The Last Invasion of Britain', 283.
11 'Mr Lloyd George votes for Fishguard', *Western Mail* (8 August 1934), 10.
12 'Eisteddfod Proclamation Ceremonial from our own Reporter', *Western Mail* (28 June 1935), 10.
13 'Round and About by "The Wanderer"', *Western Mail* (18 July 1936), 13.
14 Llewellyn Evans, 'The Tragi-Comedy of February 1797. Eye-witness's account of the French Invasion and Surrender', *Western Mail* (3 August 1936), 22.
15 *Western Mail* (3 August 1936), 23.
16 Edward James, 'National Eisteddfod opens on a high note', *Western Mail* (4 August 1936), 13. This is the same burial record annotated by Samuel Fenton, the vicar of Fishguard, with his personal reminiscences of her, see Chapter 4.
17 H. L. Ap Gwilym, *An Authentic Account of the Invasion by French Troops on Carrig Gwasted Point near Fishguard* (Haverfordwest, 1842), p. 39; J. E. Thomas, *Britain's Last Invasion: Fishguard 1797* (Stroud, 2007), p. 154.
18 Earl Richard [Lloyd George], *Lloyd George* (London, 1960), p. 18.
19 'Listener-in', *Western Mail* (16 November 1935), 15.
20 'LLOYD GEORGE AT WELSH EISTEDDFOD AT FISHGUARD' (1936), *www.britishpathe.com/asset/226485/* (last accessed 6 August 2024).
21 'Mr Lloyd George's Unfinished Symphony. Speech cut short because amplifiers were out of commission', *Western Mail* (7 August 1936), 6.
22 David Dutton 'Sir John Simon (Viscount Simon), 1873–1954' *The Journal of Liberal History*, *https://liberalhistory.org.uk/history/simon-john-viscount-simon/* (last accessed 6 August 2024).
23 John Simon, *Retrospect: The Memoirs of the Rt Hon Viscount Simon Viscount Simon* (London, 1952), p. 14.
24 Simon, *Retrospect*, p. 16.
25 *Western Mail* (6 August 1936). Before the Eisteddfod, Simon wrote to the Librarian at Windsor Castle for information held in the Royal Archives on the invasion and received copies of the letters from Portland to the

King, subsequently published by Aspinall. Pembrokeshire Archives D/SIM/52.
26 'Story of French Invasion', *Western Mail* (6 August 1936), 11. See also his attack on C. F. Shepherd for an article on 'Fishguard and the National' in the *Narberth Weekly News* (23 and 30 July 1936), Pembrokeshire Archives D/Sal/169.
27 'Fishguard Invasion Story', *Western Mail* (13 August 1936), 11.
28 David Salmon, 'Histories of the French Invasion of Pembrokeshire', *Journal of the Welsh Bibliographical Society*, 5/1 (August 1937), 41–8.
29 Mark Rawlinson, 'Invasion! Coleridge, the defence of Britain and the cultivation of the public's fear', in Philip Shaw (ed.) *Romantic Wars: Studies in Culture and Conflict, 1793–1822* (Aldershot, 2000), p. 116.
30 'Singeing the Beard. A War Newsletter no xlvi', *The Sphere*, 20 July 1940, 66.
31 Richard Brooke, *Liverpool as it was during the last quarter of the eighteenth century 1775–1800* (Liverpool, 1853), p. 538.
32 Liverpool Museums, 'Coming Danger', *www.liverpoolmuseums.org.uk/coming-danger* (last accessed 6 August 2024).
33 'Invading Liverpool! When the city got a rude shock. What happened in 1797', *The Liverpool Echo* (12 January 1940), 6.
34 *The Liverpool Echo* (12 January 1940), 6.
35 'Liverpool Volunteers', *The Liverpool Echo* (17 June 1940), 4.
36 'An Earlier Threat', *The Liverpool Echo* (13 May 1941), 4.
37 Herbert Richmond, *The Invasion of Britain: An Account of Plans, Attempts and Counter-measures from 1586 to 1918* (London, 1941).
38 Richmond, *The Invasion of Britain*, p. 37.
39 Richmond, *The Invasion of Britain*, p. 42.
40 'Welsh women scared Britain's last invaders. French mistook them for troops', *Midland Daily Telegraph* (which became the *Coventry Evening Telegraph* in 1941) (22 February 1940), 7; the headline in the *Liverpool Echo* was 'Welsh Women Scared Frenchmen. Comedy of Last Attempt to Invade Britain', *Liverpool Echo* (22 February 1940), 2. The same article also appeared in the *Ormskirk Advertiser* (11 July 1940), 5.
41 Quoted in the above, for example, *Ormskirk Advertiser* (11 July 1940), 5.
42 'How Glamorgan reacted to invasion threat by Edgar Chappell', *Western Mail* (4 June 1940), 4.
43 'Invasions of England: only small and quickly suppressed landings have taken place. None successful since 1066', *The Sphere* (29 June 1940), 29.
44 'Invaded Britian', *The Spectator* (9 February 1940), 177.
45 *The Spectator* (9 February 1940), 177.
46 'Letter from Mr Powell', *The Spectator* (22 March 1940), 417.
47 'Invaded Britain', *The Spectator* (29 March 1940), 452.
48 *The Spectator* (29 March 1940), 452.

49 Pembrokeshire Archives D/Sal /169, Correspondence dated 16 February, 29 March, 1 April 1940.
50 *The Spectator* (29 March 1940), 452.
51 'Invaded Britain', *The Spectator* (5 April 1940), 486.
52 'A Brief Escape from this War', *The Sphere* (10 August 1940), 30.
53 'A Brief Escape from this War', *The Sphere* (10 August 1940), 30.
54 'Attempts to invade Britain', *The Times* (4 January 1941), 2.
55 Derek Hudson, 'Attempted Invasions', *The Times* (6 January 1941), 5.
56 The story appeared under the same headline of 'BRITAIN'S LAST INVASION' in the *Liverpool Daily Post* (22 February 1941), 2; *Yorkshire Evening Post* (24 February 1941), 4; *The Nottingham Evening Post* (24 February 1941), 4.
57 South Wales Miners' Library, 'International Women's Day: Educate, Agitate, Organise – Elizabeth Andrews', *https://minerssite.wordpress.com/2018/03/07/international-womens-day-educate-agitate-organise-elizabeth-andrews/* (last accessed 6 August 2024).
58 Elizabeth Andrews, 'WOMEN OF WALES, Incidents of the 1797 Invasion', *The Glamorgan Gazette* (23 May 1941), 4; 'Nothing New under the Sun', *South Wales Gazette* (10 October 1941), 8.
59 *The Flintshire County Herald* (23 May 1941), 2.
60 *The Flintshire County Herald* (23 May 1941), 2; *The Glamorgan Gazette* (23 May 1941), 4.
61 *The Flintshire County Herald* (23 May 1941), 2; *The Glamorgan Gazette* (23 May 1941), 4.
62 *South Wales Gazette* (10 October 1941), 8.
63 Elsie Towyn Jones, New Quay, 5 May, 'Women of Wales', *Western Mail* (9 May 1942), 3
64 'Wales and Invasion', *Western Mail* (5 May 1942), 2.
65 J. Warner, *We laughed at Boney: (or; We've been through it all before) How our forefathers laughed defiance at the last serious threat of invasion-by Napoleon: a striking parallel with our present position* (London, 1943).
66 Warner, *We Laughed at Boney*, p. 38.
67 Elizabeth Edwards, *English-Language Poetry from Wales 1789–1806*, (Cardiff, 2013), no. 31, pp. 164–5. Edwards gives the title as 'The Victory of Fishguard. A favourite Song. The Words by the Revd Dr Morgan whose Countrymen were forward to repel the French Invaders, who very lately made a Descent in Wales (London, 1797)'. Another title to his song was 'The Victory of Fishguard a favourite song, the words by the Revd Dr Morgan, whose brothers were the foremost to repel the French Invaders who very lately made a descent on Wales'. The reference to 'brothers' could mean countrymen, but it could also literally mean brothers or brothers in arms, particularly as Morgan was from Haverfordwest.
68 R. G. Thorne and R. Howell, 'Pembrokeshire in Wartime 1793–1815', in Elwyn Davies and David Howell (eds), *Pembrokeshire County History*,

vol. 3: *Early Modern Pembrokeshire 1536–1815* (Haverfordwest, 1987), pp. 382–3.
69 E. H. Stuart Jones, *The Last Invasion of Britain* (Cardiff, 1950), p. 291.
70 Stuart Jones, *The Last Invasion of Britain*, p. 292.
71 National Library of Wales Minor Deposits 1145, Programme of 1946 ceremony.
72 'Facts of the French Landing at Fishguard' *Western Mail* (15 February 1947), 3.
73 'Wales Day by Day', *Western Mail* (1 May 1946), 2.
74 His surname was Stuart Jones (not hyphenated). He owed his surname to his famous father, Henry Stuart Jones. Originally, Stuart was his father's second forename, but he and his wife generally prefixed it to their surname, and he was knighted in 1933 as Stuart Jones.
75 Stuart Jones, *The Last Invasion of Britain*. Stuart Jones's father was the formidable and admired scholar Henry Stuart Jones, Camden Professor of Ancient History at Oxford 1920–7 and Principal of University College of Wales, Aberystwyth 1927–34, knighted by King George V in 1933. He married the daughter of the Revd Edwyn Henry Vaughan from Pembrokeshire and they settled in Saundersfoot in 1905. Their son, born in 1896, was named Edwyn after his maternal grandfather.
76 Biographical information comes from his obituary 'Commander E. H. Stuart Jones', *Central Somerset Gazette* (29 April 1966), 2.
77 'Summons', *Central Somerset Gazette* (11 February 1938), 3.
78 E. H. Stuart Jones, *An Invasion that Failed: The French Expedition to Ireland 1796* (Cardiff, 1950), p. 163.
79 Stuart Jones, *The Last Invasion of Britain*, p. vii.
80 Stuart Jones, *An Invasion that Failed*, p. 29.
81 Stuart Jones, *The Last Invasion of Britain*, pp. 70–9.
82 Stuart Jones, *The Last Invasion of Britain*, pp. 110–11.
83 Stuart Jones, *The Last Invasion of Britain*, p. 111.
84 Stuart Jones, *The Last Invasion of Britain*, p. 119.
85 Stuart Jones, *The Last Invasion of Britain*, p. 104.
86 'W. Richards, *Cwyn y Cystuddiedig* (translation)', in Stuart Jones, *The Last Invasion of Britain*, footnotes 30 and 35 p. 268. It is unlikely that Stuart Jones translated the Cwyn himself, he would have arranged someone to translate the work for him.
87 Stuart Jones, *The Last Invasion of Britain*, p. 97.
88 Stuart Jones, *The Last Invasion of Britain*, pp. 293–4.
89 'Review of E. H. Stuart Jones, The Last Invasion of Britain', *Dock Leaves*, 1–4 (1949), 107.
90 Sir Frederick Rees 'Bookshelf, Review of The Last Invasion of Britain', *Western Mail* (13 September 1950), 4.
91 Evan David Jones (2001), 'REES, Sir JAMES FREDERICK (1883–1967), Principal of the University College at Cardiff', in *Dictionary of*

Welsh Biography, https://biography.wales/article/s2-REES-FRE-1883 (last accessed 12 February 2021).

92 Sir Frederick Rees 'Bookshelf, Review of The Last Invasion of Britain', *Western Mail* (13 September 1950), 4.
93 David Williams, *A History of Modern Wales* (Cardiff, 1950), pp. 174–5.
94 J. J. Evans, *Dylanwad y Chwyldro Ffrengig ar Lenyddiaeth Cymru* (Liverpool, 1928), pp. 65–111, 112–34, 135–72, 173–92. This compartmentalisation annoyed Gwyn A. Williams, a student and admirer of David Williams, so much that it later provided the methodological stimulus for his revisionist approach, 'these Welsh phenomena of the 1790s were one'. See Gwyn A. Williams, 'Welsh Indians: the Madoc Legend and the first Welsh radicalism', *History Workshop Journal*, 1/1 (Spring 1976), 149.
95 Williams, *A History of Modern Wales*, p. 173.
96 Williams, *A History of Modern Wales*, p.174.
97 For example, Elisabeth Inglis Jones, *The Story of Wales* (London, 1955), p. 192; Wynford Vaughan Thomas, *Wales: A History* (London, 1985), p. 196; John Davies, *Hanes Cymru* (London, 1990), p. 327. It is also the intellectual source for Gwyn A. Williams's hostility towards the Fishguard Invasion in his work *When was Wales* (London, 1985), p. 170.
98 David Williams, 'Wales and the French Revolution', in A. J. Roderick, ed., *Wales through the Ages* Vol 2: *Modern Wales* (Llandybie, Carmarthenshire, 1960), p.123
99 For national defence patriotism, J. E. Cookson, *The British Armed Nation 1793-1815* (Oxford, 1997), pp. 91, 212

Chapter 10

'Little Fishguard for Ever!' Two Hundred Years and Counting, 1950–97

The period after the War saw great social and cultural change, along with new tensions and also new reconciliations. Memories of an event that took place nearly two centuries earlier remained strong, despite the scepticism from some parties about the story of the women: 'This generation is inclined to scoff at the story of the Fishguard women', reported the *Western Mail* in 1950.[1] Nonetheless, the *Western Mail* in the 1950s still published stories how the red shawls of their ancestors were still treasured in north Pembrokeshire and south Cardiganshire.[2] Local memories and material relics continued to contest and defy public doubt.

In 1952, a plaque was finally unveiled on Goodwick beach to commemorate the French Invasion. The military were heavily represented. The plaque mentioned the unconditional surrender to the first Baron Cawdor and the units under his command: there was no mention of the local people, let alone the women. Richard Elley commenced his article in the *Western Mail* in 1957 with a long quotation from the by now famous Mathias letter of 27 February 1797, which seemed to him to prove the presence and contribution of women. But he wrote: 'Historians take another view.'[3] However, there were signs of change.

Major Francis Jones, writing in 1958, commemorated the part played by Wales in the history of the Territorial Army, which was celebrating its fiftieth anniversary.[4] Several significant changes had taken place since the Territorial Army was formed, not least the incorporation of women. The inclusion of women had been fully justified by the results 'of the women of Fishguard whose gay shawls and petticoats baffled the intelligence service of the French invaders in 1797'. The role of the women was also mentioned in in Lt Col. R. L. Howell's *History of the Pembroke Yeomanry* in 1966.[5]

New, modern tensions revived old debates and memories of these debates. There was local anger and opposition when a NATO accordance agreed in Paris that the fledgling German forces could use the 5,000-acre range at Castlemartin. The legend of the women was brought into the public debate and mentioned by *The Times* in a leading article on 11 August 1961. Derek Hudson returned to the discussion and the story was again retold.[6] The journalist, still only fifty, concluded that 'non-proven is still the best verdict'.[7] The inevitable reply came. The correspondent had been reading Ap Gwilym (1842) and, unusually, Charles Dickens's weekly magazine *Household Words*. He attributed Wilkie Collins's piece of 1859 to Dickens and quoted from it in the context of the debate over military land and preparedness for war: 'In view of present events in Pembrokeshire, Dickens's conclusion is worth quoting; "If we are to be invaded again and on a rather larger scale, let us not be so ill prepared, the next time, as to take refuge in our wives' red petticoats."'[8]

Memories of the Fishguard National Eisteddfod endured long after the event and bore a creative harvest even as late as the 1970s. One visitor to Fishguard in 1936 came after the end of the Eisteddfod, but the atmosphere of the event still permeated through the town, so much so that the memory of it would stay with him for years. This visitor was the writer and poet Harri Webb, accompanied by his mother. The trip was the original inspiration for Webb's popular comic ballad 'The Women of

Fishguard'. The poem appeared in his anthology *Rampage and Revel* in 1977 but may have been written earlier.[9]

Webb's recollections of Fishguard and his mother were found in his unpublished papers by Meic Stephens, written around 1974. Harri and his mother visited Fishguard a few weeks after the Eisteddfod; the people of Fishguard were still basking in its memory and they welcomed the visitors from Swansea. Harri took a photograph of his mother who did not have much longer to live: 'I remain grateful to the people of Fishguard and the quiet of that day and their cheerful talk about their Eisteddfod. It was the last of such occasions for a woman who didn't have many such treats.'[10]

His mother died three years later in 1939, when he was a student at Oxford. The poem is a tribute to the power of womanhood and maternalism in their Welsh context, the Welsh 'Mam', but set in a local and recognisably historic context, a composite of the strong mother of the Day-Old Baby, Jemima, the red-flannelled women and memories of his own mother. The comic impact of the poem depends on knowledge and appreciation of the historical images that form this composite, through which Webb's genius permeates.

Stuart Jones had written what came to be known as the definitive account of the Invasion, but this did not deter later historians from exploiting the commerciality of the story, its romance and uniqueness as the 'last invasion' and writing new histories aimed at a popular, non-academic audience. Some of these histories, published in local Pembrokeshire or small Welsh publishing houses, were better than others but all had important contributions to make in developing and memorialising the narrative. The first of the popular histories aimed at a new general audience was John Kinross's *Fishguard Fiasco: An Account of the Last Invasion of Britain* (1974). The greatest drawback of the book was the title itself. There had been a long tradition of calling it a fiasco; Kinross quoted Edward Laws from almost 100 years earlier: 'Thus ended the great fiasco of the French invasion. What did it all mean?'[11] 'Fiasco' is, however, a deeply misleading term, since the Fishguard Invasion was far too serious and terrible to be called that. It trivialises the fate of Mary Williams. In his first edition, written in the chauvinistic and sexist 1970s, John Kinross writes of Mary Williams and her pension: 'She lived on a fat government pension until she was 89 so by the time she died she had gained £2240 from the incident *which made it well worth while*' (my italics).[12] In the 2007 reprint the phrase 'which made it well worth while' was thankfully dropped.[13]

The subject also attracted the attention of the social historian Pamela Horn. Her *History of the French Invasion of Fishguard 1797*, even at only twenty-four pages, is still the best introduction to the Invasion. The new and significant contribution made by Horn was the examination of the records of the accounts of Irish officers Barry St Leger, Robert Morrison and Nicholas Tyrrell taken at Whitehall on 5 March 1797.[14] These documents provided unique insights into the tensions between the Irish officers and Tate, and information about the lack of control over the troops, their desire to capitulate and the unease of Morrison in committing treason by fighting against his own country. The best description of Fishguard as a port and economic centre in 1797 was also written by Pamela Horn.[15]

The histories of Kinross and Horn, one a general account for a popular audience, another a work of carefully researched social history, were both written in a British framework. In 1982, Marianne Elliott provided a perspective that was both Irish and French as a result of her diligence and command of the French sources. Elliott laid out the precise composition of the 'patchwork expedition' that was Tate's *Legion Noire*.[16] Both of Stuart Jones's books appeared in Elliott's footnotes and bibliography. Elliott went on to write a biography of Wolfe Tone, published in 1989, which was the first non-hagiographic work on the great Irish patriot.[17]

Marianne Elliott had written from a French and Irish perspective. Geraint H. Jenkins's lecture to the Welsh Medical

Society at the Fishguard National Eisteddfod in 1986 (exactly fifty years after the first time the National Eisteddfod was held at Fishguard) was delivered from the Welsh and Welsh-language perspective.[18] He opened his lecture with the words of Philip Dafydd from his ballad, welcoming his listeners to hear how the ungodly French host landed in Pembrokeshire and how God kept His people.[19] Jenkins knew that the story had been told and retold, but considered it worth telling again in light of recent studies on the nature and background to the event. The French did not realise how deep the Welshman's prejudice was against foreigners and how deep their hatred was towards Papism.[20] He was the first since J. J. Evans to quote the Welsh ballads as a source in relation to the French Invasion, and to use them to describe how the French stole and guzzled sheep and pigs, stole the wheat as well as the cattle and calves in droves, before descending to the cellars to get good strong beer.[21] In this lecture we see the welcome return of Nansi Jones, Llanybydder, and the fate of Mary Williams is described carefully without naming names, the perpetrator described as being an Irish officer who came here only 'for that amusement' (this from Rutland's Diary). Geraint H. Jenkins stated unequivocally that she was raped in front of her husband, presumably using the 1803 source of *Specimens of French Ferocity*, although his source for this is not stated: as a lecture there were no footnotes.[22] T. Cunllo Griffiths is mentioned for the continuation of anti-Catholic and anti-French prejudice into the latter years of the nineteenth century, as well as Jemima and the poetry of Thomas Evans (Tomos Glyn Cothi), which combined anti-Gallican feeling with praise for the bravery of the Welsh (note: as Welsh, not as Ancient Britons: 'y Cymry dewrion').[23] Jenkins sees the French Invasion as the catalyst that deepened the hatred of the Welsh people for the French as foreigners and Papists, but not as an antidote for radicalism.[24]

The same year as the Geraint H. Jenkins lecture, T. Llew Jones also told the French Invasion story from a Welsh perspective, for a popular audience and young adults in particular.[25] The narrative was familiar, based on Stuart Jones with few new facts, but told in T. Llew Jones's inimitable style as a storyteller *par excellence*. T. Llew Jones gave more attention than any English-language version of the story to those who were persecuted, an episode of injustice against local Welsh Dissenters and ordinary people. No other book, certainly not one in English, would have included a photograph of the Baptist chapel at Llangloffan as an illustration of the French Invasion. Were the hands of Lord Cawdor so clean he wondered?[26] He also ventured that there was no smoke without fire and whether a few of the Welsh did in fact welcome the French Revolution.

A new, American perspective was provided by the writer John D. Ahlstrom in an article on William Tate in the *South Carolina Historical Magazine*. The article, which relied heavily on Stuart Jones's research for Tate's later career, introduced this fascinating character to his own people.[27] Tate's nationality had long been a matter of speculation, was he Irish or American? In 1797, some Irishmen and women were in open rebellion against Britain but remained subjects of the British Crown and therefore culpable of treason. Rutland believed Tate was Irish, Ap Gwilym had him as a 'native of Wexford' 'who called himself an American', Laws described him as the 'Hiberno-Franco-American General Tate'.[28] Stuart Jones, from Tate's personal dossier in the *Archives de la Guerre* established that he was born in America.[29]

Since the Second World War more books and references in print had appeared on the Fishguard Invasion than in any other period. It was a subject of academic discourse and taught in schools. However, this public attention did not replace the intense personal and family memories still held by the people of, or with roots in, Pencaer. Oral traditions, family and personal memories were rarely published, but this did occur, as in the remarkable case of Syd Walters. Walters, often dismissed as a crank and eccentric, was also an authentic remembrancer, through family memories, of the Fishguard invasion. Memories do not have to be accurate or reasonable or reliable to be authentic. There is much in Syd Walters's account that tallies with the contemporary evidence, and he is to be commended for writing his books at his own expense, which included the vivid memories of the women in his family.[30]

Syd Walters had impressive Fishguard Invasion family credentials. He was the sixth generation in a Llanferran family who had maintained a rich oral tradition of the Invasion. He had, by his mother's own 'word of mouth', 'words which had originated from a person alive at the time of the landing'.[31] When he was later courting his wife to be, his mother told his fiancée the real reason why the women of Pencaer had congregated together in such numbers on Garn Fawr: 'the mothers were determined to defend themselves and their daughters from being molested, raped or taken away by the invaders.'[32] There is no reason to doubt Syd Walters's mother's memory that the women and young girls gathered for protection on high vantage points given what we know about the ordeal suffered by Mary Williams. Other sources also confirm that the country people were in hiding, keeping vigil and massing against the enemy in Pencaer. The women folk are the heroines in the Walters family, notwithstanding inevitable family tensions. Syd Walters lists his maternal grandmothers with their dates in a roll of honour.[33]

Walters returned to the topic of the Last Invasion again in 1992 in a privately printed *Truthful History of the Last Invasion of Britain*, in which he articulated his anti-Catholic, anti-Irish, utterly repugnant and fantastic conspiracy theories. His anti-Catholic opinions were not unique to him but were commonplace in certain Protestant, Nonconformist and Welsh mindsets and communities.[34] The prejudices expressed in his later privately printed works were his alone, and peaked in 1995 with a publication that had, on its home-produced cover, the effigy of the Baptist minister Henry Davies being burnt in Fishguard square in 1798 by the Irish Catholics.[35] Syd Walters and his evidence is clearly problematic. However, among the warped interpretations, conspiracy theories and fantasies, the memories of his mother are authentic, his black-and-white photographs of Pencaer and Fishguard and Goodwick before the harbour development are superb, his sketches are helpful and he also provides a cache of letters from the Invasion that are valuable, authentic and new. He occasionally employed a professional researcher to do his research, and a number of new government documents were identified from the Public Record Office, including those relating to the King's Warrants, which mentioned that the widows of the three Welshmen killed – Anne Howell, Mary Davies and Anne Llewellyn – received pensions in compensation.

The same year as Syd Walters's second *Truthful History*, Phil Carradice published his more professional and academic, but less emotive and personal work, which also had *The Last Invasion* in the title.[36] 'The Last Invasion' as a concept had now been fully embraced by all those writing on the subject, and virtually every book now described the French Invasion as the 'Last Invasion', with Fishguard appearing as a subtitle.

A major historiographical advance was provided by Roland Quinault of the University of North London, a professional historian writing for a general audience during the Bicentenary of the Fishguard Invasion. His article was published in 1999, but had appeared as an earlier draft in 1997 as a paper delivered to the Fishguard Historical Society.[37] This was not another retelling of the story but a reassessment of its contemporary and retrospective significance. He was at pains to establish from the outset that the invasion was a serious affair not 'the mixture of French farce and Welsh flannel', a description that commentators had used to denigrate and belittle the event. As we have seen, ridicule of the Invasion was almost as old as the Invasion itself.

The role that the ordinary people played in combating the invasion had been neglected in some respects, exaggerated in others. Quinault made the point that may seem obvious, but is not commonly discussed, that it was primarily self-interest rather than loyalty to 'king and country' that made the people of Pembrokeshire oppose the French.[38] The exaggerated element, according to Quinault, was the role of the women. He implied that the story of the women dressed in red flannel being mistaken for soldiers was an echo of an earlier incident, the case of Betty Gammon in Ilfracombe, who it was said rallied local women with red petticoats draped around their shoulders to parade on War Hill in the hope of deterring the French, and quoted Stuart Jones as his evidence for this statement. The evidence does not bear this interpretation. Stuart Jones in the reference cited was simply saying that there was a tradition in Ilfracombe of local women rallying around Betty Gammon.[39] There is no evidence that contemporary knowledge of the Ilfracombe story had travelled across the Bristol Channel to affect the creation of the Fishguard story; indeed, there is argument for travel in the other direction at a much later date. Red petticoats around the shoulders is more reminiscent of Wilkie Collins than Fishguard. Quinault's interpretation was fresh and insightful; he also addressed the memorialisation of the invasion up to the 1997 bicentennial, noting how the invasion saga, embellished by myth and art, had long served as a focus for local pride and as a tourist asset.[40] The article was a step change in the understanding of the place of the invasion in its contemporary context and its later significance.

The 1997 bicentenary promoted both the history and the heritage of the place where the French had invaded in 1797, and the myths and memories associated with it, through a series of events that would both commemorate and celebrate 1797. In the run up to the bicentenary, two local Fishguard historians, Bill Fowler and Richard Davies, researched, taught and raised local awareness generally about the events that they would soon celebrate. The focus was scholarship with a light and popular touch. In less than a year they published six articles in *Pembrokeshire Life*.[41] Bill Fowler, history graduate of the University College of Wales Aberystwyth (and proud of it) and head of sixth and the head of history at Fishguard County School, produced an educational resource for thirteen to fourteen-year-olds on behalf of Dyfed County Council Education Department.[42] The questions posed as part of the resource pack were questions that have concerned generations of historians, such as the composition of the French force and the rationale for the surrender, as well as the legend of the women.[43]

Bill Fowler became the chairman of the Bicentenary Committee. The events and activities of the bicentenary were varied, appealing to all age groups. The French Invasion had been celebrated and commemorated in many ways over the centuries: thanksgiving services, military dinners, town parades, processions of young and not-so-young women in national costume. The 1997 bicentenary was very much in the community tradition, run by a committee of local people in the same way as the centenary had been organised, with a similar under-representation of women. But 1997, unlike 1897, had the backing of the Welsh Tourist Board. The bicentennial was promoted by the Tourist Board as 'one of the most significant events to be held in West Wales for years'. The *Bicentenary Newsletter* of December 1996 promised a 'kaleidoscope of activity to thrill all tastes'.[44] The timetable of events had entertainment, the march from Stackpole, a commemorative church service and Welsh TV hymn-singing programme, *Dechrau Canu, Dechrau Canmol*.[45]

The people of Fishguard and Goodwick were encouraged to turn out in period costume on the day – the heroine, of course, was Jemima Nicholas, played by Yvonne Fox who then made the role her own for the next thirteen years and became a 'Civic Jemima'. Interesting facts surfaced about Jemima in the process: it was claimed that she was more than six foot tall, whereas in contrast Yvonne was only five foot and three inches.[46] Between 3,000 and 4,000 people turned out to greet the marchers from Stackpole on the Sunday afternoon, 23 February 1997.[47]

Permeating and underpinning the celebrations were the many works of historical enquiry. Pieces were reproduced as part of the bicentenary memorabilia. The past was a commercial asset: Ap Gwilym's *An Authentic Account of 1842* was reproduced

'Little Fishguard for Ever!'

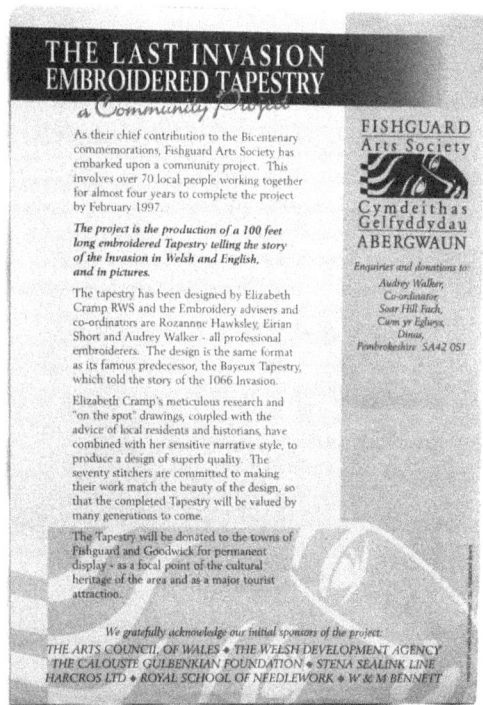

Figures 22a and 22b: Example of a promotional leaflet produced for the bicentenary of the Fishguard Invasion in 1997

in facsimile for Pembrokeshire County Cultural Services in 1997, and reproductions of Propert's map were sold again as souvenirs in as they had been in 1897. Promotional flyers such those shown in Figure 21 contained historical information, as well as publicising the events of the bicentenary.

The most fascinating and enduring legacy of the bicentenary was the specially commissioned tapestry that represented the event in a totally different, but very effective way, as a permanent memorial. Designed and sewn by around eighty local women, it is a similar format and size to the Bayeux tapestry; it took four years to complete and is on permanent display in a purpose-built gallery attached to the Library in Fishguard Town Hall. The tapestry, although designed and sewn by women, acknowledges the uncertainty of the story of the red cloaks and has 'The Myth' embroidered under the colourful scene of the women marching around the Bigney.[48] The tapestry is an eloquent tribute to the strength of the women and the community, in the same proud civic tradition of the ladies in their red shawls, the *Merched* or *Gwragedd Abergwaun*. The contours of the mythology and remembrance have changed in the telling and with the historical context. We see memory and memories, but also forgetting.

Nansi Jones has quietly and almost imperceptibly disappeared from the memory and memorialisation of the French Invasion. She was not mentioned by Salmon or Stuart Jones. There were two reasons for her fading away: the decline of revivalist Welsh Nonconformity and teetotalism, and the rise of Jemima. Nansi Jones was known almost exclusively to Welsh-speaking Nonconformists, and the decline of Welsh Nonconformity as a revivalist movement and Nansi Jones went hand in hand. Jemima was closely associated with her hometown of Fishguard whereas Nansi Jones's links were more remote in faraway Llanybydder. Jemima has thrived while the anti-Jemima, a more recent creation, has not.

Jemima and her pitchfork have now become a 'brand' in the twenty-first century.[49] Jemima's image is used to sell tea and beer.⁵⁰ She has her own page on Wikipedia. The National Museum of Wales has Jemima as one of the ten objects signifying the History of Wales, incorrectly designating Jemima as a cobbler's wife.⁵¹ Jemima is also listed in the top 100 Welsh Women,⁵² and social media will often have references to the French Invasion and Jemima on the anniversary, 22 February, each year when the people of Fishguard celebrate and commemorate as a community. People associate the French Invasion with Jemima and not Cawdor; the brand name *Cawdor* is well known but for different reasons.

This survey of more than 200 years of Remembering the French Invasion has proved one thing: the sheer persistence of the remembrance. The French Invasion stories possess significant Pembrokeshire, Welsh, British, Irish, French and other transnational dimensions. The French Invasion and its story have had an impact on the histories of Liverpool, Leeds, Bristol, Haverfordwest and Carmarthen, as well as on incidents of popular fear of invasion, and not only at a time of war. In terms of the curation of memory, the stories belong to the people of Fishguard, Goodwick and Pencaer, and are intrinsic to their history and heritage. The conflict against the French in 1797 was fought by local people with an emotional intensity of popular fury that was not a war of ideas. The people were fighting with God on their side to protect their lives, their families and their livestock. People were killed on both sides, there were atrocities, there was compensation. The resulting persecution and recrimination were remembered for generations. The community lived on, wary of strangers, still nervous of war, and, for the women of Fishguard in particular, proud of their role in causing the downfall of the enemy and represented collectively by the folk hero Jemima.⁵³

The community memory attests to the resilience of these communities and to the strength of their women. A people who liberated themselves from the enemy in 1797 and have not forgotten.

Endnotes

1. 'Wales Day by Day', *Western Mail* (11 October 1950), 2.
2. 'Wales Day by Day', *Western Mail* (24 February 1951), 2; *Western Mail* (21 September 1954), 4.
3. Richard Elley, 'Welsh troops who stopped Boney', *Western Mail* (22 February 1957), 7.
4. Major Francis Jones, 'Wales Plays Her Part in a Great Record', *Western Mail* (28 June 1958), 5.
5. Lt Col. R. L. Howell, 'The Pembroke Yeomanry', *The Pembrokeshire Historian*, 2 (1966), 76. The women were also included again very briefly in R. G. Thorne and R. Howell, 'Pembrokeshire in Wartime 1793–1815', in Elwyn Davies and David Howell (eds), *Pembrokeshire County History, vol. 3: Early Modern Pembrokeshire 1536–1815* (Haverfordwest, 1987), p. 395.
6. 'The Best Safeguard. Letter to the Editor', Derek Hudson, *The Times* (18 August 1961), 9.
7. Derek Hudson, *The Times* (18 August 1961), 9.
8. 'The Best Safeguard. Letter to the Editor', R. W. Lewis, *The Times* (29 August 1961), 9.
9. Harri Webb, 'The Women of Fishguard', *Rampage and Revel* (Llandysul, 1977), p. 301.
10. Harri Webb, 'Memories of the Eisteddfod', in Meic Stephens (ed.), *A Militant Muse: Selected Literary Journalism 1948–1980* (Bridgend, 1998), pp. 141–2.
11. Edward Laws, *The History of Little England Beyond Wales*, quoted in John Kinross, *Fishguard Fiasco: An Account of the Last Invasion of Britain*, 1st edn (Tenby, 1974), p. 59.
12. Kinross, *Fishguard Fiasco* (1974), p. 58.
13. John Kinross, *Fishguard Fiasco: An Account of the Last Invasion of Britain*, 2nd edn (Little Logaston, 2007), p. 45.
14. Pamela Horn, *History of the French Invasion of Fishguard 1797* (Fishguard, 1980), Appendix A, B and C, pp. 19–23, PRO PC.1/37, A.114.
15. Pamela Horn, *The Building of Fishguard Fort* (Fishguard, 1982), pp. 2–3.
16. Marianne Elliott, *Partners in Revolution: The United Irishmen and France* (Yale CT, 1982), p. 116.
17. Marianne Elliott, *Wolfe Tone* (Yale CT, 1989) p. 323; Roland Quinault, 'The French Invasion of Pembrokeshire in 1797: A Bicentennial Assessment', *Welsh History Review*,1–4 (1998–9), 626.
18. Geraint H. Jenkins, 'Glaniad y Ffrancod yn Abergwaun yn 1797', lecture given at the National Eisteddfod in Fishguard in 1986, published in his collection of articles *Cadw Ty mewn Cwmwl Tystion* (Llandysul, 1990), pp. 256–72.

19   Jenkins, 'Glaniad y Ffrancod yn Abergwaun yn 1797', p. 257. The ballad was Philip Dafydd, 'Anogaeth I Foliannu Duw', see Ffion Jones, *Welsh Ballads of the French Revolution 1793–1815* (Cardiff, 2012) no. 19, p. 204.
20   Jenkins, 'Glaniad y Ffrancod yn Abergwaun yn 1797', p. 262.
21   Jenkins, 'Glaniad y Ffrancod yn Abergwaun yn 1797', p. 263; Anon, 'Praise to the Welsh, the men of Pembrokeshire', no. 15 in Jones, *Welsh Ballads of the French Revolution*, p. 178.
22   Jenkins, 'Glaniad y Ffrancod yn Abergwaun yn 1797', p. 265.
23   Jenkins, 'Glaniad y Ffrancod yn Abergwaun yn 1797', p. 270. The Thomas Evans poem cited by Jenkins is 'Penillion ar Diriad y Ffrancod yn Abergwaun', see *Gardd Aberdar yn cynwys y cyfansoddiadau buddugol yn Eisteddfod y Carw Coch, Aberdar, Awst 29, 1853*, (Carmarthen, 1854), p. 105.
24   Jenkins, 'Glaniad y Ffrancod yn Abergwaun yn 1797', p. 271.
25   T. Llew Jones, *Berw Gwyllt yn Abergweun* (Llanrwst, 1986).
26   Llew Jones, *Berw Gwyllt yn Abergweun*, p. 25.
27   John D. Ahlstrom, 'Captain and Chef de Brigade William Tate: South Carolina Adventurer', *The South Carolina Historical Magazine*, 88/4 (October 1987), 183–91.
28   H. L. Ap Gwilym, *An Authentic Account of the Invasion by French Troops* (Haverfordwest, 1842), p.8; Edward Laws, 'The French Landing at Fishguard', *Archaeologia Cambrensis*, 4th ser., 14/56 (October 1883), 313.
29   E. H. Stuart Jones, *The Last Invasion of Britain* (Cardiff, 1950), p. 276.
30   Walters's oeuvre is large, containing two different books with the same title, *Truthful History of the Last Invasion* (Sutton Coldfield, 1989; and Glastonbury, 1992); there are at least sixteen works on the Fishguard Invasion and related topics published between 1988 and 1996. Some of the titles give an indication of their content; for example, *My Indictment of the Catholic Treachery: Endured by the Welsh-Speaking Non-conformists since February 1797* (Glastonbury, 1996).
31   Syd Walters, *Illustrated Commentary on the History of Fishguard and Goodwick from c.1750 to 1987* (privately printed, 1988), p. 5.
32   Walters, *Illustrated Commentary*, p. 20.
33   Walters, *Illustrated Commentary*, pp. 20–1.
34   See Paul O'Leary, *Immigration and Integration: The Irish in Wales, 1798–1922* (Cardiff, 2000) and on the general question of whether Wales was a tolerant nation, Chris Williams, Neil Evans and Paul O'Leary, *A Tolerant Nation? Revisiting Ethnic Diversity in a Devolved Wales* (Cardiff, 2015); Paul O'Leary, 'When Was Anti-Catholicism? The Case of Nineteenth- and Twentieth-Century Wales', *The Journal of Ecclesiastical History*, 56/2 (April 2005), 308–25.
35   Syd Walters, *Fishguard and French Invasion: Cheating and Obtaining Funds by False Pretences* (privately printed, 1995), jacket cover.
36   Phil Carradice, *The Last Invasion: The Story of the French Landing in Wales* (Pontypool, 1992).

The Last Invasion

37 Quinault, 'The French Invasion of Pembrokeshire in 1797', 618–42.
38 Quinault, 'The French Invasion of Pembrokeshire in 1797', 628.
39 Stuart Jones, *The Last Invasion*, p. 69, note 24.
40 Quinault, 'The French Invasion of Pembrokeshire in 1797', 641.
41 Bill Fowler and Richard Davies, 'The Story of Nonconformist Thomas John ... Almost a martyr', *Pembrokeshire Life*, December 1995, 44; Bill Fowler and Richard Davies, 'Who was William Tate?', January 1996, 41; Bill Fowler, 'End of a Dream: part 2', *Pembrokeshire Life*, February 1996, 35; Bill Fowler, 'A Redoubtable Local Heroine', *Pembrokeshire Life*, May 1996, 20; Bill Fowler, 'Who Sails in the Sunset?', *Pembrokeshire Life*, April 1996, 7; Bill Fowler, 'The Invasion was Halted ... The Power Struggle was Just Beginning', *Pembrokeshire Life*, July 1996, 34–5; Bill Fowler, 'Twisting the Knife', *Pembrokeshire Life*, August 1996, 6–7; Bill Fowler, 'Truth or Legend', *Pembrokeshire Life*, October 1996, 16.
42 The target audience information from Bill Fowler himself.
43 Bill Fowler, *The French Invasion at Fishguard* (Dyfed Education Department, 1989), p. 6.
44 *The Bicentenary of the Last Invasion of Britain Newsletter*, no. 1 (Fishguard, December 1996), p. 1.
45 *Bicentenary Newsletter*, p. 1.
46 Jo Knowsley, 'Beware, big Welsh girls in high hats', *The Sunday Telegraph* (12 January 1997), 13.
47 *The Official Souvenir Brochure of the Last Invasion of Britain* (Fishguard, 1997), p. 37.
48 *The Story Behind a Community Project: The Last Invasion Tapestry* (Fishguard, 1997). See also *https://lastinvasiontapestry.co.uk/the-tapestry/* (last accessed 6 August 2024).
49 For changing visual representations of Jemima, see Rita Singer, 'Why, Why, Why, Jemima? Picturing the French Invasion of Fishguard', 22 January 2021, *https://bydbach.hcommons.org/why-why-why-jemima/* (last accessed 31 July 2024).
50 The beer is promoted with a snippet of history concerning Jemima and 1797. www.glamorganbrewing.co.uk/our-beers/jemimas-pitchfork-cask (last accessed 6 August 2024).
51 See *www.wales.com/about/culture/history-wales-ten-objects* (last accessed 6 August 2024).
52 See *www.100welshwomen.wales/* (last accessed 6 August 2024).
53 A recent illustration of the collective women's memory, see 'Merched Jemeima', *Cwlwm Mudiad Chwiorydd Undeb Bedyddwyr Cymru*, 58 (September 2017), 11–12.

Bibliography

Ballads and Poetry

Am y Waredigaeth ryfeddol a gafwyd gan yr Arglwydd oddiwrth y Ffrancod yn y flwyddyn 1797, gan Ebenezer Richard (bachgenyn pymtheg mlwydd oed) wedi ei chyfansoddi yn yr un flwyddyn, sef 1797, Hen Faledau, *The London Kelt*, 20 March 1897 and 3 April 1897. Select verses from it appeared in the sons' eulogy for their father in 1839.

Anon., 'The False Alarm', in Elizabeth Edwards, *English-Language Poetry from Wales 1789–1806* (Cardiff, 2013), no. 30, pp. 162–3.

Brigstocke, Anne, *God and Gideon or, the valour of ancient Britons displayed* (no date but NLW has c.1797).

Evans, Thomas, *Penillion ar Diriad y Ffrancod yn Abergwaun; Gardd Aberdar yn cynnwys y Cyfansoddiadau Buddugol 1853* (Carmarthen, 1854), p. 105.

Fenton, Richard, 'A POEM, Written at Fishguard by a Spectator to the French Invasion', in J. Baker, *Visions, A Poetic Essay; hastily sketched for the present juncture of danger, to assist in forming the national spirit in AN UNION OF LOYALTY AND PATRIOTISM, to which is added, A BRIEF AND FAITHFUL NARRATIVE OF THE RECENT FRENCH INVASION, UPON THE COAST OF WALES NEAR FISHGUARD* (Bath, 1803), pp. 10–12.

Griffiths, T. Cunllo, 'Glaniad y Ffrancod yn Abergwaun', *Glaniad y Ffrancod yn Abergwaun. Darlith* (Ystalyfera, 1885), pp. 49–50.

Harries, John, 'The Land of the Leek', *Welsh Patriotism: Or, the Landing of the French at Fishguard* (Haverfordwest, 1875), p. 24.

Hughes, John Ceiriog, 'Y Baban Diwrnod Oed', *Oriau'r Hwyr: sef Gweithiau Barddonol* (1860); p. 57, lines 48–55.

Owen, T. E., 'Anglesey Volunteer Song', *Chester Courant*, 31 October 1797, p. 3. The song was republished as the 'Welsh Volunteer Song' in 1804, *Chester Courant*, 3 July 1804; *Hereford Journal*, 11 July 1804, p. 222.

Owen, T. E., 'Anglesey Volunteer Song', in Elizabeth Edwards, *English-Language Poetry from Wales 1789–1806* (Cardiff, 2013), no. 49, pp. 221–3, 303–4.

Reade, Joseph, 'Invasion! A Poem' (1804), in Elizabeth Edwards, *English-Language Poetry from Wales 1789–1806* (Cardiff, 2013), no. 47, pp. 211–19.

Richards, N. Neander, on the 'Canmlwyddiant', Glamorgan Free Press, 24 July 1897.

The French Invasion, two English-language ballads, one from Jeffreston, the other from Corston, made available to Wheeler and Broadley by Laws and published by them, *Napoleon and the Invasion of Britain* (1908), pp. 70–5; and by Stuart Jones as Appendix 1 in *The Last Invasion of Britain* (1950), pp. 269–74.

'"The Victory of Fishguard. A favourite Song". The Words by the Revd Dr Morgan whose Countrymen were forward to repel the French Invaders, who very lately made a Descent in Wales' (London, 1797), in Elizabeth Edwards, *English-Language Poetry from Wales 1789–1806* (Cardiff, 2013), no. 31, pp. 164–5. Another title to his song was '"The Victory of Fishguard, a favourite song". The words by the Revd Dr Morgan, whose brothers were the foremost to repel the French Invaders who very lately made a descent on Wales'.

Webb, Harri, 'The Women of Fishguard', *Rampage and Revel* (Llandysul, 1977), p. 301.

Ballads numbered as they appear in Jones, *Welsh Ballads of the French Revolution*

Jones, Ffion Mair, *Welsh Ballads of the French Revolution 1793–1815* (Cardiff, 2012).

[12] Dienw, 'Cân newydd am y waredigaeth fawr a gafodd yr hen Frytainiaid trwy law Duw [a] Lord Cawdor oddi wrth lu o lardon Ff[rein]ig yn y flwydd 1797' (1797).
[14] Dienw, 'Cân o ddiolchgarwch i'r Arglwydd am Ei waredigaeth hynod, yn ein cadw rhag fflangell ein gelynion pan tiriasant yn ein tir' (1797).
[15] Dienw, 'Clôd i'r Cymry, gwyr Sir Benfro, am gymeryd y rheibus elynion cythreulig, ysglyfyddwyr mileinig, sef Ffrancod pan diriasant yn Abergwaun' (1797).
[18] Nathaniel Jenkins, 'Annerch i'r Cymry, i'w hannog i edifarhau am eu pechodau at Dduw, ac i'w glodfori am ein gwared o grafangau'r Ffrancod didrugaredd' (1797).
[19] Phillip Dafydd, 'Annogath i foliannu Duw am y waredigaeth fawr a gafodd y wlad pan tiriod 1,400 o'r Ffrancod echryslon yn Pencaer yn sir Benfro i oresgyn ein tir trwy ladd a losgi ei cyd-wladwyr' (1797).
[20] Richard Roberts, 'Dau bennill yn rhoi ychydig o hanes y gelynion a diriasant i borthladd Abergwaun yn sir Benfro' (1797).
[21] Thomas Francis, 'Cân am y waredigaeth a gafodd y Brytainiaid o ddwylaw'r Ffrancod gwaedlyd' (1797).
[22] G. S., 'Cân o glod i'r Arglwydd am ein holl fuddugoliaethau ar fôr ac ar dir' (1799).
[23] George Stephens, 'Can o ganmoliaeth i volunteers y tair sir, sef sir Benfro, sir Aberteifi a sir Gaerfyrddin' (1799).
[24] Dafydd Evan Morgan, 'Cân o glod i foluntiers Glan Teifi a'u hoffisers' (1800).

Performances: Music, Drama, Cabaret, Radio and Television

1801, Thomas Dibdin, St David's Day: or, the Honest Welchman (London, 1801).
c.1896, Glaniad y Ffrancod yn Abergwaun: neu 'Madame Dumas' (chwareugerdd) y geiriau gan D. Cynwal Davies, y gerddoriaeth gan D. W. Rowlands (1908), English translation by Samuel Williams (Snell, Swansea, c.1936).

1929/30, Welsh-language London-Welsh Cabaret held at the Hotel Russell in London on New Year's Eve 1929/1930, the *pièce de résistance*, an item titled 'Merched Abergwaun', a dance by a bevy of pretty girls dressed in white satin with scarlet cloaks and tall Welsh hats purporting to portray the deception of the French at Fishguard in 1797, *Western Mail*, 1 January 1930.

1930, RADIO DRAMA, Ernest Velindre, French Invasion of 1797 in four acts, played by the Cardiff Radio Players, *The Daily Herald*, 11 February 1930.

1937, DRAMA, Grace Roberts, *Llongau'r Gelyn*, performed by the Trecynon Society at the Abercynon Little Theatre in May 1937. Welsh Historical Play Fishguard Invasion the Background, *Western Mail*, 8 May 1937.

1949, DRAMA, *Glaniad y Ffrancod yn Abergwaun*.

1950, RADIO DRAMA, *Proud Foot of the Conqueror* (advertised in Western Mail 10 February 1950).

1953, RADIO DRAMA, *The Trial of Thomas John* (reviewed *South Wales Gazette*, 17 July 1953).

1972, Ryan Davies, NAPOLEON vs MAM, recitation of Webb's *Women of Fishguard*, BBC Wales Poems and Pints, BBC Wales Archive.

2022, Matthew Sturgis, *The Last Invasion*, Theatr Gwaun, Fishguard.

2022, Rob Taylor, *Conquest of the World*, Theatr Gwaun, Fishguard.

Newspapers and Journals

1797–8
Bath Herald
Caledonian Mercury
Cambridge Intelligencer
Chester Courant
Chester Chronicle
Cumberland Paquet

Derby Mercury
Dublin Evening Post
Gloucester Journal
Hampshire Chronicle
Hereford Journal
Hull Advertiser
Ipswich Journal
Kentish Chronicle
Leeds Intelligencer
Manchester Mercury
Newcastle Courant
Norfolk Chronicle
Northampton Mercury
Staffordshire Advertiser
The Saunders's News-letter
The Times

1798–1860
Baner ac Amserau Cymru
Bury and Norwich Post
Cardiff and Merthyr Guardian
Charles o'r Bala sef cyhoeddiad pythefnosol at wasanaeth crefydd, llenyddiaeth ac addysg
Eddowe's Journal
Evening Mail
Falkirk Herald
Hereford Journal
Hereford Times
Illustrated Berwick Journal
Lancashire Gazette
Monmouthshire Beacon
Monmouthshire Merlin
Pembrokeshire Herald
Seren Gomer
Suffolk Herald

Sun (London)
The Cambrian
The Morning Advertiser
The Times
The Welshman
Volunteer Service Gazette
Weekly Dispatch
Worcestershire Chronicle
Y Bedyddiwr
Y Diwygiwr
Y Genhinen
Yr Haul

1861–1914
Aberdare Echo
Army and Navy Gazette
Barry Herald
Birmingham Daily Post
Cardiff Times and South Wales Weekly News
Cardigan and Tivy Side Advertiser
Cardigan Observer and General Advertiser
Cardigan Reporter
Cymro a'r Celt Llundain
Daily Mail
Evening Express
Evening News
Haverfordwest and Milford Haven Telegraph and General
Herald of Wales
Islington Daily Gazette
London Evening Standard
Manchester Courier
Merthyr Telegraph
Merthyr Times and Dowlais Times
Newcastle Courant
Pembroke County Guardian

Bibliography

Pembrokeshire Herald and General Advertiser
Potter's Electric News
Seren Cymru
South Wales Daily News
South Wales Daily Post
South Wales Echo
Tarian y Gweithiwr
The Athenaeum
The Cambrian
The Central Sussex Gazette
The County Echo
The Daily Telegraph
The Globe
The Herald of Peace and International Arbitration
The Kerry Evening Post
The Llanelly Mercury and South Wales Advertiser
The London Kelt
The Musical Herald
The Penny Illustrated Paper
The Shields Daily News
The Sphere
The Tatler
The Tenby Observer
The Treasury a monthly miscellany and missionary reporter in connection with the Calvinistic Methodist church
The Weekly Mail
The Welshman
Volunteer Service Gazette
Votes for Women
Waterford Standard
The Western Mail
Wellington Journal and Shrewsbury News
Western Daily Press
Witney Gazette
Worthing Gazette

Y Brython Cymreig
Y Gwladgarwr
Y Llan
Yorkshire Post
Young Wales
Y Tyst Cymreig
Y Tyst a'r Dydd

1914–1997
Aberdare Leader
Birmingham Daily Post
Carmarthen Weekly Reporter
Central Somerset Gazette
Daily Chronicle
Daily Mail
Flintshire County Herald
London Daily News
Leeds Mercury
Liverpool Echo
Londonderry Sentinel
Midland Daily Telegraph
Notes and Queries
Northern Whig
Nottingham Evening Post
Ormskirk Advertiser
South Wales Gazette
The Daily Telegraph
The Glamorgan Gazette
The People
The Scotsman
The Spectator
The Sphere
The Studio
The Sunday Telegraph
The Times

The Western Mail
The Westminster Gazette
Y Llan
Y Llenor
Yorkshire Evening Post
Western Daily Press

Manuscripts

In addition to the documents marshalled by Broadley and Wheeler, David Salmon, E. H. Stuart Jones, Pamela Horn:

British Library
'"Hanes Llu o Filwyr Ffraingc a ddaeth I fewn I Ddeheudir Cymru, A D 1797": Edward Charles Welsh Poems 1790–1814', BL Add MS 14,959.

Carmarthenshire Record Office
Cawdor Collection, box 223.
Milford to David Edwardes, 24 February 1797, Carmarthenshire Record Office, facsimile of original in Syd Walters, *Fishguard and French Invasion: Cheating and Obtaining Funds by False Pretences* (1995), pp. 5–7.

Historical Society of Pennsylvania
Richards to Samuel Jones, 19 March 1798, Mrs Irving H. McKesson Collection (Jones section).

National Archives
Portland correspondence PRO 42-40-1, 42-40-2, 42-40-3, 42-40-4; PRO PC.1/37, A.114 8 March 1797; Examination of Barry St Ledger PRO PC.1/37, A.114; Pamela Horn, History of the French Invasion of Fishguard 1797 (1980) Appendix A, B and C, pp. 1–23.

National Library of Wales
At Y Cymry NLW 13232E (Mysevin 12) William Owen (-Pughe) MISCELLANEA.

Diary of John Davies, Ystrad 1796–9, NLW MS 12350A.

Henry Owen Papers NLW 1419.

Iolo Morganwg to William Owen Pughe, 7 March 1797, NLW MS13222.fo.13 –4.

List of Books in Evan Jones Library, NLW ex 1780. For influence on Salmon, see NLW Salmon Correspondence 7351C, letters dated 16 and 17 September 1929. Sir Evan Jones had bought manuscripts also from Broadley's Collection. Undated David Salmon letter, NLW MS 19439B.

Mr M.-A. Tour to South Wales, August 1801 NLW MS 1340C

Diary of John Davies, Ystrad 1796–9 NLW MS 12350A.

Programme of 1950 ceremony in NLW Minor Deposits 1145.

Prospectus: Historical Records of the Yeomanry Regiments (1908), NLW Minor Deposits 1145 B.

The Press Copy F. C. Meyrick and B. F. M. Freeman, *History of the Pembroke or Castlemartin Regiment of Imperial Yeomanry 1794–1907*, cuttings from the newspapers where the History had appeared in advance of publication arranged in chronological order with handwritten additions and deletions are in the NLW Minor Deposits 1145B.

Transcripts by E. A. Lewis of documents in the PRO relating to the trial, PRO W.R. Miscellanea 208D, in NLW MS Henry Owen Papers 1419C.

Pembrokeshire Archives
D/Sal/169 papers of Principal Salmon
D/Sal/173 papers of Principal Salmon
D/Sal/175 papers of Principal Samon
D/Sal/176 papers of Principal Salmon
D-Sim/52 Simon correspondence with the Royal Archives
HDX/990/27 Brut y Bobl
HDX/1009/108 Draft article and correspondence

Printed Material: Narratives of the French Invasion

1797–1815

An Address to the People of the United Kingdom of Great Britain and Ireland on the Threatened Invasion, Addendum: Specimens of French Ferocity and Brutality in Wales (London, 1803).

An History of Real and Threatened Invasions of England from the first landing of the Danes to the present period, including the descent on the coast of Wales in 1797 (London, 1797; 2nd edn 1798).

Annual Register, or a View of the History, Politics and Literature for the Year 1797, vol. 39 (1798, 2nd edn 1807).

Anon [William Richards], *Cwyn y cystuddiedig, a griddfanau y carcharorion dieuog: neu, Ychydig o hanes dyoddefiadau diweddar Thomas John a Samuel Griffiths, y rhai goddef gorthrymder tost a chaethiwed caled, dros chwech neu saith o fisoedd yn ddi-achos, a gawsant eu rhyddhau, o'r diwedd, yn yr uchel Eisteddfod, neu y Sessiwn mawr diweddaf, yn Hwlffordd: er dirfawr Siomedigaeth I'w Gelynion gwaedlyd a dideimlad* (Carmarthen, 1798).

'A Welsh Minister's Address', *The Loyalist*, xii (15 October 1803), pp. 204–5.

A Word in Season; or, A Few Plain Admonitions and evaluations on the Present State of Public Affairs, Addressed to the Inhabitants of Wales and Translated from the Welsh Language by the Author T.J. (Holywell, 1798).

Ayton, Richard, and William Daniell, *A voyage round Great Britain undertaken in the summer of 1813 and commencing from Land's End, Cornwall. By Richard Ayton; with a series of views. drawn and engraved by William Daniell* (London, 1814).

Baker, James, *A Brief Narrative of the French Invasion near Fishguard Bay Including a Perfect Description of that Part of the Coast of Pembrokeshire, on which was effected the LANDING OF THE FRENCH FORCES, on the 22nd of February, 1797, and of their surrender to the Welch Provincial Troops, HEADED BY LORD CAWDOR (Worcester, 1797).*

Baker, James, *Visions, a Poetic Essay; hastily sketched for the present juncture of danger, to assist in forming the national spirit in AN UNION OF LOYALTY AND PATRIOTISM to which is added A BRIEF AND FAITHFUL NARRATIVE OF THE RECENT FRENCH INVASION upon the coast of Wales* (Bath, 1803).

Baker, J., *Picturesque Guide through Wales and the Marches; Interspersed with the Most Interesting Subjects of Antiquity in that Principality. The Second Edition; with Considerable Alterations and Additions* (Worcester, 1795).

Baker, J., *The Imperial Guide with Picturesque Plans of the Great Post Roads, containing Miniature Likenesses* (London, 1802).

Clifford, Robert, *Application of Barruel's Memoirs of Jacobinism, to the secret societies of Ireland and Great Britain* (London, 1798).

Cornish, Joseph, *A Brief History of Nonconformity from the Reformation to the Revolution: with Remarks on Church-Establishments* (London, 1797).

Davies, Edward, *Cyfarch i Bobl Prydain Fawr ar fygythion y Ffrangcod i ruthro i'w gwlad; wedi ei gyfiethu o'r Saesneg. Esiamplau o ymddygiad creulon anifeilaidd y Ffrangcod y'Nghymru* (London, 1804).

Evans, John (ed.), *Remains of William Reed, late of Thornbury; including rambles in Ireland* (London, 1815).

Fenton, Richard, *A Historical Tour through Pembrokeshire* (London, 1811).

Fenton, Richard, 'A Historical Tour through Pembrokeshire', *The Eclectic Review*, 8/2 (September 1812), 869.

Richard Fenton, *Poems by Mr Fenton*, vol. 2 (London, 1790).

Fenton, Richard, *Tour in Quest of Genealogy through several parts of Wales, Somersetshire and Wiltshire in a series of letters to a friend in Dublin, interspersed with a description of Stourhead and Stonehenge together with various anecdotes, and curious fragments from a manuscript collection ascribed to Shakespeare (London)* (London, 1811).

Heweston, W. B., *History of Napoleon Bonaparte: And Wars of Europe* (1815) vol. 1.

Bibliography

'Instructions for Col Tate', *The Anti-Jacobin*, number 14 (12 February 1798), in William Gifford (ed.), *The Anti-Jacobin or Weekly Examiner*, vol. 1 (New York, 1970), p. 480.

[Jones, Theophilus] Cymro, 'Cursory remarks on Welsh Tours or Travels', *Cambrian Register*, 1796 (London, 1799).

[Jones, Thomas], *Gair yn ei Amser at drigolion Cymru gan Ewyllysiwr da at ei wlad* (Caerlleon, 1798).

Knox, Thomas, *Some account of the proceedings that took place on the landing of the French near Fishguard, in Pembrokeshire, on the 22nd February 1797* (London, 1800).

Lewis, Titus, *Hanes Wladol a Chrefyddol Prydain Fawr o'r Amser y daeth Brutainaid i wladychu iddi gyntaf hyd at yn bresennol* (Carmarthen, 1810).

Lipscomb, George, *Journey into South Wales through the counties of Oxford, Warwick, Worcester, Hereford, Salop, Stafford, Buckingham, and Hertford; in the year 1799* (London, 1802).

Malkin, Benjamin Heath, *The Scenery, Antiquities and Biography of South Wales from Materials Collected During Two Excursions in the Year 1803* (London, 1804).

Manners, John Henry, Duke of Rutland, *Journal of a Tour through North and South Wales, the Isle of Man* (London, 1805).

Meyrick, Samuel, *The History and Antiquities of the County of Cardigan* (London, 1808).

Nicholson, George (ed.), *The Cambrian Travellers' Guide in every direction containing remarks made during many excursions in the Principality of Wales and bordering districts, augmented by extracts from the best writers* (London, 1813).

Price, Uvedale, *Thoughts on the Defence of Property: Addressed to the County of Hereford* (1797).

'Review of Lipscomb, Journey into South Wales', *Monthly Review, or, Literary Journal* (1805), 205.

'Review of New Publications, Journey into South Wales 1799', *The Gentleman's Magazine*, 74/2 (1804), 743.

Skrine, Henry, *Two Successive Tours throughout the whole of Wales: with several of the adjacent English counties* (London, 1798).

'Specimens of French Cowardice and Brutality in Wales', *The Loyalist*, 5 (1803), 89.

The Bishop of Llandaff's Thoughts on the French Invasion (London n.d. but 1798), invasion scenario extract from the above.

The Critical Review: or, Annals of Literature, 19 (1797).

The Universal Magazine, March 1797.

The New Annual Register, or General Repository of History, Politics and Literature for the year 1797 (London, 1798).

Watson, Richard, *A Charge Delivered to the Clergy of the Diocese of Llandaff in June 1798* (London, 1798).

Watson, Richard, *Address to the People of Great Britain* (London, 1798).

1816–63

Alison, Archibald, *History of Europe from the Commencement of the French Revolution in 1789 to the Restoration of the Bourbons in 1815*, 10 vols (1833–43).

An Account of Tenby, containing An Historical Sketch of the place compiled from the best authorities and a description of its present state (Pembroke, 1818).

'A Native. How the French Fared at Fishguard, 1797 A.D.', *Chambers's Journal of Popular Literature* (14 January 1860), 17–21.

Anon [Wilkie Collins], 'The Great (Forgotten) Invasion', *Household Words* (12 March 1859), 19.

Anon [David Meyler], Adgofion Tiriad y Ffrancod yn Swydd Benfro, *Y Traethodydd*, 12 (1856).

Ap Gwilym, H. L., *An Authentic Account of the Invasion by French Troops on Carrig Gwasted Point, near Fishguard, 1797* (Haverfordwest, 1842).

Blunt, Humphrey, *Perils and Panics of Invasion in 1796–7–8, 1804–5 and at the present time* (London, 1860).

Brooke, Richard, *Liverpool as it was during the last quarter of the eighteenth century 1775–1800* (Liverpool, 1853).

Caradoc of Llancarfan, *History of Wales*, topographical notes supplied by Richard Llwyd (Shrewsbury, 1832).

Bibliography

Collins, Wilkie, 'The Great (Forgotten) Invasion, Nooks and Corners of History: II', in *My Miscellanies*, vol. 1 (London, 1863).

Creasy, E. S., *The Invasions and the Projected Invasions of England from the Saxon Time with Remarks on the present Emergencies* (London, 1852).

Cust, Edward, *Annals of the Wars of the Eighteenth Century compiled from the most authentic histories of the period*, vol. 5 1796–1799 (London, 1862).

De Bonnechose, Emile, *Lazare Hoche: General de Chef ... sous la Convention et le Directoire 1793–1797* (Paris, 1867).

Gifford, C. H., *History of the Wars occasioned by the French Revolution from the commencement of hostilities in 1792 to the end of 1816*, vol. 1 (1817), 129–30.

James, William, *The naval history of Great Britain from the declaration of war in 1793 to the accession of George IV*, vol. 2 (London, 1820).

Jones, David, *Hanes y Bedyddwyr yn Neheubarth Cymru* (Carmarthen, 1839).

Jones, John Emlyn (gol), *Hanes Prydain Fawr yn wladol a chrefyddol gan y diweddar Barch Titus Lewis wedi ei ddiwygio a'I helaethu* (Carmarthen, 1857).

McGregor, John James, *History of the French Revolution and of the wars resulting from that event* (Waterford, 1816).

Price, Y Parch Thomas, 'Carnhuanawc', *Hanes Cymru a Chenedl y Cymry, o'r Cynoesoedd hyd at farwolaeth Llewelyn Ap Gruffydd* (Crickhowell, 1842).

Scott, Walter, *Life of Napoleon vol. III, Appendix no. 2: Descent of the French in South Wales under General Tate* (London, 1827).

Stephens, Thomas, *The Literature of the Kymry: Being a Critical Essay on the History of the Language and Literature of Wales* (Llandovery, 1849).

Tales and Traditions of Tenby (Tenby, 1858).

'The French at Fishguard in 1797', *The United Service Magazine and Naval and Military Journal*, 41/171 (February 1843), 202–13.

Thomas, Thomas, *Memoirs of Owen Glendower (Owain Glyndwr) With a Sketch of the History of the Ancient Britons From the*

Conquest of Wales by Edward the First to the present time (Haverfordwest, 1822).

Williams, H. L., *An Authentic Account*, 2nd edn (Haverfordwest, 1853).

1864–1918

Anon [M. E. James], *The Fishguard Invasion of 1797. Some Passages taken from the Diary of the Reverend Daniel Rowlands, sometime Vicar of Llanfihangelpenybont* (London, 1892).

Baring-Gould, S., *The Book of South Wales* (London, 1905).

Bradley, A. G., *Highways and Byways in South Wales* (London, 1903).

Broadley, A. M., *Chats on Autographs* (London, 1910).

Brown, John (alias for Christopher Cobbe-Webb), (revised by Philipps and Warren), *The History of Haverfordwest with that of Some Pembrokeshire Parishes* (Haverfordwest, 1914).

Cobbe-Webb, Christopher, Gentleman, *Old Pembrokeshire parishes in the Hundred of Roose or Haverfordwest and its Story with Old Pembrokeshire Parishes* (Haverfordwest, 1882).

Desbrière, Edouard, *1793–1805, Projets et Tentatives de Debarquement aux Isles Britanniques*, 5 vols (Paris, 1900–2)

Edwardes, Charles, 'The French Invasion of 1797', *Chambers's Journal* (February 1898), 187–9.

Edwards, O. M., *Wales: The Story of the Nations* (London, 1901).

Farrar, Mrs John, *Recollections of Seventy Years* (Boston, 1866).

Fenton, Ferrar, 'Landing of the French at Fishguard in 1797', *Pembrokeshire Antiquities* (Solva, 1897), 63–7.

Fishguard 1797–1906: The story of the last invasion of England, as told from the original MSS with a note on modern Fishguard (GWR, 1906).

Foord, Edward, and Gordon Home, *England Invaded* (London, 1913, reissued 1915 as *The Invasions of England*).

For Travellers of All Nations: Historic Sites (GWR, 1910).

Great Western Railway, *South Wales: The Country of Castles* (London, 1905).

Bibliography

Griffiths, T. Cunllo, 'At Etholwyr Ceredigion', *Ye Brython Cymreig* (17 June 1892), 1.

Griffiths, T. Cunllo, *Glaniad y Ffrancod yn Abergwaun* (Ystalyfera, 1885).

Griffiths, T. Cunllo, *Lloffion y Beirdd* (Wrexham, 1879).

Guillon, E., *La France et l'Irlande pendant la Revolution* (Paris, 1888).

Harries, John (Cymro Sir Benfro), *Welsh Patriotism: Or, The Landing of the French at Fishguard on the 22nd of February, 1797 compiled from authentic sources* (Haverfordwest, 1875).

Historic Sites and Scenes of England, 1st edn (GWR, 1909).

'How the French Fared at Fishguard [By a Native]', *The Red Dragon*, 7 (1885), 235–45.

Hozier, H. M., *The Invasions of England: A History of the Past with Lessons for the Future* (London, 1876).

James, D. (Defynnog), *Ein Gwlad: neu Cymru-ei daear, ei hanes, ei llen:at wasanaeth ysgolion ac efrydwyr* (Newport, Mon., 1905).

James, M. E., *The Fishguard Invasion by the French in 1797*, centenary edn (London, 1897).

Laws, Edward, 'The French Landing at Fishguard', *Archaeologia Cambrensis*, 4th ser., 14/56 (October 1883), 311–24.

Laws, Edward, *The History of Little England Beyond Wales, the Non-Kymric Colony Settled in Pembrokeshire* (London, 1888).

Maurice, W., *History of the French Invasion of Fishguard in 1797* (Echo Offices, Fishguard no date but approx. 1910).

Rees, T. Mardy, *Notable Welshmen* (Caernarfon, 1908).

Rhys, Daniel, 'Peryglon Pencaer, NEU FFWDAN Y FFRANCOD YN ABERGWAUN', *Papur Pawb*, weekly instalments 14 July to 3 November 1894.

Rose, J. Holland, *Pitt and the Great War* (London, 1911).

Tiriad y Ffrangcod yn y flwyddyn 1797 ynghyda dewrder a chyfrwysdra y Cymry yn eu gwrthsefyll a'u cymeryd yn garcharorion (Hugh Humphreys, Caernarfon, Llyfrau Ceiniog rhif 74, *c*.1878).

Wheeler, H. F. B., *The French Revolution from the Age of Louis XIV to the Coming of Napoleon* (London, 1913).

Wheeler, H. F. B., *The Story of Napoleon* (London, 1910).

Wheeler, H. F. B., and A. M. Broadley, *Napoleon and the Invasion of England* (London, 1908, republished with modern introduction, 2007).

Williams, George, 'Landing of the French at Fishguard 1797', *Pembrokeshire Antiquities* (Solva, 1897), 61–3.

Williams, William, 'Am y ddaeargryn a ddygwyddodd mewn amryw o deyrnasoedd helaeth yn y fwyddyn 1755 a 1756', *Gweithiau Williams Pantycelyn* (Holywell, 1887).

1919–

Ahlstrom, John D., 'Captain and Chef de Brigade William Tate: South Carolina Adventurer', *The South Carolina Historical Magazine*, 88/4 (October 1987), 183–91.

Broster, D. K., *Ships in the Bay!* (London, 1931).

Carradice, Phil, *The Last Invasion: The Story of the French Landing in Wales* (Pontypool, 1992), reissued as *Britain's Last Invasion: The Battle of Fishguard* (Barnsley, Yorkshire, 2019).

Davies, David, *The Influence of the French Revolution on Welsh Life and Literature* (Carmarthen, 1926).

Davies, H. M., 'Terror, Treason and Tourism: The French in Pembrokeshire 1797', in Mary-Ann Constantine and Dafydd Johnston, *Footsteps of 'Liberty and Revolt': Essays on Wales and the French Revolution* (Cardiff, 2013), pp. 247–70.

Davies, L. Twiston, and Averyl Edwards, *Women of Wales* (London, 1935).

Edwards, Richard, *Hanes Llangloffan* (Solva, 1932).

Elliott, Marianne, *Partners in Revolution: The United Irishmen and France* (Yale CT, 1982).

Evans, John James, *Dylanwad y Chwyldro Ffrengig ar Lenyddiaeth Cymru* (Liverpool, 1928).

Evans, R. B., *An Account of the Last Invasion of Britain 1797 a.d.* (Goodwick, 1997).

Fishguard and French Invasion: Cheating and Obtaining Funds by False Pretences (privately printed, 1995).

Fowler, Bill, *The French Invasion at Fishguard* (Dyfed County

Council Education Department, 1992).

Freeman, Michael, 'Fishguard Invasion', https://welshhat.wordpress.com/chronological-survey/1790s/the-fishguard-invasion/ (last accessed 30 July 2024).

Grey, Charlotte, *The Last Invasion* (London, 1982).

Gore, John, 'The Last Invasion of Britain', *Quarterly Review* (April 1935), 270–83.

Horn, Pamela, *The Building of Fishguard Fort* (Fishguard, 1982).

Horn, Pamela, *History of the French Invasion of Fishguard 1797*, also titled *The Last Invasion of Britain Fishguard 1797* (Fishguard, 1980).

Ifans, Dafydd, 'Llythyr am Laniad y Ffrancod ger Abergwaun', *National Library of Wales Journal*, 29/4 (Winter 1996), 469–70.

Jenkins, Geraint, 'Glaniad y Ffrancod yn Abergwaun ym 1797, Darlith Eisteddfod Genedlaethol Abergwaun 1986', *Cadw Tŷ mewn Cwmwl Tystion; Ysgrifau hanesyddol ar grefydd a Diwylliant* (Llandysul, 1990), pp. 256–72.

John, Lyn, 'Llanelli and the Fishguard Invasion' (2016), www.llanellich.org.uk/files/356-llanelli-fishguard-invasion (last accessed 30 July 2024).

Jones, E. D., 'The French Landing at Fishguard, 1797', *National Library of Wales Journal*, 6/3 (Summer 1950), 303.

Jones, Major Francis, 'An Echo of 1797', *The Pembrokeshire Historian, Journal of the Pembrokeshire Local History Society*, 3 (1971), 81–2.

'Landing of the French: AD 1797', *Carmarthenshire Antiquarian Society Transactions*, 8/23–4 (1912–13), 79–80.

Last Invasion of Britain: Illustrated Film Script (privately printed, 1994).

Lewis, Sian, *Jemima Nicholas-Heroine of the Fishguard Invasion*, Welsh Women Series, vol. 5 (Gwasg Carreg Gwalch, 2012).

Llew Jones, T., *Berw Gwyllt yn Abergweun* (Llanrwst, 1986).

Kinross, John, *Fishguard Fiasco: An Account of the Last Invasion of Britain* (Tenby, 1974, revised 2007).

Kleinman, Sylvie, 'Initiating Insurgents Abroad: French Plans to

"Chouannise" Britain and Ireland 1793–1798', in B. Heuser, *Small Wars and Insurgents Theory and Practices 1500–1850* (London, 2016), pp. 48–77.

Morton, H. V., *In Search of Wales* (London, 1932).

Oman, Carola, *Britain Against Napoleon* (London, 1942).

Quinault, Rowland, 'The French Invasion of Pembrokeshire in 1797: A Bicentennial Assessment', *WHR*, 19/1–4 (1998–9), 618–42.

Rees, W. (Arianglawdd), 'Bedyddwyr Penfro: Glaniad Y Ffrancod 1797', *Trafodion Cymdeithas Hanes Bedyddwyr Cymru*, (1933), 1–2.

Richmond, H. W., *The Invasion of Britain: An Account of Plans, Attempts and Counter-measures from 1586 to 1918* (London, 1941).

Roberts, Gomer M., 'The Year 1797 in the life of the Rev David Jones, Llangan', *Cylchgrawn Cymdeithas Hanes y Methodistiaid Calfinaidd*, 23 (1938), 100–9.

Roberts, Tony, *French Invasion at Fishguard/Glaniad y Ffrancod yn Abergwaun* (Cardigan, 1997).

Rose, Richard, 'The French at Fishguard: Fact, Fiction and Folklore', *Transactions of the Honourable Society of Cymmrodorion*, 2002 new series, 9 (2003).

Salmon, David, 'A Sequel to the French Invasion of Pembrokeshire', *Y Cymmrodor: The Magazine of the Honourable Society of Cymmrodorion*, 43 (1932), 62–92.

Salmon, David, *Fishguard Invasion 1797: The Descent of the French on Pembrokeshire* (Carmarthen, 1930).

Salmon, David, *French Invasion of Pembrokeshire 1797* (Carmarthen, 1930).

Salmon, David, 'Histories of the French Invasion of Pembrokeshire', *Journal of the Welsh Bibliographical Society*, 5/1 (August 1937), 41–8.

Salmon, David, 'The French Invasion of Pembrokeshire in 1797', *West Wales Historical Records*, 14 (1929), 136–209.

Singer, Rita, 'The last invasion of Britain wasn't in 1066' (2023), https://bydbach.hcommons.org/the-last-invasion-of-britain-wasnt-in-1066/ (last accessed 30 July 2024).

Stuart Jones, Commander E. H., *The Last Invasion of Britain* (Cardiff, 1950).

The Bicentenary of the Last Invasion of Britain Newsletter, no. 1 (Fishguard, December 1996). 'The Cwmgwili Manuscripts (continued)', *Transactions of the Carmarthenshire Antiquarian Society*, 29 (1939), 19.

The Official Souvenir Brochure of the Last Invasion of Britain Fishguard, Goodwick and Pencaer (Fishguard 1997).

The Story Behind a Community Project: The Last Invasion Tapestry (Fishguard, 1997).

Thomas, J. E., *Britain's Last Invasion: Fishguard 1797* (Stroud, 2007).

Vaughan, William, *The Black Legion* (Aberystwyth, 2008).

Walters, Syd, *Illustrated Commentary on the History of Fishguard and Goodwick from c.1750 to 1987* (privately printed, 1988).

Walters, Syd, *Truthful History of the Last Invasion of Britain* (privately printed, 1992).

Werner, Jack, *We laughed at Boney: (or; We've been through it all before) How our forefathers laughed defiance at the last serious threat of invasion-by Napoleon: a striking parallel with our present position* (London, 1943).

Wheeler, H. F. B., *Napoleon 1769–1821* (London, 1921).

Whitehouse, Doug, 'The Last Invasion of Britain 1797' (1995), *www.waterlooassociation.org.uk/2018/07/26/the-last-invasion-of-britain/* (last accessed 30 July 2024).

Selected Secondary Sources

Aaron, Jane, 'Hoydens of Wild Wales: Representations of Welsh Women in Victorian and Edwardian Fiction', *Welsh Writing in English: A Yearbook of Critical Essays* (1995).

Aaron, Jane, *Nineteenth -Century Women's Writing in Wales: Nation, Gender and Identity* (Cardiff, 2007).

Aaron, Jane, *The Welsh Survival Gene: The 'Despite Culture' in the Two Language Communities of Wales*, Institute of Welsh Affairs National Eisteddfod Lecture, Meifod 2003 (Cardiff, 2003).

Arts and Sciences: or, Fourth Division of the English Encyclopedia, vol. 8 (1868).

Aspinall, A. (ed.), *The Later Correspondence of George III, vol. 2: February 1793 to December 1797* (Cambridge, 1963).

Association for the Preservation of Liberty and Property, *An Address to the People of the United Kingdom of Great Britain and Ireland on the Threatened Invasion* (London, 1803).

Association for the Preservation of Liberty and Property, *Important Considerations for the People of this Kingdom, published July 1803. And sent to the officiating Minister of every Parish in England* (London,1803).

Association for the Preservation of Liberty and Property, *Ystyriaethau Pwysfawr I Bobl y Deyrnas Hon, a gyhoeddwyd yn y Gorphenaf, 1803. Ac a ddanfonwyd at bob Gweinidog Eglwys trwy Loegr* (Liverpool, 1803).

Ballinger, John, 'An Artist topographer', *The Library*, 7/26 (April 1916), 116–43.

Baring, Mrs Henry, *The Diary of the Right Hon. William Windham 1784 to 1810* (London, 1866).

Bassett, T. M., *The Welsh Baptists* (Swansea, 1977).

Beiner, Guy, *Forgetful Remembrance: Social Forgetting and Vernacular Historiography of a Rebellion in Ulster* (Oxford, 2018).

Beiner, Guy, *Remembering the Year of the French: Irish Folk History and Social Memory* (Madison WI, 2007).

Ben-Israel, Hedva, *English Historians on the French Revolution* (Cambridge, 1968).

Brake, Laurel, and Marysa Demoor (eds) *Dictionary of 19th Century Journalism in Great Britain* (London, 2009).

Bullen, M., *Milford Marathon: The Story of the Customs Officers who Helped to Repel the French Invasion of Pembrokeshire in 1797* (London, 1997).

Burke, Edmund, *A Third Letter to a Member of the Present Parliament on the proposals for Peace with the Regicide Directory* (London, 1796).

Carnot, Nicolas Léonard Sadi, 'Instructions pour l' Etablissement d'une Chouannerie en Angleterre, Carnot's Plan for Invading England', *Fraser's Magazine*, 15 (1877), 201–2.

Carter, Louise, 'Scarlet Fever: Female Enthusiasm for Men in Uniform 1780–1815', in Kevin Linch and Matthew McCormack, *Britain's Soldiers: Rethinking War and Society, 1715–1815* (Liverpool, 2014), pp. 155–79.

House of Lords Library, T. Robin, *The Oxford Literary History of Wales, vol 2: Writing in Welsh 1740–2010: A Troubled Heritage* (Oxford, 2020).

Chapman, T. Robin, 'The Turn of the Tide Melancholy and Modernity in Mid-Victorian Wales', *Welsh History Review*, 27/3 (June 2015), 503–27.

Charnell-White, Catherine (ed.), *Welsh Poetry of the French Revolution 1789–1805* (Cardiff, 2012).

Clarke, William, *The Secret Life of Wilkie Collins* (London, 1988).

Colley, Linda, *Britons: Forging the Nation 1707–1837* (Yale CT, 1992).

Constantine, Mary-Ann, 'Celts and Romans on Tour: Visions of Early Britain in Eighteenth-Century Travel Literature', in Francesca Kaminski-Jones (ed.), *Celts, Romans and Britons Classical and Celtic Influence in the Construction of British Identities* (Oxford, 2020), pp. 117–39.

Cookson, J. E., *The British Armed Nation 1793–1815* (Oxford, 1997).

Cottle, Joseph, *The Fall of Cambria* (1808).

Cowsill, Miles, *Fishguard Rosslare* (Kilgetty, 1990).

Cruttwell, Clement, *A Tour through the whole island of Great Britain divided into journeys, vol. 3: Wales* (London, 1801)

Csengei, Ildiko, 'The Literature of Fear in Britain *Coleridge's Fears in Solitude* and the French Invasion of Fishguard in 1797', *English Literature*, 5 (December 2018), 183–206.

Dale-Jones, Edna, 'Arrivals and Departures-Carmarthen 1797', *The Carmarthenshire Antiquary*, 33 (1997), 106–14.

Davies, D. Russell, *Hope and Heartbreak: A Social History of Wales and the Welsh 1776–1871* (Cardiff, 2005).

Davies, Damian Walford, 'Mapping Invasion: Cartography,

Caricature, Frames of Reading' in Sally Bushell and Julia S. Carlson and Damian Walford Davies (eds), *Romantic Cartographies: Mapping, Literature, Culture 1789–1832* (Cambridge, 2020) pp. 101–21.

Davies, Damian Walford, *Presences that Disturb: Models of Romantic Identity in the Literature and Culture of the 1790s* (Cardiff, 2002).

Davies, Hywel M., 'Loyalism in Wales', *Welsh History Review*, 20 (2001), 687–716.

Davies, Hywel M., *Transatlantic Brethren: Revd Samuel Jones and his Friends, Baptists in Wales, Pennsylvania and Beyond* (Bethlehem PA, 1995).

Davies, Hywel M., 'Wales in English Travel Writing 1791–1798: the Welsh Critique of Theophilus Jones', *Welsh History Review*, 23/3 (June 2007), 65–93.

Davies, J. E., *The Changing Fortunes of a British Aristocratic Family 1789–1976: The Campbells of Cawdor and their Welsh Estates* (Woodbridge, 2019).

Davies, J. H., 'Bibliography of Welsh Ballads', *Transactions of the Honourable Society of Cymmrodorion*, 304 (1908–11), 111.

Dugdale, Thomas, assisted by W. Burnett, *Curiosities of Great Britain: England and Wales Delineated: Historical, Entertaining and Commercial*, vol. 2 (London, 1830).

Dyck, Ian, *William Cobbett and Rural Popular Culture* (Cambridge, 1992).

Edwards, Elizabeth, *English-Language Poetry from Wales 1789–1806* (Cardiff, 2013).

Edwards, Elizabeth, *Richard Llwyd, Beaumaris Bay and other Poems* (Nottingham, 2015).

Edwards, Huw Meirion, 'The Lyric Poets', in Hywel Teifi Edwards, *A Guide to Welsh Literature c.1800–1900* (Cardiff, 2000), pp. 97–125.

Ein Gwlad neu Cymru – Ei Daear, Ei Hanes, A'i Llen, 3rd edn (Newport, 1911).

Elliott, Marianne, *Wolfe Tone* (Yale CT, 1989).

Ellis, E. L., *The University College of Wales, Aberystwyth 1872–1972* (Cardiff, 1972).

Evans, Paul, 'The Flintshire Loyalist Association and the Loyal Holywell Volunteers', *The Journal of the Flintshire Historical Society*, 33 (1992), 62.

Evans, Thomas, *Cambrian Itinerary or Welsh Tourist* (London, 1801).

Fenton, Richard, *The Tears of Cambria* (1773).

Fowler, Bill, 'A Redoubtable Local Heroine', *Pembrokeshire Life*, May 1996.

Fowler, Bill, 'End of a Dream: part 2', *Pembrokeshire Life*, February 1996.

Fowler, Bill, 'The Invasion was Halted … The Power Struggle was Just Beginning', *Pembrokeshire Life*, July 1996.

Fowler, Bill, 'Who Sails in the Sunset?', *Pembrokeshire Life*, April 1996.

Fowler, Bill, and Richard Davies, 'Who was William Tate?', *Pembrokeshire Life*, January 1996.

Fowler, Bill, and Richard Davies, 'The Story of Nonconformist Thomas John … Almost a martyr', *Pembrokeshire Life*, December 1995.

Freeman, Michael, 'Lady Llanover and the Welsh Costume Prints', *The National Library of Wales Journal*, 34/2 (2007), 235–51.

George, W. R. P., *The Making of Lloyd George* (London, 1976).

Green, Daniel, *The Great Cobbett: The Noblest Agitator* (Oxford, 1985).

Gwyndaf, R., 'The Welsh Folk Narrative Tradition: Continuation and Adaption', *Folk Life*, 26 (1987–8), 78–100.

Hancock, Simon, 'The Great War at Sea' (2019), *www.stdavidshistoricalsociety.org.uk/Great%20War%20at%20Sea.pdf* (last accessed 30 July 2024).

Hassall, Charles, *General View of the Agriculture of the County of Pembroke* (London, 1794).

Herbert, Trevor, and Gareth Elwyn Jones (eds), *The Remaking of Wales in the Eighteenth Century* (Cardiff, 1988).

Howell, David, 'Society 1660–1793', in Elwyn Davies and David Howell (eds), *Pembrokeshire County History, vol. 3: Early Modern Pembrokeshire 1536–1815* (Haverfordwest, 1987), pp. 256–98.

Hughes, John, *Methodistiaeth Cymru Sef Hanes Blaenorol a Gwedd Bresenol y Methodistiaid Calfinaidd*, vol. 2 (Wrexham, 1854).

Hughes, W. J., *Wales and the Welsh in English Literature from Shakespeare to Scott*, (Wrexham, 1924).

Humphreys, Maggie, and Robert C. Evans (eds), *Dictionary of Composers for the Church in Great Britain and Ireland* (London, 1997).

Inglis-Jones, Elisabeth, *Peacocks in Paradise* (Llandysul, 2006 reprint).

Jarvis, Branwen, 'Ceiriog a Chymru', *Transactions of the Honourable Society of Cymmrodorion* (1987), 85–104.

Jenkins, Bethan M., *Between Wales and England: Anglophone Welsh Writing of the Eighteenth Century* (Cardiff, 2017).

Jenkins, Geraint, 'Clio and Wales: Welsh Remembrancers and Historical Writing', *Transactions of the Honourable Society of Cymmrodorion*, 2001 new series, 8 (2002), 119–36.

Jenkins, Geraint H., '"Taphy-land historians" and the Union of England and Wales 1536–2007', *Journal of Irish and Scottish Studies*, 1/2 (2008), 1–27.

Jenkins, Geraint H., *The Foundations of Modern Wales 1642–1780* (Cardiff, 1987).

Jenkins, G. H., 'An Uneasy Relationship: Gwallter Mechain and Iolo Morganwg', *The Montgomeryshire Collections*, 97 (2009), 80.

Jenkins, R. T., *Hanes Cymru yn y Bedwaredd Ganrif ar Bymtheg* (Cardiff, 1933; repr. 1972).

Jenkins, R. T., 'J. J. Evans, Dylanwad y Chwyldro Ffrengig', *Y Llenor*, 8/1–4 (1929), 126–8.

Jenkins, R. T., 'William Richards o Lynn', *Trafodion Cymdeithas Hanes Bedyddwyr Cymru* (1930), 17–68.

Jenkins, R. T., and H. Ramage, *A History of the Honourable Society of Cymmrodorion* (London, 1951).

Jenkins, Terry, 'The Orsini Affair and the Crisis of 1858', *History Today*, 58/2 (February 2008).

Johnes, Martin, *Wales: England's Colony* (Cardigan, 2019).

Jones, Dafydd Glyn, *Agoriad yr Oes: erthyglau ar lên, hanes a gwleidyddiaeth Cymru* (Talybont, 2001).

Jones, David Ceri, and Eryn Mant White, *The Elect Methodists: Calvinistic Methodism in England and Wales*, vol. 2 (Cardiff, 2011).

Jones, Ffion M., *Welsh Ballads of the French Revolution 1793–1815* (Cardiff, 2012).

Jones, Ffion M., '"The silly expressions of French revolution", the experience of the Dissenting community in south-west Wales, 1797', in D. Andress (ed.), *Experiencing the French Revolution* (Oxford, 2013), pp. 245–62.

Jones, Ffion M., *Welsh Correspondence of the French Revolution 1789–1802* (Llandysul, 2018).

Jones, Francis, 'Harries of Tregwynt', *Transactions of the Honourable Society of Cymmrodorion* (1943–4, 1946), 108–19.

Jones, Francis, 'The Vaughans of Golden Grove', *Transactions of the Honourable Society of Cymmrodrion*, 1 (1966), 149–238.

Jones, Iorwerth, *David Rees y Cynhyrfwr* (Swansea, 1971).

Jones, Matthew C., '"Weak Heads and Worse Principles?" Church and State, Conservatism and Identity n Welsh Calvinistic Methodist Literature, 1797–1802', *The Journal of Religious History, Literature and Culture*, 4/1 (June 2018), 79–99

Jones, Rhian E., *Petticoat Heroes: Gender, Culture and Popular protest in the Rebecca Riots* (Cardiff, 2015).

Jones, R. Tudor, *Congregationalism in Wales* (Cardiff, 2004).

Jones, William, *Hanes Cymmanfa y Bedyddwyr Neillduol yn Nghymru, o'i dechreuad hyd y flwyddyn 1790* (Cardiff, 1831).

Kaminski-Jones, Rhys, '"Where Cymry United, Delighted Appear": The Society of Ancient Britons and the celebration of St David's Day in London 1715–1815', *Transactions of the Honourable Society of Cymmrodorion*, new ser., 23 (2017), 56–68.

Kennedy, Catriona, *Narratives of the Revolutionary and Napoleonic Wars: Military and Civilian Experience in Britain and Ireland* (Basingstoke, 2013).

Lewis, Jacqueline, 'Passing Judgements-Welsh Dress and the English Tourist', *Folk Life: Journal of Ethnological Studies*, 33 (1994), 29–47.

Lewis, Saunders, *Yr Artist yn Philistia 1: Ceiriog* (Aberystwyth, 1929).

Lewis, T. H., 'Y Mudiad heddwch yng Nghymru', *Transactions of the Honourable Society of Cymmrodorion* (1957–8), 87–127.

Linnard, William, 'John Perkins of Llantrithyd. The Diary of a Gentleman Farmer in the Vale of Glamorgan 1788–1801', *Morgannwg*, 31 (1987), 26–7.

Lloyd George, Richard, *Lloyd George* (London, 1960).

Lloyd Morgan, Ceridwen, 'From Temperance to Suffrage?', in Angela V. John, *Our Mothers' Land: Chapters in Welsh Women's History 1830–1939* (Cardiff, 2011), pp. 134–56.

Löffler, Marion, *The Literary and Historical Legacy of Iolo Morganwg 1826–1926* (Cardiff, 2007).

Löffler, Marion, *Welsh Responses to the French Revolution: Press and Public Discourse 1789–1806* (Cardiff, 2012).

Löffler, Marion, with Bethan Jenkins, *Political Pamphlets and Sermons from Wales 1790–1806* (Cardiff, 2014).

Markus, Radvan, *Echoes of the Rebellion: The Year 1798 in Twentieth-Century Irish Fiction and Drama* (Bern and Oxford, 2015).

Lyons, Martin, *France under the Directory* (Cambridge, 1975).

Mather, F. C., *High Church Prophet: Bishop Samuel Horsley (1733–1806) and the Caroline Tradition in the Later Georgian Church* (Oxford, 1992).

McDowell, Sara, 'Heritage, Memory and Identity', in Brian Graham and Peter Howard (eds), *The Ashgate Research Companion to Heritage and Identity* (Aldershot, 2008), pp. 37–54.

'Merched Jemeima', *Cwlwm Mudiad Chwiorydd Undeb Bedyddwyr Cymru*, 58 (September 2017), 11–12.

Miles, Dillwyn, 'Richard Fenton, Pembrokeshire Historian 1747–1821', *Journal of the Pembrokeshire Historical Society*, 7 (1996–7), 51–65.

Moffat, Alistair, *Sea Kingdoms: The Story of Celtic Britain and Ireland* (London, 2001)

Moody, T. W., R. B. McDowell and C. J. Woods, *The Writings of Theobald Wolf Tone 1763–1798* (Oxford, 2007).

Morgan, K. O., 'Wales and the Boer War – A Reply', *Welsh History Review*, 4/1–4 (1968–9), 367–80.

Morgan, Prys, *The Eighteenth-Century Renaissance* (Llandybie, 1981).

Morris-Suzuki, Tessa, *The Past Within Us: Media, Memory, History* (London and New York, 2005).

Oddy, J. A., *The Writings of the Radical Welsh Baptist Minister William Richards (1749–1818)* (Lampeter, 2008).

O'Leary, Paul, *Immigration and Integration: The Irish in Wales, 1798–1922* (Cardiff, 2000).

O'Leary, Paul, 'When Was Anti-Catholicism? The Case of Nineteenth- and Twentieth-Century Wales', *The Journal of Ecclesiastical History*, 56/2 (April 2005), 308–25.

O'Leary, Paul, 'Arming the Citizens: The Volunteer Force in Nineteenth-Century Wales', Matthew Cragoe and Chris Williams (eds), *Wales and War: Society, Politics and Religion in the Late Nineteenth and Twentieth Centuries* (Cardiff, 2007) pp. 63–81.

O'Neill, Philip, *Wilkie Collins: Women, Property and Propriety* (London, 1988).

Parry, Edward, *Cambrian Mirror or A New Tourist Companion Through North Wales*, 2nd edn (1846).

Phillips, L., 'The Naval Family Mends of Haverfordwest', *Dyfed Family History Journal*, 10/7 (December 2010), 26–7.

Philp, M., 'The British Response to the Threat of Invasion 1797–1815', in M. Philp (ed.), *Resisting Napoleon: The British Response to the Threat of Invasion 1797–1815* (Aldershot, 2006).

Pugh, Edward, *Cambria Depicts: A Tour through North Wales illustrated with Picturesque Views by a Native Artist* (London, 1816).

Prescott, Sarah, *Eighteenth Century Writing from Wales: Bards and Britons* (Cardiff, 2008).

Pryce, Huw, *J. E. Lloyd and the Creation of Welsh History: Renewing a Nation's Past* (Cardiff, 2011).

Pryce, Huw, *Writing Welsh History: From the Early Middle Ages to the Twenty-First Century* (Oxford, 2022).

Quinault, R., 'The Cult of the Centenary c.1784–1914', *Historical Research*, 7/176 (1998), 303–23.

Ramsey, Neil, *The Military Memoir and Romantic Literary Culture 1780–1835* (London, 2011).

Rawlinson, Mark, 'Invasion! Coleridge, the defence of Britain and the cultivation of the public's fear', in Philip Shaw (ed.), *Romantic Wars: Studies in Culture and Conflict, 1793–1822* (Aldershot, 2000), pp. 110–37.

'Red Shawls and French Invaders. An Historical Anecdote for the Ladies', *The Republic: A Monthly Magazine of American Literature*, 3/3 (March 1852).

Rees, Dr D., Bronant, 'Cymru Fu. Ebenezer Richard', *Y Negesydd* (1 May 1896), 1.

'Review of E. H. Stuart Jones, The Last Invasion of Britain', *Dock Leaves*, 1–4 (1949), 107.

'Review of Fenton, A Historical Tour through Pembrokeshire. Reprint. Brecknock 1903', *Archaeologia Cambrensis: the Journal of the Cambrian Archaeological Association*, 6/6 (1906), 71.

Richard, Edward W., and Henry Richard, *Bywyd y Parch. Ebenezer Richard* (London, 1839).

Roberts, Gwyneth Tyson, *The Language of the Blue Books: The Perfect Instrument of Empire* (Cardiff, 1998).

Semmel, Stuart, *Napoleon and the British* (Yale CT, 2004).

Sherrington, Emlyn, 'Welsh Nationalism, the French Revolution and the Influence of the French Right 1880–1930', D. Smith (ed.), *A People and a Proletariat: Essays in the History of Wales 1780–1980* (London, 1980) pp. 127–47.

Shrimpton, Jayne, *Victorian Fashion* (London, 2016).

Simon, John, *Retrospect: The Memoirs of the Rt Hon Viscount Simon* (London, 1952).

Singer, Rita, 'Some Thoughts on Margaret Ellen James: The Fishguard Invasion by the French in 1797 (1892)', (last accessed 31 July 2024).

Singer, Rita, 'Why, Why, Why, Jemima? Picturing the French Invasion of Fishguard', 22 January 2021, *https://bydbuch.licommons.org/why-why-why-jemima/* (last accessed 31 July 2024).

Solar, Peter M., 'Shipping and Economic Development in

Nineteenth Century Ireland', *The Economic History Review*, 59/4 (November 2006), 717–42.

Stephens, Meic (ed.), *A Militant Muse Harri Webb: Selected Literary Journalism 1948–1980* (Bridgend, 1998).

Stuart Jones, E. H., *An Invasion that Failed: The French Expedition to Ireland 1796* (Cardiff, 1950).

The Welsh Academy Encyclopaedia of Wales (Cardiff, 2008).

Thomas, J. E., *Sabine Baring-Gould: The Life and Work of a Complete Victorian* (Stroud, 2015).

Thomas, J. E., *Social Disorder in Britain, 1750–1850: The Power of the Gentry, Radicalism and Religion in Wales* (London, 2011).

Thomas, M. Wynn, *Eutopia: Studies in Cultural Euro-Welshness 1850–1980* (Cardiff, 2021).

Thorne, R. G., *The History of Parliament: The House of Commons 1790–1820*, vol. 3 (London, 1986).

Thorne, R. G., 'The Pembrokeshire Elections of 1807 and 1812', *The Pembrokeshire Historian*, 6 (1979), 7–24.

Thorne, R. G., and R. Howell, 'Pembrokeshire in Wartime 1793–1815', in Elwyn Davies and David Howell (eds), *Pembrokeshire County History, vol. 3: Early Modern Pembrokeshire 1536–1815* (Haverfordwest, 1987), pp. 382–3.

Vandrei, Martha, *Queen Boudica and Historical Culture in Britain: An Image of Truth* (Oxford, 2018).

Walker, Margaret S., 'The Reverend Henry Vincent, 1793–1865: A Neglected Pembrokeshire Antiquarian', *Journal of the Pembrokeshire Historical Society*, 6 (1994/5), 69–78.

Warner, J., *We laughed at Boney: (or; We've been through it all before) How our forefathers laughed defiance at the last serious threat of invasion-by Napoleon: a striking parallel with our present position* (London, 1943).

Watson, Richard, *Anecdotes of the Life of Richard Watson: Written by Himself at Different Intervals and Periods in 1814* (London, 1817).

Williams, Carl, 'Ein Treftadaeth Fedyddiedig:De-orllewin Penfro', *Traodion Cymdeithas Hanes Bedyddwyr Cymru* (1998), 1–22.

Williams, Carolyn D., *Boudica and Her Stories: Narrative transformations of a Warrior Queen* (Cranbury NJ, 2009).
Williams, Chris, Neil Evans and Paul O'Leary, *A Tolerant Nation? Revisiting Ethnic Diversity in a Devolved Wales* (Cardiff, 2015).
Williams, David, *A History of Modern Wales* (Cardiff, 1950).
Williams, Gwyn A., 'Welsh Indians: the Madoc Legend and the first Welsh radicalism', *History Workshop Journal*, 1/1 (Spring 1976), 149.
'Yr Hybarch William Davies, Abergwaun. Gan y Parch D. Bateman, Rhosycaerau', *Y Cronicl (Cronicl y cymdeithasau crefyddol)*, 48/565 (May 1890), 130.

Unpublished Theses

Bennett, A. D., 'The Great Western Railway and the Celebration of Englishness' (DPhil thesis, University of York, Institute of Railway Studies, October 2000).
Huws, Bethan Angharad, 'Gwell Cymro, Cymro oddi cartref? Cymhlethdod meddwl a Gwaith John Ceiriog Hughes' (MPhil thesis, Cardiff University, 2015).
Kaminski-Jones, Rhys, 'True Britons: Ancient British Identity in Wales and Britain' (PhD thesis, University of Wales, 2016).
Shapiro, S. J., 'The British Army in Home Defense, 1844–1871: Militia and Volunteers in a Liberal Era' (PhD dissertation, Ohio State University, 2011).

Index

A
Aberayron 203
Aberdare 190
Aberdaugleddyf 147
  see also Milford Haven
Aberdare Leader 236
Aberystwyth 57
Academic discourse 7
Academic doubt 217
'Adroddiad y Nadolig' 148
  see also 'Y Baban Diwrnod Oed'
SS Aguila 236
Ahlstrom, John D. 296
  see also Tate, Col. William
'A Laddo a Leddir' 169, 188
Algiers 279
American Revolution 245
Amiens, Peace of 95–6
An Address to the People of the United Kingdom of Great Britain and Ireland on the Threatened Invasion (1803) 83, 215
  Addendum: *Specimens of French Ferocity and Brutality in Wales* 84, figure 6, 85, 86, 87
  see also Cyfarch i Bobl Prydain Fawr ar Fygythion y Ffrangcod
Ancient (or 'Antient') Britons, regiment of fencible cavalry in Ireland (1797–8) *see* Williams Wynn, Sir Watkin, 5th baronet
Ancient Britons 24, 28, 29
  Kaminski-Jones, Rhys 28
  Society of Ancient Britons 33
  Gendered identity 33–4
Andrews, Elizabeth 275
Anglicans 7

'An Heroic Single Woman' 169
  see also Ap Gwilym, H. L.
Annual Register, The 32
anti-Catholic prejudice 297, note 34
Anti-Jacobin, The 70
anti-Jemima 1
Ap Gwilym, H. L. 91, 114–21, 151, 168, 177–8, 265, 268, 292
  An Authentic Account of the Invasion by the French Troops on Carrig Gwasted Point near Fishguard (1842) 91, 114–20, 171, 173, 300
  see also Williams, Henry Lewis
Ap Iorwerth, Twm 174
Archaeologia Cambrensis 172
Archives Nationales 281
Armed peasantry 23, 30, 54
  fear of 20–1, 54–6
Aribi Pasha 214
Archives de la Guerre 281–2
'Articles of capitulation' 115–16
'Arwresau bro fy mebyd' *see* James, David Emrys (Dewi Emrys)
Association for the Preservation of Liberty and Property 82
'Adgofion Tiriad y Ffrancod yn Sir Benfro' 129–32
  see also Y Traethodydd; Meyler, Revd David
Athenaeum, The 161, 219
Attorney General 62
Authenticity 2, 49
Ayton, Richard 54, 100–3
  A Voyage round Great Britain undertaken in the summer of 1813 (1814) 100–2
  see also Daniell, William

B

'Y Baban Diwrnod Oed' 119, 180, 224
Baker, James 28, 47, 53, 86, 89, 91, 208, figures 15–16, 216
  Picturesque Guide through Wales and the Marches (1795) 47
  Brief Narrative of the French Invasion near Fishguard Bay (1797) 47–8
Ballads 49–53, 295
  Clod i'r Cymry 51
  English language ballads 52, 218
Bank of England 17
Baptist(s) 7, 182, 219–20, 239
  Southwestern association 68
  see also Colby, John; Manners, John, Duke of Rutland
Bantry Bay 2–3, 219, 281
Baring-Gould, Sabine 207, 242
  Book of South Wales (1905) 207
Barlow, Hugh 35, 62
Barry territorials 222
Bath Herald 25
Beiner, Guy 9, 153
  see also memory, social
Beracah 110
Bethany, Goodwick 203
Bethel, Fishguard 203
Bicester Advertiser 144
Bigney Hill 140, 266
Birmingham curiosity shop 206
Birmingham Daily Post 162
Bicentenary (1997) 299–302
  Bicentenary Newsletter 300
'Black enemies' ('gelynion duon') 50
'rhai o'r blacks a rhai o'r tonis' 50
'Black legion' 215
Blaenavon, vicar of 251
Blaenrhondda Dramatic Society 202
Blair, William 90
  see also *The Loyalist*
The Blitz 274
Blue Books 139–40, 184–7
Bonnechose, Emile de 177
Boudica 170, 276
  see also Buddug
Bowen, James 118, 178

Bowen, Major William 55
Bowling, Major George R. 114
'Brave Women of Fishguard' 190
  'The Brave Women of 1797' 187
  'The Heroes and Heroines of 1797' 187
Brestgarn clock 117–18, 176
Brief Narrative of the French Invasion Near Fishguard Bay see Baker, James
Brigstocke, Anne 53
Bristol 3, 8, 58, 214, 271
Bristol Baptist Academy 63
British Empire 17
Broadley, Alexander Meyrick 207, 214, 216–19
  Napoleon and the Invasion of England: The Story of the Great Terror 207, 214
  see also Wheeler, Harold F. B.
Brooke, Richard 268
  Liverpool as it was during the last quarter of the eighteenth century 268
Brown, Joseph 35
Burke, Edmund 17, 245
Bulgarian atrocities 157
By-election (1908) 220

C

Cabaret, Hotel Russell (1929) 241
Cambrian 111, 169
Cambrian Archaeological Association 171–2
Cambrian News 203
The Cambrian Traveller's Guide 103
Campbell, John, Lord Cawdor 4–6, 15, 16, 18, 21, 22, 23, 24, 25, 26, 31, 32, 36, 52, 61, 62, 111, 115, 189, 206, 213, 283, 296
  Correspondence 206–7
Cardiff and District Pembrokeshire Society 241
Cardiff Free Library 216
Cardiff Times and South Wales Weekly News 183–6
  Centenary Anniversary Special (27 February 1897) 184

Index

Cardigan Bay 3, 18
Cardigan farmers 202
　see also 'Dai a Wil'
Cardiganshire militia 53, 111
Cavendish-Bentinck, Home Secretary
　see Portland, 3rd Duke of
Caerlem 4, 57
Carmarthen 34
　Mayor of 21
Carn Coch 31
Carn fawr 297
Carn Gelli 4, 6
Carn Wnda 116
Carnhuanawc see Price, Thomas
Carradice, Phil 298
Carreg Goffa (Memorial Stone)
　192–4, figure 11, 193
Carreg Wastad 4, 17, 89, 100, 265
Carter, Louise 38
Carnot, Nicolas Léonard Sadi 4
'Caru yn y gwely' 139
Castagnier, Jean Joseph 217, 281
Castlemartin range 292
Castlemartin troop 16
Castlemartin yeomanry 145, 213, 279
　see also Pembrokeshire yeomanry
Castleton 35
　see also Brown, Joseph
Caswilia 31
Cavalry Week (1850) 112
Cawdor see Campbell, John, Lord Cawdor
Cawdor as brand name 303
Cawdor, first Earl (son of Lord Cawdor) 146–7
Cawdor, third Earl, chairman of GWR (great-grandson) 218
Cawdor, fourth Earl 262
　see also Gore, John
Cawdor diary 263
Cawdor jug 254–5
　see also Western Mail
Ceiriog see Hughes, John Ceiriog
Centenaries 180–1
Centenary of Invasion (1897) 8, 176, 180–94, 223
　'The Brave Women of 1797' 187

'The Heroes and Heroines of 1797' 187
Centenary Anniversary Special see Cardiff Times
Centenary commemoration medal
　figures 8–9, 188
Chapman, Robin 178
Chambers's Journal (1860) 126–7, 236
　'How the French fared at Fishguard in 1797 A.D. By a Native' 126–7, 236
Charleston 4
'Chouannerie' 4, 47
Chappell, Edgar 271
'Charming Welshes' 146
　see also Tate, Edouard
Chester 271
Chester Courant 25, 58, 61
Cilgerran 48
Civic loyalty 7
Cobb, Richard 281
Cobbett, William 82, 86
Colburn, Henry 121
Colby, Col. John 31, 62, 67, 125
　see also Baptists
Cold War 283
Collins, Wilkie 142–4, 162, 186, 207, 242, 292
　Household Words 142, 292
　'The Great (Forgotten) Invasion' 142–4
　My Miscellanies (1863) 142
Corbet, Edward 58
Corston 52
Cotts 118–19, 147–9
　see also 'Y Baban Diwrnod Oed'; Hughes, John Ceiriog
Country of Castles (GWR) 212
Counter-revolution in Brittany 247
　see also Quiberon
Cowbridge 58
Crawshay 271
Creasy, Edward 215
Crug-y-bar 150
'Crug-y-bar' (hymn tune) 150
Cruttwell, Clement 93
Cumberland Paquet 34
Cwmllynfell 182

Cwmllynfell Operatic Society 183
Cwyn y Cystuddiedig 63, figure 5, 69, 244–5, 283, 285
  see also Richards, William
Cyfarch i Bobl Prydain Fawr ar Fygythion y Ffrangcod 86, note 28
  see also *An Address to the People of the United Kingdom*; Davies, Edward
Cymru Fydd 7, 185–6
Y Cymmrodor 252, 273

D
Dafydd, Henry
Dafydd, Philip 51, 53, 54, 68, 244, 295
'Dai a Wil' 158
'Dai Ben Frenchman' 224
Daniell, William 54, 100–3
  see also Ayton, Richard
Davies, Canon David 265
Davies, David (Penarth) 239–41, 246
Davies, Edward (Rector of Llanarmon) 86
  Cyfarch o Bobl Prydain Fawr 86, note 28
Davies, Henry (the elder, minister at Llangloffan) 110, 128, 241, 244, 297
Davies, Henry (the younger, minister at Llangloffan) 128–9
Davies, John Lloyd 141
Davies, Leonard Twiston 252–3
  see also *Women of Wales* (1935)
Davies, Llewellin 227
Davies, Mary (musician, folksong collector) 252
Davies, Mary (widow in receipt of pension in compensation for death of husband in the Invasion) 298
Davies, Morlais 181
Davies, Parry 186, 192
Davies, Peter 185
Davies, Richard 299
Davies, Thomas 31

Davies, William (Independent minister at Fishguard) 54–5
Davies, William (veteran of Bunker Hill) 173
  see also Cardiganshire farmers; Griffiths, T. Cunllo
'The Day Old Baby' 173, 178, 181, 221, 293
  see also 'Y Baban Diwrnod Oed'
Dechau Canu, Dechrau Canmol 300
Democratic folk movement 192–3
Denman, George 145–6
Desbrière, Edouard 215–7
  Projets et Tentatives de Debarquement aux Isles Britanniques (Paris 1900–2) 215–16
'Descent in Wales' 17
Despair 49–53
'Dewrion ferched Abergwaun' 177
  see also Fishguard parish council
Dickens, Charles 292
  see also *Household Words*
Dictionary of Welsh Biography 244
Discord 59–70
Dissenters 61
Diwygiwr, Y 149–50
Dock Leaves 283
Dunbar, George, Mayor of Liverpool 58, 88, 268
  see also Liverpool
Dundas, Henry, Viscount Melville 17
Dungleddy troop 16
Dyfed County Council Education Department 299
'Dychryn' 48
  see also Lewis, Titus; Terror
Dylanwad y Chwyldro Ffrengig ar Lenyddiaeth Cymry (1928) 242–5
  see also Evans, John James (J.J.)

E
East Grinstead 272
The Eclectic Review 99–100
Edwardes, Francis 57
  see also Haverfordwest
Edwards, Averil 252–3
Edwards, Elizabeth 278
Edwards, O. M. 221

Index

Wales, Story of the Nations (1900) 221
Elley, Richard 291
  see also Western Mail
Elliott, Marianne 294
Ellis, T. E. 186
Emigration to Pennsylvania 60
English Encyclopedia 132
English government inspector 109
Entente Cordiale 213
Ethé, Herman 245
Evans, John James (J.J.) 242–5, 246, 281, 284, 295
Evans, Llewellyn 265, 267
Evans, Thomas (travel writer) 93
Evans, Thomas (Tomos Glyn Cothi) 295
Evening Express 191–2, 194
Evening Mail, The 146

F
Fear 53, 56–9
Feminists 9
Fenton, Richard 53–4, 89, 96–7, 172
  see also A Historical Tour through Pembrokeshire (1811)
Fenton, Ferrar 194
'Ferocious Demetians' 33
  see also Williams, Edward (Iolo Morganwg)
First World War 233–8
  U-boat threat 235–6
Fishguard 4–7, 21, 32, 35, 48, 53–4, 58–9, 81, 92–9, 117, 140, 171, 206, 236
  'A Fishguard Fencible' caricature 3, 39, 40, 246, 283
  'Battle of Fishguard' 6
  'Fishguard' battle honours 10, 201, 279
  Fishguard County School 242, 299
  Fishguard, disdain for 95
  Fishguard fencibles 4, 17
  Fishguard Historical Society 298
    Fishguard Fiasco: An Account of the Last Invasion of Britain (1974) 293–4
  The Fishguard Invasion by the French in 1797 (1892) 177, 208–9
  The Fishguard Invasion or Three Days in 1797 (1897) 215
  Fishguard as a moment to prove civic loyalty 7
  Fishguard Parish Council 177
  Fishguard-Rosslare route 238
  Fishguard National Eisteddfod (1936) 264–5, 292
  Fishguard National Eisteddfod (1986) 295
  Fishguard Show (1884) 174
  growing prosperity 202–3, figures 13–14, 204
  St Mary's Church, Fishguard 5
  tourist accounts 92–9
  see also James, M. E.; Kinross, John; Malkin, Benjamin Heath; 'Merched Abergwaun'; Salmon, David; *South Wales: The Country of Castles*
Flemingston, Vale of Glamorgan
  see Williams, Edward (Iolo Morganwg)
Flight 53–4
Flintshire County Herald 274
Fowler, Bill 299–300
Fox, Yvonne *see* Nicholas, Jemima
Freeman, B. F. M. 210
Freeman, Michael 223, note 95, 240, note 37
French 28, 30–2, 60
  French Directory 2
  French 'mischief' 88
  French 'Other' 79
  'French principles' 284–5
  'French Walk' 182
The French at Fishguard (1843) 124
French Revolution 7
French Revolution and Wales 79, 238–40, 244–5
'FRIEND TO HIS COUNTRY' 58
furze (hiding in) 96, 124
  see also A Historical Tour through Pembrokeshire (1811); *The French at Fishguard* (1843)

G

Gair yn ei Amser (1798) 69–70
  see also Jones, Thomas
'Gallant Little Wales' 7, 183, 186
Gammon, Betty 298
Y Geninen 183
Gentleman's Magazine 70
George, Ann 118, 261
George, David Lloyd 186, 192, 220, 264–6
German, enemy 7, 235–6
Glamorgan Gazette 274
Glaniad y Ffrancod yn Abergwaun (1885) 158–61
  see also Griffiths, T. Cunllo
Glaniad y Ffrancod (operetta) 182, 202
  see also Madam Dumas
Gloucester 21, 31
Gloucester Journal 21
Godre'r Mynydd 150
  see also Jones, Nansi
Goodwick 7, 11, 32, 298
  Goodwick Harbour Village 203, figure 12, 204
  Goodwick sands or beach 6, 27, 116–17, 279, 291
  Goodwick sands, Thanksgiving Services 69, 109–10
Gore, John 262–3, 273
Grays, Essex 36
  see also Mends, John
The Great Forgotten Invasion 142–4
  see also Collins, Wilkie
Great Western Railway (GWR) 7, 190, 203
  tourism literature 205–7, 237
Griffith, Samuel 7, 30–2, 61–2, 240
Griffiths, Ann 170
Griffiths, T. Cunllo 157–61, 202, 295
  see also *Glaniad y Ffrancod yn Abergwaun* (1885)
Gwenny Vaughan: or the French Invasion 184
  see also Meredith, Gwyn
Gymraes, Y 139–40

H

Hanes Tiriad y Ffrancod (1856) 127–8
  see also *Hanes Prydain Fawr*; Lewis, Titus
Hanes y Bedyddwyr yn Neheubarth Cymru (1839) 110
  see also Jones, David
Harmony, Baptist chapel, Fishguard 244
Harries, John 154–7, 170
  'The Land of the Leek' 156
  Welsh Patriotism (1875) 154–6, 161
Harries, Mrs (of Tregwynt) 54
Haul, Yr 149
Haverfordwest 4, 19, 20, 21, 26, 36–7, 53, 61, 65, 220, 279
  Haverfordwest and Fishguard, tensions over Centenary 181
  Haverfordwest Castle dungeons 61
  Haverfordwest, Mayor of 115
'Hen Wlad fy Nhadau' 187, 201–2
Herald of Peace 189
Herald of Wales 174
Hereford Journal 25, 60
Heritage 181
Historiography 1
Historic Sites and Scenes of England (GWR) 224–5
A Historical Tour through Pembrokeshire (1811) 89, 96–9
  'Baptists' and 'fanatics' 99
  'brutal excess' 97–8
  furze (hiding in) 97
  see also Fenton, Richard
A History of Modern Wales (1950) 284
  see also Williams, David
history
  folk history 161
  military history 2, 81
  'official' history 11, 26
  popular history 1
  public history 1
History of Little England Beyond Wales 172, 174–5
  see also Laws, Edward
History of the French Invasion of Fishguard (1980) 294
  see also Horn, Pamela

Index

History of the Pembroke Imperial Yeomanry 210
   never published figure 18, 212
   press copy 213
History of the Pembroke Yeomanry (1966) 292
   see also Howell, R. L., Lieut. Col.
Hay 34
historical
   criticism 213
   culture 1
   enquiry 227
   fiction 121, 236–7
   memory 1
   tourists 92–9
The Historical Association 274
Hitler, Adolf 8
Hoche, Louis Lazare 2, 183, 246, 281
Hook colliers 20, 53
Horn, Pamela 294
Horsley, Samuel, bishop St David's 57
Howell, Anne (widow received pension in 1797) 298
Howell, R. L., Lieut. Col. 292
Hozier, Henry 215
Hudson, Derek 271–4, 292
   'Invaded Britain' 272
Hughes, John Ceiriog (Ceiriog) 119, 147–9, 183, 221, 224
   'Y Rheiffl Gorau' 148
   see also ' Y Baban Diwrnod Oed'; 'The Day-old baby'
Huws, Capten 180

I

Ilfracombe 298
Imaginary landings/invasions 56–9
Important Considerations for the People of this Kingdom (1803) 82–3, 86–7
   see also Hudson, Derek; *Ystyriaethau Pwysfawr*
Independents 7
The Influence of the French Revolution on Welsh Life and Literature 239
   see also Davies, David (Penarth)

Intertextual connections 9
Invasion
   'official documents' 18–21
   propaganda 83–9
   threats 142
In Dewisland 207
   see also Baring-Gould, Sabine
Ireland 2, 7, 79–81, 183, 203, 223
Society of United Irishmen 2
   see also Ancient Britons, fencible regiment in Ireland 1797–8; Bantry Bay

J

Jabet, George 162
Jacobin 79
James, David (Defynnog) 221
   Ein Gwlad neu Cymru – ei Daear, ei Hanes, a'i Llen 221
James, David Emrys (Dewi Emrys) 261–262
James, Margaret Ellen 177, 180, 185, 187, 209, 212, 215, 216, 222
   see also *The Fishguard Invasion of 1797*
Jeffreston 52
   see also Ballads, English
Jenkins, Mr (Hay) 34–5
Jenkins, Geraint H. 294–5
Jenkins, R. T. 244, 284
Jewin Street (Welsh chapel) 221
Joan of Arc 220
John, Augustus 266
John, Thomas 'traitor' 7, 30–1, 37, 56, 60, 61, 64, 110, 240, 244, 247, 273
   see also *Cwyn y Cystuddiedig*, Richards, William
Johnes, Jane, Hafod 57
Jones, David (Baptist historian) 110
Jones, David, Llangan 125, 254
   see also Western Mail
Jones, Elsie Towyn, New Quay 276
Jones, Evan (Gurnos) 175–6, 222
Jones, Sir Evan 246, 250
Jones, Major Francis 292
Jones, Mathew C 69

Jones, Messrs of Newport (Trefdraeth) 176
Jones, Nansi 1, 7, 9, 149–51, 161, 178, 244, 251, 261–2, 295, 300
   see also anti-Jemima; Griffiths, T. Cunllo; James, David Emrys (Dewi Emrys)
Jones, Samuel (Pennepek, nr Philadelphia) 67
Jones, T. Llew 295–6
Jones, Theophilus 93
Jones, Thomas 69–70
   see also Gair yn ei Amser
'Jubilee of the Surrender of the French troops at Fishguard' 112

K
Kentish Chronicle 23–4
Kentish Gazette 37
King's Lynn 63
   see also Richards, William
Kinross, John 293
Knight, Ann 37–8
Knox, Thomas 4, 5, 7, 16, 26, 40, 55, 59–60, 111, 114–15, 170–1
   Some Account of Proceedings that took place on the landing of the French (1800) 208, 281

L
Ladies of Llangollen 252
Ladysmith, relief of 201
'Last Invasion' 8, 111, 267–8
   'Last Foreign Invasion of Britain' 188
   see also Gore, John
The Last Invasion of Britain (1950) 279–84
   see also Stuart Jones, E. H.
Laws, Edward 172–4, 177, 183, 189–90, 209, 215, 216–18, 293
   see also *History of Little England Beyond Wales*
Le Brun, Chef de Bataillon Jacques Philippe Rochemure (second in command to Tate) 27, 281
Leeds 237
Leeds Intelligencer 53, 88

Leeds Mercury 237–8
Légion Noire 3, 5, 219, 270, 281, 294
Lewis, Edward Arthur 247
Lewis, Titus 48
   see also *Hanes Prydain Fawr*
Lipscomb, George 94
'Little England beyond Wales' 205
'Little Britain beyond Wales' 205
'Little Fishguard for Ever' 291–303
Liverpool 3, 8, 58, 269, 271
Liverpool Blitz 269
Liverpool Echo 269–70
Liverpool and Fishguard 268–270
Llan, Y 224, 226
Llanelli, lady from 125
Llanelli 149, 221
Llanferran 297
Llangloffan Baptist chapel 296
Llangwm, ladies of 220
Llanrwst, Rector of 58
Llansamlet 201
Llanstinan 16
Llanwnda 5, 26, 53, 124, 126
   see also Emigration to Pennsylvania; *The French at Fishguard* (1843)
Llanybydder 302
Llewellyn, Anne (widow received compensation in 1797) 298
Lloyd, J. E. 246
Llwyd, Richard 113
   see also *Topographical Notes*
London 15, 37
London Gazette 17–19, 217
The Loyalist 217

M
Mabon, William Abraham 192
Macheret, Pierre Joseph Romain 281
Madam Dumas 182
   see also *Glaniad y Ffrancod*
Maenclochog 224
Malkin, Benjamin Heath Malkin 95, 126
Manchester Church and King club 29
Manners, John, Duke of Rutland 32, 61–2, 90–1, 295
   Journal of a Tour in Wales in 1797 90–1

Index

Mansell, Mr (carried the news to London via Gloucester) 21, 31
Massy, Rosamund 220
Mathias A. G. O. 254
Mathias, Henry 89–90
Mathias, John and Mary 162
   Mathias letter (dated 27 February 1797, to sister of above) 35, 264, 273, 291
   see also Jabet, George; *Western Mail*
Mathias, Roland 283
Mathry 4
SS Mauretania 223–4, 264
Mends, John 36, 38, 226, 272
memory
   Social memory 90, 110
   Military memory 121–7
'Merched Abergwaun' 300
   Cabaret 241
Meredith, Gwyn 184
   see also Gwenny Vaughan
Merthyr Times 175
Merthyr Tydfil 271
Methodists 66
Methodist Revival 239
Meyler, David 91–2, 109, 129–32, 158
   see also Adgofion Tiriad y Ffrancod
Meyler, Hugh (owner of guard house that became the 'Royal Oak') 25–7, 30, 33
Meyler, William 25
Meyrick, Col. F. C. 210, 212
   see also History of Pembroke Yeomanry
Meyrick, Samuel Rush 95
Midland Daily Telegraph 270
Milford, Lord *see* Phillips, Richard
Milford Haven 57, 66, 236
   see also Aberdaugleddyf
Monmouthshire Merlin 126
Monte Cassino 279
Morgan, Caesar 278
   see also Victory of Fishguard
Morgan, Kenneth 201
Morgan, Mary 278
   Tour to Milford Haven (1795) 254, 278
Morgan, Owen (Morien) 170–1, 175

Morgan, Prys 69
Morgan, Thomas, Hyde Park, Scranton 169
Morrison, Robert 294
Mortimer, John 17, 131, 173
Morton, H. V. 253
   In Search of Wales 253

N

Napoleon 8, 52, 82, 183, 267, 270, 278
Narberth 35
NATO accordance 292
Nevern 233
Newport, Pembs (Trefdraeth) 53, 140, 182
New York 7, 140, 223
Nicholas, Jemima 1, 5, 7, 11, 114, 119–20, 161, 169–70, 178, 182, 194, 209, 220–2, 234–5, 242, 261, 265, 281, 275, 279, 293, 295
   as a brand 302–3
   'descendants' of Jemima 222
   first Jemima 100–2
   Hanes Tiriad y Ffrancod 127–8
   Yr Haul 150
   'Sali' in Peryglon Pencaer 180
   'Spirit of ancient Cambria' 120
   Yvonne Fox 300
   see also anti-Jemima; Ap Gwilym, H. L.; Griffiths, T. Cunllo; James, David Emrys; Meyler, David; Harries, John; James, M. E.; Salmon, David; Vincent, Henry James
Nicholson, George 103
   The Cambrian Travellers' Guide 103
Nonconformity 140
North Africa Corps 279
Notes and Queries (Birmingham) 162
Notes and Queries 234

O

Oral tradition 159, 218, 297–8
   see also Walters, Syd
Order of St David 81
Owen, Henry 247
Owen, John, Pontiago 89
   see also Baker, James

Owen, Thomas Ellis 80, 82
  'Anglesea Volunteer Song' 80
Oxford 293

P

Paine, Tom (in translation) 284
Pall Mall Gazette 226
Palmerston 112
Pankhurst, Emmeline 220, 242
Papur Pawb 179–80
Parry, Edward 113
'Peisiau cochion' 244
  see also Red petticoats
Pembroke prison 21
Pembroke County Club 189
Pembroke County Guardian 210, 219
Pembrokeshire 1–4, 7, 10, 28, 34, 38, 172
  ballads reflecting divides 52
  Pembrokeshire men 8, 15, 93, 189
  'Pembrokeshire Plains' 81
  Pembrokeshire pride 154–5
  'Some Pembrokeshire Worthies' 174
  Tensions between north and south 59–60, 173–4
  South Pembrokeshire dialect 35
  see also Ap Iorwerth, Twm; Harries, John; Laws, Edward
Pembrokeshire Herald 126, 162, 219
Pembrokeshire Life 299
Pembrokeshire Yeomanry 15, 110–12, 128, 170, 201, 209–10
Pencaer 2, 4, 7, 28, 30, 155–6, 298
Pencaer, Niclas 180
The Penny Illustrated Paper 186
Pentre Public Hall 202
The People 236
Personal Injuries (Civilians) Act (1941) 276
Philipps, Charles, Lord Lieutenant Haverfordwest 174
Phillips, Eleanor (Nelly) 177, 216–17
Philipps, John Wynford 226
Phillips, Richard, Baron Milford 15, 16, 19–23, 89, 29, 217
Picton, Sir Thomas 169
Pimlico 145

Piozzi, Hester Thrale 252
Pitt, William 16
Pontardawe 202
Pontgynon, Crosswell 157
Pontycymmer 175
popular fury 23–33
popular Welshness 186
Portland, 3rd Duke of 18, 22–3, 58, 62, 89, 171, 206, 217
Potter, Joseph, High Street, Haverfordwest 114
Powell, Miss, Glamorgan Street, Brecon 162
Price, Isaac, Crug-y-bar 150
Price, Thomas (Carnhuanawc) 113
  Hanes Cymru (1836–42) 113
Priestley, Joseph 245
Primary sources, new 214
Princess Gwenllian 276
Proces Verbal (7 Ventose, An 2) 281
Propert, Thomas (his map) 193, 300
Prudhomme, Charles 31, 36–7, 61, 242, 273
  see also John, Thomas
Public Record office 298
Pwllcorn, Jaci 224
Pwllheli eisteddfod 239

Q

Quiberon 3, 246–7
Quinault, Roland 2, 298–9

R

rape 88–9
  propaganda 83, 86–7, 90
Rawlinson, Mark 1–2, 267
Rebecca Riots, 112, 128
  'Castlemartins' 112
'The Redcoats of 1797' 224, figure 19, 225, 226
'Red-cloak heroines' 221
'Red cloak legend' 264–5
Red Dragon 127
Red petticoats 141–5, 170, 241, 292, 298
Red shawl 201
Rees, Sarah Jane 170
Rees, Sir Frederick 283–4

Index

Rees, T. Mardy 234
   Notable Welshmen 221, 234
Rees, William (Arianglawdd) 244
Reeves, John 82–3
Reynolds, John 22, 88–9, 110
Rhosycaerau 54
Rhydybont (nr Llanybydder) 150
Rhys, Daniel 179–80
   Peryglon Pencaer 179–80
Richard, Ebenezer 50–2
Richards, William, Lynn 63, 67–8, 244, 245, 283, 285
   Reflections on French Atheism and English Christianity 66
   see also *Cwyn y Cystuddiedig*
Richmond, Sir Herbert William 270, 274
Ridgway, Alexander 146
Roach, John 56
Robertson, Sir Charles Grant 27
Roderick, A. J. 285
   Wales through the Ages 285
Rooke, Lieutenant-General James 55
Rose, John Holland 226
Rosslare 7, 202
Roux, Madame 177
Rowlands, D. W. 183, 202
   see also *Glaniad y Ffrancod* (operetta)
Rowlandson, Thomas 94
Royal Oak 6, 115, 191, 251–2
Royal Welch Fusiliers 242
Rustic weapons, 25–7, 29, 30, 40

S

Saint Gwyndaf church 5
'Saints' (three GWR vessels) 238
Salmon, David 215, 233–5, 262, 265, 266, 281, 272–4, 300
   claims 'The French at Fishguard' is a work of fiction 121
   Fishguard Invasion in 1797: The Descent of the French in Pembrokeshire (1930) 250–1
   see also Hudson, Derek; Nicholas, Jemima; West Wales Historical Records
'Scientific' historians 181, 214
   'scientific' historical method 162

The Scotsman 235
Scott, Sir Walter 79
Seabrooke, J. H. 226
Second World War 267–79
Seren Gomer 110, 128
Simon, Sir John 266–7
Slebech 16
Solva 52, 140
South African War 201
South Carolina 3
   South Carolina Historical Magazine 296
South Wales: The Country of Castles (GWR) 205
South Wales Weekly News 184
Specimens of French Ferocity and Brutality in Wales 84, figure 6, 85, 86–7, 90, 295
   see also Jenkins, Geraint H.
The Spectator 272–4
The Sphere 271
South Wales Daily Post 183–4
The Stage 183
St Davids 53, 57
   St David's Cathedral 61
St Leger, Barry 4, 5, 26, 90–1, 294
Stephens, Meic 293
Stephens, Thomas 141
Strumble Head see Pencaer
Stuart Jones, Edwyn Henry 35–7, 114–15, 298, 300
   An Invasion that Failed: the French Expedition to Ireland 1796 (1950) 280
   The Last Invasion of Britain (1950) 279–84
Stuart Jones, Henry 280
Suffragettes 220–1
Summertown 31
Surrender of the French (1797) 21–3, 25–8
Swansea 36, 57
Swansea Pembrokeshire Society 242
Swansea Training College for Women 233
Swete, Dr H. Lawton 181, 191
Sylwedydd, Y 139

T

Talbot Hotel, Aberystwyth 209
Tapestry 300
  see also Bicentenary
Tarian y Gweithiwr 186
Tate, Col. William 2–4, 6–7, 8, 18, 22, 27–8, 30, 55, 95, 101, 111, 115, 124–6, 144, 205, 209, 215, 246, 264, 271–2, 274, 281
  'Madame' Tate 125–6, 178
  'Nazi imitators' 268
  Instructions (1798) 70, 219, 240, 243, 271
  Tate, Edouard 146
  see also Ahlstrom, John D.
Tenby 10, 140
  Tenby correspondent 241–2
Tenby Observer 176–7, 223
Terror, 5, 48
  see also 'Dychryn'
Thomas, John (Haverfordwest trader) 66
Thomas, Thomas (Rector of Aberporth) 113
  Memoirs of Owen Glendower (1822) 81–2
Thomas, William, Mathry 86
Times, The 16, 18, 92, 115, 146, 292
  see also Hudson, Derek
Tone, Theobald Wolfe 2, 3, 246, 281, 294
tourism 7, 176, 203
Treason 60
Y Traethodydd 130
Trefdraeth see Newport
Trefin 50
Tregwynt 54, 59
  see also Harries, Mrs; Vaughan, Col. Daniel
Trefwrgi Lane 5, 26
Treherbert Public Hall 202
Trehowel (French HQ) 4, 17, 28, 59, 116
'Treleaze' (Trellys) 124
Tresinen or Tresinwen 265
Tyrrell, Nicholas 294

U

Union between Britain and Ireland 81
United Service Magazine (formerly *United Service Journal and Military Magazine*) 120–1
  'The French at Fishguard in 1797' 120–7
  see also *Chambers's Journal, Red Dragon*
Upper Cwmtwrch 183

V

Vandrei, Martha 1, note 3
Vaughan, Col. Daniel 54
  see also Tregwynt
Vaughan, John, Golden Grove 56
Vendée 3, 47
  see also Quiberon
Vengeance (ship of Commander Castagnier) 217
Victoria 253
Victoria's Diamond Jubilee 194
Vincent, Henry James 152–4
Volunteers 147
Volunteer forces 144
  Rifle Corps 7, 145
  'Y Rheiffl Gorau' 148
Volunteer Service Gazette 210

W

Wad, Shemi 224
Wakefield, Gilbert 64
Walters, Syd 296–8
  Truthful History of the Last Invasion of Britain (1989 and 1992) 297
Warlow, G. H. 252
  see also *Y Cymmrodor* (1932)
Warren, Frederick 242
Washington, George 3
Webb, Harri 292–3
  'The Women of Fishguard', *Rampage and Revel* (1977) 292–3
Weekly Dispatch (London) 126
Wellington Journal, The 213
Wells, Somerset 280
'Welsh Amazons' 126–7

Index

Welsh 'country people' 24–5, 28, 30–1
   see also Mends, John
Welsh defiance of Hitler 276
Welsh expression of Britishness 83
'Welsh Heroine' 234
Welsh Home Rule 7
   see also Cymru Fydd
Welsh loyalty to the Crown 81
Welsh militia in Ireland 245
Welsh national anthem
   see also 'Hen Wlad fy Nhadau'
Welsh national costume 186, figure 10, 191, 264
Welsh national fiction in English 184–5
Welsh Nonconformity 158–61, 300
Welsh patriotism 117, 170, 172
   see also Harries, John
Welsh working-class men 162
Welsh working-class women 274–6
The 'Welsh Tour' 93–4
Welsh Tourist Board 300
Welshman 187, 210
Werner, Jack 277–8
   We Laughed at Boney (1943) figure 21, 277
Westminster Gazette 209
Western Mail 170, 180, 183–4, 187, 235, 241–2, 251, 252, 253, 254–5, 261, 264, 266, 276, 279, 283, 291
West Wales Historical Records 246
Wheeler, Harold F. B. 207, 214, 216–18, 226, 234, 246
   'H.F.B.' 226
   see also Broadley, Alexander Meyrick
Whitney, Thomas Richard 140
   The Republic: A Monthly Magazine of American Literature 140
Witness statements 30–2
Williams, David 284–5
   History of Modern Wales (1950) 285
Williams, Edward (Iolo Morganwg) 33, 35, 56, 79
Williams, Gwyn A. 284, note 94, 285, note 97

Williams, Henry Lewis 114, 127, 186
   see also Ap Gwilym, H. L.
Williams, John Ceulanydd 149
Williams, Mary, Caerlem 4–5, 109, 114–15, 118–19, 121, 122–5, 173, 183, 268, 276, 294–5
   'Matty Carham' 268
   The French at Fishguard in 1797 120–7
   victim of rape 90–2
   see also Williams, Thomas
Wiliams, Peter of Carnachenllwyd Isha 114
Williams, Thomas, Trelethin (magistrate and 'first sighter') 114–15
Williams, Thomas, Caerlem (husband of Mary Williams) 4, 5, 122–4
   see also Williams, Mary
Williams, William, Pantycelyn 151
Windy Hill farm 116, 182
Windham, William, Secretary at War 17, 62
Women
   'Cyflwr Cymdeithasol a Moesol Merched Penfro' 139
   'Dewrion Ferched Abergwaun' 177
   in red 33–9, 141–2
   'Legend of the women' 7, 233–5, 250–4
   'old women' 34–5, 109
   'Women of Fishguard' 7, 141, 144, 162, 175, 187, 206, 220, 252, 292–3
   'Women of Pembrokeshire' 139–40, 154–5, 187
   Women of Wales 252–3
   'Women with red cloaks' in Invasion propaganda 84–6
Wood, Sir Charles 141
Woodward, G. M. 39
Wynn, Sir Watkin Williams, 5th Baronet 79–81

Y
York, Duke of 28, 59
Young Wales 207
'Ystyriaethau Pwysfawr i Bobl y
    Deyrnas Hon (1803) 82–3

Z
Zeppelins 237